CICERO'S *DE FINIBUS*

Cicero is increasingly recognized as a highly intelligent contributor to the ongoing ethical debates between Epicureans, Stoics and other schools. In this work on the fundamentals of ethics his learning as a scholar, his skill as a lawyer and his own passion for the truth result in a work which dazzles us in its presentation of the debates and at the same time exhibits the detachment of the ancient sceptic. Many kinds of reader will find themselves engaged with Cicero as well as with the ethical theories he presents. This collection takes the reader further into the debates, opening up new avenues for exploring this fascinating work.

JULIA ANNAS is Regents Professor of Philosophy at the University of Arizona. She has worked in ancient ethics and in the increasingly large area of contemporary virtue ethics, which has stimulated an interest in ancient ethics other than Aristotle. She wrote the introduction and notes to the recent translation of the *De Finibus* by Raphael Woolf.

GÁBOR BETEGH is Laurence Professor of Ancient Philosophy at the University of Cambridge, and Fellow of Christ's College. He has worked on various aspects of ancient philosophy, including Hellenistic philosophy and ethics.

CICERO'S *DE FINIBUS*

Philosophical Approaches

EDITED BY

JULIA ANNAS AND GÁBOR BETEGH

CAMBRIDGE
UNIVERSITY PRESS

CAMBRIDGE
UNIVERSITY PRESS

University Printing House, Cambridge CB2 8BS, United Kingdom

Cambridge University Press is part of the University of Cambridge.

It furthers the University's mission by disseminating knowledge in the pursuit of
education, learning and research at the highest international levels of excellence.

www.cambridge.org
Information on this title: www.cambridge.org/9781107074835

First published 2016

Printed in the United Kingdom by Clays, St Ives plc

A catalogue record for this publication is available from the British Library

Library of Congress Cataloguing in Publication data
Cicero's *De Finibus* : philosophical approaches / edited by Julia Annas, Gábor Betegh.
pages cm
Includes bibliographical references and index.
ISBN 978-1-107-07483-5 (hardback)
1. Cicero, Marcus Tullius. *De Finibus* bonorum et malorum.   2. Ethics, Ancient.
3. Good and evil.   4. Epicurus.   5. Stoics.   I. Annas, Julia, editor.
II. Betegh, Gábor, editor.
BJ214.C6D4333   2015
171–dc23   2015022586

ISBN 978-1-107-07483-5 Hardback

Contents

Contents

Contributors

JULIA ANNAS is Regents Professor of Philosophy at the University of Arizona.

THOMAS BÉNATOUÏL is Professor of Ancient Philosophy at the Université de Lille.

GÁBOR BETEGH is Laurence Professor of Ancient Philosophy at the University of Cambridge and Fellow at Christ's College.

CHARLES BRITTAIN is Susan Linn Sage Professor of Philosophy and Humane Letters at Cornell University.

DOROTHEA FREDE is Emeritus Professor of the University of California, Berkeley.

CHRISTOPHER GILL is Emeritus Professor of Ancient Thought at the University of Exeter.

MARGARET GRAVER is Aaron Lawrence Professor of Classics at Dartmouth College.

BRAD INWOOD is Professor of Philosophy and Classics at Yale University.

ANNA MARIA IOPPOLO is Emeritus Professor of Ancient Philosophy at Università di Roma La Sapienza.

PIERRE-MARIE MOREL is Professor of the History of Ancient Philosophy at Université Paris I – Panthéon-Sorbonne and Institut Universitaire de France.

JAMES WARREN is a Reader in Ancient Philosophy at the University of Cambridge and Fellow and Director of Studies in Philosophy at Corpus Christi College.

Introduction

Julia Annas
University of Arizona

Cicero's abilities as a philosopher have become much better appreciated in recent years. It is no longer innovative to treat his philosophical works as serious contributions to the philosophical debates of his day, rather than uncritical pastings together of various sources which scholars need to pick apart. Historians of philosophy now generally realize that Cicero had a first-rate philosophical education, grasping not only the positions of the major schools of his day but the crucial assumptions and argumentative moves structuring those positions. It's also widely accepted that he was philosophically sharp and astute enough to put this education to good effect in organizing arguments, systematizing positions and evaluating debates between philosophical schools. This is not surprising when we consider his famous forensic skills; Cicero, if anyone, is well equipped to understand the use, power and limitations of argument.

Cicero's self-presentation as an Academic sceptic also makes a great deal more sense against the background of the recent rediscovery and reassessment of the ancient sceptical schools. We can see how congenial Academic scepticism would be to someone to whom forensic practices of arguing were familiar, encouraging the thought that argument for and against a position was a good way to approach the truth of a matter, while encouraging intellectual modesty in the arguers as to their own grasp of it. As an Academic sceptic, Cicero is able to exercise his argumentative skills to the utmost while remaining, for the moment, detached from the position being argued for. And this involvement in the argument combined with detachment from its conclusions is also congenial to Cicero's very firm grasp of his own identity as a Roman *consularis*, someone as skilled as the Greeks in practising philosophy but maintaining gentlemanly aloofness from the idea of philosophy as an earnest full-time way of life. Cicero, after all, turned his literary attention to philosophy only, as he frequently reminds us, when unable to practise in the field of Roman political activity.

Cicero's use of the dialogue form in his philosophical works has also come to be appreciated far more in recent years. Comparison with Plato has generally been unfavourable, despite the rather lively Platonic conversation of the unfinished *De Legibus*. Cicero in his later philosophical dialogues explicitly makes use of the 'Aristotelian' format whereby philosophical positions are explicitly laid out in an organized way to be contrasted as wholes (rather than having to be partly inferred from more interactive dialogue) and in which the author himself appears as one of the speakers. Malcolm Schofield's pathbreaking article on Cicero's use of dialogue has enabled us to see Ciceronian dialogues as open-ended, in contrast to many of Plato's, and as exhibiting many of Cicero's strongest points. 'Working through the arguments on either side not only suited his tastes and skills as an advocate, but gave him the opportunity to enact and perfect the judiciousness and hesitation of the Academic method that were second nature to him.'[1]

Given all these recent advances, the time is now ripe for philosophical reassessment of the *De Finibus*, the most theoretical of Cicero's ethical dialogues. This work has been made more accessible by two recent new editions of the text, as well as increased interest in and understanding of Hellenistic philosophy and its developments in the first century BC.[2] It is our best continuous source for the different ethical theories current in the first century BC and their relationships, and the best source for our knowledge of the ethical theories of the Epicureans, Stoics and Antiocheans, which are here presented and contrasted in their own right and not merely within the framework of the larger *Weltanschauungen* of these schools. Ethics was important for all these schools – indeed the increasing importance of ethics in all the philosophical schools is noteworthy – and the *De Finibus* allows us to see the schools' ethical positions discussed at length. We find the eudaimonist approach to ethics, in which theories are defined by their account of our final end, a fascinating alternative approach to the one we find in doxographical sources, where ethics tends to be presented in its metaphysical background.

Aspects of the work which have been found problematic in the past can now be seen as less so. The absence of Plato's and Aristotle's ethical theories makes sense in terms of the philosophical situation of the first century BC. So does the stress we find in the work on the impasse between virtue and pleasure as candidates for the final end, and the impasse between the Stoic and the Peripatetic positions on the place of items other than virtue in our final end. Cicero's use of rhetorical devices is easily understood

---

[1] Schofield 2008: 65.
[2] Reynolds 1998, Moreschini 2005. There is a recent English translation, Annas and Woolf 2001.

within the way he contrasts positions as an Academic; it does not have to be seen as an expression of personal bias or as a retreat from 'purely' philosophical modes of argument. The heavy use he makes, throughout the work, of Carneades' classification of ethical theories in terms of their final ends, is also best seen not as reliance on stock arguments but as a creative approach to a debate about ethics which defines the various theories in terms of their final ends.[3]

As Cicero does not hesitate to remind us, he is doing something new in Latin literature. He is aware of his role as a mediator, doing in Latin something hitherto done only by specialists in philosophy in Greek. He is consciously translating a tradition from one culture to another (contrasting in this with Seneca[4]). He is not writing as a philosopher with a theory of his own to develop and defend. He writes as a Roman *consularis* discussing with his peers, in a leisurely fashion and in attractive settings, ideas which they find important and difficult, which have been developed most profoundly by Greeks. As an Academic sceptic, he can present himself, as 'Cicero' the interlocutor, attacking and defending, but never committed to any of the positions under discussion. Marcus Tullius Cicero, the politician and writer, uses all his philosophical and forensic skill to present to us the arguments for and against the most important positions of his day. He leaves us with much to discuss about the positions themselves and his presentations of them.

The *De Finibus* was the subject of the twelfth Symposium Hellenisticum, held in Budapest in June 2010. The programme of the Symposium was as follows:

James Warren (Cambridge University): Epicurean Pleasures in Cicero's *De Finibus*.

Pierre-Marie Morel (Ecole Normale Supérieure, Lyon): Cicero on Epicurean Virtues (*Fin.* 1–2).

Dorothea Frede (University of California, Berkeley): Epicurus on the Importance of Friendship in the Good Life.

Margaret Graver (Dartmouth College): Cato, Honor and the Honorable.

Brad Inwood: The Voice of Nature.

Thomas Bénatouïl: Structure, Standards and Stoicism in *De Finibus* 4.

---

[3] See Annas 2007a.
[4] As Brad Inwood reminds us, Inwood 2005: 18–22. See Powell 1995c for an appreciative discussion of Cicero's translations of Greek philosophical terms, and Powell 2007 for a perceptive overview of Cicero as philosopher, Academic and writer of dialogues, as well as a Roman statesman.

Anna-Maria Ioppolo (Università di Roma La Sapienza): *Sententia explosa*: la critica all'etica stoica nel *IV* libro de *De Finibus*.
Christopher Gill (University of Exeter): Antiochus' Theory of *oikeiōsis*.
Charles Brittain (Cornell University): Cicero's Sceptical Approach in the *De Finibus*.
The discussants at the Symposium were:
Keimpe Algra (University of Utrecht)
Gábor Betegh (Central European University)
István Bodnár (Eötvös University/Central European University)
John Cooper (Princeton University)
Ingo Gildenhard (Durham University)
Katerina Ierodiakonou (University of Athens)
Péter Lautner (Pázmány Péter Catholic University)
Anthony Long (University of California, Berkeley)
Malcolm Schofield (Cambridge University)
David Sedley (Cambridge University)
Emidio Spinelli (Università di Roma La Sapienza)
Gisela Striker (Harvard University)
Svavar Hrafn Svarvarsson (University of Iceland, Reykjavik)
Teun Tieleman (University of Utrecht)
Raphael Woolf (King's College, University of London)

We would like to thank Tony Long for his speech in memory of Jacques Brunschwig, one of the founders of the series of Symposia Hellenistica, who had recently died.

The meeting was funded by the ERC_HU BETEGH09 research project, the C. J. De Vogel Foundation and the Central European University. Special thanks are due to András Szigeti for his efficient help in organizing the Symposium. We are especially grateful to Ákos Brunner, Máté Veres and Mariapaola Bergomi for their committed and expert assistance in the editorial tasks for preparing this volume for publication.

The authors' contributions follow the order in which Cicero discusses the theories: Epicurus, the Stoics, Antiochus. The theories are treated not as the results of a doxographical approach, but in each case with awareness of the relevance of Cicero's position as an Academic sceptic, and the implications of this for his treatment of the theories in question. It is thus useful to begin with the paper on Cicero's sceptical method by Charles Brittain. The reader may find it useful to return to this after reading the contributions focused on the different theories of our final end, since it is only to be expected that different points of view are to be found on this issue.

Brittain dismisses the view that Cicero is giving us either a neutral doxography or a dogmatically Antiochean position. Cicero explicitly represents himself as an Academic sceptic; the serious question is what kind of sceptic he is, a mitigated sceptic tending to Antiochean views, or a radical Carneadean sceptic? Brittain defends the latter. He argues that features of the dialogue suggesting commitment to Antiocheanism are superficial, and that Cicero's self-characterization as an Academic sceptic does not determine what kind of sceptic he is; Brittain then offers positive evidence that Cicero's scepticism is Carneadean, that is, that he finds some positions more persuasive than others, but does not take this to indicate objective grounds for taking these to be more likely to be true than other, conflicting positions. He then shows how Cicero's overall sceptical stance is consistent with what strikes many readers as a problem for it, namely that in the dialogue the character Cicero's evaluations of the three theories are hardly neutral; sometimes they are heavily weighted. Brittain first points to various features of the dialogue framework which heighten our sense that the characters' judgements are 'subjective', representing their own individual viewpoints; this includes the character Cicero, whose apparently changing positions across the dialogues express dramatically the writer Cicero's own changes of mind, warning us not to ascribe to him a consistent commitment to any of the views discussed. Secondly, Brittain lays out a philosophical motivation for what appear to be his changing commitments: Cicero is, and represents himself as being, both a Roman to whom the Roman way of life and appeal to heroic examples of virtue are deeply important, and also someone committed to philosophy as the best rational way to achieve happiness. Given this, his rejection of Epicurean ethical views, and his vacillation between Stoic and Antiochean views of happiness, are readily understandable. The paper concludes by drawing a parallel with Cicero's epistemological vacillations in the *Academica*.

Cicero's presentation of the Epicurean theory of the final end in Books 1 and 2 has regularly been taken to be a textbook example of unfairness. Torquatus, the Epicurean spokesman, is portrayed as loyally committed to his position but unpractised in argument, and Cicero takes the opportunity to run down Epicurus' whole philosophy as amateur and clumsy. Many have got the impression that Cicero is not giving Epicurus a fair positive presentation before presenting his criticisms. Three of the authors take up issues from these books and give us a more nuanced interpretation, in which Cicero's critical attitude is seen as philosophically motivated.

James Warren focuses on Cicero's criticism of the Epicurean account of pleasure. Cicero presses home in Book 2 the claim that Epicurus vacillates fatally between two positions about our final end, that it is pleasure and that it is painlessness or tranquillity, *ataraxia*. Only the first of these, Cicero claims, is hedonism. Warren argues that Cicero here gives us a serious argument which indicates a real problem in the theory presented in Book 1. He examines in some detail the passage in Book 1 (29–41) where Torquatus is given scope to present Epicurus' account of pleasure and the claim that the final end of painlessness actually is the highest pleasure. Warren goes carefully through the stages of this passage, paying particular attention to the section about Chrysippus' statue and the argument it is held to illustrate. He argues in detail that Torquatus' presentation of the thesis that painlessness is the highest good does not link it persuasively to the idea of pleasure as a felt stimulation. When Cicero in the opening part of Book 2 (5–17) outlines the dilemma for Epicurus which he relentlessly presses, Warren argues that he is not foisting unargued premises, or ordinary opinions about pleasure, on Epicurus: the dilemma can be produced from his own words and some of his further assumptions. The dilemma is that whether Epicureans hold that the final end is pleasure or painlessness they don't succeed in establishing a *distinctive* position. If they hold that the final end is pleasure, they fall into the Cyrenaic position; if they hold that it is painlessness, they fall into the position of the obscure Hieronymus of Rhodes. They try to avoid this by claiming that painlessness *is* pleasant, indeed the most pleasant state; but the Book 1 moves show that they are committed to thinking that painlessness is not the kind of felt stimulation that they characterize as pleasure. Warren concludes that Cicero's procedure is highly damaging to Epicurus, who fails successfully to link painless living with pleasant experience.

Pierre-Marie Morel discusses the Epicurean account of the virtues. Although Cicero rejects Epicurean ethics wholesale, he is impelled to discuss the Epicurean account of virtue in its own right, not just as an implication of the rejected hedonism. This is, Morel holds, because Cicero thinks that the Epicureans are independently mistaken about the nature of virtue and its place in the happy life. Morel points out that Torquatus' account of the virtues differs from our other sources in presenting the standard four virtues, wisdom, temperance, courage and justice, something which sits uneasily with Epicurus' insistence elsewhere on the centrality of prudence to virtue (treated as a unity), with the institutional account of justice we find elsewhere and with the fact that Torquatus' temperance appears to have the role and features central to Epicurus' prudence. Morel concludes that Torquatus is, with mixed results, adapting the school account of *virtue* to what he takes to be inter-school assumptions about the *virtues*. Morel also highlights Cicero's claims that Epicurus' position on virtue falls into inconsistencies, and also plain errors, about the *honestum*, in a way which severely damages his theory, but at the same time develops ideas about the importance of consistency, and of a non-instrumental conception of the *honestum*, which will dominate the dialogues with the Stoics and with Antiochus. Cicero's encounter with Epicurean ethics brings it into the spotlight as the 'negative image' of a true conception of virtue and happiness; the theory fascinates Cicero as one that both allows no compromise with it and is indispensable in ethical debate for the way that refuting it brings out important truths about virtue and happiness, which will figure in the debates between Stoics and Antiocheans.

Dorothea Frede takes up the issue of friendship. Her paper, like Morel's, emphasizes that here Cicero is unique among our sources in the extent and character of his discussion. Cicero's presentation of the account through Torquatus, as well as its criticism by Cicero the speaker, focus on a standard and central problem for Epicurus: if my final end is my pleasure and tranquillity, surely the place of others in my life will be restricted to their instrumental value for achieving my pleasure? Torquatus vigorously disputes this, giving three Epicurean arguments to the conclusion that friendship has intrinsic value for the happy life. These do not impress Cicero, and the second and third do not impress Frede either, but she gives an interesting detailed discussion of the first, which extracts from Torquatus' careless formulation an intriguing and forceful argument (making it all the more unfortunate that Cicero does not reply adequately to it). Cicero's criticisms of Epicurean friendship in general, and of these three arguments in particular, reveal his unwillingness to allow that for Epicureans friendship could be anything other than an instrumental good. Frede concludes that, although Cicero is unfair in implying that for Epicureans friendship would be weighed against the advantages of wealth, nevertheless it emerges that there are problems for Epicurus in explaining 'what friends *are* to each other'. What would friends actually *do* together in a settled Epicurean life? We have little indication of what this would be, other than the sharing of the pleasures of everyday activities such as sports and other social activities. But in these, given the Epicurean insistence on tranquillity as the overall aim, particular friends would appear to be fungible.

Two papers on the presentation of Stoicism in Book 3 explore Cicero's handling of two central and difficult Stoic concepts, virtue and nature.

Margaret Graver begins from the fact that Cicero uses, as a correspondence for the Greek *kalon*, the Latin term *honestum*, which has a rather different social profile, suggesting the praise and esteem of others rather than a harmonious state internal to the person. Graver argues that for Cicero this point, far from being a disadvantage, indicates that *honestum* is 'uniquely suited to mediate between the shared values of Rome's political elite and the rationally grounded values of philosophical ethics'. (Compare Morel's conclusions about *honestum*.) *Honestum*, while it can be used interchangeably with *virtue*, marks out the quality of virtue which *merits esteem*, whether or not that is actually given. Graver examines Cato's brief arguments from choiceworthiness and happiness to praiseworthiness (as well as their responses in Book 4) and concludes that, while they do not show as much as Cato hopes, they indicate interesting Stoic assumptions about the relation between what is truly valuable and what is truly honourable, the relation usefully indicated in Cicero's use of the term *honestum*. Why is there such a notable gap between what is truly honourable and what society actually honours? Graver examines the Stoic explanations of our widespread error, especially about honour and glory, and the tendency of leading politicians to value glory, an indifferent, for its own sake (a mistake he finds particularly in Caesar). Graver concludes with an examination of Cicero's optimism about human capacity to come to appreciate the value of virtue along with an understanding of truly honourable conduct.

Brad Inwood focuses on a passage, 3.62, where the Stoic Cato makes a claim about the naturalness of parents' care for their offspring, and claims that in observing the behaviour of other animals we hear 'the voice of nature'. Inwood's concern is the character of the Stoic appeal to nature as normative. The first part of the paper takes a 'detour' by a path that Cicero does not take though it is prominent in other Stoics. In the 'cradle argument' both Epicureans and Stoics appeal to nature to explain the motivations of pre-rational children. A proffered explanation has to show that it is not just *a* good explanation but defeats rivals, and we find an argument, from Chrysippus to Hierocles, which goes: nature must do one of three things to an animal – make it dear, or indifferent, or hostile to itself. But the second and third options are foreclosed by the fact that (Stoic) nature is a teleological system, which cannot have self-undermining or pointless products. Nature then supports the first option, given the teleological conception of nature. Inwood points out that it is puzzling that Cicero appeals to this type of argument neither in Book 2 (against the Epicurean 'reading' of the cradle argument) nor in Book 3. Cicero has Cato appeal to nature rather in 3.62 ff, where he argues to the conclusion that humans are naturally social animals, inclined by their nature to bonding in social units, from observation of non-human animals, together with an appeal to the 'voice' of (teleological) nature. Inwood goes carefully through this argument, concluding that Cato's analogy with non-human animals does not do the work he thinks it does, and that the supplementary arguments do not offer strong independent support.

Anna Maria Ioppolo's intricate paper on Book 4 pays close attention to the role and affiliation of different views which are generally brought together as previously refuted by Carneades in his classification of ethical theories. Ioppolo traces especially the position of Aristo of Chios, referred to in Book 4 and elsewhere as a *sententia explosa*. This position is notorious for its 'indifferentism' – its dismissal of differences of value among Stoic indifferents. In Book 4 we find Cicero, arguing from an Antiochean point of view against the position of the 'orthodox' Stoa by presenting it with a dilemma, one horn of which reduces it to the position of Aristo. Ioppolo reminds us that underlying this are previous arguments within the Stoa itself, in which Chrysippus argued that Aristo's view differed from that of the Stoic ethics which was to become orthodox, in particular because Aristo left us with no rational basis for choice among indifferents. Ioppolo carefully traces the ways in which Aristo's position figures in the arguments of Book 4, and casts light on notorious puzzles in the book – the way in which Cicero presents a number of Stoic accounts of the *telos* as though they obviously came to the same thing, and the way in which the Antiochean criticisms in the book fail to match up with Cato's positive presentation of Stoic ethics in Book 3. Introducing selection in accordance with nature into accounts of the *telos*, she argues, is a response to Carneadean arguments which themselves respond to Chrysippus' arguments against Aristo, and thus are a product of both inter- and intra-school argument. Chrysippus himself 'left the content of moral action undefined with his formula of the end'. Thus we should not infer that all the Stoic accounts of the *telos* come to the same thing, as their listing by Cicero may lead us to think; we should be sensitive to arguments both among and within philosophical schools.

Thomas Bénatouïl's paper on Book 4 gives us a number of fresh ideas about the structure and arguments of this book, which has regularly been criticized for structural deficiencies. Chief among these are the puzzling facts that Book 4 contains a rather restricted number of anti-Stoic arguments, which are repeated somewhat relentlessly. Further (as Ioppolo also notes) the arguments of Book 4 do not respond to the positive account of

Stoicism laid out by Cato in Book 3, in the way that the negative arguments of Book 2 do respond to the account in Book 1; many of the Book
3 points are apparently ignored. Bénatouïl rejects the adequacy of previous explanations which leave Cicero as an incompetent or oblivious
paster-together of different sources. Rather, he sees Cicero as consciously
using a fresh and more appropriate method against the Stoics, whose
ideas require not point-by-point refutation but a general opposition of
systems. Bénatouïl's careful examination of the structure of the book finds
three stages in which Stoic ethics are confronted: arguments from common sense; arguments from the 'Old Academy'; and 'remaining' arguments, which are mainly internal to Stoic ethics itself. This corresponds,
he claims, to the standards of criticism provided by the initial account of
'Old Academy' doctrine (something which has been thought redundant
in light of Book 5). The Stoics are judged to be failures from the rhetorical
point of view (hence the conflicts with common sense), from the logical
point of view (issues of consistency by contrast with the 'Old Academy')
and from the 'physical' point of view (the 'remaining arguments', where
Stoic doctrines are shown not to be in agreement with the relevant phenomena). Bénatouïl then gives his attention to the awkward absences of
Book 3 ideas from Book 4, particularly *oikeiōsis*, and points up the relevance of Cato's presence as defender of Stoic ethical views. Cato's relation
to Stoicism is complex and indicative of Cicero's own ambivalence about
Stoicism and 'Old Academy' positions on the final good.

Christopher Gill's paper on Book 5 brings out clearly two distinct, but
related issues: the underlying rationale of Antiochus' account of ethical
development, and its relation to his position on the good (both clarified
by reference to the contrasting Stoic account), and also Cicero's own attitude to this Stoic–Antiochean debate. Gill discusses the recent attempt
by Tsouni[5] to revive in strengthened form Dirlmeier's claim for a basic-
ally Aristotelian provenance of the Book 5 account, but he goes on to
maintain the position that this extended account of ethical development
is intended as a replacement for a Stoic version of *oikeiōsis*, one which is
in line with Antiochus' stress on the development of a human being *as a
whole*. Gill discusses, carefully and clearly, the comparative advantages and
problems that each school's account runs into, both in attempting to give
a convincing account of human nature and in aiming to describe ethical
development consistently with the theory of value, especially the account
of the final end. Antiochus' more plausible account of human ethical

---

[5] In Sedley 2012: 131–150.

development comes at the cost of complexity in his account of happiness, since he holds that virtue is sufficient for happiness, while other kinds of good thing add an 'extra' kind of happiness, forcing him to distinguish between the 'happy' and the 'happiest' life, an overall position which Gill's thorough discussion shows to be a deeply problematic one. Cicero as speaker in this dialogue points out some problems for the Antiochean theory, and Gill discusses the issue of Cicero's own position (with reference to the differing view of Brittain). Gill sees Cicero as presenting the Stoic and Antiochean theories in ways carefully designed to bring out their respective strengths and weaknesses; the accessible but structurally weak theory presented in Book 5 prepares us to be left with a 'dialectical standoff' between the theories which reflects Cicero's own difficulty in committing himself to either side.

Cicero's sceptical methods
The example of the De Finibus

Charles Brittain
Cornell University

Introduction

In this chapter I will argue that the dialogue form in Cicero's later works serves the essential philosophical function of expressing his radical Academic scepticism. The form is essential to this purpose, not just as a matter of structure – the pattern of paired arguments *pro* and *contra* – but all the way through, including the characterization, the narrative *persona*, and the focus on the Roman context of the conversations the dialogues represent. I use the *De Finibus* as an example, in part because it is a hard case: if it can be shown that Cicero's presentation of Hellenistic ethics in this dialogue is an expression of his deep scepticism, the case for the sequence it belongs to should be relatively easy. The specific case I will try to make is that reading *De Finibus* in the light of Cicero's discussion of epistemology in the *Academica* explains how Cicero's sceptical outlook produced the attitudes towards goods and ethical ends that we find his character adopting in the *De Finibus*. In particular, I will argue that Cicero's apparent vacillation in the *De Finibus* over the unique goodness of virtue is parallel to his vacillation, in the *Academica*, over the correctness of the Stoic conditions on rational assent – and that this vacillation stems from the same sceptical stance in both the epistemological and ethical cases.

On my account, then, Cicero represents himself as deeply attracted to several conflicting ethical positions, and so in a state of intractable doubt about which one be correct: his scepticism thus emerges from the dramatization of his own unresolved doubts. In the *Academica*, the form of his own scepticism is dramatized in the same way, and mostly clearly in *Ac.* 2.66, where Cicero (in character) asserts the pull of both mitigated and radical

I thank Tad Brennan for his invaluable and supererogatory (even for him) help in writing this paper. I am also very grateful for the extremely helpful comments from the participants of the Symposium in Budapest and from audiences in Würzburg, Yale, and Oxford, especially from Gábor Betegh, Katerina Ierodiakonou, and Th omas Bénatouïl, as well as for the inordinate generosity of the editors of this volume, Julia Annas and Gábor Betegh.

scepticism in claiming that he is a *magnus opinator*, but the sage is not.[1] The ethical parallel – Cicero's conflicting views about the value of goods subject to fortune – is sketched there too, in *Ac.* 2.134, but only very briefly.[2] To see how this is dramatized on the large scale, we need to look at the *De Finibus*.

This chapter has three parts. In the first section, I lay out some rival interpretations of Cicero's position in the *De Finibus*, and quickly rule out one that does not allow that he writes as a sceptic of any kind. In the second section, I consider what kind of sceptic Cicero is, and argue that he is not a mitigated sceptic, but rather a radical or, as I shall describe him, a Carneadean sceptic. In the final section, I try to show how Cicero's sceptical approach emerges from the dialogue as a whole, and I elaborate the parallel mentioned above, between Cicero's attitude towards assent and his attitude towards goods subject to fortune.

1 Three interpretative options (one dismissed)

1.1 Interpretative options

There are clearly other ways in which one can interpret Cicero's stance in the dialogue. I used to think, as many scholars still do, that Cicero espoused in *De Finibus* an unexciting form of mitigated scepticism which allowed him to endorse dogmatic views – and in particular, the central Antiochian ethical claims his character argues for in *Fin.* 4 and Piso expounds in *Fin.* 5.[3] I will consider in detail and reject that option in

---

[1] *Ac.* 2.66: [Cicero:] *Nec tamen ego is sum qui nihil umquam falsi adprobem qui numquam adsentiar qui nihil opiner; sed quaerimus de sapiente. ego vero ipse et magnus quidam sum opinator (non enim sum sapiens) ... eo fit ut errem et vager latius. Sed non de me, ut dixi, sed de sapiente quaeritur.* ('Not that I am someone who never approves anything false, never assents, and never holds an opinion; but we are investigating the wise person. In fact, I myself am a great opinion-holder: I'm not wise ... As a result, I err or wander further afield. But it's not me, as I said, but the wise person we are investigating.')

[2] *Ac.* 2.134: [Cicero:] *sed <et> ille [Zeno] vereor ne virtuti plus tribuat quam natura patiatur, praesertim Theophrasto multa diserte copioseque dicente, et hic [Antiochus] metuo ne vix sibi constet, qui cum dicat esse quaedam et corporis et fortunae mala tamen eum qui in his omnibus sit beatum fore censeat si sapiens sit: distrahor, tum hoc mihi probabilius tum illud videtur, et tamen nisi alterutrum sit virtutem iacere plane puto.* ('But in Zeno's case I worry that he ascribes more to virtue than nature allows, especially in the light of Theophrastus' many learned and eloquent arguments; and in Antiochus' I'm afraid that he is scarcely consistent when he says that there are bodily and external circumstances that are bad, and yet believes that someone subject to all of them will be happy if he's wise. I am torn: now one, now the other view seems more persuasive to me, and yet I think that virtue will utterly collapse unless one of them is right.') On Cicero's aporetic stance on ethical questions in *Ac.* 2, see Algra 1997 and esp. 130–138.

[3] Brittain 2001: 258–259. The strongest proponent of this view of the work in recent years has been Woldemar Görler, in whose honour I call it the 'standard view'; see, e.g., Gawlick and Görler 1994: 1038–1040, and, most recently, Görler 2011. It is also endorsed, more tentatively, by John Glucker; see Glucker 1988: 60–69 and 1995: 133–137.

section 2 below. Another view some readers have adopted is that Cicero provides an essentially neutral exposition of Greek ethics, a doxography that is not designed to express his own ethical commitments. For ease of reference, I will call these three options (which indicate, I hope, the basic range open to philosophical readers of the dialogue):

1   the doxographical reading,[4]
2   the mitigated sceptical reading, expressing his qualified endorsement of a set of philosophical views – in this case, ethical views, and in particular, the Antiochian doctrines about goods, and[5]
3   the Carneadean sceptical reading, expressing intractable doubt about such philosophical views – and in particular, systematic philosophical views about goods – through the dialogue as a whole.[6]

---

[4] A variant on this is what we can call 'the dogmatic reading', on which Cicero is a dogmatic Antiochian (or Stoic or Peripatetic) in ethics. I am not sure if anyone really holds this view. A number of source critics have treated him as if he were, because they think that his material is drawn almost entirely from Antiochus' On Ends. But this is not a reading of the dialogue, but rather a guess about its origins. It would amount to an interpretation if one thought that Cicero regards ethical views as somehow insulated from scepticism. I discount this view here, though, because it suffers from the same defect as the doxographical view: it is hard to see how to reconcile it with Cicero's explicit representation of himself as an Academic of some kind both in the frames of the set of dialogues from 45–44 BC that come before and after *Fin.* (see n. 12) and as a *persona* in the arguments of the dialogues, including in *Fin.* 5; see section 1.2.

[5] Chris Gill offers a *Stoic* variant of this view in section 4 of his chapter in this volume, on the basis of his evaluation of the relative philosophical weight of the criticisms of the Stoics and of Antiochus offered by the Cicero-character in *Fin.* 4 and 5, and because, in his view, Cicero takes a consistently Stoic line on goods in *Tusc.* and *Off.* This seems less an interpretation of the dialogue as such – which is my object here – than a philosophical response to it, since it ignores the array of dialogic structures (including arguments) described in sections 2–3 below. It is easy to see how one might infer – invalidly, I argue below – from Cicero's *persona*'s criticisms of Antiochus' consistency in *Fin.* 5 that Cicero rejects his view; but if that inference is valid, one should also infer from the same *persona*'s criticisms of the Stoics' view as incompatible with human nature in *Fin.* 4 that Cicero rejects their view too (see n. 6). Cicero's stance in *Tusc.* and *Off.* (and other late dialogues) also strikes me as more complicated than Gill suggests. The cross-reference to *Fin.* 4 in *Tusc.* 5.32–34 in fact presupposes that (the interlocutor thinks that) 'Cicero' did *not* take a Stoic line in *Fin.* as a whole, since otherwise he would not now be 'changing his mind'. But 'Cicero's' response in *Tusc.* 5.34 (and the rest of the book; cf. *Tusc.* 5.76, 5.85, 5.120) is not that he now *accepts* the Stoic view on goods, but that he has been *using* it in *Tusc.* to pursue a complex persuasive strategy; see Görler 2004a. And Cicero may be adopting a similar strategy in *Off.* by using the Stoic line as a counter-weight to his son's Peripatetic studies (*Off.* 3.11): the Stoic line offers an impossible ideal (*Off.* 3.13–17), but one that is pedagogically useful owing to its clarity (*Off.* 3.20–22, 3.33).

[6] Another possibility I do not consider in detail here is the view that Cicero *is* a mitigated sceptic in *Fin.*, but nevertheless chooses *not* to endorse an ethical position or set of doctrines in this dialogue; see, e.g., Bringmann 1971: 138–157 (cf. Süss 1966 52–64) and Annas and Woolf 2001. I allow that this view is a serious contender, as David Sedley and Malcolm Schofield pointed out in Budapest. But I don't discuss it here for three reasons. (1) As I argue in sections 2.2.2–2.3.1 below, the evidence for taking Cicero to be a mitigated sceptic of this sort in *Fin.* is also compatible with his being a radical sceptic. But since Cicero represents himself as a Clitomachian follower of Carneades, i.e., radical sceptic, in *Ac.*, and since he refers readers back to his discussion there when the nature of his scepticism is in question (*Fin.* 5.76; cf. *ND* 1.11–12; *Div.* 2; *Off.* 2.8), the radical, Carneadean interpretation is preferable, *ceteris paribus*. (2) In section 3 I argue that the dramatization of Carneadean

In the remainder of this section, I will give a few rapid arguments against the first reading (section 1.2), in order to set the scene for the more difficult question I want to investigate in the main body of this chapter: whether we should think of Cicero's approach in *De Finibus* as that of a mitigated sceptic or as sceptical in a deeper, more Carneadean, way.

1.2   *Against the doxographical reading*

I think it has been true of most ancient philosophers in the last 100 years (myself included) that they have often treated Cicero's dialogues as merely doxographical sources of information about earlier Greek schools and sources. To the extent that this reflects an *interpretation* of the dialogue, it supposes that the dialogue form – the argumentative structure, the characterization and so on – is an irrelevant packaging for the exposition of ethical systems. Or, more plausibly, perhaps it acknowledges that the *structure* provides a way of giving a properly critical presentation of ethics on the model of an adversarial legal case, with argument on either side. But all the other features of the dialogues – the narrative frame, the Roman contexts of the conversations, their locations and dates, and their characters, etc. – are philosophically irrelevant. On this view, there are *characters*, and they express and criticize views, but it makes no sense to wonder how they are characterized or what they think or whether they are supposed to have consistent views: if 'Cicero' asserts 'P' and 'not-P' in a dialogue, it is merely a function of the exposition. (This may explain, one might think, apparent inconsistencies in Cicero's characterization of his own *persona*, e.g., between his endorsement of Antiochian ethical views in *Fin.* 4 and his attraction to incompatible Stoic views in *Fin.* 5.[7])

scepticism actually requires characters – such as the Cicero-character in *Fin.* 4–5 – who are torn, i.e., committed to incompatible views. This means that we can't infer from even the Cicero-character's apparent endorsement of a view that the view is endorsed by Cicero or the work as a whole. Thus I take it that, for example, the apparently strong endorsements of views by Cicero-characters at the end of some dialogues (*ND* 3.95 and *Div.* 2.148–150) are not evidence of the works' mitigated scepticism, but structural devices, designed to temper the inclination to rash assent to negative dogmatism inspired by the slashing critiques of Stoic theology by Cotta and 'Cicero' (see e.g. Schofield 1986 on *Div.* and Pease 1914 and Wynne 2014 on *ND*). (3) My aim in this chapter is to show that reading the dialogue as a Carneadean work is fully consistent with the text and makes good sense of the full range of dialogic features it contains. But both readings agree on the central claim that the work isn't designed to endorse any of the views it discusses, and allowing that is enough to put the Carneadean interpretation in play.

[7] Smith 1995 suggests a sophisticated version of a legal model of this sort, on the basis of passages like *Pro Cluentio* 139: *Sed errat vehementer, si quis in orationibus nostris quas in iudiciis habuimus auctoritates nostras consignatas se habere arbitratur. Omnes enim illae causarum ac temporum sunt, non hominum ipsorum aut patronorum. Nam si causae ipsae pro se loqui possent, nemo adhiberet oratorem.*

But a decent respect for Cicero's own descriptions of his methods and aims, in the dialogues and elsewhere, shows that this sort of doxographical view is untenable. It doesn't fit Cicero's manifest interest in characterization or the subtlety of his literary hermeneutics (see, e.g., *Ad Att.* 13.19, *Ad Q. fr.* 3.5.1).[8] Nor, to stick to the dialogues themselves, does it fit with the explicit claims in the prefaces about his aims in writing. In *De Finibus* itself, Cicero as narrator is very clear in *Fin.* 1.6 that his aim is to apply his own *iudicium* or *critical judgement* to the views he sets out.[9] And this is further spelled out

Nunc adhibemur ut ea dicamus, non quae auctoritate nostra constituantur sed quae ex re ipsa causaque ducantur. ('But anyone who thinks that he has my own attested opinions from claims made in my forensic speeches is very much mistaken. All such claims belong to the cases and the moment they are made, not to the advocates themselves or their clients. For if cases could speak for themselves, no one would need an orator. As it is, we are sought not to say what we have established on our own authority but what one can glean from the facts and the case itself.') But, while Cicero and his characters often use legal metaphors to describe their arguments, and often in interesting ways (see e.g. *Fin.* 4.1, 4.61; more complex metaphors are used in *Div.* 2.46 and *Tusc.* 5.32, see n. 11 below), in my view, this is an analogy or metaphor, rather than Cicero's model for his enterprise as a whole.

[8] Cicero's interest in dialogue form and especially characterization remains under-studied in modern scholarship, despite the early start made in Hirzel 1895: 457–552, and resumed in Levine 1958, Douglas 1962 and 1995 (cf. Dyck 1998), Zoll 1962, and Leeman 1963, and again in the twin articles on *Div.* by Beard 1986 and Schofield 1986. But things are changing: see Steel 2005, Schofield 2008, and Baraz 2012, and the individual studies in Fox 2000 (on *Rep.*), Fantham 2004 (on *De Or.*), and Gildenhard 2007 (on *Tusc.*). Cicero's formal interest in these issues is clear (*inter alia*) from the remarks he makes on these issues in passing in his letters. From four such passages we can glean the following: (1) He tries to avoid temporal anachronism with characters (*Att.* 14.16.2; cf. *Brutus* 217–218). (2) He also tries to avoid inconsistency of characters with respect to content, such as a Lucullus giving complex arguments (*Att.* 13.19.4). (3) Likewise with personality, such as Scaevola's not remaining to listen to *De Or.* 2–3, which Cicero avoids for the same reason he takes Plato to have avoided having Cephalus stay for *Rep.* 2–10 (*Att.* 14.16.3). (4) His prefaces (cf. *Att.* 16.6.4 for his *volumen* of them) are first-personal, like Aristotle's, and so allow for different temporal settings (*Att.* 14.16.2). (5) He distinguishes three kinds of setting: ones with historical characters on the model of Heraclides (*Rep.*); ones set at a remove from the present but in living memory (*De Or.* – cf. *Fam.* 1.9.23); and ones set in his own times, but preferably with the other characters dead (*Fin.*, *Ac.*) – and in the latter, Aristotelian, kind, the conversation is organized so that it is under the control of the narrator (*ita sermo inducitur ceterorum ut penes ipsum sit principatus*, *Att.* 13.19.4). (6) He allows that ancient characters imply fictionality and so loss of perceived authorial authority (*Q.Fr.* 3.5). (7) Likewise that the actual conversations in non-ancient dialogues are fictional, though ideally suited to their characters' interests and views (*Fam.* 9.8.2). We can also see from his works that Cicero was aware of a wide range of interpretations of Platonic dialogues. The most notable among these are: (a) an Antiochian view that divides historical Socratic dialogues from Pythagorean ones which don't represent what Socrates thought but rather what Plato later on thought (*Rep.* 1.15–16, cf. *Fin.* 5.87); (b) a sceptical interpretation, that takes Socrates as an aporetic character and takes the dialogues as a whole to be aporetic (*Ac.* 2.74 and 1.46); and (c) a proto-Platonist one that takes Plato as dogmatic and Socrates' occasional disclaimers of knowledge as ironic (*Ac.* 1.15–16, 2.15). See Long 1995b.

[9] *Fin.* 1.6: *Quid? si nos non interpretum fungimur munere, sed tuemur ea quae dicta sunt ab iis quos probamus eisque nostrum iudicium et nostrum scribendi ordinem adiungimus, quid habent, cur Graeca anteponant iis quae et splendide dicta sint neque sint conversa de Graecis?* ('What of it, if I do not perform the task of a translator, but preserve the views of those whom I consider worthwhile, while contributing my own judgement and order of composition? What reason does anyone have for preferring Greek to that which is written with brilliance and is not a translation from Greek?') NB: All

in his somewhat enigmatic remark in *Fin.* 1.12 that he has 'gone through not only the view(s) I approve but those of each of the philosophical schools individually'.[10] This tells us, at least, that Cicero approves some, but not all, of the philosophical views he will present: he does not claim – in his authorial voice – to be neutral between them.

When we try to work out *how* Cicero presents his own views in the dialogues, it seems reasonable to assume that he does so at least partly through his own *personae* in the narrative frame and in the subsequent conversations. It is true this involves his holding inconsistent *views*, but it turns out that when Cicero is explicitly charged with inconsistency, he – or, at least, his *persona* – does not adduce the legal model to explain it away. Rather, he always appeals to the freedom of the Academic to say what he thinks at the moment, even if it isn't what he thought at some other time; see *Div.* 2.46 and *Tusc.* 5.32 – the latter referring to *Fin.* 4 (see section 3.1 below).[11] Of course, the Cicero-character might

---

translations from *Fin.* are based on Raphael Woolf's excellent translation, in Annas and Woolf 2001, with minor changes. All other translations are my own. The Latin text is Reynolds' 1998, although Reid 1925 and especially Madvig 1876 [1839] remain useful. As Patzig 1979: 308–310 argued against Reid 1925 *ad loc.*, Cicero's *iudicium* here is clearly his own philosophical judgement. (The sequel of 1.6 shows that Cicero takes his work to be as original as Posidonius' or Panaetius' versions of Chrysippian ethics; and in *Fin.* 1.11 Cicero says he is looking for the best and *truest* of the incompatible views of philosophers on ethics.)

[10] *Fin.* 1.12 *Nos autem hanc omnem quaestionem de finibus bonorum et malorum fere a nobis explicatam esse his litteris arbitramur, in quibus, quantum potuimus, non modo quid nobis probaretur sed etiam quid a singulis philosophiae disciplinis diceretur persecuti sumus.* ('For my part, I consider that this work gives a more or less comprehensive discussion of the question of the highest goods and evils. In it I have gone through not only the view(s) I approve but those of each of the philosophical schools individually.') This needn't assert more than that the book includes views Cicero does not approve. It is notable that Cicero sensibly drops the clause about what he finds plausible in his summary of *Fin.* in *Div.* 2.2.

[11] *Div.* 2.46. '*Tu igitur animum induces' sic enim mecum agebas 'causam istam et contra facta tua et contra scripta defendere?' Frater es; eo vereor. verum quid tibi hic tandem nocet? resne quae talis est an ego qui verum explicari volo? itaque nihil contra dico, a te rationem totius haruspicinae peto.* ('"How can you bring yourself," you argued, "to defend this position, which is contrary to both your record and your writings?" You're my brother, so I will be polite. But, really, what is the problem here? Is it the case itself, which is a difficult one, or me, who just wants to set out the truth? So I'm not going to respond to this charge – I'm just going to ask you for a causal explanation for haruspicy.') *Tusc.* 5.32: *sed tua quoque vide ne desideretur constantia. Quonam modo? Quia legi tuum nuper quartum de finibus; in eo mihi videbare contra Catonem disserens hoc velle ostendere – quod mihi quidem probatur – inter Zenonem et Peripateticos nihil praeter verborum novitatem interesse ...* [33] *Tu quidem tabellis obsignatis agis mecum et testificaris, quid dixerim aliquando aut scripserim. cum aliis isto modo, qui legibus impositis disputant: nos in diem vivimus; quodcumque nostros animos probabilitate percussit, id dicimus, itaque soli sumus liberi.* ('"But aren't you losing your own consistency, too?" – How's that? – "I read recently the fourth book of your *De Finibus*, and in your argument with Cato there you seemed to me to want to show (something I at any rate accepted) that there was no difference between Zeno and the Peripatetics except the verbal innovations <of the former> ..." You are adducing sealed documents and testimony as to what I once said or wrote. That's an OK approach with other philosophers, who argue under oath <to be faithful to their school doctrines>. But we

not represent *Cicero* as such in these passages. Still, on the only account given in the dialogues, these inconsistencies are resolved as distinct temporal episodes in the thought of a single character, and one whose Academic philosophical views are echoed in the narrative frame.[12] The doxographical model thus seems incompatible with some basic features of the dialogue.

2   Is Cicero a mitigated sceptic with Antiochian views or a Carneadean sceptic?

This rapid rebuttal of a non-sceptical reading leaves me free to argue against the view I used to hold, that Cicero's approach in the *De Finibus* was that of a mitigated sceptic, who endorsed the central doctrines of Antiochian ethics. My aim here is to argue the other side, to the effect that the dialogue reflects or dramatizes a deeper form of scepticism in the tradition of Carneades.

Readers have taken Cicero to be a mitigated sceptic with Antiochian leanings because it looked as though he was an Antiochian in ethics and it looked as though this was compatible with the form of mitigated scepticism he appeared to hold. In this section of the chapter I will examine some basic features of the dialogue that have given rise to these (false) appearances. But I will start by saying a bit more about what I mean by 'mitigated scepticism with Antiochian leanings', and the view I prefer, 'Carneadean scepticism' (section 2.1). Then I will examine the evidence for the former and show why it does not hold up (section 2.2). Finally, I will add some positive reasons to prefer the Carneadean reading to the mitigatedly sceptical Antiochian reading (section 2.3).

2.1   *Mitigated and Carneadean scepticism*

'Mitigated sceptic with Antiochian leanings' is a short way to describe 'a follower of the mitigated interpretation of Academic scepticism, who approves sceptically of the central doctrines of Antiochian ethics'. A mitigated sceptic – at least, as I have argued elsewhere – is a follower of the Academy who takes the Philonian interpretation of Carneades (before the

---

live for the day – we say whatever strikes our minds as persuasive, and for that reason, we alone are free.') On the function of these and similar passages in Ciceronian dialogues, see Schofield 2008: 74–83.

[12] Cicero characterizes his aims in dialogues as Academic (*inter alia*) in, e.g., prefaces such as *Ac.* 2.7–9, *ND* 1.10–12, *Tusc.* 1.7–9, 2.1–9 and 5.11, *Div.* 2.1–7, and *Fat.* 3–4.

Roman Books).[13] Mitigated sceptics accept the Stoic conceptual analysis of knowledge, according to which it requires assent to cognitive impressions. Like the Stoics, they refuse their (unqualified) assent to impressions that are not cognitive, but, unlike the Stoics, they do not think that there are any cognitive impressions. Thus knowledge is unavailable, in their view, and (unqualified) assent should never be given. (See the classic formulation in *Ac.* 2.104, cited in n. 13.) However, they use the 'persuasive' (*probabilis* or *pithane*) impression as a *provisional* criterion of the truth, on the grounds that, if generated in appropriately rational ways, such impressions give better guidance, and are more likely to be true, than impressions that are not 'persuasive'. Thus, despite withholding (unqualified) assent, mitigated sceptics are free to approve the views that, after rational scrutiny, strike them as more 'persuasive' – for instance, the set of views constituting the Antiochian doctrine of the goods. They may also do so consistently on the basis of arguments for the superiority of these views to other ethical tenets, provided that they recognize that the grounds for their approval are never conclusive, i.e., are never grounds for (unqualified) assent.

A 'Carneadean sceptic', by contrast, is a follower of Carneades who takes the Clitomachian – and in my view, correct – interpretation of their eponymous scholarch. The Carneadean sceptic is someone who has considered the claims of rationalist philosophy and found them to be compelling but inconclusive – indeed, no more compelling than their negations. Unlike the mitigated sceptic, then, the Carneadean sceptic is not rationally committed to the Stoic view that knowledge requires

---

[13] Brittain 2001, drawing on Frede 1987b and 1987c and Barnes 1989. Brittain 2006: xix–xxix gives a short version of this view. The main evidence for both kinds of Academic sceptic is *Ac.* 2.32–36 and 2.98–114. (Note that I gloss over here the issue of the mitigated sceptics' 'qualified assent' (mentioned in *Ac.* 2.59, 2.67, 2.78, and 2.148), although this is one way of distinguishing their position from the Clitomachian view.) On the Academic notion and classification of 'persuasive impressions', see further Allen 1994. The central text is *Ac.* 2.104: *adiungit dupliciter dici adsensus sustinere sapientem, uno modo cum hoc intellegatur, omnino eum rei nulli adsentiri, altero cum se a respondendo ut aut adprobet quid aut inprobet sustineat, ut neque neget aliquid neque aiat. id cum ita sit, alterum placere ut numquam adsentiatur, alterum tenere ut sequens probabilitatem, ubicumque haec aut occurrat aut deficiat, aut 'etiam' aut 'non' respondere possit.* ('Clitomachus added: "The wise person is said to suspend assent in two senses: in one sense, when this means that he won't assent to anything at all; in another, when it means that he will restrain himself even from giving responses showing that he approves or disapproves of something, so that he won't say 'yes' or 'no' to anything. Given this distinction, the wise person accepts suspension of assent in the first sense, with the result that he never assents; but holds on to his assent in the second sense, with the result that, by following what is persuasive wherever that is present or deficient, he is able to reply 'yes' or 'no'."") I should perhaps note here that I disagree with Gawlick and Görler 1994: 1092–1099 and Görler 2004a: 285–288 on Cicero's originality in using the *probabile* as a way of conducting philosophical investigations. This seems to me to be built in explicitly to Clitomachus' description of the original notion in *Ac.* 2.104.

assent to cognitive impressions, since there are arguments in favour of this view, but there are strong arguments against it as well. Nor is the Carneadean rationally committed to the doctrine of the Socratic tradition, whether Stoic or Antiochian, that philosophy can provide an art of living that will elevate its practitioners above the vagaries of fortune. This too is a compelling vision, but there are compelling arguments against it as well. So the Carneadean sceptic finds himself in a state of profound *aporia* about the best rational response to such philosophical questions. But this doesn't mean that a Carneadean sceptic will never find one view more 'persuasive' than another, and so never act in accordance with what strikes him as good or bad, and so on. (Again, see Clitomachus' formulation in *Ac.* 2.104.) It just means that he or she does *not* consider the fact of their finding an impression 'persuasive' to give objective grounds for assuming that it is more likely to be true than another impression. Like the Sextan sceptic we meet in *PH* 1, the Carneadean follows impressions as a practical criterion of life, *not* as a dogmatic – or as a provisional – criterion of truth.[14]

2.2   *Is Cicero a mitigated sceptic with Antiochian leanings? Evidence for and against*

The basic evidence in favour of taking Cicero in the *De Finibus* as a mitigated sceptic with Antiochian leanings comes in two parts: the work's Antiochian structure and the sceptical methods of Cicero as both narrator and character.

2.2.1   *The dialogue is not structured to favour Antiochian ethics*

I start with the Antiochian leanings. The main reason for thinking that Cicero endorses the central doctrines of Antiochian ethics in *Fin.* is that the structure of the dialogue seems weighted heavily in favour of Antiochus:

(a) for, in *Fin.* 1–2, Cicero seems to rule out Epicurean ethics, leaving Stoic and Antiochian ethics as his and our remaining options;

(b) in *Fin.* 3–4, Cicero adopts an Antiochian approach to ethics in his critique of the Stoics;

---

[14] The arguments grounding the possibility of Carneadean scepticism are examined in detail in Bett 1989 and 1990.

(c) and *Fin.* 5 is skewed in favour of the Antiochian Piso, since there is no *Fin.* 6 criticizing his view – Cicero makes only a few critical remarks against it in *Fin.* 5 and Piso still gets the last word.[15]

(d) Some people think that Cicero's critique of the Epicureans in *Fin.* 2 is also Antiochian; if so, 2, 4, and 5 are all (allegedly) Antiochian.[16]

But further reflection shows that the dialogue is in fact structured in an extremely complicated way, and not one that leads to an Antiochian interpretation. It is well known that it consists of three distinct conversations, with three sets of characters, held at three different times, and in three different places, linked together in a frame address/letter/quasi-conversation with someone else and set in another time.

Fin. 1–2: Torquatus (Epicurean) vs. Cicero, with Triarius (Stoic) attending – set in 50 BC at Cicero's house in Cumae, when Torquatus was praetor-elect (*Fin.* 2.78).

Fin. 3–4: Cato (Stoic) vs. Cicero – set in 52 BC, the year of Pompey's law on court procedures (*Fin.* 4.1), and in the library of Lucullus Jr's house in Tusculum (*Fin.* 3.7).

Fin. 5: Piso (Antiochian) vs. Cicero, with Atticus, Q. Cicero, and L. Cicero attending – set in 79 BC, when they were students in Athens (*Fin.* 5.1f).

Frame: Cicero to Brutus (Antiochian), set 'now', presumably in 45 BC (*Fin.* 1.1–13, *Fin.* 3.1–6, *Fin.* 5.1 and 5.8).

But I don't think that the implications of this complicated structure have been noticed. Given that there are four different Ciceronian characters or *personae* here, reconstructing his overall position requires some interpretative work. So we can't just infer from the representation of his anti-Antiochian argument of thirty-five years ago or his anti-Stoic argument of seven years ago that the contemporary Cicero of the frame – or that *Cicero* himself – has the same view.[17] The structure in fact complicates things in four ways:

(a) as above, by putting side by side four potentially distinct Cicero-slices,

(b) by its narrative/frame order, which progresses, with comments, from *Fin.* 1 to *Fin.* 5,

[15] See Leonhardt 1999: 13–88, whose argument that the order and length of speeches determine which is more persuasive to Cicero is justly criticized in Graver 2000.

[16] The strongest variant of this is the pre-war source-critical orthodoxy that identified Antiochus' *On Ends* as the source for Cicero's arguments in *Fin.* 2 and 4 as well as Piso's in *Fin.* 5 (which explicitly relies in some measure on Antiochian material, *pace* Giusta 1990); see Hirzel 1883 II: 630–668, Philippson 1939: 1132–1141, and, e.g., Nikolsky 2001: 462–464. But see *ad* n. 29 below: if Antiochus came up with the common strategy of *Fin.* 2 and *Fin.* 4, he somehow failed to notice how well the same strategy fits his own position. This is one reason for thinking that the strategy is Carneadean.

[17] The frame in *Fin.* 3.1–6 does tell us, though, that Cicero-now agrees with Cicero-in-50 BC about Torquatus' argument; see *ad* n. 50.

(c) by its temporal order, which progresses in the opposite direction, from *Fin.* 5 to *Fin.* 1, and

(d) by the different associations of the shifts in location, from home to Athens.

One could argue that the contrast between (b) and (c) and (d) is supposed to show us Cicero's evolution, so that we learn by reading backwards why the anti-Antiochian arguments of Cicero the philosopher in Athens in 79 BC are wrong in the light of the arguments made by Cicero the consular in Italy in 52 BC. But I don't think that this is what we actually find in the text. It seems rather, as I will argue, that Cicero designed the structure exactly in order to prevent such a simple 'reading-off' of his position. My suggestion is thus that these complexities are designed to dramatize for us the depth of Cicero's sceptical *aporia*, in the way that he sketches in *Ac.* 2.134 (see section 3).[18] At any rate, the structure of the dialogue can't be taken as evidence of Cicero's Antiochian leanings.

2.2.2 *The sceptical methods in the dialogue are compatible with radical scepticism*

The second part of the standard case for taking Cicero in the *De Finibus* as a mitigated sceptic with Antiochian leanings is based on the claim that Cicero's methods and stance in it seem to be identified as those of a mitigated sceptic:

a   the method of exposition in the dialogue – argument 'on either side' – is the standard method of the mitigated sceptic (especially when the protagonist's view is palpable but not made explicit); see, e.g., *Fin.* 2.1–2 and the many parallel passages, such as *ND* 1.11, *Ac.* 2.7–9, 2.60;[19]

---

[18] *Ac.* 2.134: [Cicero:] *sed <et> ille [Zeno] vereor ne virtuti plus tribuat quam natura patiatur, praesertim Theophrasto multa diserte copioseque dicente, et hic [Antiochus] metuo ne vix sibi constet, qui cum dicat esse quaedam et corporis et fortunae mala tamen eum qui in his omnibus sit beatum fore censeat si sapiens sit: distrahor, tum hoc mihi probabilius tum illud videtur, et tamen nisi alterutrum sit virtutem iacere plane puto.* ('But in Zeno's case I worry that he ascribes more to virtue than nature allows, especially in the light of Theophrastus' many learned and eloquent arguments; and in Antiochus' I'm afraid that he is scarcely consistent when he says that there are bodily and external circumstances that are bad, and yet believes that someone subject to all of them will be happy if he's wise. I am torn: now one, now the other view seems more persuasive to me, and yet I think that virtue will utterly collapse unless one of them is right.') Cf. *Ac.* 2.139: [Cicero:] *Sit sane ita* [viz. Chrysippus' view that there are only three possible ends] *– quamquam a Polemonis et Peripateticorum et Antiochi finibus non facile divellor nec quicquam habeo adhuc probabilius.* ('Maybe that's right – though it's not easy to tear myself away from the end adopted by Polemo, the Peripatetics, and Antiochus, and so far I don't find anything else more persuasive.')

[19] *Fin.* 2.2: [Cicero:] *Sed et illum quem nominavi et ceteros sophistas, ut e Platone intellegi potest, lusos videmus a Socrate. Is enim percontando atque interrogando elicere solebat eorum opiniones quibuscum*

b Cicero is explicitly characterized as an Academic in *Fin.* 5.76, viz. he holds
the core views that: (1) the Stoic definition of 'cognition' rules out knowledge (cf. *Ac.* 2.112–113); (2) the Academic can nevertheless adopt 'persuasive' views, e.g., Antiochian ones in ethics; (3) the Academic is peculiarly
'free' to argue for whatever strikes him as persuasive.[20] These are the standard set of views that Cicero uses to characterize the Academics in the prefaces to *ND* 1, *Ac.* 2, *Off.* 2, etc. – and the ones he elaborates in more detail
in *Ac.* 2.65–113.

---

*disserebat, ut ad ea quae ii respondissent si quid videretur diceret. Qui mos cum a posterioribus non esset
retentus, Arcesilas eum revocavit instituitque ut ii qui se audire vellent non de se quaererent sed ipsi dicerent quid sentirent; quod cum dixissent, ille contra. Sed eum qui audiebant, quoad poterant, defende-
bant sententiam suam. Apud ceteros autem philosophos qui quaesivit aliquid tacet; quod quidem iam fit
etiam in Academia. Ubi enim is qui audire vult ita dixit: 'Voluptas mihi videtur esse summum bonum',
perpetua oratione contra disputatur, ut facile intellegi possit eos qui aliquid sibi videri dicant non ipsos
in ea sententia esse sed audire velle contraria.* ('But we know from Plato that Gorgias and the other
sophists were mocked by Socrates. Socrates' own technique was to investigate his interlocutors by
questioning them. Once he had elicited their opinions in this way, he would then respond to them
if he had any view of his own. This method was abandoned by his successors, but Arcesilaus revived
it and laid it down that anyone who wanted to hear him speak should not ask him questions but
rather state their own opinion. Only then would he *speak against it.* Now Arcesilaus' audiences
would defend their position as best they could. But the practice with other philosophers is that
a member of the audience states a view, and then is silent. This is in fact what currently happens
even in the Academy. One who wants to hear the philosopher's view says perhaps "In my opinion
pleasure is the highest good." The philosopher then puts the contrary position in a continuous discourse. Evidently, then, the one who had declared that such-and-such was their view did not really
hold that opinion but simply wanted to hear the opposing arguments.')

[20] *Fin.* 5.76: *Tum Lucius: Mihi vero ista valde probata sunt, quod item fratri puto. Tum mihi Piso: Quid
ergo? inquit, dasne adolescenti veniam? An eum discere ea mavis quae cum plane perdidiceriti nihil
sciat? Ego vero isti, inquam, permitto. Sed nonne meministi licere mihi ista probare quae sunt a te dicta?
Quis enim potest ea quae probabilia videantur ei non probare? An vero, inquit, quisquam potest probare
quod perceptum, quod comprehensum, quod cognitum non habet? Non est ista, inquam, Piso, magna
dissensio. Nihil enim est aliud, quam ob rem mihi percipi nihil posse videatur nisi quod percipiendi
vis ita definitur a Stoicis ut negent quicquam posse percipi nisi tale verum quale falsum esse non possit.
Itaque haec cum illis est dissensio, cum Peripateticis nulla sane. Sed haec omittamus; habent enim et
bene longam et satis litigiosam disputationem.* ("I am completely won over", exclaimed Lucius, "and
I believe that my cousin is too." "Well then, does the young man have your consent?" Piso asked
me. "Or do you prefer that he learn a system which will leave him knowing nothing when he has
mastered it?" "I give him his head", I replied, "but are you forgetting that it is quite legitimate for
me to bestow my approval on what you have said? After all, who can fail to approve what seems
persuasive?" "Yet who can approve anything that is not something he has cognized, grasped or
known?" "There is no great disagreement here, Piso", I said. "There is only one thing that makes
me deny the possibility of cognition, and that is the Stoics' definition of its scope. They claim that
nothing can be cognized except that which is true and could not be false. So it is with the Stoics
that this disagreement arises, and clearly not with the Peripatetics. But let us put this matter to one
side, since it involves a rather long and pretty contentious debate.") Cf. *Ac.* 2.112–113: [Cicero:]
*Si enim mihi cum Peripatetico res esset, qui id percipi posse diceret quod inpressum esset e vero, neque
adhaerere illam magnam accessionem 'quo modo inprimi non posset a falso', cum simplici homine
simpliciter agerem nec magno opere contenderem atque etiam si, cum ego nihil dicerem posse conpre-
hendi, diceret ille sapientem interdum opinari, non repugnarem, praesertim ne Carneade quidem huic
loco valde repugnante ... ut omittam alia, haec duo de quibus agitur quis umquam dixit aut veteris*

But further reflection suggests that the characterization of Cicero's scepticism in the dialogue is also less favourable to the mitigated reading than these quick remarks suggest. They indicate only that Cicero is an Academic sceptic, not that he is a mitigated rather than Carneadean sceptic.

a Closer examination of *Fin.* 2.1–3 and other parallel passages shows that there are three basic Academic methods: the Socratic, the Arcesilian, and the Carneadean.[21] To put it briefly: Socrates is represented here and elsewhere as a mitigated sceptic, who has his own views, but, for pedagogical reasons, he does not foreground them; Arcesilaus is represented as a radical sceptic, who isn't committed to any views he adduces; and Carneades' distinctive *pro* and *contra* argument is compatible with both forms of scepticism – and indeed with dogmatism as Piso points out in *Fin.* 5.10. If so, however, we can't infer which view Cicero holds just from the formal method of the dialogue: the format of argument 'on either side' is inconclusive evidence.[22]

b The characterization of Cicero in the dialogue is also more complicated than the mitigated reading suggests, and in a way that seems compatible with both mitigated and unmitigated scepticism. The complexity derives from the various ways in which Cicero has characterized himself in the three conversations: in *Fin.* 1–2, he is represented as distancing himself from contemporary sceptical Academics (see *Fin.* 2.1–3 and 2.43),[23] but also gives a 'manifesto' for a rational inquiry into the

---

Academiae aut Peripateticorum, vel id solum percipi posse quod esset verum tale quale falsum esse non posset, vel sapientem nihil opinari: certo nemo. horum neutrum ante Zenonem magno opere defensum est; ego tamen utrumque verum puto, nec dico temporis causa, sed ita plane probo. ('After all, if I were arguing with a Peripatetic, I would deal straightforwardly with a straightforward person. If he said that an <impression> can be grasped when it is from a true <state of affairs> without adding that significant qualification 'and stamped in a way it couldn't be by a false <state of affairs>', I wouldn't contest this very seriously. And even if his reply to my claim that nothing can be cognized were that the wise person would sometimes hold opinions, I wouldn't rebut his view – especially since even Carneades didn't fight strongly on this issue … I'll leave out my other objections; but which Old Academic or Peripatetic ever made either of these claims: that the only <impression> that could be grasped was a true one of a kind a false <impression> couldn't be, or that a wise person wouldn't hold opinions? None of them, clearly: neither of these views was seriously defended before Zeno. I, on the other hand, think each is true, and this is not just an *ad hoc* claim, but the position I openly approve.')

[21] See Douglas 1995 and Brittain 2001: 233–243 on the various forms of argument 'on either side'. See Brittain 2001: 191–219 on the radical and mitigated sceptical Academic interpretations of Socrates and Plato.

[22] See section 3.1 below on the criticisms of the Academic format of argument 'on either side' in e.g. *Fin.* 2.3, 2.17, and 3.14.

[23] *Fin.* 2.43 [Cicero:] *Restatis igitur vos; nam cum Academicis incerta luctatio est, qui nihil affirmant et quasi desperata cognitione certi id sequi volunt quodcumque veri simile videatur.* ('There remains your

highest good which reads like a précis of the sceptical inquiry we get from Cicero the author in *Fin.* 3–5 (although his decisive rejection of Epicurean ethics rests on Carneadean dialectic; see *Fin.* 2.38[24]); in *Fin.* 3–4, he is represented as agreeing with the central Antiochian views about ethics (see *Fin.* 3.10; cf. *Fin.* 4.80),[25] but still as an Academic, from Cato's perspective (see 'Carneades tuus' in *Fin.* 3.41);[26] and in *Fin.* 5, he is characterized as a sceptical Academic and critic of Antiochian ethics by himself and Piso in *Fin.* 5.1–8 (and as a 'New' Academic by Piso in 5.7) and in *Fin.* 5.75–76 and 5.85 (cited in nn. 20 and 53 respectively). But the various hints throughout the dialogue that Cicero is a sceptical Academic – and one who maintains positive, though incompatible, views in Books 1–2, in 3–4, and in 5 – do not by themselves clarify the form of his scepticism. To determine that we would need to know if he finds the distinct views he upholds in each conversation to be objectively or subjectively 'persuasive' – these being the two interpretations of Carneades' espousal of *probabilia* or *pithana* in *Ac.* 2.104 (cited in n. 13), and implying, respectively, mitigated or unmitigated scepticism.

<Epicurean> position. (A contest with the Academics has little purpose, since they affirm nothing and as if despairing of certain knowledge propose to follow whatever is truth-like.)')

[24] *Fin.* 2.38: [Cicero:] *Ita relinquet duas de quibus etiam atque etiam consideret. Aut enim statuet nihil esse bonum nisi honestum, nihil malum nisi turpe, cetera aut omnino nihil habere momenti aut tantum ut nec expetenda nec fugienda, sed eligenda modo aut reicienda sint, aut anteponet eam quam cum honestate ornatissimam, tum etiam ipsis initiis naturae et totius perfectione vitae locupletatam videbit. Quod eo liquidius faciet, si perspexerit rerum inter eas verborumne sit controversia.* ('This leaves just two views. After thorough consideration of each, reason may determine that only what is honorable is good, and only what is dishonorable is bad, all else being of no importance or of so little importance that it should be neither chosen nor shunned, but merely selected or rejected. Or else reason might prefer the theory which is seen to include not just the honorable in all its splendor, but also the riches of nature's primary objects and of a perfectly rounded life. The verdict will be all the clearer if it has first been established whether the difference between these two theories is substantive or merely verbal.')

[25] *Fin.* 3.10 [Cato:] *Quam vellem, inquit, te ad Stoicos inclinavisses! Erat enim, si cuiusquam, certe tuum nihil praeter virtutem in bonis ducere.* – [Cicero:] *Vide, ne magis, inquam, tuum fuerit, cum re idem tibi quod mihi videretur, non nova te rebus nomina inponere. Ratio enim nostra consentit, pugnat oratio.* ('"If only," exclaimed Cato, "you had made cause with the Stoics! You if anyone, should surely believe that there is nothing good except virtue." "Perhaps you Stoics ought not to have dressed up the same ideas in new terminology", I replied, "given that I have the same view as you. Our arguments coincide; it is merely in their form of expression that our dispute arises."')

[26] Note, however, that Piso's remark that 'Your Arcesilaus ... was ours, too' in *Fin.* 5.94 shows that Academics New and Old can be considered to belong to the same Academic tradition at times. (I take it that Cato's failure to include a reference to Cicero in his explicit mention of the Academics in *Fin.* 3.31 is not problematic, since he explains that he is only giving a doxographical report of what 'some Academics' (Arcesilaus?) are supposed to have thought.)

2.3   Positive evidence for Cicero's Carneadean scepticism

After trying to neutralize the evidence for Cicero's being a mitigated sceptic with Antiochian ethical leanings, I now want to give a positive reason to think that Cicero's approach is sceptical in an unreserved sense.
I should preface this argument, however, by making it explicit that by
'*Cicero's* approach' I mean the overall stance that Cicero presents dramatically *through* the dialogue. To suggest that his approach is Carneadean is
thus not to claim that any particular *persona* in the dialogue is sceptical in
this sense. The idea is rather that Cicero's scepticism is an emergent property of the dialogue as a whole: it is the upshot of his dramatization of his
attraction to several incompatible positions.[27]

The positive argument is derived from the nature and origin of the
structuring arguments Cicero deploys in *Fin.* 2 and 4. To put it briefly,
I suggest:

a   The main arguments in *Fin.* 2 are parallel to the main arguments in
    Fin. 4.
b   Carneades came up with these arguments.
c   The same arguments are clearly applicable to the Antiochian/Peripatetic
    view in *Fin.* 5.
d   So, even though Antiochus used Carneades' *divisio* to bolster his
    own ethical view, the Cicero-character is actually using Carneadean
    arguments against the Epicureans, the Stoics, *and* the Peripatetics/
    Antiochus.

---

[27] The idea that Cicero's philosophical position is an emergent property of the dialogue as a whole
is not anachronistic; see Schofield 1986. Cicero knew that this was how the radical sceptics interpreted Plato's position, on the basis of his dialogues (cf. *Ac.* 1.46, 2.74). Needless to say, Cicero
was also aware of several other general interpretations of Plato's dialogues – his works contain two
proto-Platonist interpretations derived from Antiochus in *Ac.* and also a proto-historicist interpretation, distinguishing 'historical' Socratic dialogues from Pythagorean dialogues where Socrates'
position is fictional (*Fin.* 5.87, *Rep.* 1.15–16) – see n. 8 above. But an emergent view of dialogue
was available to him. The main problems for the emergent view are: (1) Unlike Plato, Cicero never
thinks of not putting himself in his 'sceptical' dialogues; but, as Schofield 2008 has shown, and
I argue here, he gets round this by putting too much of himself in the dialogues for one to infer
that he endorses any one first-order position. (2) His characterization of the Aristotelian form
of dialogue (*Att.* 13.19.4) seems not to allow for a distinction between Cicero the character and
Cicero the narrator and the author. But this is a formal constraint only, not a content constraint.
(3) Cicero or his characters all seem to share the standard view that if a main character says 'P'
then the author thinks 'P' too (this is true for *all* the various interpretations of Plato he notes).
But the sceptical interpretation I am proposing in fact *relies* on this feature: I argue in section 3.2
that Cicero's commitment to the various views his character endorses is the basis of the sceptical
impasse he finds himself in.

That's to say, I think that we can see from the general form of the criticisms the Cicero-character uses against each school that Cicero dramatizes a consistent, sceptical approach, based on a well-known set of arguments proposed by Carneades. (I am not sure how controversial this is.)

In a bit more detail:

a The main arguments in *Fin.* 2 and 4 share the following features, I think:

  1 They are pretty clearly based on Carneades' *divisio* of ethical ends (*Fin.* 2.16, 19, 34–44; 4.49–50).

  2 They drive 'a final dilemma: either their view reduces to a different standard dogmatic position or their view is equivalent to a heretical dogmatic position. So the Epicurean is reduced to either the position of Aristippus or of Hieronymus (*Fin.* 2.15–20): the Epicurean is either a simple hedonist or takes the goal to be lack of pain. And the Stoic is reduced to either the position of the Peripatetics or of Aristo (*Fin.* 4.68–73) – viz. either she accepts the existence of non-moral goods or she denies that any non-moral state is preferable to another.

  3 In order to produce these dilemmas, the dogmatist is accused of a fatal ambiguity at the basis of their position – for the Epicurean, conflating two sorts of pleasure (*Fin.* 2.5–15), for the Stoic, treating non-moral goods sometimes as goods and sometimes as indifferents (*Fin.* 4.20–25);

  4 and also of identifying a highest good that is incompatible with the range of primary object of impulse they accept: the Epicureans take *indolentia* as their *summum bonum* but accept ordinary pleasure as the first object of appetition (*Fin.* 2.20–24, 30–32); the Stoics take virtue as their *summum bonum* but accept the primary natural objects as the first objects of appetition (*Fin.* 4.78, 4.24–43).

  5 As a result of their confusions ((2)–(4) above), the dogmatists are easily accused of hypocrisy (*Fin.* 2.28, *Fin.* 4.23, 4.56–60);

  6 and in fact the best exemplar of the dogmatic view in question signally fails to live in accordance with their confused theoretical views – so Epicurus was a better man than he was an Epicurean (*Fin.* 2.96–105), and Panaetius is too clever to use Stoic doctrine in practice (*Fin.* 4.23, 4.79).

b I think that these arguments are Carneadean because they result from his *divisio* and have the right structure for a Carneadean argument to the general effect that dogmatic ethics fails to produce the art of life (attested in Sextus, though not ascribed to any particular sceptic).

The argument is that the dogmatists make happiness impossible either because it is subject to fortune since it requires non-moral goods or because there is no practical way to attain it since all non-moral states are equally indifferent. The direct evidence we have doesn't prove that the argumentative structure derives from Carneades; but *Tusc.* 5.119–20 and *Fin.* 3.41 do show that Carneades deployed the core points ((1)–(2) above) against the Stoics.[28]

c   Cicero's argument against Piso in *Fin.* 5 conforms to the basic Carneadean argument above: he argues that – owing to a fatal ambiguity over the status of non-moral goods – the Antiochian position either reduces to the Stoics' or to the heretical view of Theophrastus (which, like Aristo's in *Fin.* 3–4, is agreed to be incapable of securing happiness); see, e.g., *Fin.* 5.83–85.

I take it, then, that the principal role of Cicero as a character in the dialogue is to advance what seems a clearly Carneadean set of arguments to the effect that all of the leading Hellenistic theories of ethics fail to secure happiness and hence none provides an art of life. This looks like a role more suited to a deeply sceptical Academic than to a mitigated sceptic with Antiochian ethical leanings.[29]

---

[28] See Annas 2007a, esp. 196. *Tusc.* 5.120: *quorum controversiam solebat tamquam honorarius arbiter iudicare Carneades. nam cum, quaecumque bona Peripateticis, eadem Stoicis commoda viderentur neque tamen Peripatetici plus tribuerent divitiis bonae valetudini ceteris rebus generis eiusdem quam Stoici, cum ea re, non verbis ponderarentur, causam esse dissidendi negabat.* ('Carneades used to adjudicate their controversy, as if he had been appointed an honorary judge. For, given that the Stoics considered everything the Peripatetics thought was good to be advantageous, and that the Peripatetics didn't ascribe more to wealth, good health, etc., than the Stoics did, when these were actually evaluated, rather than just described – given that, Carneades denied that there was any reason for their disagreement.') Cf. *Fin.* 3.41: *Carneades tuus egregia quadam exercitatione in dialecticis summaque eloquentia rem in summum discrimen adduxit, propterea quod pugnare non destitit in omni hac quaestione quae de bonis et malis appellatur non esse rerum Stoicis cum Peripateticis controversiam sed nominum.* ('Your beloved Carneades, however, with his exceptional proficiency in dialectic and his powerful eloquence, brought the matter to a real head. He would tirelessly contend that on the whole issue known as "the problem of good and evil" there was no dispute between the Stoics and the Peripatetics other than a verbal one.') Sextus' arguments against an art of life are given in *PH* 3.239–278 and *M.* 9.168–256. Some indirect evidence for the probability that Carneades attacked the Peripatetic view as well as the Stoic and Epicurean views is found in *Tusc.* 5.50, where Cicero dismisses 'the balance of Critolaus' as an adequate defense of the Peripatetic claim that non-moral goods are actual goods or constituents of happiness; see also *Tusc.* 5.47, where the 'identity' of the Peripatetic non-moral goods with the Stoic preferred indifferents is questioned. (Critolaus was a contemporary of Carneades: both went on the notorious philosophers' embassy to Rome in 155 BC.) That Peripatetics were potential targets for Academic scepticism is clear from Diogenes' report that Clitomachus had expertise in Peripateticism as well as Stoicism and Academicism (DL 4.67).

[29] This also seems to rule out the idea that Antiochus is Cicero's principal source for the work, since the suggestion that Antiochus devised a form of argument to which his own view was obviously liable is not a nice compliment to his acuity.

3 Emergent scepticism: a parallel between 'cognition' and goods subject to fortune

So far I have given some general arguments which I hope have made some headway against the view that Cicero represents himself as a mitigated sceptic who is strongly committed to Antiochian ethics, and I have given one positive argument to the effect that his scepticism is unmitigated. A natural objection to the more sceptical interpretation of *Fin.*, however, is that Cicero's evaluations of the Epicurean, Stoic, and Antiochian views still seem very clearly weighted. But if he is committed to the position that the Epicurean view is wrong, the Stoic view is implausible, and hence that the Antiochian view, for all its flaws, is overall the most persuasive, the mitigated sceptical reading is correct. So now I want to explain how that impression of the Cicero-character's evaluative stance in the various conversations is compatible with Cicero having a more sceptical overall approach in the work. The second part of this section will give a philosophical argument to this effect; but first I want to suggest that the dialogic framework introduces various forms of subjectivity that are designed to undermine our dogmatic commitment to any conclusions we or the characters may be inclined to make.

3.1 Subjective elements in the dialogue

One way in which the dialogue highlights the subjectivity of any conclusions we may derive is through the representation of critical judgements and assessments that frame the conversations and the discussion as whole. It is a principle of Academic scepticism of all kinds that an Academic teacher or writer does not interpose his own judgement on the student/ reader, but rather leaves the latter free to make judgements on rational grounds (see, e.g., *Ac.* 2.7–8[30]). But this is not what we find in the dialogue.

---

[30] *Ac.* 2.8: *hoc autem liberiores et solutiores sumus, quod integra nobis est iudicandi potestas nec ut omnia quae praescripta et quasi imperata sint defendamus necessitate ulla cogimur. Nam ceteri primum ante tenentur adstricti quam quid esset optimum iudicare potuerunt; deinde infirmissimo tempore aetatis aut obsecuti amico cuidam aut una aliquoius quem primum audierunt oratione capti de rebus incognitis iudicant et ad quamcumque sunt disciplinam quasi tempestate delati ad eam tamquam ad saxum adhaerescunt.* ('But we are freer and less constrained because our power of judgement is intact and we aren't compelled by any necessity to defend a set of views which have been prescribed and practically imposed on us by someone else. In fact, the other philosophers <labour under two constraints>. First, they are held in place by bonds formed before they were able to judge what was best. Secondly, they made their judgements about subjects they didn't know at the weakest point in their lives following the lead of a friend or captivated by a single speech from someone they heard for the first time; so, because they were driven by storm, as it were, to whichever philosophical system it is, they hang on to it as their <salvific> rock.')

a   Take the case of Torquatus: at *Fin.* 1.15 he seeks Cicero's judgement on his argument for Epicurean ethics, since he regards Cicero as a fair judge (*iudicem aequum*), and he invites it again at *Fin.* 1.72.[31] But at *Fin.* 2.119, after his own speech, Cicero suggests Triarius – a partisan Stoic – as a fair judge, though Torquatus strongly disagrees.[32] It doesn't seem a stretch to suggest that by highlighting the theme of fair judgements, the dialogue invites us to wonder how fair a judge Cicero the character is. And if we do wonder about this, we are likely to be rather dismayed by the start of *Fin.* 3 (3.1–6), where Cicero the narrator (in 45 BC) straightforwardly asserts the complete correctness of Cicero-in-50 BC in his arguments in *Fin.* 1–2 such as *Fin.* 2.38 (cited in n. 24).[33] If there is more to be said, as Torquatus makes clear that there is, should the narrator be doing this?

b   A second case is that of Brutus, in the frame narrative. Cicero characterizes Brutus as a proficient judge and philosopher in *Fin.* 1.2, *Fin.* 1.8, and especially in *Fin.* 3.6.[34] But Cicero does not tell us until *Fin.*

---

[31] *Fin.* 1.72: *Quae cum dixisset [Torquatus], Explicavi, inquit, sententiam meam, et eo quidem consilio, tuum iudicium ut cognoscerem, quae mihi facultas, ut id meo arbitratu facerem, ante hoc tempus numquam est data.* ('I have set out my own view, with the intention of learning your judgment on it. I have never before now been given the opportunity to do so, at least not <when I was allowed to explain it> in my own way.')

[32] *Fin.* 2.119: [Cicero:] *Sed erat aequius Triarium aliquid de dissensione nostra iudicare.* [Torquatus:] *Eiuro, inquit adridens, iniquum, hac quidem de re; tu enim ista lenius, hic Stoicorum more nos vexat.* ('But it would be fairer for Triarius to make a judgment about our disagreement.' 'I don't accept him as a fair judge, at least on this matter. For you criticize us more gently, but he does it in the Stoic fashion.')

[33] *Fin.* 3.2: *Quaerendum est enim, ubi sit illud summum bonum quod reperire volumus, quoniam et voluptas ab eo remota est et eadem fere contra eos dici possunt qui vacuitatem doloris finem bonorum esse voluerunt; nec vero ullum probetur summum bonum quod virtute careat, qua nihil potest esse praestantius. Itaque quamquam in eo sermone qui cum Torquato est habitus non remissi fuimus, tamen haec acrior est cum Stoicis parata contentio.* ('We must investigate where that supreme good that we want to discover is to be found. Pleasure has been eliminated from the inquiry, and pretty much the same objections hold against those who maintained that the ultimate good was freedom from pain. Indeed no good should be declared supreme if it is lacking in virtue, since nothing can be superior to that. We were forceful enough in our debate with Torquatus. But a still fiercer struggle with the Stoics is at hand.')

[34] *Fin.* 3.6: *De ipsis rebus autem saepenumero, Brute, vereor ne reprehendar cum haec ad te scribam, qui cum in philosophia, tum in optimo genere philosophiae tantum processeris. Quod si facerem quasi te erudiens, iure reprehenderer. Sed ab eo plurimum absum neque ut ea cognoscas quae tibi notissima sunt ad te mitto, sed quia facillime in nomine tuo adquiesco et quia te habeo aequissimum eorum studiorum quae mihi communia tecum sunt existimatorem et iudicem. Attendes igitur ut soles diligenter, eamque controversiam diiudicabis quae mihi fuit cum avunculo tuo, divino ac singulari viro.* ('Turning to the subject itself, Brutus, I am in constant fear that I will be reproached for addressing this work to you, who are such an erudite student of philosophy in general and the best *kind* of it in particular. If I were doing so as if to instruct you, then the reproach would be justified. But that is far from my intention. Nor am I sending you this work to let you know what you already know very well. Rather, I take the greatest comfort in associating it with your name. And I regard you as the most impartial evaluator and judge in those fields of study where we share an interest. Pay

5.8 that Brutus – the expert he calls on to adjudicate the conversation between Cicero *qua* supporter of Antiochian ethics and Cato, Brutus' Stoic uncle – is himself an Antiochian.[35] Again, it doesn't seem a stretch to suggest that the theme of objective judgement is simultaneously underlined and undermined.

A second way in which the dialogue highlights the subjectivity of any conclusions we may derive from it is by its representation of the actual effect of the arguments on the participants.[36] Cicero stresses in each conversation that he can be 'converted' – he could be an Epicurean (*Fin.* 1.28), or a Stoic (*Fin.* 4.2), or an Antiochian/Peripatetic (*Fin.* 5.95) – if his interlocutor can just persuade him of a crucial point.[37] But the only characters who change their minds at all in the dialogue are the avowedly inexpert characters, Lucius Cicero – who is represented as a young novice, mainly interested in oratory (see *Fin.* 5.5–6 and *Fin.* 5.76) – and Quintus Cicero – who is represented as primarily interested in poetry and the value of philosophical writing for a liberal education (see *Fin.* 5.3 and *Fin.* 5.96). This is underlined by the evident lack of persuasion in the more philosophically competent speakers, especially Cato (e.g. at *Fin.* 4.80) and Cicero (e.g. at *Fin.* 5.95, where he notes that Piso needs to strengthen his crucial case 'again and again' if he wants to persuade him). It also seems designed to undermine, in the light of the Academic critique of dogmatic 'conversions' by youths (see *Ac.* 2.7–8, cited in n. 30).

A third way in which the dialogue highlights the subjectivity of any conclusions we may derive from it is by its representation of the gap between the theory and practice of argumentative method adopted by

---

close attention, then, and be the judge in the disagreement I had with your uncle, a wonderful and unique man.')

[35] *Fin.* 5.8: *Cuius oratio attende, quaeso, Brute, satisne videatur Antiochi complexa esse sententiam, quam tibi, qui fratrem eius Aristum frequenter audieris, maxime probatam existimo.* ('Please concentrate, Brutus, and see if his talk adequately captures the philosophy of Antiochus. I know that you are a particular adherent of his views, and have often heard lectures by his brother Aristus.')

[36] On these issues, see Schofield 2008 and Inwood 1990.

[37] *Fin.* 1.29: [Cicero:] *Certe, inquam, pertinax non ero tibique, si mihi probabis ea quae dices, libenter assentiar.* ('Rest assured that I will not be willful. If you persuade me of your claims, I shall gladly agree with you.') *Fin.* 4.2: [Cato:] *Easdemne res? inquit; an parum disserui non verbis Stoicos a Peripateticis sed universa re et tota sententia dissidere? Atqui, inquam, Cato, si istud obtinueris, traducas me ad te totum licebit.* ('"The same doctrines?" exclaimed Cato. "Have I failed to drive home the point that the difference between the two schools is not verbal but a matter of substance at each and every turn?" "Well" I said, "if you can establish that, you have a right to claim me as a complete convert to your cause."') *Fin.* 5.95: *Atqui iste locus* [virtue is sufficient for *beate vivere*] *est, Piso, tibi etiam atque etiam confirmandus, inquam; quem si tenueris, non modo meum Ciceronem sed etiam me ipsum abducas licebit.* ('"This position of yours, Piso, is in urgent need of strengthening", I said. "But if you can defend it, I will let you steal not just my cousin Cicero but my own self."')

(especially) the Cicero-character. In *Fin.* 2.3, Cicero makes an elaborate argument in favour of the Socratic/Arcesilian method of question and answer, using this to draw conclusions from points conceded by the interlocutor.[38] He also distinguishes this method from two others:

a   continual speech (*perpetua oratio*), which is now common even in the Academy, he says in *Fin.* 2.2; and
b   dogmatic philosophical methods, i.e., Stoic syllogisms (*consectaria*), which, though they are consistent dialectical arguments, are not inferred from premises conceded by their interlocutors (*Fin.* 4.50, cf. 4.52, 4.7); and Epicurean arguments, which aren't honed by dialectic, and hence are often invalid (see, e.g., *Fin.* 1.22).[39]

But in the event, Cicero's own arguments rarely conform to these ideals. First, Cicero drops the question and answer format in a few pages, by *Fin.* 2.17, and uses *perpetua oratio* in the 'later' book *Fin.* 4 without any hint of discomfort with the method. And both Torquatus (*Fin.* 2.17) and Cato (*Fin.* 3.14) object to Cicero's actual practice of question and answer as a captious method that is inappropriate in aim, viz. not a method that works *ex concessis*.[40] Secondly, the alternative Torquatus argues for

---

[38] *Fin.* 2.3 [Cicero:] *Nos commodius agimus; non enim solum Torquatus dixit quid sentiret, sed etiam cur. Ego autem arbitror, quamquam admodum delectatus sum eius oratione perpetua, tamen commodius, cum in rebus singulis insistas et intellegas quid quisque concedat, quid abnuat, ex rebus concessis concludi quod velis et ad exitum perveniri. Cum enim fertur quasi torrens oratio, quamvis multa cuiusque modi rapiat, nihil tamen teneas, nihil apprehendas, nusquam orationem rapidam coerceas.* ('Our procedure, though, is a better one. Torquatus stated not only what he thought, but why he thought it. I believe, however, much as I enjoyed hearing him speak uninterrupted, that it is nonetheless more manageable if one stops after each individual point and ascertains what each of the listeners is happy to concede, and what they would reject. One can then draw the inferences one wishes from the points conceded and reach one's conclusion. When, on the other hand, the speech races on like a torrent, carrying with it all manner of material, then there is nothing the listener can grasp or get hold of. There is no way to check the raging flood.')

[39] *Fin.* 4.50: [Cicero:] *Iam autem Callipho aut Diodorus quomodo poterunt tibi istud concedere, qui ad honestatem aliud adiungant quod ex eodem genere non sit? Placet igitur tibi, Cato, cum res sumpseris non concessas, ex illis efficere quod velis?* ('Are you happy, then, Cato, to draw the inferences you wish from points that have not been conceded?') See Schofield 1983 on this charge against Stoic syllogisms.

[40] *Fin.* 2.17: [Torquatus:] *Tum ille: Finem, inquit, interrogandi, si videtur; quod quidem ego a principio ita me malle dixeram hoc ipsum providens, dialecticas captiones. Rhetorice igitur, inquam, nos mavis quam dialectice disputare? Quasi vero, inquit, perpetua oratio rhetorum solum, non etiam philosophorum sit ... Obsequar igitur voluntati tuae dicamque si potero rhetorice, sed hac rhetorica philosophorum, non nostra illa forensi, quam necesse est, cum populariter loquatur, esse interdum paulo hebetiorem.* ('At this Torquatus said, "An end to questioning, if you please. I told you my own preference right from the beginning, precisely because I foresaw this kind of dialectical quibbling." "So you prefer to debate in the rhetorical rather than dialectical style?" I asked. "As if," he replied, "continuous discourse is only for orators and not for philosophers." "... I bow, then, to your wishes, and will use, if I can, the rhetorical style, but it shall be the rhetoric of philosophers rather than

and Cicero grudgingly accepts at *Fin.* 2.17 is supposed to be a form of philosophical rhetoric that is distinct from Ciceronian forensic rhetorical modes. But Cicero makes overt use of forensic rhetorical modes, e.g., in *Fin.* 4.61 – where he puts a speech into the mouths of the ancients, which appeals explicitly to their authority – and he is called on it in *Fin.* 4.62 by Cato.[41]

The fact that we find the same mismatch between ideal and practice in the representation of each of these three aspects of the conversations in the dialogue indicates that they are not accidental features. The idea that we are supposed to pick up on the subjectivity of the methods and especially of the judgements they produce can also be supported by some general features of the representation of 'Cicero' *across* various dialogues. (At least, it can if we allow our readings of one dialogue to guide those of another, which seems plausible for the set *Hort., Ac., Fin., Tusc., ND, Div.,* and *Fat.*, since they contain explicit cross-references to each other.[42]) That is, we can read the vacillations of 'Cicero' across dialogues on the issue of the sufficiency of virtue for happiness as a dramatization of his uncertainty in the face of the arguments in *Fin.* This vacillation is represented directly in *Ac.* 2.134 (cf. 2.138), as mentioned above. It is also made explicit in *Tusc.* 5 in two ways:

a   *Tusc.* 5 as a whole argues first that the Stoic view is uniquely correct and secondly that all the philosophers can be seen to be correct on this issue – so it repeats the vacillations of *Fin.* taken as a whole.

lawyers. The latter is designed for a popular audience, and so is sometimes of necessity a little lacking in subtlety.") *Fin.* 3.14: [Cato:] *Non ignoranti tibi, <inquit,> quid sim dicturus, sed aliquid, ut ego suspicor, ex mea brevi responsione arripere cupienti non respondebo ad singula: explicabo potius, quoniam otiosi sumus, nisi alienum putas, totam Zenonis Stoicorumque sententiam.* ("You know well what I shall say," he replied. "And I suspect you cannot wait to seize upon some point or other if I make a brief response. So I will not reply point by point. Instead, since we have plenty of leisure, I will expound the whole system of Zeno and the Stoics – unless you would rather I did not.")
41 *Fin.* 4.61–62: [Cicero:] *Quid si reviviscant Platonis illi et deinceps qui eorum auditores fuerint et tecum ita loquantur? 'Nos cum te, M. Cato, studiosissimum philosophiae, iustissimum virum, optimum iudicem, religiosissimum testem, audiremus ...' Ea cum dixissent, quid tandem talibus viris responderes?* [4.62] [Cato:] *Rogarem te, inquit, ut diceres pro me tu idem qui illis orationem dictavisses, vel potius paulum loci mihi ut iis responderem dares, nisi et te audire nunc mallem et istis tamen alio tempore responsurus essem, tum scilicet cum tibi.* ('Imagine that those pupils of Plato, and their follower in turn, were to come back to life and address you in the following manner: "Marcus Cato, most devoted student of philosophy, most just of men, most honorable of judges, most scrupulous of witnesses ..." Well, Cato, what response could you make to the words of men like these? "I would request," said Cato, "that having put this speech into their mouths you make one on my behalf too. In fact I prefer to listen to you, and I intend to reply to these distinguished figures – meaning yourself – on another occasion. Otherwise I would have asked you to give me a little breathing-space to make my reply.") On Cicero's forensic use of *exempla*, see van der Blom 2010.
42 In *Fin.*, however, the only explicit cross-reference is to the *De re publica* (*Fin.* 2.59).

b *Tusc.* 5.32 makes Cicero's vacillations on this as a character explicit, by
directly pointing out the inconsistency between his current support for
the Stoic view and his argument against it in *Fin.* 4.[43]

Finally, the way in which Cicero argues for the consistency of the
Antiochian view on the sufficiency of virtue for happiness in *Tusc.* 5.83–87
itself seems to reinforce the suggestion that we should be wary of his conclusions here and in *Fin.* For in *Tusc.* 5.83–87, Cicero uses exactly the same
two arguments in favour of the Antiochian view that the Cicero of *Fin.*
5.95 had found inadequate when they were given by Piso in *Fin.* 5.86–94.
(These are the arguments from predominant characteristics (*Fin.* 4.91–92;
Tusc. 5.85–86) and that virtue is sufficient for living happily if not in perfect happiness (*Fin.* 4.93–94, *Tusc.* 5.85–87).) When Cicero concluded in
Fin. 5.95 that Piso needed to 'strengthen this case again and again' to persuade him, it seems unlikely that he meant that merely repeating it with
a rhetorical argument that non-moral evils aren't really evil would secure
Cicero's rational commitment to the Antiochian view.[44] So the way Cicero
represents his own changes of mind on this issue seems to undermine
fairly clearly any inference from his temporary conclusions here or there
to a strong commitment to this or that conclusion.

3.2   A philosophical motivation for Cicero's apparent commitments

The earlier sections have argued that we don't need to interpret Cicero's
approach in *Fin.* as mitigatedly sceptical and why we might want to interpret it as more deeply sceptical. I will end by sketching a philosophical
argument for a more deeply sceptical interpretation of his apparently dogmatic judgements and relative evaluations of the Epicurean, Stoic, and
Antiochian positions in the dialogue. The idea here is that we can see
the real function of these apparent commitments by reconstructing an
unstated meta-argument in which they serve as premises for a sceptical
conclusion.[45]

The first step towards a plausible explanation for the explicit judgements Cicero makes concerning the three dogmatic schools in *Fin.* 1–5 is
to see that he starts out with two sorts of commitment.

---

[43] See *Tusc.* 5.32–33, cited in n. 11 above.
[44] See *Fin.* 5.95, cited in n. 37 above.
[45] This may sound dubious, but it is a standard way of interpreting the arguments of radical sceptics
such as Arcesilaus and Carneades, and yields powerful results in their cases, I think; see e.g. Striker
1980 and Frede 1987b and 1987c.

a   Cicero is committed in principle, I think, to the views of 'ordinary life', i.e., what Sextus calls *bios* and what the Romans in the late Republic called the *mos maiorum*.[46] His attachment to ordinary life is indicated by two pervasive themes in the dialogue. The first is the characterization of Cicero and the other interlocutors, which clearly presents them as *Romans* and as therefore in some sense *non*-philosophers.[47] (*Romanitas* is stressed most notably in *Fin.* 1.1–13; the interlocutors' status as civilians in philosophy is expressed explicitly by Cicero in *Fin.* 2.1 and Piso in *Fin.* 5.8 and indirectly through the repeated avowal that 'we' – including Torquatus – are interested in philosophy as part of the liberal education suitable for elite Romans; cf. *Fin.* 1.13, 3.7–8, 5.1–8.) The second is the constant appeal to Roman *exempla*, which is most relentless in the first conversation (see below), but also present in *Fin.* 3–4 and in 5. If correct, this is important because ordinary life and the *mos maiorum* are deeply committed to two claims about goodness:

1   virtue is a primary and intrinsic good,
2   there are also other kinds of good, which are subject to fortune.

b   Cicero, like all the protagonists in the dialogue, is also committed in principle to philosophy as the source for both a rational method and the art of life, i.e., as the best means of securing happiness. (Cicero's commitment is given in the narrative frame at *Fin.* 3.4 (cf. 1.3 and 1.11–12).[48] The commitment of the others to their philosophical school as offering an art of life is made explicit for the Epicureans at *Fin.* 1.42, for the Stoics at *Fin.* 3.12, and for the Antiochians at *Fin.* 5.16.[49]) Thus,

---

[46] Though there is a difference between content and attitude: I am not of course suggesting that Roman citizens in the late Republic took the sceptical attitude to the content of the *mos maiorum* that Sextus takes to the content of *bios*.

[47] *Fin.* 2.1: [Cicero:] *Hic cum uterque me intueretur seseque ad audiendum significarent paratos, Primum, inquam, deprecor ne me tamquam philosophum putetis scholam vobis aliquam explicaturum, quod ne in ipsis quidem philosophis magnopere umquam probavi.* ('At this point they both looked at me and signaled that they were ready to hear me. I began by saying, "Let me first of all beg you not to expect me to expound a formal lecture to you like a philosopher. Indeed, this is a procedure I have never greatly approved of even in the case of philosophers."') *Fin.* 5.8: [Piso:] *Dat enim id nobis solitudo, quod si qui deus diceret, numquam putarem me in Academia tamquam philosophum disputaturum.* ('Since the Academy is deserted, I have the chance to discourse in it like a philosopher, which I would never have believed possible had even a god foretold it.')

[48] *Fin.* 3.4: *Quo magis hoc philosopho faciendum est; ars est enim philosophia vitae, de qua disserens arripere verba de foro non potest.* ('Philosophy is the art of life, and it cannot take ordinary language as the basis for its discussions.')

[49] *Fin.* 1.42: [Torquatus:] *Ut enim medicorum scientiam non ipsius artis, sed bonae valetudinis causa probamus, et gubernatoris ars, quia bene navigandi rationem habet, utilitate, non arte laudatur, sic sapientia, quae ars vivendi putanda est, non expeteretur si nihil efficeret: nunc expetitur quod est tamquam artifex conquirendae et comparandae voluptatis.* ('We value medical science not as an art in itself but because it brings us good health; navigation too we praise for providing the techniques for steering a ship – for its utility, not as an art in its own right. In the same way wisdom, which

to the extent that Cicero is committed to philosophy, he is also deeply attached to these two principles of Hellenistic philosophy:

3   there are norms of rationality one should adhere to,
4   there is a rational means for securing happiness.

The idea, then, is that we can explain Cicero's apparent ethical commitments and differential evaluations of ethical views in the dialogue – i.e., the way in which he, first, entirely rules out the Epicureans, and, secondly, seems to favour the Antiochians over the Stoics, without accepting either – by appealing to the two sorts of antecedent commitment outlined above. Or, to put it crudely, we can explain the first problem – Cicero's rejection of the Epicurean view – by his ordinary-life commitment to the goodness of virtue ((1) above), and the second problem – his differential attachments to the Stoic and Antiochian views – as an intractable *aporia* induced by the equipollent demands of his commitments to the existence of goods of fortune and to the possibility of securing happiness against fortune by rational means ((2) and (4) above).

The first *explanandum* is Cicero's flatly ruling out the *Epicurean* view of the *telos* in character in the conversation with Torquatus, e.g., in *Fin.* 2.37–38, which is given additional weight by its confirmation in the narrative frame in *Fin.* 3.1–3.[50] The fundamental motivation here seems clear, since, as Brad Inwood has noted, the sequence of *exempla* deployed by Cicero in *Fin.* 1–2 is designed to demonstrate that the intrinsic goodness of virtue is a basic tenet of the *mos maiorum* (cf. *Fin.* 1.23–24, 1.36, 2.60–68, and Inwood 1990). Cicero's stance is thus explained by a familiar sceptical move: we would need much stronger theoretical arguments than

---

should be considered the art of living, would not be sought if it had no practical effect. As things are, it is sought because it has, so to speak, mastered the art of locating and obtaining pleasure.') *Fin.* 3.11: [Cato:] *Nam nisi hoc obtineatur, id solum bonum esse quod honestum sit, nullo modo probari possit beatam vitam virtute effici; quod si ita sit, cur opera philosophiae sit danda nescio. Si enim sapiens aliquis miser esse possit, ne ego istam gloriosam memorabilemque virtutem non magno aestimandam putem.* ('Unless it is maintained that what is honorable is the only good, there is no way of establishing that it is virtue that brings about the happy life. And if this is so, then I do not see why we should trouble ourselves with philosophy. If it were possible for a wise person to be unhappy, I fear I would set little value on glorious and wonderful virtue.') *Fin.* 5.16: [Piso:] *Cognitis autem rerum finibus, cum intelligitur quid sit et bonorum extremum et malorum, inventa vitae via est conformatioque omnium officiorum, cum <ex->igitur, quo quidque referatur; ex quo, id quod omnes expetunt, beate vivendi ratio inveniri et comparari potest.* ('Once, however, we understand the highest ends, once we know what the ultimate good and evil is, then we have a path through life, a model of all our duties, to which each of our actions can thereby be referred. And it is from this that the thing everyone seeks, the method for living happily can be found and acquired.') External evidence for the Hellenistic philosophers' commitment to an art of life is found e.g. in Sextus *M.* 9.169 (Epicurus), 9.170 (Stoics), and 9. 173 (Peripatetics).
[50] See *Fin.* 2.38 cited in n. 24 above and *Fin.* 3.2 in n. 33.

the Epicureans can provide to dislodge our pre-theoretical commitment to the goodness of virtue. When dogmatic arguments fail, the sceptic returns to his default practical criteria for life.

The second *explanandum* is Cicero's conflicting responses to the Stoic and Antiochian doctrines about the good in *Fin.* Cicero's evaluations of the *Stoic* position in *Fin.* 4 and 5 are not entirely uniform. But it doesn't seem a stretch to note that he identifies three positive features in it: it looks like a consistent philosophical system, it tries to fulfill the promise of philosophy by providing an art of life strong enough to secure happiness ((4) above), and it gives a rigorous interpretation of the ordinary view that virtue is somehow primary ((1) above). The main problem he identifies, however, is clear: the Stoics can secure happiness only by claiming that all genuine goods are immune to fortune, which is contrary to common sense – i.e., to (2) above (see *Fin.* 4.55).[51] Since their conclusions appear to be both manifestly false and produced by valid arguments, the premises must be false (see *Fin.* 4.55, 4.67–68).[52] That is to say that ordinary people cannot believe that the sage is happy on the rack: they consider the existence of goods and bads subject to fortune to be self-evident.

Cicero's explicit judgement on the *Antiochian* position is that it strikes the wise (*prudentes*) as inconsistent because it tries to maintain both the implausible Stoic thesis of the possibility of happiness based on immunity of virtue to fortune and the ordinary view that there are other kinds of goods and bads that are subject to fortune (*Fin.* 5.85).[53] Yet Antiochus' view has the real advantage, I think, of recognizing the commitment of the

---

[51] *Fin.* 4.55: [Cicero:] *Sensus enim cuiusque et natura rerum atque ipsa veritas clamabat quodam modo non posse adduci ut inter eas res quas Zeno exaequaret nihil interesset.* ('Common sense, the facts of nature, and truth herself proclaimed the impossibility of being persuaded that there was really no difference between all the things which Zeno made equal.')

[52] *Fin.* 4.67–68: [Cicero:] *Utrum igitur tandem perspicuisne dubia aperiuntur, an dubiis perspicua tolluntur? Atqui hoc perspicuum est, vitia alia aliis esse maiora, illud dubium, ad id quod summum bonum dicitis ecquaenam possit fieri accessio. Vos autem cum perspicuis dubia debeatis illustrare, dubiis perspicua conamini tollere ... [4.68] Teneamus enim illud necesse est, cum consequens aliquod falsum sit, illud cuius id consequens sit non posse esse verum.* ('Well now: should the evident clarify the doubtful or be refuted by it? This at any rate is evident, that some vices are worse than others. Whether or not what you call the supreme good admits of any increase is open to doubt. But you Stoics try to overturn the evident with the doubtful, when you should be illuminating the doubtful with the evident ... We must hold to the principle that when a conclusion is false, its premises cannot be true.')

[53] *Fin.* 5.85: [Cicero:] *Tibi hoc incredibile, quod beatissimum: quid? tuum credibile? Si enim ad populum me vocas, eum qui ita affectus sit beatum esse numquam probabis; si ad prudentes, alterum fortasse dubitabunt, sitne tantum in virtute ut ea praediti vel in Phalaridis tauro beati sint, alterum non dubitabunt quin et Stoici conveniente sibi dicant et vos repugnantia.* ('You find it incredible that this [being on the rack] is a state of complete happiness. Well then: is your own view credible? If you make me dispute your case before an audience of ordinary people, you will never convince them that a person so afflicted is even happy. Put me before experts [*prudentes*], and they will have two

maiores to both the primacy of virtue and the existence of other significant goods ((1) and (2) above). We can thus see it as an attempt to systematize the views of ordinary life in Republican Rome or the *mos maiorum*. But the result is that it looks false to ordinary people for the same reason the Stoic view did – i.e., because a sage on the rack isn't happy – as well as inconsistent to the wise in its ambivalent claims about the immunity of goods to fortune.

Viewed in this light, we can see, I hope, how Cicero's apparently dogmatic judgements and evaluations in his criticisms of the Epicurean, Stoics, and Peripatetics/Antiochians in *Fin.* serve a serious sceptical function in the 'meta-argument' that the dialogue as a whole dramatizes. That argument is a standard sceptical argument from equipollence about the kinds and attainability of goods. *Fin.* plays out for us the drama of Cicero's deep commitment to the ethical presuppositions of both ordinary life and philosophical rationalism – a drama that leads to intractable, perhaps irresoluble doubt, but gets there through a set of apparently dogmatic scenes, which one might easily mistake as the product of the author's confusion or inconstant devotion to properly philosophical concerns.

One reason to think that something like this may be correct in the ethical case, is that (as I mentioned above) we find a strongly parallel situation in the realm of sceptical epistemology, in Cicero's *Academica*. The basic commitments that generate the intra-Academic sceptical dilemma dramatized in the *Lucullus* (and no doubt in the lost first book, the *Catulus*) may be summarized, crudely, I think, as:

a   a commitment to the possibility of knowledge, derived from ordinary life; and
b   a rationalist, philosophical commitment to immunity from error (or infallibility of assent).

As in the ethical case, we can use the range of Academic responses to these basic, but competing, constraints to explain the attraction of the three incompatible Academic positions Cicero identifies in the *Academica*. The *radical*, Carneadean, sceptic recognizes the force of the Stoic definition of 'cognition' in setting out plausible conditions on assent to an impression, but doesn't find any appropriate impressions. As a result, the radical sceptic has to give up her rational pretensions to knowledge ((a) above),

---

reactions. Firstly, they will perhaps have doubts that virtue is so powerful that those endowed with it would be happy even when inside the bull of Phalaris. But, secondly, they will have no doubt that the Stoic system in consistent, whereas yours is self-contradictory.')

but is able to preserve an immunity from error by avoiding assent ((b) above). The contrary response is found in the *fallibilist* position avowed by Philo in his heretical 'Roman Books'. For in that work (or so I have argued), Philo rejected the Stoic definition of 'cognition' and its stringent conditions of assent – and thus argued for the ready availability of ordinary knowledge, and consequently the inevitability of error. The *mitigated* sceptic represents, unsurprisingly, a compromise view on the Stoic assent conditions: she accepts the Stoic conditions for knowledge – and accordingly, denies its possibility – but then argues for a set of weaker conditions for provisional assent (or rationally warranted approval). This puts her in the same position as the Antiochian in ethics: one can see provisional assent either as a clever strategy for preserving immunity from error without giving up on one's commitment to rationalism, or as a compromise that fails in both respects, since, given that provisional assent can't secure immunity from *practical* failure, the mitigated sceptic rules out both knowledge and inerrancy.

It would take a long time, and more acuity than I have, to try to spell out in any detail more precise parallels between the ethical positions in *Fin.* and the epistemological positions in *Ac.* (Though I hope that the analogies between mitigated scepticism and Antiochian ethics, and between Roman Philonian fallibilism and Theophrastus' ethical heresy, are more or less apparent.) But for our purpose, this is perhaps enough to indicate that there is – in Cicero's presentations – a fundamental conceptual tension between two sets of demand: the demand of ordinary life for a ready and plentiful supply of (fallible) knowledge, and the demand of rationalism for a hard-won and rare supply of infallibility or immunity from error – just as there is a basic tension in ethics between a biotic conception of goods as ready to hand and plentiful and a rationalist understanding of goods as hard-won and rare in being immune from fortune.

This tension is, I think, what generates the intra-Academic drama of the *Academica*, i.e., the (mostly lost) disputes between Catulus, Catulus *père*, and Cicero, about the plausibility of radical and mitigated scepticism. It is also what generates the internal vacillation Cicero manifests in his speech in the *Lucullus*, and most clearly (as I said at the start) in *Ac.* 2.66, between the rationalist demands embodied by the sceptical 'sage's' suspension of assent and the requirement for epistemic action derived from the conceptual commitments of ordinary life.[54]

---

[54] See *Ac.* 2.66, cited in n. 1 above.

The conclusion I want to draw from this parallel is simple. If we looked at *Fin.* in isolation, it would be easy to underestimate Cicero's philosophical sophistication, because it is sometimes hard to see how many of the elements of the dialogue – and, not least, many of the judgements and evaluations he makes *in propria persona* – contribute to the philosophical arguments of the work. But the parallel with the epistemological case in the *Academica* shows, I think, that Cicero's self-presented vacillations should be understood as a dramatization of the philosophical tension between two kinds of fundamental commitment. If this is right, Cicero's scepticism in *Fin.* is a lot deeper, and much more interesting, than I used to think, and his dialogues are more artful, and worth a lot more study, than many of their readers have assumed.

CHAPTER 2

Epicurean pleasure in Cicero's De Finibus

James Warren
Corpus Christi College, Cambridge

The first two books of Cicero's *De Finibus* are devoted to the presentation and criticism of Epicurean ethics and, because the Epicureans are hedonists, some of this presentation and criticism is rightly devoted to the Epicurean conception of pleasure. I am not particularly concerned here with the task of establishing whether Cicero's presentation of the Epicurean view is fair and accurate by comparing *Fin.* with all the various other sources of evidence we have for the Epicurean conception of pleasure; my primary concern is the structure and presentation of the argument in *De Finibus*. My general contention is that in his discussion with Torquatus in Book 2 Cicero raises a serious and significant challenge for the Epicureans and that this challenge is well motivated by the presentation of the Epicurean position in Book 1. In particular, *Fin.* 1 sets out Torquatus' case for Epicurean hedonism in a way that leaves space for Cicero to exploit a possible distinction between the state of painlessness and the experience of pleasure. I concentrate on two passages: the first is the opening of Torquatus' presentation of Epicurean ethics (1.29–41) in which we are offered the Epicurean argument in favour of the goodness of pleasure and some explanation why painlessness should be counted as the highest pleasure; the second is the brief interchange between Cicero and Torquatus at the beginning of Book 2 (2.5–17) in which tensions and difficulties in Torquatus' initial exposition are emphasised.

Book 1

It is evident from the outset that Torquatus will have a difficult task persuading Cicero that there is anything much worth accepting in Epicurean

I would like to thank the participants at the *Symposium Hellenisticum* for their useful reactions to an earlier version of this essay. Some of these ideas were first aired at meetings of the 'Greco-Roman philosophy in the 1st century BC' seminar which was part of an AHRC-funded research project in Cambridge 2005–2009. Other sections emerged from what became Warren 2007.

ethics. Cicero makes clear that he is very well informed about the school's views, having accompanied Atticus to hear lectures by the Epicurean scholarchs Phaedrus and Zeno (1.16). Cicero claims a secure grasp of the school's system and thinks he is therefore immune from the possible criticism that his disagreement with them stems from a misunderstanding. The Epicurean theory is nevertheless a useful place for the discussion to begin, he says, since it will allow the participants to warm up by thinking first about a simple philosophy that is very well known before passing to the more interesting cases of the Stoics and Antiochus.[1]

Almost immediately the discussion focuses on the account of pleasure, a topic which Torquatus himself offers as the central concern of Epicurean ethics (1.28: *de qua omne certamen est*). This sets the terms of the contest: if the Epicureans are as confused about pleasure as Cicero assumes, then their whole ethical system is flawed. The atmosphere is combative and adversarial: Torquatus hails Epicurus as the lone guide to the truth (1.14) while Cicero is confident that Epicurus is mistaken not only in his approach to physics (1.17–21) and his meagre thoughts on logic (1.22) but also, and perhaps especially, when it comes to ethics and the topic of pleasure and pain. For Cicero, not only is it simply false, indeed 'unworthy of a human being', that we all by nature pursue pleasure and avoid pain, but also Epicurus is not even the clearest and most plausible philosophical hedonist; that dubious honour goes to the Cyrenaics (1.23). The first criticism is sharpened further by making the discussion intensely personal. Cicero turns to Torquatus' own ancestors and their noble and virtuous deeds (1.24–25) and claims they are counterexamples to the Epicurean account of human nature. In promoting Epicureanism, Torquatus appears to be undermining the grounds of his own family's prestige, indeed the grounds of his own *cognomen*.

Torquatus' exposition was therefore never very likely to win much favour. It is served up to a hostile and prejudiced interlocutor as a preparatory exercise before the more serious contenders to come. Nevertheless, Torquatus is allowed to offer a relatively lengthy exposition. The treatment of pleasure in Book 1 can conveniently be divided into two sections. First, Torquatus offers a set of remarks designed to secure the conclusion that pleasure is the highest good and should be the end of all our actions (1.29–36). Then he turns to offer a more detailed characterisation of the kind of pleasure that is the goal of life, namely the absence of pain (1.37–41).

[1] 1.13: *ut autem a facillimis ordiamur, prima veniat in medium Epicuri ratio, quae plerisque notissima est.*

Foundations: pleasure as a natural good: 1.29–36

Torquatus takes the view that the to-be-pursued nature of pleasure and the to-be-avoided nature of pain are axiomatic. Epicurus, Torquatus says, simply asserted these claims as self-evidently true and in no more need of justification than, for example, the assertion that 'fire is hot'. No doubt, Epicurus was himself aware that they do not however command universal assent: some think that only some pleasures are good and others think that no pleasures are good. And the Epicureans, as we shall see, have something to say about why it is that not everyone recognises these truths. But it is expected that, on reflection, every reasonable person should accept that pleasure is naturally to be pursued and pain to be avoided. Torquatus does note a degree of controversy between different Epicureans on the correct form in which they ought to present this starting-point of their ethical system and outlines two principal factions (1.31). Inevitably, Torquatus insists that the interpretation he favours is in fact consonant with what the founder of the school originally intended. He prefers an economical approach. To his mind, it is not necessary to offer a fully fledged rational defence of the goodness of pleasure to bolster the evidence of perception. Nor does he think it necessary to posit some kind of innate conception of the goodness of pleasure.[2] He does concede that, on occasion, there may be the need to set straight a misconception born of philosophical confusion about this central truth, and there is a good example of him doing just that later in the text (see 1.39). But with this exception, he seems prepared to assert that the evidence of the senses alone should be sufficient at least for the initial step. He characterises Epicurus' stance as follows:

> omne animal, simul atque natum sit, voluptatem appetere eaque gaudere ut summo bono, dolorem aspernari ut summum malum et, quantum possit, a se repellere, idque facere nondum depravatum ipsa natura incorrupte atque integre iudicante. itaque negat [*sc.* Epicurus] opus esse ratione neque disputatione quam ob rem voluptas expetenda, fugiendus dolor sit: sentiri haec putat, ut calere ignem, nivem esse albam, dulce mel, quorum nihil oportere exquisitis rationibus confirmare, tantum satis esse admonere.

(1.30)

Every animal as soon as it is born seeks pleasure and rejoices in it, while shunning pain as the highest evil and avoiding it as much as possible. This is behaviour that has not yet been corrupted, when nature's judgement is pure and whole. Hence he denies that there is any need for justification or

---

[2] See Sedley 1998: 139–142.

debate as to why pleasure should be sought, and pain shunned. He thinks
that the truth is perceived by the senses, as fire is perceived to be hot, snow
white, and honey sweet. In none of these examples is there any call for
proof by sophisticated reasoning; it is enough simply to point them out.

(Trans. R. Woolf)

The first sentence offers what has come to be known as a 'cradle argument'.[3] Using the behaviour of pre- and non-rational creatures as a reference point for determining the natural human good is an interesting
tactic.[4] Clearly, the Epicureans wish to point to cases in which observed
behaviour cannot possibly be influenced by any beliefs about value and
therefore use examples of actions taken by creatures which either can have
no beliefs at all or do not yet have any such beliefs. Torquatus is particularly interested in showing what we would all value if only we could strip
away various misconceptions and corruptions that get in the way. One
of the central contentions of the Epicurean ethical project is that adult
humans have generally acquired various beliefs about what to value and
what to avoid which actively prevent the efficient pursuit of the natural
goal. These may be beliefs held as a result of some kind of philosophical commitment to an explicit and theorised set of axiological claims.
But they may also be more mundane or conventional beliefs. The belief,
for example, that political power is something to be pursued interferes
with an individual's attainment of the natural goal by generating desires
which contribute nothing to attaining that natural goal and instead produce pain and discontent.

There is a danger that the Epicureans may be misunderstood to be
critical in general terms of the role played by reason and belief in adult
human behaviour. Torquatus does not, in fact, hold up infants and beasts
as ideals on which we might model ourselves entirely, but uses them only
as evidential support for the more restricted claim that pleasure is a natural object of pursuit and pain a natural object of avoidance; the particular form of pleasure that ought to be the natural human *telos* can be made
clear later.[5] It is true that in many cases, as reason develops and humans
acquire beliefs as a result of education and acculturation, the resulting set

[3] The term is inspired by Antiochus' observations at *Fin.* 5.55. See Brunschwig 1986 and Chapter 6 by Inwood in this volume.
[4] It is not an Epicurean innovation. See Eudoxus' argument at Aristotle *Eth. Nic.* 1172b9–15 and cf. Warren 2009: 252–265. For other reports of the Epicurean argument see Sext. Emp. *Pyr.* 3.194 and *Math.* 11.96.
[5] Cicero interprets the cradle argument as making a stronger claim and therefore thinks that Epicurus goes on inconsistently to assert that the absence of pain is the natural good: see *Fin.* 2.31–35.

of opinions prevents one from attaining the ideal life. All the same, reason has an essential role to play in the good human life and is itself part of adult human nature. As Torquatus will later insist, the correct use of prudential reasoning is essential for the proper pursuit and maximisation of pleasure over time. Further, reason is an essential tool for the correct understanding of the universe, on which much of the perfect Epicurean's happiness depends, and there are certain pleasures, for example the pleasures of philosophical discussion, which can be experienced only through the employment of reason. Reason and belief, in short, can be misguided and become sources of pain and obstacles to the good life. But used properly they are essential tools for the acquisition and maintenance of the best human life.

This more positive appraisal of reason can be set aside for now, however, since uppermost in Torquatus' mind is the importance of showing that pleasure is good and to be pursued. Indeed, as the direction of inference in 1.30 shows (*itaque*), the 'cradle argument' is explicitly made to serve as evidence for the foundational claim that the value of pleasure is simply and directly perceived (*sentiri*). Since the creatures in question are incapable of having any other means of recognising value and evidently do engage in pursuit and avoidance, it surely must be the case that perception alone is determining those responses, free from the interference of any beliefs. Moreover, this passage as a whole shows that in Epicurus' view there is an important continuity between the reactions of animals and infants and those of adult humans; for both groups, he insists, the goodness of pleasure is immediately revealed by perception in such a way that there ought to be no need of any further argument in its favour.

It is hard to overstate the importance of this insistence, both for the Epicurean ethical theory itself and also for Cicero's critical engagement with it in the rest of the text. Indeed, the question of the relationship between Epicurean pleasure and the senses is perhaps the central point of disagreement between Torquatus and Cicero. Time and again, Cicero will argue that the stronger the Epicureans make the link between pleasure (specifically, the goodness of pleasure) and the senses, the less plausible will be the Epicureans' assertion that painlessness is the highest pleasure since, Cicero supposes, the pleasure that is directly perceived by the senses as good is not the so-called pleasure which the Epicureans eventually attempt to install as the *telos*. That disagreement will become more and more explicit as the text proceeds, but it is important to note how its seed is planted at the very outset of Torquatus' position and is apparently required as the epistemological underpinning of the Epicurean conception of value. And throughout Torquatus' exposition, the Epicurean is made to refer to the senses as the arbiters of the goodness of pleasure or the means by which we recognise that we are in pleasure or pain. Cicero, therefore, is carefully exploiting what he takes to be a tension between the purported initial justification of Epicurean axiology and its eventual developed form.

A robustly empiricist approach to value is encapsulated in the Epicureans' identification of the *pathē* as one of the criteria of truth (Diog. Laert. 10.31). Torquatus – apparently following Epicurus himself – is clearly relying on some basic points of Epicurean empiricism since, still in 1.30, he happily compares the question of the goodness of pleasure with other examples of things supposedly made clear and evident simply via the senses. For example, that honey is sweet needs no defence since honey is simply perceived to be so.[6] Torquatus thereby brushes familiar sceptical concerns aside. The grounds for the sceptics' caution is generally as follows: given that honey may not appear sweet to some people at some times, it is not wise to infer that honey is indeed sweet by nature and perhaps not wise to think it is sweet even in the cases when it does indeed appear such to the senses. It is not immediately clear, however, how an analogous argument might function in the case of pleasure that might have provoked this Epicurean response. It is possible to see how the same object or activity may not always produce pleasure in all perceivers and that therefore it might be wise not to infer immediately that such and such a thing is pleasant. But the argument here concerns not whether some particular thing is pleasant but the choiceworthiness of pleasure itself. The sceptical argument ought to be that some experiences of pleasure appear choiceworthy while others do not, and as a result of this observation we should suspend judgement about the choiceworthy nature of pleasure itself. In that case, the principal Epicurean answer should account for the false appearance of non-choiceworthy pleasures and show how these are not to be taken as evidence against the initial perception of pleasure as good. Indeed, this is precisely what Torquatus goes on to do at 1.32–33 by offering an argument which defends the goodness of pleasure while allowing that certain pleasures are not to be pursued on hedonistic grounds. A properly prudential approach to one's choices will reveal that some pleasures, while good, are not to be chosen because of their longer-term painful consequences while some pains, while bad,

---

[6] See, e.g., Xenophanes B 38, Diog. Laert. 9.105 (Timon of Phlius), Sext. Emp. *Pyr.* 1.20. For his part, Cicero also has qualms about allowing something as important as the nature of the good to be assigned to the judgement of the senses although he does concede that the senses can judge authoritatively qualities including sweetness: *Fin.* 2.36–38.

should be chosen because of their longer-term pleasant consequences. Torquatus' brief account of a form of hedonic calculus does little to further the explanation of the nature or value of pleasure.[7] It does, however, allow Torquatus a first attempt at explaining the behaviour of the famous Torquati mentioned first by Cicero at 1.23–25 as *prima facie* counterexamples to a general thesis of psychological hedonism.[8]

Pleasure and the absence of pain

The insistence on the evident and perceived goodness of pleasure takes the Epicureans only part of the way to their desired hedonist conclusion. It shows that pleasure is something we find naturally good and pain something we find naturally bad. It does not show that pleasure is the only or highest good and pain the only bad. Nor does it offer very much in the way of an elaboration of what pleasure is: what, for example, is its precise relationship to pain, to perception and to desire. Nor yet does it say very much about how the Epicurean observations about the goodness of pleasure are meant to offer a goal for a recognisably eudaimonist ethical theory, a theory which will specify a conception of a good life which is somehow complete and satisfying as a whole.[9] The next step, and the step which appears to offer answers to all these rather pressing questions, is the claim that the absence of pain in a living organism is itself a pleasure. Further, and more controversial still, they claim that the absence of all pain is the greatest possible pleasure (*maxima voluptas*: 1.37; *summa voluptas*: 1.38).

Alongside this pleasure identified with the absence of pain the Epicureans also recognise pleasures associated with episodes of removing pain (e.g., drinking when thirsty). And they agree that it is possible while experiencing no pain to experience qualitatively different pleasures (e.g., sipping some wine when not at all thirsty), the latter being what Torquatus seems to mean when he talks of merely embellishing but not increasing an already pleasant state of painlessness. In both these cases, the pleasure appears to be associated with some change in the perceiver's state

---

[7] For more discussion see Warren 2001.

[8] The general assumption of Cicero's presentation and criticism of the Epicureans in *Fin.* 1 and 2 is that they are psychological hedonists. See Woolf 2004, *contra* Cooper 1999a. Cooper may well be right, however, to note that Epicurus' *Letter to Menoeceus* is not evidently committed to this general descriptive thesis.

[9] Cf. Annas 1993: 339. Compare the Epicureans' eudaimonism with the difficulties apparently faced by the hedonist Cyrenaics: see Diog. Laert. 2.87. There is some debate whether the Cyrenaics ought to be counted as eudaimonists: see in particular Tsouna 2002.

in the form either of the removal of a pain or of the qualitative alteration of a present state.

These two broad categories – the pleasure of painlessness and the pleasures of change or removal of pain – are what in some sources are probably meant by the terms 'katastematic' and 'kinetic' pleasures respectively. As our sources repeatedly note, the recognition of katastematic pleasure is what sets Epicureanism apart from rival theories such as Cyrenaicism.[10] Although the distinction is not mentioned explicitly by Epicurus himself in either the *Letter to Menoeceus* or the *Kyriai Doxai*, there is little reason to question its authenticity despite some recent doubts.[11] The precise nature of and the relationship between the two forms of pleasure remain obscure, however, and continue to be a subject of considerable debate.[12] Cicero does not offer anything like a clear categorisation, perhaps because he is deeply suspicious about whether katastematic pleasure is really pleasure at all. Torquatus instead tends to talk of pleasure *in motu* in contrast with pleasure identified with the absence of pain, which is described by various different expressions (see e.g. 1.37–38 and 2.9, discussed further below).

There are two important consequences of this recognition of katastematic pleasure which guide the presentation and criticism of Epicurean ethics in *De Finibus*. First, it follows that there is no intermediate state between pleasure and pain. This again contrasts the Epicurean view sharply with that of the Cyrenaics, and indeed most other thinkers who had turned their attention to the nature of pleasure and pain and had recognised the existence of a state of feeling neither pleasure nor pain.[13]

---

[10] For further discussion and comparison see Diog. Laert. 2.87–89; 10.136–137 and Aristocles *ap.* Eus. *Praep. evang.* 14.18.31ff. Cf. Purinton 1993, 252ff., Warren 2001, O'Keefe 2002, Sedley 2002.

[11] It would be imprudent to rest too much on the obscure and controversial phrase from Epicurus' *On Choices* (Us. 2) cited at Diog. Laert. 10.136: ἡ μὲν γὰρ ἀταραξία καὶ ἀπονία καταστηματικαί εἰσιν ἡδοναί· ἡ δὲ χαρὰ καὶ ἡ εὐφροσύνη κατὰ κίνησιν ἐνεργείᾳ βλέπονται. However, Metrodorus appears to have distinguished clearly kinetic and katastematic pleasure and to have used those very terms to mark the distinction (also at Diog. Laert. 10.136, from Metrodorus' *Timocrates*: νοουμένης δὲ ἡδονῆς τῆς τε κατὰ κίνησιν καὶ τῆς καταστηματικῆς ... = fr. 29 Körte). For accounts which deny the authenticity of the distinction see Gosling and Taylor 1982: 367–394 (who take the insistence on the distinction to be part of Cicero's generally hostile and uncharitable approach) and Nikolsky 2001 (cf. Wolfsdorf 2009: 240–246). Both accounts rely heavily on a passage from Epicurus' *On the Telos*, quoted by Cicero at *Tusc.* 3.41 and *Nat. D.* 1.111 and by Athenaeus 546e (Us. 67), in which he says that he cannot conceive (νοήσω, *intellegam*) of the good without what are conventionally thought of as kinetic pleasures: of eating, drinking, sex and the senses. It is not clear, however, whether the pleasures listed here are constitutive of the ideal life, necessary means to it or inevitable concomitants of it.

[12] See Merlan 1960, Diano 1974, Rist 1974, Gosling and Taylor 1982, Giannantoni 1984, Hossenfelder 1986, Mitsis 1988, Striker 1993, Erler and Schofield 1999, Wolfsdorf 2009 and 2013: 147–167.

[13] *quibusdam* at 1.38 refers to all these.

Second, if the Epicureans' account is accepted as plausible, it allows them to promote katastematic pleasure, and the chance of attaining this as a stable state of living, as a much more promising candidate for a eudaimonistic *telos* than the conventional view of merely episodic pleasure; they go on to claim that this painless state of living is somehow 'complete' in that its value is not increased as it is prolonged. Even Cicero recognises that this is part of the Epicureans' intention in offering their peculiar account of pleasure, although he thinks that it is a doomed attempt: *Fin.* 2.86–89. Already by Epicurus' time, there was a long tradition of criticism of pleasure as a candidate for the *telos* precisely because it was assumed to be somehow remedial or otherwise connected with the process of restoration of some good state (and therefore not itself a final good) or else in some other way necessarily inconstant or impermanent. Certainly, the Epicureans – with the notable support of Aristotle – dissent from perhaps the majority ancient view of pleasure as essentially a *kinēsis* and therefore not something which can be complete or sufficient in the way that *eudaimonia* ought to be.

It is reasonably clear why the Epicureans might have wanted to defend their unorthodox view of pleasure and it is also clear why they might have had difficulty in doing so. Certainly, it is not immediately clear from the phenomenology of everyday experience that the state of the absence of pain is itself pleasant. We need not be as obtuse in our response as a Callicles or some of the later critics of Epicureanism who object that it is absurd to say that a corpse or a stone experiences the highest pleasure. We might instead ask the simple question whether it is plausible, for example, to claim that since someone is feeling no physical pain, he is therefore experiencing the greatest physical pleasure. Cicero evidently thought that this simple question drives at the heart of the Epicureans' confusion. But in order to demonstrate that confusion he first allows Torquatus to set out the Epicurean view and to try to mount a case for it. This is the topic of 1.37–41. In these chapters Torquatus sets out to explain to Cicero the Epicurean view of the nature of pleasure (*nunc autem explicabo voluptas ipsa quae qualisque sit*: 1.37). The explanation has three parts: (1) in 37–38 Torquatus offers what appears to be an argument for the conclusion that painlessness is itself pleasant and the denial of an intermediate state; (2) in 39 Torquatus tackles an objection from Chrysippus which he takes to be a further opportunity to explain the Epicurean position in contrast to the Cyrenaics; (3) in 40 Torquatus offers a picture of the ideal Epicurean life which he assumes will be attractive and also illustrative of the points he has tried to explain in (1) and (2).

1   The pleasure of painlessness: 1.37–38

It is not easy to find any explicit Epicurean arguments for the conclusions that the state of the absence of all pain is the highest pleasure and that there is no intermediate state between pleasure and pain. That this is what they did indeed conclude is evident enough, but precisely how they thought they might persuade anyone of this conclusion is much less clear.[14] Perhaps the most promising extant text is an argument at 1.37–38.[15]

> non enim hanc solam sequimur, quae suavitate aliqua naturam ipsam movet et cum iucunditate quadam percipitur sensibus, sed maximam voluptatem illam habemus, quae percipitur omni dolore detracto, nam quoniam, cum privamur dolore, ipsa liberatione et vacuitate omnis molestiae gaudemus, omne autem id, quo gaudemus, voluptas est, ut omne, quo offendimur, dolor, doloris omnis privatio recte nominata est voluptas. ut enim, cum cibo et potione fames sitisque depulsa est, ipsa detractio molestiae consecutionem affert voluptatis, sic in omni re doloris amotio successionem efficit voluptatis. [38] itaque non placuit Epicuro medium esse se quiddam inter dolorem et voluptatem; illud enim ipsum, quod quibusdam medium videretur, cum omni dolore careret, non modo voluptatem esse, verum etiam summam voluptatem. quisquis enim sentit, quem ad modum sit affectus, eum necesse est aut in voluptate esse aut in dolore. omnis autem privatione doloris putat Epicurus terminari summam voluptatem, ut postea variari voluptas distinguique possit, augeri amplificarique non possit.

We do not simply pursue the sort of pleasure which stirs our nature with its sweetness and produces agreeable sensations in us: rather, the pleasure we deem greatest is that which is felt when all pain is removed. For when we are freed from pain, we take delight in that very liberation and release from all that is distressing. Now everything in which one takes delight is a pleasure (just as everything that distresses is a pain). And so every release from pain is rightly termed a pleasure. When food and drink rid us of hunger and thirst, that very removal of the distress brings with it pleasure in consequence. In every other case too, removal of pain causes a resultant pleasure. Thus Epicurus did not hold that there was some halfway state between pain and pleasure. Rather, that very state which some deem halfway, namely the absence of all pain, he held to be not only true pleasure, but the highest pleasure. Now whoever is to any degree conscious of how he is feeling must to that extent be in pleasure or pain. But Epicurus thinks that the absence of all pain constitutes the upper limit of pleasure.

---

[14] See, e.g., Epic. *Ep. Men.* 131 and *RS* 3: 'The removal of all pain is the limit of the magnitude of pleasures. Whenever pleasure is present, as long as it lasts, pain or distress or their combination is absent.'

[15] See also Striker 1993: 11–14; Sedley 1998: 142–144.

Beyond that limit pleasure can vary and be of different kinds, but it cannot be increased or expanded.

(Trans. R. Woolf)

This account introduces the Epicurean view that there are two general kinds of pleasure. The first sentence describes certain pleasures characterised by a kind of smooth or delightful motion registered by the senses. These would seem to be 'kinetic pleasures'; the pleasure experienced in taking a drink and removing a thirst would be a paradigmatic example. Torquatus seems to take these as agreed and uncontroversial since he offers them as a contrast with some other kind of pleasure. This second kind, which seems to be what is often termed 'katastematic pleasure', is what is felt in the state of feeling no thirst. This picture is then supplemented by the suggestion that kinetic pleasures can also be experienced by someone who is already experiencing katastematic pleasure. In this case, however, since katastematic pleasure is the greatest possible, any kinetic pleasure does not increase but merely 'embellishes' the pleasure already being experienced.[16] So, taking a sip of wine when he is not thirsty does not add to an agent's pleasure but merely alters the quality of the pleasure already being experienced. We should note that this demonstrates that not all kinetic pleasures therefore involve the restoration of a physiological lack, although these basic physiological pleasures are the most obvious and recognisable cases of kinetic pleasure. It is also, we should note, not stated that kinetic pleasures are all 'sensory' or otherwise confined to bodily sensations. The Epicureans' use of physical replenishments as paradigm cases of kinetic pleasures may have encouraged this view, but it is easy to imagine mental kinetic pleasures too: for example, the joy and relief felt by someone realising that his fear of death is misplaced. (Contrast this with the pleasant state of not fearing death, a state which can be 'embellished' from time to time by recalling and considering novel expressions of arguments for this conclusion or by the renewed recognition of the absence of anxiety.)[17]

---

[16] Here *variari distinguique*; cf. 2.10: *variari* and Epicurus *RS* 18: 'The pleasure in the flesh does not increase when once the pain of need has been removed, but it is only varied (ποικίλλεται). And the limit of pleasure in the mind is produced by rationalizing those very things and their congeners which once used to present the mind with its greatest fears.'

[17] See also Lucr. *DRN* 2.1ff. It is pleasant to recognise what pains you do not suffer, but not in the sense of adding to the pleasantness of your painless state. Nevertheless, the conscious recognition of the fact of being without pain can produce a noticeable effect. (Perhaps this conscious recognition is what is referred to as χαρά: see scholion to Diog. Laert. 10.66 and Konstan 2006.)

Does Torquatus offer any argument for the conclusion that katastematic pleasure is the highest possible? The passage I have just quoted contains a great deal of plain assertion of familiar Epicurean principles, but there might be an argument here after all. If there is, then the crucial justificatory moves are in 1.37:

> nam quoniam, (i) cum privamur dolore, ipsa liberatione et vacuitate omnis molestiae gaudemus, (ii) omne autem id, quo gaudemus, voluptas est, ut omne, quo offendimur, dolor, (iii) doloris omnis privatio recte nominata est voluptas.

The opening words (*nam quoniam*) show that some sort of inference is being offered and the impression that this is intended to be something along the lines of a formal argument is supported by the reuse of crucial terms in the premises and conclusion (*privamur/privatio* and *gaudemus*). The argument as a whole would seem to run as follows:

> Since (i) when we are freed from pain (*cum privamur dolore*), we rejoice in the actual freedom and absence of all distress (*ipsa liberatione et vacuitate molestiae gaudemus*)
> and (ii) everything in which we rejoice (*gaudemus*) is pleasure, just as everything that distresses us is pain.
> then (iii) the absence (*privatio*) of all pain (*doloris omnis*) is rightly called pleasure.[18]

This ought to deduce the desired Epicurean conclusion about katastematic pleasure from some agreed and plausible premises. Unfortunately, on that account the important claim in (i) is easily dismissed as either implausible or else the inference from (i) and (ii) to (iii) relies on an ambiguity in some of the central terms. A term such as *liberatio*, for example, can mean both a process (the process of freeing something) and a result (the final state of having been freed); we might say something similar about *detractio* and *privatio*. While we might expect everyone to agree that the process of removing a pain is pleasant, it is certainly not universally agreed that the resulting state of the absence of pain is pleasant; indeed, that is precisely what the Epicureans wish to argue and in doing so they are themselves recognising that it requires some defence. So if *liberatio* in (i) is read as meaning the resulting state of freedom from pain, then (i) is *prima facie* false, or else is obviously true only for the immediate period of relief. But if *liberatio*

---

[18] Or, possibly, taking *omnis* as a nominative: (iii*) 'Every absence of pain is rightly called pleasure'; but cf. *omni dolore detracto*, and *omnis molestiae* earlier in this section.

in (i) is read as meaning the process of removing a pain, then coupling (i) and (ii) will not give the desired Epicurean conclusion, only the less controversial claim that every process of removing some pain is pleasant. One term in this section, however, is not so evidently prone to this process/result ambiguity: *vacuitas* is the state of the absence of something detrimental.[19] This makes it more likely that the conjoined term *liberatio et vacuitas* is here also referring to the end state of freedom from pain.

Charity, therefore, and the weight of the lexical evidence seem to require us to conclude that Torquatus is arguing here in 1.37–38 from the claim that every absence of pain is pleasant to the conclusion that the absence of all pain is most pleasant. What we would need first, in that case, is some reason to believe the opening claim: that every absence of pain is pleasant.[20] Do I feel pleasure simply by not being thirsty? Not, one would think, in any usual sense of 'pleasure'. It is possible, however, that the next sentence is intended to make this assumption more palatable:

> ut enim, cum cibo et potione fames sitisque depulsa est, ipsa detractio molestiae consecutionem affert voluptatis, sic in omni re doloris amotio successionem efficit voluptatis.

Similar concerns about process/result ambiguity plague this section too but the general point seems clear enough. In cases of removing hunger or thirst there is no sense in saying that first pain is removed and then, only once all pain is gone, pleasure arises and thereafter can begin to increase. Rather, there is an immediate succession between pleasure and pain and the very removal of pain (either the very process of removing pain or the end result of pain having been removed) immediately generates pleasure. This claim leads directly to Torquatus making explicit an important consequence of such a view, namely that there is no intermediate state between pleasure and pain. All the same, it is hard to think that this kind of consideration would be particularly persuasive, since it is perfectly possible to hold that pleasure is best thought of as some kind of motion or change which can occur both in cases of restoring a pain and also in cases of a positive motion or change from an already pain-free state.[21] This would explain the phenomenon of pleasure being experienced in the very process

---

[19] See *OLD* s.v. 2 which cites Cic. *Tusc.* 5.42: *securitatem ... appello vacuitatem aegritudinis.*

[20] Cf. Striker 1993: 13: 'Admittedly, this only shifts the difficulty with this passage from one step to another.'

[21] This, roughly speaking, is Plato's general view. He seems to be committed to the notion that pleasures are always restorations of some kind of lack but that only some lacks are noticed or painful so only some pleasures are removals of pain.

of removing the pain of hunger but would not require the conclusion that a state of being hunger-free is similarly pleasant since at that stage there is no longer any relevant motion or change.

Before moving on from this argument we should also note that it threatens an implicit distinction between freedom from pain and pleasure which would presumably be embarrassing to the Epicureans if it were emphasised. When Torquatus asserts that 'we rejoice in the very freedom and absence of pain' (*ipsa liberatione et vacuitate omnis molestiae gaudemus*) the message might be that the absence of pain is some kind of object in which we take joy (*gaudium*). It is also not clear whether the absence of pain is already a pleasure and the *gaudium* is therefore some kind of second-order pleasure – a pleasant appreciation of one's already pleasant and pain-free state – or whether the *gaudium* is, so to speak, what makes the pain-free state pleasant: the pleasure of being pain-free consists in the joy which we take in it. I shall return to this general question at the end of this essay since some recent interpretations of Epicurean hedonism argue for this latter alternative. It is worth noting for now that Torquatus can reasonably be interpreted as offering this very view, although it remains to be seen whether it is a coherent or helpful line for him to take. The end of this brief section also points to the same issue:

> quisquis enim sentit quem ad modum sit adfectus eum necesse est aut in voluptate esse aut in dolore.

Torquatus employs a distinction between 'how one is affected' and the perception of how one is affected. The perception is then related to the fact of one's being 'in pleasure' or 'in pain'. We are told only that any perception of how one is affected necessarily results in being in pleasure or pain. Unfortunately, Torquatus does not elaborate further on the precise relationship between the three important elements in this picture. It is not clear, for example, whether perception of how one is affected is *necessary* for a person to be in either pleasure or pain; if it is not then someone might be in pain but not notice it. Torquatus says only that the perception of how one is affected is sufficient for being in either pleasure or pain. It is similarly unclear whether we necessarily perceive how we are affected. Finally, we might want to ask whether the perception of how one is affected referred to here is in fact meant to be identical with the *pathos* of pleasure or pain or somehow causes or gives rise to it.[22]

---

[22] In the discussion of this essay at the Budapest meeting, a number of people suggested that what is intended or needed here is some notion of basic 'consciousness' such that Torquatus means here that anyone who is at all self-conscious will register pleasure or pain. This might well be a helpful

A possible account of the missing details would be the following. Torquatus intends this comment to explain why there is no intermediate state by insisting that agents always register or perceive how they are affected. This proprioception, furthermore, necessarily registers one's current state with either pleasure (if the state is not lacking) or pain (if it is lacking). Since one's bodily state must either be lacking or not lacking then one will necessarily experience either pleasure or pain. In that case, pleasure and pain are the results of some kind of necessary self-perception and one's current state is the constant object of that self-perception. This will rule out the possibility of experiencing neither pleasure nor pain simply because one is not perceiving 'how one is affected'.[23] This interpretation helps to explain why this comment is thought by Torquatus to offer grounds for (*enim*) the previous assertion that the highest pleasure is the absence of pain. If we imagine the self-perception involved here not only to be constant but also comprehensive then the conscious agent will continuously register how he is affected throughout his nature. If it is agreed that pleasure is the absence of pain then an agent entirely lacking pain throughout his nature will register this pleasant state via a comprehensive proprioception and, since there remains no pain to remove, there is no possibility of any further pleasure beyond this state.

2 *Chrysippus' statue*

At 1.39 Torquatus outlines and then rejects an argument from Chrysippus for the conclusion that pleasure is not a good. The argument is supposed to have been embodied and depicted by a statue of Chrysippus to be found in Athens.[24] Torquatus introduces the argument by recalling discussions with his father who would mock Chrysippus' argument and explain how it failed to refute the Epicurean account of pleasure.

This detail of the family life of the Torquati is, despite initial appearances, far from irrelevant to the overarching argument between Torquatus and Cicero since the consistency of the behaviour of the Torquati with Epicurean theory has been raised by Cicero as an important testing ground for Epicurean ethics most generally. Two great men from the family's past have been invoked so far and both, importantly, are renowned

line for him to take but it seems to me to be open to the counterclaim that it is possible for a self-conscious agent to be experiencing neither pleasure nor pain and, in any case, we need to notice that in Cicero's presentation of Torquatus' position, the awareness in question is once again being characterised as a straightforward form of perception.

[23] Such an assumption might be behind the puzzling claim at 1.30: *detractis de homine sensibus reliqui nihil est.* This interpretation is also suggested by Striker 1993: 16–17.
[24] Other evidence for the statue in the Ceramicus: Diog. Laert. 7. 182. See von den Hoff 1994: 96–111.

for the stern and harsh treatment of their own sons. T. Manlius Torquatus won the cognomen in 361 BC for his courage in fighting a Gaul in single combat and taking a torque from the dead Gaul's neck. He then had a very distinguished career marked later, in 340 BC, by the decision to order the decapitation of his own son for military disobedience. Both events are invoked by Cicero at 1.23 as evidence of cases in which a person's behaviour surely contradicts the Epicurean assertion that people act in the pursuit of pleasure. Another Torquatus (Titus) is then invoked in 1.24 as having dealt in a similarly stern fashion with his son. Both cases seem to have passed into general Roman elite consciousness as *exempla* of a kind of unswerving virtue which does indeed appear hard to square with the psychological hedonism which *Fin.* ascribes to the Epicureans.[25] It would certainly be difficult for Lucius Torquatus, Cicero's interlocutor, to criticise the behaviour of his noble ancestors and he therefore has to make some attempt at offering an account of their famed actions which follows his own Epicurean psychological and ethical principles. For his part, Lucius tries bravely to claim that it is hardly to be thought that his noble ancestors would have undertaken such extraordinary actions had they not had in mind some kind of advantage they might receive (1.34–35): T. Manlius, Lucius assures us, fought the Gaul in order not to be killed himself; he then sacrificed his son in order to retain the military discipline on which his own life depended.

The move to his own past, however, allows Lucius to offer a more positive picture of a Torquatus and his son not only acting consistently with Epicurean principles but doing so without the least sign of inter-generational conflict and indeed with apparent enjoyment.[26] This warm familial joking certainly adds to the tone of what is to come, but we need also to consider closely the logic of both Chrysippus' supposed argument and Torquatus' response. The description of the exchange is as follows:

> at etiam Athenis, ut e patre audiebam facete et urbane Stoicos irridente, statua est in Ceramico Chrysippi sedentis porrecta manu, quae manus significet illum in hac esse rogatiuncula delectatum: 'numquidnam manus tua sic affecta, quem ad modum affecta nunc est, desiderat?'– nihil sane. – 'at,

---

[25] See Val. Max. 2.6.7, Livy 8.7 (T. Manlius): Langlands 2008: 170–171 notes other references (see nn. 45 and 46) and comments: 'His deed is the paradigmatic *exemplum* of *severitas* in Roman tradition and his name a byword for *disciplina* as well as *severitas*'; Val. Max. 5.8.3 (Titus). Cicero clearly enjoys invoking this image and returns to it at *Fin.* 2.105, albeit only in passing.

[26] It is not clear whether Lucius' father was also an Epicurean or whether he simply had no taste for this particular Stoic argument.

si voluptas esset bonum, desideraret.'– ita credo. – 'non est igitur voluptas bonum.' hoc ne statuam quidem dicturam pater aiebat, si loqui posset.
conclusum est enim contra Cyrenaicos satis acute, nihil ad Epicurum. nam
si ea sola voluptas esset, quae quasi titillaret sensus, ut ita dicam, et ad eos cum
suavitate afflueret ei illaberetur, nec manus esse contenta posset nec ulla pars
vacuitate doloris sine iucundo motu voluptatis. sin autem summa voluptas est,
ut Epicuro placet, nihil dolere, primum tibi recte, Chrysippe, concessum est
nihil desiderare manum, cum ita esset affecta, secundum non recte, si voluptas
esset bonum, fuisse desideraturam. idcirco enim non desideraret, quia, quod
dolore caret, id in voluptate est.

(1.39)

   My father used to mock the Stoics with wit and elegance by telling me how,
in the Cerameicus at Athens, there is a statue of Chrysippus sitting with an
outstretched hand, that hand symbolizing the delight Chrysippus took in the
following little piece of argument: 'Does your hand, in its present condition,
want anything?'[27] 'Not at all.' 'But if pleasure were a good, it would be wanting
it.' 'I suppose so.' 'Therefore pleasure is not a good.' My father remarked that
not even a statue would produce such an argument, if it could speak. Though
the reasoning has some force against a Cyrenaic position, it has none whatso-
ever against Epicurus. If pleasures were simply the kind of thing which, so to
speak, titillated the senses and flooded them with a stream of sweetness, then
neither the hand nor any other part of the body could be satisfied with the
mere absence of pain and no delightful surge of pleasure. But if, as Epicurus
maintains, the highest pleasure is to feel no pain, well then, Chrysippus, the
initial concession, that the hand in its present condition wants nothing, was
correct; but the subsequent one, that if pleasure were a good the hand would
have wanted it, is not. For the reason that it did not want it was that to have
no pain is precisely to be in a state of pleasure.

(Trans. R. Woolf)

The outstretched hand of the statue is taken here by Torquatus and his
father to be a sign of the perverse joy (*delectatum*) taken by Chrysippus in
this argument, perhaps ironically given the overall anti-hedonist import
of the line of thought. But presumably Chrysippus was just gesturing by
way of example, holding out his own hand and encouraging his interlocutor to do the same and, more important, consider how the hand
currently feels. Certainly, the presentation gives the argument an authentically Stoic flavour, from the careful exposition in terms of a full dialectical question-and-answer format to the familiar Stoic use of hand gestures

---

[27] *desiderare* here should not be taken to imply that the hand itself has desires of any kind. Instead it
means simply 'need', 'want', 'lack'. Cf. Cic. *Nat. D.* 1.99.

to illustrate philosophical points.[28] Chrysippus' argument seems to be as follows:[29]

1 Your hand – in the state it is currently in – wants nothing. (*numquidnam manus tua sic affecta, quem ad modum affecta nunc est, desiderat? – nihil sane*).
2 Your hand does not want pleasure (*a fortiori*).
3 If pleasure were a good, your hand would want it (*at, si voluptas esset bonum, desideraret*).
4 Pleasure is not a good (*non est igitur voluptas bonum*).

Torquatus is clearly not impressed; nor was his father. Torquatus (junior) concedes that this argument is sound against a Cyrenaic conception of pleasure since it is perfectly plausible to say that, at this particular moment, assuming all is well and healthy, your hand neither is experiencing nor requires some sort of pleasant tactile stimulation. However, this merely offers a useful opportunity to attempt to demonstrate the significant distinction between Cyrenaic and Epicurean hedonism. The point Chrysippus is interested in making is that the hand is currently in no pain and furthermore is also not feeling pleasure. Since it is not in any need, it is in no need of pleasure. From this he thinks that it must follow that pleasure is not good, since the hand would want pleasure if pleasure were really good.[30] The crucial assumption, already noted, is that it is possible to be neither in need or pain nor experiencing pleasure and that the hand in question is in that very state. This intermediate state was indeed recognised by the Cyrenaics and therefore they are vulnerable to Chrysippus' objection whereas the Epicureans, as Torquatus made clear in 1.38, deny that there is such a painless and pleasure-free position. On the basis of this denial, they will object to Chrysippus' argument simply by denying that the condition in 3 is always true. Most importantly, it is false in a case in which a hand – or even a person – is already in a state of painlessness since the Epicureans will assert that in that case the hand already has all the pleasure that it might need. But in this case the lack of need should not cast doubt on the goodness of pleasure.

---

[28] Hand gestures: Cic. *Acad.* 2.145, Sext. Emp. *Math.* 2.7. Note also Torquatus' use of Stoic logical terminology to refer to the distinct premises (*primum ... secundum ...*).

[29] For other Stoic arguments for the conclusion that pleasure is not a good see, e.g., Diog. Laert. 7.103 (*SVF* 3.156): Hecato in Book 9 of *On Goods* and Chrysippus in *On Pleasure* argue that some pleasures are shameful and nothing shameful can be good.

[30] The Epicureans allow that sometimes pleasures, though good, are not to be chosen. Here we must assume that this potential complication is not relevant.

Argument 3 is also not always false, of course, since the Epicureans agree that there are cases in which someone would desire the good, namely pleasure, but these are cases in which a person is in a state of pain. Epicurus makes this perfectly clear at *Ep. Men.* 128: 'We have need of pleasure at that time when we are in pain as a result of the absence of pleasure.' From this perspective, Chrysippus' mistake is rather subtle. He is certainly not mistaken to assume that the hand in question fails to be experiencing pain; nor is he mistaken to assume that in the case in which a hand fails to be experiencing pain it also will not experience a need for pleasure. Rather, his mistake is to assume that the hand is not – in its current state – already in a state of pleasure.

The important and contentious point, in that case, is precisely what is meant by the qualification in 1 above: *sic adfecta quem ad modum adfecta nunc est.* But on this point there is also a large degree of agreement between the two parties. Chrysippus and Torquatus can agree that the hand is currently in a state of not being in pain and also that Chrysippus is therefore, as Torquatus says, right to say that the hand currently wants nothing. They also agree that therefore the hand does not want active pleasant sensory stimulation. The one point of disagreement, indeed the significant point of disagreement, is the controversial Epicurean insistence that the painlessness is itself a kind of pleasure. And this, Torquatus must think, is what has been demonstrated in the previous section and can be relied upon here.

One final observation remains to be made on Torquatus' response which is very important to bear in mind when considering the role of this passage in the overall strategy of *Fin.* 1 and 2. If the Epicurean defence of their own conception of pleasure is at all successful against Chrysippus' objection then they can use the Stoic argument against their hedonist rivals, the Cyrenaics. Based on their distinction between the pleasure of painlessness which, on their preferred account, Chrysippus' contented hand is experiencing, and the sensory stimulation which the hand neither is experiencing nor desires, they can proceed to endorse the conditional noted as 3 in the above reconstruction as true for pleasure in the sense of the Cyrenaics' *telos* of 'pleasure in motion' or pleasure *quae quasi titillaret sensus*. If that were good then Chrysippus' hand would indeed want it even when the hand is free from pain. But since there is no such want then the Cyrenaics must be wrong to think that such pleasure is good. Torquatus notes this rather pleasing double result: *conclusum est enim contra Cyrenaicos satis acute, nihil ad Epicurum*; Chrysippus can come to the Epicureans' aid in rubbishing their hedonist rivals but his argument

fails to touch Epicurus' own brand of hedonism. The choice of terminology to describe this alternative kind of pleasure is also worth noting
since again it demonstrates not only that Cicero has been paying close
attention to Epicurean usage but also the extent to which his criticisms
in Book 2 look back towards Torquatus' exposition here. The Epicureans
have to put clear water between themselves and the Cyrenaics in order
to escape Chrysippus' argument and their means of doing so, as we have
seen, involves them accepting and endorsing the strength of the argument
against the goodness of a certain kind of pleasure. If, as he hopes, Cicero
is successful in the second book in showing that this is indeed the *only*
proper sense in which we should understand pleasure then the Epicureans'
reaction to Chrysippus' argument will come back to haunt them. Either
they will be forced to abandon their pretensions to be offering a recognisable brand of hedonism or they will be forced to admit that, despite
attempts to the contrary, they are in fact merely parroting a brand of
Cyrenaic hedonism and, what is more, that they have already endorsed a
strong refutation of that very position.

The important characteristics of the pleasure for which Chrysippus'
refutation is understood to be relevant are the following:

i   it affects the senses in a pleasing way (*quasi titillaret sensus*);
ii it floods them with a pleasant feeling (*cum suavitate adflueret ei
    inlaberetur*);
iii it is a kind of motion or change (*iucundus motus*).

Torquatus is happy to allow the pleasure which conforms to this set of
descriptions to be distinguished from the good. In fact, those same three
characteristics – the role of perception, *suavitas* and *iucunditas*, and the
notion of motion or change – have already been invoked by Torquatus at
1.37 (cited above) to describe the kind of pleasure which the Epicureans
do not *solely* pursue, in contrast with the greatest kind of pleasure which
is found in the absence of all pain.[31] That this is not the *only* pleasure
worthy of pursuit is certainly important: the Epicureans do not wish to
deny that pleasure of this kinetic kind is indeed sometimes to be chosen.
But it is certainly not the good or the *telos* and the pleasure that is to be
identified as the *telos* should be sharply distinguished from it. This argument with Chrysippus further reinforces the conclusion – a conclusion

---

[31] 1.37: *non enim hanc solam sequimur, quae **suavitate** aliqua naturam ipsam **movet** et cum **iucunditate** quadam **percipitur sensibus**.*

endorsed wholeheartedly by the Epicureans themselves – that pleasure of this kinetic kind cannot be the good.

In making Torquatus set out his view in this way, Cicero has very carefully constructed a position in preparation for his own criticisms of the Epicurean stance in Book 2. When in that book the character Cicero shows his own hand, he allies himself with both Chrysippus and the Cyrenaics in the belief that anything that is truly and comprehensibly a pleasure must conform to these characteristics of kinetic pleasure. In that case, he says, given that Torquatus himself has already agreed with Chrysippus that such an understanding of pleasure would indeed be incompatible with its being good, then the Epicureans are either deeply confused about hedonism and ought to listen more carefully to the Cyrenaics and to what is the obvious and commonsensical notion of pleasure or else are merely disguising an old view that the absence of pain is the *telos* under a thin hedonist disguise.

As we shall see, in the exchanges at the beginning of Book 2 Cicero repeatedly insists that pleasure must be understood as a kind of sensory stimulation or motion, and uses vocabulary clearly designed to be reminiscent of the characterisation of pleasure rejected here by Torquatus.[32] As part of this strategy of demonstrating that the Epicureans are inconsistent in both condemning pleasure and advocating hedonism, Cicero has evidently been careful to give Torquatus' response using authentically Epicurean vocabulary. Much of his case in Book 2 will rest on what he takes to be the proper meaning of terms for pleasure, but it remains important that he at least give the impression that the Epicureans are being condemned from their own mouths. The verb *titillare*, in particular, seems to have been carefully chosen. As Cicero himself makes clear at *Nat. D.* 1.113 in Cotta's reply to the Epicurean Velleius, *titillatio* is intended to be a recognisably Epicurean term and was apparently used to make just the point on which Torquatus currently insists:

> at has leviores ducis voluptates, quibus quasi titillatio (Epicuri enim hoc verbum est) adhibetur sensibus.
>
> (*Nat. D.* 1.113)

> But you consider inferior those pleasures from which arise a sort of tickling (for that is Epicurus' term) of the senses.

---

[32] For example, see 2.6: *quia voluptatem hanc esse sentiunt omnes, quam **sensus** accipiens **movetur** et **iucunditate** quadam perfunditur*; 2.8: *omnes enim **iucundum motum**, quo **sensus** hilaretur. Graece* ἡδονήν *Latine voluptatem vocant*; 2.13: *huic verbo omnes, qui ubique sunt, qui Latine sciunt, duas res subiciunt, laetitiam in animo, **commotionem suavem iucunditatis** in corpore.*

Titillare (and perhaps *hilare* at *Fin.* 2.8) is probably Cicero's translation for Epicurus' γαργαλίζω. It recurs in Cicero's paraphrase of Epicurus' notorious assertions in his *On the Telos* about not being able to conceive of the god without the pleasures of tastes or sex at *Tusc.* 3.47 and when Athenaeus cites the original Greek he notes at the outset that Epicurus often mentioned such 'ticklings' (γαργαλισμοί).[33] This is a rather delicate point for the Epicureans: they clearly want to maintain the notion that these kinds of sensory stimulation are to be included in the good life and may even be useful indicators of the goodness of pleasure in general but they nevertheless do not want to identify such pleasures as the good. It is not hard to see why critics seized upon this as a weakness in the overall theory. Cicero's combination of Torquatus' exposition and his own later response offers the most sophisticated example of that general strategy.

One final point must be noticed about the Epicurean treatment of this argument. Their response seems to involve their agreement that (i) Chrysippus is perceiving the state of his hand and (ii) is perceiving that it is not in pain but also (iii) is failing to recognise the pleasure that he is thereby experiencing. Chrysippus is correct, *ex hypothesi* to say that he is not in pain. He is right, furthermore, that he is not experiencing pleasure in the sense of sensory stimulation. But he is mistaken when he says that he is not experiencing pleasure. There remains in that case the important fact that, according to the Epicurean response to his argument, Chrysippus is somehow mistaken about the hedonic state of his hand. This is potentially troubling if we remember that the Epicureans assert that perceptions and *pathē* – pleasure and pain – are criteria of truth and we might therefore wonder whether they ought to be saying anything that suggests a person is anything but an incorrigible witness to his own hedonic state.[34] In fact, the Epicureans do not need to make such a strong claim. Although Torquatus himself, in just the previous chapter, has claimed that 'whoever feels the way in which he is affected must necessarily be either in pleasure or in pain' (*quisquis enim sentit quem ad modum sit adfectus, eum necesse est aut in voluptate esse aut in dolore*, 1.38), this falls short of saying that anyone sensing his own state will correctly recognise whether he is in pleasure or pain, making clear merely that anyone so aware must be in one or other of these two states. It remains open, therefore, for the Epicureans to explain the sense in which Chrysippus is mistaken in the following way.

---

[33] See Plutarch *Lat. viv.* 1129B, *An seni sit res publica gerenda* 786C, Athenaeus 12 546E–7A. Also compare: Sen. *Ep.* 92.6, 99.27.
[34] Gosling and Taylor 1982: 369 take this to be part of Cicero's criticism.

His hand *is* in fact *in voluptate*, we can surmise, since his hand is indeed experiencing no pain. But he does not realise that it is because he has an incorrect intellectual grasp on what pleasure is. Just as it is always the case that our senses provide true information about the world but we are all too capable of forming false beliefs on their basis, so too it is evidently the case that someone may be experiencing pleasure but yet fail to believe that he is doing so.

This error is in addition to Chrysippus' other mistake of failing to recognise the goodness of pleasure, a topic which Torquatus has already broached at 1.30ff. when he discussed Epicurus' own insistence that the goodness of pleasure is immediately presented in the experience of pleasure in just the same way that, he insists, fire is immediately recognised as hot, honey as sweet, and so on. Presumably the Epicureans will say that there are some people who are sufficiently divorced from the plain evidence of their senses and *pathē* that they promote beliefs which are inconsistent with these truths. Just as there are people who – often as a result of falling in with an unfortunate philosophical crowd – are misguided enough either to believe that honey is not sweet or else to resist forming the belief that honey is sweet, so too there are people like Chrysippus whose axiological theory forces them to overlook the plain evidence of their *pathē*. Indeed, this passage conforms very well to a methodological principle introduced earlier. Torquatus himself insisted at 1.31 that, in the face of all manner of philosophical objections to the goodness of pleasure, the Epicureans ought not to be over-confident in the power of the evidence of the *pathē*. Chrysippus would appear to be a good example of a kind of philosophical misconception to which the Epicureans should respond not only by pointing to what they took to be the self-evident goodness of pleasure but also by tackling the various misguided or confused arguments set in the way of this truth.

3   *The ideal life: 40–41*

Finally, Torquatus attempts to persuade us of the excellence of the life he promotes by contrasting two characters. One of them lives a life free from mental or physical pain and is perturbed by no fear of death or anxiety about the divine; his memories are clear and provide a constant source of pleasures and he recognises that pain will either be brief or endurable. The other is subject to the greatest mental and physical pains, with no prospect of relief. The argument seems to be the rather feeble one that if this second life is thought to be the worst possible human existence then the first life, in some sense or other clearly its opposite, must therefore be the best possible human life. There is more that could be said about this passage, particularly its reintroduction of the important point that the pleasures and pains being discussed throughout this section are not merely physical or bodily pleasures and pains, but for present purposes its opening is what matters:[35]

> constituamus aliquem magnis, multis, perpetuis fruentem et animo et corpore voluptatibus nullo dolore nec impediente nec inpendente, quem tandem hoc statu praestabiliorem aut magis expetendum possimus dicere?

> Let us imagine someone enjoying a large and continuous variety of pleasures, of both mind and body, with no pain present or imminent. What more excellent and desirable state could one name but this one?
>
> (Trans. R. Woolf)

What is striking in this account of a perfect pleasant life is Torquatus' use of the plural *voluptates*. The excellence of the life appears to derive not only from the fact that such a person is constantly experiencing pleasure but that this person is also experiencing pleasures which are great (or perhaps intense), many and constant.[36] The general tone of this characterisation is that of a life whose goodness depends on the presence of a plurality of intense pleasures free from any prospect of pain. Perhaps Torquatus is speaking rather loosely as he tries to produce a rhetorically effective climax to this section, but there is a clear sense in which this brief characterisation does make the Epicureans sound much closer to the Cyrenaics than they might wish. Does this passage imply that such a life is good because it contains a large number of pleasures? Is a life better the more pleasures it contains? The more intense or varied the pleasures it contains? The Epicureans will surely wish to resist accepting any of these possibilities but, Cicero will say, they ought to accept them if they are to be recognisably hedonist in their outlook. The parallel passage in Epicurus' *Ep. Men.* 133 makes no reference to 'pleasure' at all, let alone 'pleasures', instead describing how such a person 'has reasoned nature's goal and grasps how the end of goods is easy to satisfy and to procure'.[37] Despite the closeness of the whole account in 1.40 to a similar passage at *Tusc.* 3.38, the content

---

[35] We might note, for example, that in the account of the ideal life Torquatus has been careful to note the gist of the first four *Kyriai Doxai* (pointed out by Annas in her note *ad loc.* in Annas and Woolf 2001).

[36] Woolf's translation renders *multis* with 'variety' which is perhaps questionable: Torquatus has tried hard to make clear that variety of itself is no marker of value when it comes to the assessment of the highest pleasure.

[37] *Ep. Men.* 133: τὸ τῆς φύσεως ἐπιλελογισμένου τέλος καὶ τὸ μὲν τῶν ἀγαθῶν πέρας ὡς ἔστιν εὐσυμπλήρωτόν τε καὶ εὐπόριστον διαλαμβάνοντος.

of which is explicitly attributed to Zeno of Sidon, it is hard to resist the idea that Cicero has deliberately cast this vision of the Epicurean good life in terms more obviously appropriate for other kinds of hedonism so as better to prepare the ground for his later criticism.[38]

Book 2

Criticism and dialogue: 2.5–17

At the beginning of *Fin.* 2 Cicero launches a dialectical onslaught against Torquatus and the Epicurean notion of pleasure that neatly relies on the various points set down in Torquatus' own exposition in Book 1. The relevant section is *Fin.* 2.5–17: one of the brief but important passages of rapid interchange in a Ciceronian dialogue before the meat of the second book begins with the marked change from what Torquatus calls the *dialecticae captiones* to a *rhetorica disputatio* which will take up the next hundred or so sections.[39]

Cicero exploits an obvious difficulty for the Epicurean position which has been signalled already in the previous book not only as unorthodox and needing support but also as the central thesis on which Epicurean eudaimonism is based, namely the claim that the absence of pain is the highest pleasure. We have already seen that in the first book the question of the exact relationship between a state of painlessness and the experience of pleasure is highlighted. Torquatus rested much of the burden of showing the value of pleasure on its directly and evidently perceived nature. But he nevertheless tried to set out a distinction between the kind of pleasure meant as the Epicurean *telos*, related closely to the state of painlessness, and the mere titillation of the senses (1.39).

When Cicero comes to offer a critical analysis of the Epicurean position, he outlines the dilemma for the Epicureans: either they hold fast to the claim that the goal of life is the highest pleasure or they must retreat

---

[38] The principal subject of *Tusc.* 3.38 is the Epicurean attitude to confidence in the future and recollection of past pleasures. It omits the specification in *Fin.* 1.40 that the pleasures enjoyed are many and large.

[39] On the distinction between and use of these forms of argumentation see Inwood 1990 and on Ciceronian dialogue in general see Schofield 2008. (And for a reading of another piece of close Ciceronian dialogue in *Tusc.* 1 see Warren 2013.) Certainly, Torquatus is not a particularly quick or skilful dialectician (something clear from *Fin.* 1.29 and 2.17 and noted as a general Epicurean characteristic at 2.18) but we should not assume that he is confused or easily bamboozled by Cicero to a degree that invalidates the success of Cicero's argument. Hedonists are generally portrayed as lacking in dialectical subtlety – think of Callicles or Philebus in Plato – but it would not suit Cicero's purpose to have an obvious dullard as an opponent.

to the claim that the goal of life is the absence of pain.[40] In both cases the Epicureans will fail to hold any new and distinctive philosophical position. If they adopt the former, hedonist, route they are no different from the Cyrenaics. If they adopt the latter route they are no different from Hieronymus of Rhodes, whose *telos* was the absence of pain and not pleasure (*Fin.* 2.8, 19).[41] Either they must persist in the claim that the absence of pain is indeed 'pleasant' in the most obvious sense of that word, or they must resort to some alternative account. This alternative, most likely, is to weaken the sense in which the Epicureans claim that this katastematic pleasure is phenomenologically pleasant in the way that most simple episodes of pleasure are. In other words, katastematic pleasure need not 'feel' pleasant in the way that it feels pleasant to sip a cool drink on a hot day; we are wrong to make too close an equation between these two very different kinds of pleasure. On this view, katastematic pleasure is, rather, the state of the well-functioning and unimpeded organism, beset by no physical pain or mental disturbance. The problem with this line of defence, of course, is that it makes it unclear why Epicurus would call this state a state of pleasure at all, let alone the highest pleasure.

Cicero works up to his dilemma with a series of careful moves. First, he points out – cleverly echoing Torquatus' own remarks at *Fin.* 1.29 – that it is important to agree upon the precise matter being discussed (2.4–5). What is needed is a degree of clarity, *patefactio* (2.5). However, despite Epicurus' apparent approval of the usefulness of beginning with a clear idea of the item under discussion, he tended not to offer definitions of his terms. Nevertheless, given the general Epicurean confidence in our ability to use language clearly, all that is needed is to make explicit what the general conception of pleasure is, since this must surely be what Epicurus himself relies upon. Torquatus is asked to supply a definition from which the discussion might begin. He tries to evade the request, saying that surely we all know what we are talking about, but this is merely an invitation for Cicero's first attack. Cicero cannot see that Epicurus himself is always consistent or, perhaps, Epicurus himself does not really know what

---

[40] Cicero's argument as a whole evidently owes a lot to Academic methodology and may have been inspired by Philo, whose interest in criticising Epicurean ethics is noted at *Nat. D.* 1.113. It is a close cousin of the similarly dilemmatic argument offered later in *Fin.* 4 against the Stoics and their notion of the value of indifferents: either they must hold fast to the view that indifferents are absolutely without moral value – in which case they collapse into the position of Aristo – or they accept they can make a positive contribution to the good life – in which case they collapse into a Peripatetic or Antiochean view.

[41] For Hieronymus see Dalfino 1993 and White 2004. On Speusippus' discussions of pleasure see Dillon 2003: 64–77.

he means by 'pleasure'. Torquatus naturally resists such a slur: surely the person who declared pleasure to be the *telos* would not be confused (2.6). Then Cicero launches his first dilemma: either Epicurus does not know what pleasure is or else everyone else does not know (2.6). A supplementary argument in 2.12–15 offers some evidence for this and crucially, since this is a case of a discussion in Latin of an originally Greek theory, for the sufficient correspondence of the Latin *voluptas* and the Greek *hēdonē*.[42]

This initial search for an agreed account and Torquatus' refusal to offer his own definition provide the opportunity for Cicero to introduce his own preferred understanding of *voluptas* (2.6):

> voluptatem hanc esse sentiunt omnes, quam sensus accipiens movetur et iucunditate quadam perfunditur.

> This is what everyone recognises pleasure to be: what arouses the senses when it is experienced and floods them with a certain delight.

The emphasis is on pleasure being a positive affection and having an intimate relationship with perception or experience. Cicero is evidently paying close attention to the preferred Epicurean account of the sensory pleasures agreed *not* to be the final good (see above on 1.37 and 39).[43] Here he is deliberately echoing the terms in which Torquatus first put the contrast between the kind of pleasure which cannot be good *per se* and the greatest pleasure, namely the absence of pain. Further, once again taking his lead from Torquatus and the idea that pleasure is sufficiently well understood not to require technical analysis, Cicero can now introduce this as what 'everyone' thinks pleasure is.

By now Torquatus is already so much on his guard against admitting that the Epicureans have an idiosyncratic notion of pleasure that he rushes to point out that Epicurus did indeed recognise *ista voluptas* (2.7). How could he not? Presumably, he has in mind Epicurus' acceptance of kinetic as well as katastematic pleasure and the opening Epicurean assertion that the goodness of pleasure is plain and manifest to everyone.[44] After all, Torquatus had indeed said that Epicureans do not pursue *only* the katastematic kind of pleasure in such a way as to imply that this is

---

[42] Gosling and Taylor 1982: 384–385 think that this reliance on 'general' usage is illicit and shows Cicero to be an uncharitable critic of Epicureanism. In particular, they are concerned that Cicero does not mention mental pleasures. Stokes 1995: 151–152 attempts to acquit Cicero first by asking how the distinction between mental and bodily pleasures would be particularly relevant here and then by saying that Cicero is avoiding distracting his readers with unnecessary detail.

[43] Notice the deliberate repetition of the cognate terms: *sentiunt ... sensus*. This might well be a gesture towards the Epicurean idea that what pleasure is, or at the very least the goodness of pleasure, is something which everyone directly *perceives* and is presented to us by the truth-telling *pathē*.

[44] See the 'cradle argument' at *Fin.* 1.30, Diog. Laert. 10.128–129 and p. 44 above. Inwood 1990: 153–154 rightly notes that Cicero can feel some justification in relying on this point.

indeed sometimes the object of choice and pursuit (1.37). (Cicero may also have in mind Epicurus' assertions about the pleasures of food and sex in his *On the Telos* that provided such fertile material for detractors such as Timocrates.)[45] But this manoeuvre simply plays into Cicero's hands, because Cicero's point is not that Epicurus *always* misused the term 'pleasure'. Rather, on some occasions – precisely when he was discussing those pleasures that move and delight the senses – Epicurus got it right. But on other occasions he resorted to an implausible and illegitimate second sense. Supported by the evidence to the effect that Epicurus did indeed recognise the pleasures of satisfying a hunger, Cicero presses on as if he had secured the Epicureans' acceptance of his initial definition of pleasure. At the very least, they accept that this does accurately describe some cases of pleasure.

The next line of inquiry focuses on painlessness (*non dolere*) which we learn (i) is the *telos* according to Hieronymus of Rhodes and (ii) according to him is distinct from pleasure (*aliud igitur esse censet gaudere, aliud non dolere*). It is this distinction between painlessness and pleasure which Torquatus wishes to deny and he quickly insists on that point. Cicero now has a clear assertion of the central point he wishes to attack.

In the subsequent rapid exchanges in 2.9, Cicero sets out the Epicurean position according to which someone experiences pleasure both:

1   when drinking when thirsty (*sitienti in bibendo voluptas*)
    and
2   when the thirst is quenched (*restincta sitis stabilitatem voluptatis habet*).

The first, as Torquatus himself notes, is universally accepted; Cicero has already won the Epicurean's admission that this is indeed a case of pleasure.[46] But (2) is much more controversial. It is, Torquatus says, pleasure 'of a different kind' (*alio genere*): 'stable' pleasure, rather than pleasure 'in motion'. Cicero simply does not see that these are similar enough to warrant their both being called pleasure. And if they cannot both be pleasure,

[45] See *Tusc.* 3.46–47.
[46] Stokes 1995: 154–155 raises doubts over whether this is indeed a true and paradigmatic case of Epicurean kinetic pleasure. Perhaps the Epicureans would distinguish between the removal of a thirst and the 'sweet motions' of the senses which would result from this process, the latter being kinetic pleasures properly speaking. This is the interpretation of kinetic pleasures championed most influentially by Diano 1974, with particular reference to Lucr. *DRN* 4.622–629. A similar view is offered by Erler and Schofield 1999: 653–657 and Wolfsdorf 2009. Even if the Epicureans did recognise a distinction between the pleasures of simply filling the stomach and the pleasant sensations of taste on the tongue it is not clear that the latter alone are what should properly to be thought of as kinetic pleasures.

but (1) – as everyone including the Epicureans agrees – certainly is, then (2) cannot be.

Here we have reached the central problem for the Epicurean account: How can they persuade us to think that painlessness is itself a pleasure, let alone the greatest pleasure? Torquatus' attempt to answer the question is brief but important. He reminds Cicero of the Epicurean notion that katastematic pleasure cannot be increased but merely varied (*variari*) (2.10): the painless state admits of pleasant variation, perhaps in an attempt to smooth the acceptance of, for example, the absence of thirst as a genuine form of pleasure. Cicero will have none of this and offers yet another dilemma. Although Torquatus mentioned this vari-ation only briefly, at *Fin.* 1.38, Cicero has remembered his Epicureanism well enough to be able to point out something which Torquatus has not stressed, namely that this variation is distinct from painlessness and in no way increases the pleasure of painlessness. (*RS* 18 is very explicit about this.) The painlessness is itself supposed to be the greatest pleasure so Cicero assumes that the variation is a 'sweet motion on the senses' (*dulcis motus sensibus*) and that it is another aspect of pleasure *in motu*: it is what happens when someone drinks although they are not thirsty. Note that Cicero does not care to insist on any distinction between the pleasures of drinking when thirsty and the variation of pleasure in drinking when not thirsty. Modern commentators tend to worry about whether either or both are genuine Epicurean kinetic pleasures, but for Cicero both are clear enough cases of sensory motions. And that is all he needs for his argument since whatever else is said about these cases they once again conform to the three characteristics of the kind of pleasure which Torquatus was so keen to denigrate in Book 1: a close connection with perception, motion and some kind of sweet or enjoyable quality.

It is worth pausing to consider what, precisely, this 'variation' might be. The exact nature of this variety or complexity of pleasures once pain-lessness is reached is not always considered in any detail. But there are two distinct possibilities. First, the variety might be a phenomenological variety: a heterogeneity sometimes stressed as an interesting character-istic of pleasures generally. Alternatively, this variety may lie in the dif-ferent causes of painlessness.[47] Cicero appears to support the latter view at *Fin.* 2.10: *voluptas etiam varia dici solet cum percipitur e multis dissi-milibus rebus* ('Pleasure is usually said to be varied when it is perceived from many unlike things'). But again, it is important to bear in mind that

---

[47] For this view see Bailey (1926) *ad RS* 18.

this is Cicero's own attempt to understand what he says is an obscurity in Epicureanism on the basis of the 'natural' understanding of the Latin *varietas*. Torquatus' initial introduction of the idea at *Fin.* 1.38 appeared to contrast the differentiation of pleasures 'by variation' from the differentiation of pleasures in terms of size or magnitude (*ut postea variari voluptas distinguique possit, augeri amplificarique non possit*), a contrast which might well point in the direction of qualitative variety.[48]

However we understand the relevant variation of pleasure, the problem for Torquatus is evident. If this variation is meant to support his claim that painlessness is rightly called a pleasure then it is not very helpful. In so far as the variation is another case of pleasure 'in motion', then it conforms to Cicero's preferred general understanding of pleasure and the kind of pleasure Torquatus does not want to classify as the good: a certain kind of motion of the senses. Further, if the pleasantness of the state of painlessness is dependent on this kind of variation, then the pleasantness of the state of painlessness threatens to be dependent on just the kind of sensory stimulation and pleasing phenomenological variety which, the Epicureans want to insist, is merely one of the two distinct kinds of pleasure and not, in fact, the kind of pleasure Epicurus wishes to offer as the *telos*. Indeed they have already propounded an argument at 1.39 which agrees with the Stoic proof that this sensory stimulation is not a good. (Other consequences might threaten which have further unfortunate consequences for their preferred account of *eudaimonia*. If they accept that painlessness is desirable only in so far as it offers the occasion for pleasant episodes of variation, it is hard to see how the Epicureans can resist the view that a life with more episodes of this variation of pleasure is better than one with fewer. And there might be relevant evaluative distinctions to be drawn between different forms of variation.) Alternatively, if this variation is merely a variation in different causes of painlessness (as Cicero suggests at 2.10) then it is of no help at all in answering Cicero's question of how painlessness is properly to be understood as a pleasure.

Torquatus' attempted explanation of the pleasure of painlessness has, it seems, backfired, and confirmed Cicero's suspicion that what is really pleasant is indeed always a certain motion or sensory stimulation. Again, Cicero will perhaps say that this just goes to show that Epicurus was on the right track a lot of the time. If only he had not persisted in the absurd

---

[48] For what it is worth, the uses of ποικίλος and other words cognate with the term for variation used in *RS* 18 in Philodemus and Epicurus suggest notions of complexity or qualitative variety as in, for example, the great variety of directions of atomic movement. See Usener's *Glossarium Epicureum* s.vv. Note also Plut. *Non Posse* 1088c.

claim that painlessness was itself a pleasure then perhaps he would have had a consistent case. Torquatus can perhaps maintain that painlessness is a necessary condition of pleasures of variation but he appears to have no means of showing that painlessness is pleasant which does not in fact confirm the hedonic priority of kinetic pleasures.[49]

General lessons

It is tempting to think that Cicero never allows Torquatus a fair chance of constructing a satisfactory Epicurean account of pleasure.[50] Cicero is certainly not an impartial reporter of Epicurean ethics. But it seems to me that he does manage to highlight a general problem in the Epicurean view that the Epicureans may not be able to avoid. We have already noted that there are occasions on which it is not clear how we should understand the relationship between various items referred to in the exposition, for example: the state of the agent ('how he is affected'), the agent's awareness of his state, and the agent's experience of pleasure or pain (see the discussion of 1.38 above). This is related to another general difficulty. Our sources often do not distinguish clearly between referring to a 'pleasure' as (i) the intentional object of some psychological state, sensation or attitude and (ii) a particular kind of positive phenomenological experience or sensation. This generates a significant difficulty when considering the central question that Cicero wants to explore: whether, and if so in what sense, katastematic pleasure ought to be considered a pleasure. It seems odd, certainly, to think of painlessness as a pleasure in sense (ii). Introspection suggests that painlessness is not identical with a positive feeling. The more familiar pleasures *in motu*, on the other hand, are perfectly plausible examples of pleasure understood in this usual way. On this interpretation, therefore, the Cyrenaics, who recognised only this species of pleasure, have a much more plausible hedonist view than the Epicureans.

---

[49] Compare Striker 1993: 16–17, who advocates this view: 'But obviously, if Epicurus is right about the pleasantness of painless affection, and life consists in being affected in one or the other way, then these states must contain innumerable pleasures of the kinetic sort, since presumably anything that affects us without disturbance would count as an object of pleasure.' Cf. Giannantoni 1984: 37: 'La polemica ciceroniana, in effete, conferma l'ammissione da parte di Epicuro del piacere cinetico, ma nello stesso tempo manifesta un' incertezza sul posto e sul ruolo che al piacere cinetico devono essere assegnati.'

[50] As, e.g., Gosling and Taylor 1982: 382–394. Cf. Inwood 1990: 149–150, who concludes (150): 'The problem is *not* that Cicero's view of the matter is wrong, but that it is not clearly correct and that his rhetorical development provides no room for clarification of this vital point.'

In Cicero's eyes, painlessness is a poor candidate for being a pleasure in sense (ii) at all, namely a kind of positive phenomenological experience or sensation, let alone the highest pleasure. Both the commonly accepted meaning of the word *voluptas* and, we are asked to agree, introspective evidence suggest that the absence of pain does not necessarily feel like a pleasure. Therefore either the Epicureans must remain hedonists, accept an intermediate state between pleasure and pain, and in all significant respects agree with the Cyrenaics or they must accept that the state of painlessness is the goal, which is to renounce hedonism, and agree with Hieronymus of Rhodes.

What if katastematic pleasure were now considered to be a pleasure in sense (i), that is as the intentional object of some psychological state or attitude? This is what two recent interpretations of Epicurean pleasure, and of Epicurean katastematic pleasure in particular – Purinton (1993) and Feldman (2004) – attempt to do.[51] Purinton tries to argue for Epicurus being – in his words – a 'sensible' hedonist, by offering a sophisticated reading of a wide range of evidence for the Epicurean position which uses in particular Plutarch's account in *Non Posse* (see, e.g., 1089D–E, 1091A–B), and the tantalising but obscure quotation from Epicurus' *On Choices* in Diog. Laert. 10.136. Purinton argues that katastematic pleasure should be understood as the object of the intentional state of 'joy' (*khara*).[52] Both katastematic pleasure and the various 'smooth motions' in body or soul identified as kinetic pleasures are to be understood as possible objects of joy in this sense. On this account, katastematic pleasure may not immediately 'feel' good but rather 'is' good and, if we think properly about what we should value, can be an object of joy.[53] This interpretation has many merits, but there are various reasons to think that it cannot be accepted immediately. First, it is important to be clear about the nature of 'joy' (*khara*), since this is a crucial part of Purinton's interpretation. One of the most important passages is a quotation from Epicurus' *On the Telos*, found at Plut. *Non Posse* 1089D (Us. 68):

τὸ γὰρ εὐσταθὲς σαρκὸς κατάστημα καὶ τὸ περὶ ταύτης πιστὸν ἔλπισμα τὴν ἀκροτάτην χαρὰν καὶ βεβαιοτάτην ἔχειν τοῖς ἐπιλογίζεσθαι δυναμένοις.

---

[51] Also cf. Splawn 2002.
[52] Cf. on Diog. Laert. 10.136: Gosling and Taylor 1982: 388–389; Stokes 1995: 152 and 159–160; Wolfsdorf 2009. Compare also Striker 1993: 16.
[53] Purinton 1993: 283–284 also cites *Fin.* 1.37 in support of his view, particularly the claim that *ipsa liberatione et vacuitate omnis molestiae gaudemus*. On his view, *gaudium* is the equivalent of χαρά and has as its object katastematic pleasure or painlessness.

For the well-settled state of the flesh and the trusted expectation of it provide the highest and most secure joy for those able to appraise it.

The first point to note is that joy is closely associated here with the capacity for some kind of calculation or reflection, a form of rational activity (described as *epilogismos*) which involves the proper assessment of one's current and likely future well-being.[54] Joy is produced when one is able rationally to reflect on the well-settled state of one's body or able to expect that well-settled state to continue in the future. Indeed, the Epicureans regularly remind us that the expectation that painlessness will persist can be a source of present pleasure and that the suspicion that it will not can cause present distress. Consider, for example, *Sent. Vat.* 33's insistence on both the present absence and the expectation of future absence of hunger and the like. Similarly, other sources regularly contrast the Epicureans and Cyrenaics in terms of the formers' distinctive acceptance that memory and anticipation can produce pleasure (see, e.g., Diog. Laert. 2.89).[55] The conclusion that 'joy' is the product of such rational activity and assessment is supported by the scholion to *Ep. Hdt.* 66 in which *khara* and *phobos*, fear, are assigned to the workings of the rational part of the soul located in the chest. Most crucially, they are said to be distinct from the *pathē* such as pleasure and pain. 'Joy', on this account, is produced by rational activity and is therefore like fear but, unlike the *pathē*, it is corrigible. One can be either correct or mistaken in such rational assessment of one's current and likely future bodily state.[56] It is likely that, if there is a contrast or distinction to be drawn between 'joy' and 'katastematic pleasure', then it is not a distinction that makes katastematic pleasure the intentional object of joy, but it is a distinction between different types or sources of pleasure. Joy, we might say, is a positive rational evaluation of one's present or future state just as its counterpart, fear, is a negative rational evaluation of one's likely future state. Fear is a kind of pain; so we can infer that joy is a kind of pleasure. But what really distinguishes joy is that it is brought about in a particular fashion. Joy, for example, is not a possible affection of non-rational creatures since they lack the psychic capacity required for the rational evaluation of their current state, let alone the consideration of their future state. But those non-rational creatures may nevertheless experience the *pathos* of pleasure, indeed the fact that they do so and that

---

[54] On *epilogismos* see Schofield 1996. Cognate terms are also used by the Epicureans to describe the proper process of assessing alternative possible courses of action for their likely overall effects on well-being. See e.g. Diog. Oin. fr. 44.II.10–III.14 and *RS* 16 and cf. Warren 2001.

[55] See Warren 2001: 174–178.

[56] See Konstan 2006: 197–198.

it encourages them to act in a particular way is part of Epicurus' opening, 'cradle', argument for the idea that pleasure is the good.

Regardless of these more or less local interpretative difficulties, the principal problem with Purinton's interpretation, at least in so far as it is being offered as a defence of Epicurus against potential misunderstandings, is that it denies any necessary connection between katastematic pleasure and positive sensation.[57] Indeed, Purinton argues (312–314) that an Epicurean would be mad to accept the offer of a painless life without kinetic pleasures, because there would be no 'feeling' in such a life. The danger here is that in trying to retain a robust sense of this being a hedonist theory by agreeing that the value and choiceworthiness of a good Epicurean life resides in the presence of episodes of joy within it (some of which will be directed at the state of katastematic pleasure), the Epicureans come perilously close to accepting the Cyrenaic account of value, differing merely in their terminology.[58] In this way, Purinton agrees with Cicero: what is pleasant about living in a painlessness state is not the painlessness itself, but the various episodes of varying pleasure – kinetic pleasure or what Purinton calls 'joy' – to which it may give rise.[59] Cicero would surely claim that Purinton's interpretation, much like Torquatus' defence, agrees that painlessness is not the highest pleasure. Rather, painlessness can, but need not, be an object of joy and it is this joy, properly speaking, which makes a life feel pleasant and be worth choosing.[60] Here we might compare Purinton's interpretation with that of Striker, who suggests that Epicurus may have envisaged a necessary link between a painless and healthy state of an organism and various kinetic pleasures. If any activity in which a person engages while in a painless state produces some kind of kinetic

---

[57] We saw in the discussion of *Fin.* 1.38 above that Torquatus is not as clear as he might have been on this issue but that he perhaps ought to insist on a necessary and necessarily pleasant or painful self-perception of how one is affected.

[58] For a similar interpretation see also Erler and Schofield 1999, especially 656–657. Note 656: 'From one point of view ... Epicurus' disagreement with Aristippus is much less than he makes it appear, since the greatest pleasure remains strictly speaking a kinetic pleasure, namely our delight in *aponia* and *ataraxia*.'

[59] Purinton also rejects the interpretation of *RS* 3 and *RS* 19 according to which pleasure is in no way increased by duration: 1993: 317: 'I take it, then, that Epicurus' position is this: all else being equal, one *does* have a reason to pursue the course of action which promises a pleasure of longer duration, but one should do so with the understanding that one will not be deprived of more pleasure if death should happen to cut one's pleasure short. For one will not have lost a chance to enjoy *more* pleasure, but only the chance to enjoy an equal pleasure for a longer period of time.' It is not clear to me that much of this depends on denying the common interpretation of *RS* 18–20. Nevertheless, I think that the common interpretation (which I discuss and support in Warren 2004: 110–115) has some difficult consequences for the Epicureans. See Warren 2004: 199–212.

[60] Consider also Torquatus' account of the ideal life at *Fin.* 1.40 noted above.

pleasure (perhaps this is the variation to which Torquatus refers) then painlessness will in fact necessarily be pleasant given that a living organism cannot entirely refrain from acting. Once again, this might not evade Cicero's most general concern since it seems that on this account painlessness is still pleasant only in a dependent sense: katastematic pleasure is pleasant in the sense that it is a state which allows one to experience pleasant activities, perhaps even a constant succession of pleasant activities.[61]

Feldman considers the Epicureans during his own defence of what he terms 'attitudinal hedonism'. This is contrasted with what he calls 'sensory hedonism' in so far as an attitudinal pleasure is not a feeling but is rather a propositional attitude adopted when one enjoys, is glad about or is delighted by some state of affairs. Although such attitudes may be accompanied by pleasant feelings, Feldman stresses that they need not be (see pp. 54ff.); pleasant feeling is not an intrinsic element or a necessary accompaniment of attitudinal pleasure. For Feldman, Epicurean katastematic (or, as he calls it, 'static') pleasure is the attitudinal pleasure a person takes at the fact of his feeling no pain or disturbance (see pp. 95ff.). Note that, on this account, painlessness is a state which becomes the object of some attitude and it is this attitude which is properly a pleasure; the painlessness is not itself a pleasure. Even then, however, Feldman holds that the attitude now identified as a pleasure need not involve any positive sensation. My concern here is not to investigate Feldman's notion of attitudinal pleasure, but rather to note simply that his interpretation – and indeed the reason he is initially attracted to an Epicurean rather than a Cyrenaic-inspired hedonism – not only distinguishes between painlessness and katastematic pleasure, but also embraces just the dissociation between katastematic pleasure and sensation about which Cicero complains; it even allows a merely contingent link between 'attitudinal pleasure' and positive sensation.[62] Like Purinton's view, Feldman's account tries to make sense of the state of painlessness as a pleasure by introducing some further factor (here the presence of a certain attitude, for Purinton the presence of 'joy') which is made to carry the burden of granting the painless state value by allowing some sort of positive sensation. But this factor is not a necessary accompaniment of painlessness.

---

[61] Cf. Striker 1993: 16–17.

[62] Feldman (2004) goes on (103ff.) to criticise the Epicurean account he has thus reconstructed. In particular, he finds it difficult to accommodate the views that a life including some 'static' pleasure is always better than a life which does not, and that the short life of 'static' pleasure is of no less value than a longer such life. The implausibility of this view is compounded, and perhaps generated, by Feldman's own understanding of Epicurean hedonism and of 'static' pleasure in particular.

In both accounts we seem to have embraced rather than avoided the dilemma expressed by Cicero. Cicero insists that the Epicureans choose either painlessness or pleasure as the *telos*. On these two accounts, we are invited to think that the Epicureans insisted that we should call a pleasure either (Purinton) the state of painlessness which causes or gives rise to 'joy' or (Feldman) the 'attitudinal pleasure' we adopt towards our painlessness; furthermore, they are supposed to have held that this state of painlessness or this attitudinal pleasure is not necessarily accompanied by certain sensory feelings. This does not seem like a persuasive line of defence. Why, in that case, should we agree to call them pleasures at all, let alone imagine they could count as a genuine hedonist *telos*? Cicero would not and he is perhaps right to resist.

Let us be clear about the upshot of all this. If Purinton, Feldman and those with similar accounts are correct in their general accounts of Epicurean hedonism, then I do not think this is good news for Epicurus. Such views make the link between painless living and pleasant experience too weak to ground an account of *eudaimonia* that we can readily recognise as hedonist. On the other hand, as Cicero himself shows, any attempt to make the link between painless living and pleasant experience strong enough to ground a hedonist *eudaimonia* strains beyond tolerance the required notion of pleasure. Cicero emerges as an honest and perceptive critic of the Epicurean view and *Fin.* 1 and 2 as a sophisticated demonstration of the central difficulty. The Epicurean attempt to combine the ideas that pleasure is the good and that painlessness is the ideal state may simply be impossible, and therefore any interpretation which tries to make coherent sense of Epicurus' hedonism will collapse into one or other side of Cicero's dilemma.

CHAPTER 3

Cicero and Epicurean virtues (De Finibus 1–2)

Pierre-Marie Morel

Université Paris I – Panthéon-Sorbonne and Institut Universitaire de France

Cicero's criticisms of Epicureanism are well known. The Epicureans are *minuti philosophi*, 'tiny philosophers',[1] and are situated at the very antipodes of Cicero's own fundamental moral values. In his eyes, they scorn politics, and hence also the civic values implicit in the *mos maiorum*;[2] they reject dialectic and rhetoric, to such an extent that Epicurus invites us to abandon *paideia*; and they profess to regulate moral conduct on the basis of pleasure, which they make the criterion for choice and action. It is in that spirit that Books 1 and 2 are written.

The attacks made in the *De Finibus* and the *Tusculans*[3] must, it is true, be appreciated in a nuanced way,[4] for two reasons. The first is historical: Cicero's master, before Philo of Larissa, was Phaedrus, who had succeeded Zeno of Sidon as head of the Garden; and he also had friendly relations with several Roman Epicureans, including Atticus, named at the beginning of the *De Finibus*.[5] The second reason is more directly philosophical: Cicero's works attest a real fascination with this opposed doctrine, and thereby recognize its centrality to current philosophical debates. Cicero's dramatic enactment of the *dissensus* among the schools requires precisely that the Epicureans be placed at centre stage, in order to be refuted.

At all events, the *De Finibus* formulates a clear and final verdict on the Epicurean ethics defended by Torquatus. The question of pleasure lies at

---

[1] *Cato maior* 85.

[2] See Lévy 1992: 424–434. The danger represented by Epicureanism in Cicero's eyes is all the greater for the fact that the Epicureans have according to him – with whatever degree of exaggeration – 'invaded the whole of Italy' (*Tusc.* 4.7, *Fin.* 2.49).

[3] See, e.g., *Tusc.* 4.7, which presents Epicureanism as a superficial doctrine, popular with the uneducated masses. On this see also *Fin.* 1.25, 2.44, 49.

[4] See Epicurus' defence in *Tusc.* 5.89–110. Lévy 2001 has thus assimilated Cicero's attitude to an 'éloge paradoxal'. See however Ferrari's reply (*ibid.*), who notes that Cicero's last word on the question, in the final pages of *De Officiis*, is clearly negative. See too Prost 2003, according to whom Cicero's opposition to Epicurus in *Fin.* implicitly brings into play the notion of personhood that Cicero wishes to promote. See also, more recently, Maso 2008.

[5] 1.16.

the very heart of the polemic: in denouncing the assimilation of pleasure
to the good itself, Cicero is denouncing a philosophy incapable of understanding the true nature of the *telos*. Here we have, from Cicero's pen, a
radical anti-hedonist argument. Epicurean ethics is not tenable, not even
partially, because it is mistaken in its supreme principle.[6]

So he rejects Epicurean ethics right from the very first pages of *De
Finibus*, even before examination of how the Epicureans define morality,
and therefore even before considering the special Epicurean conception
of the virtues. The disagreement is not about a particular conception of
virtue which might be wrong but still relies on acceptable principles. It is
much more radical: by subordinating morality to pleasure, Epicurean ethics starts out from an unacceptable principle and therefore leads, regardless of its doctrinal content, to disastrous consequences.

In Book I, Cicero condemns Epicureanism at 23–24, and the question
of virtue is discussed by Torquatus at 1.42–54. In Book 2, the refutation
focuses first on pleasure (6–44), and only at a second stage on the *honestum* and the virtues (45–77). Cicero will also be able to say, at 2.44, that
the debate is not between Cicero and Torquatus, but between virtue and
pleasure. Then comes a third section, on friendship (2.78–85), followed by
various arguments on pleasure and pain (2.86–119). So one might think
that the question of Epicurean virtues is secondary to the anti-hedonist
argument, because it seems polemically less decisive: the moral system of
the Epicureans is already in a state of collapse even before its conception
of virtue is refuted.

Yet the question of the virtues extolled by the Epicureans is at the centre of the polemic conducted by Cicero in the first two books of the work,
and also probably beyond. I see three reasons for this.

First, the question of the virtues is inseparable from the anti-hedonist
argument: if pleasure cannot be the true *telos*, it is because only genuinely
moral or honourable conduct, the *honestum*, can be considered the end
per se. The fundamental error of the Epicureans is precisely to consider the
virtues means and not ends. What is at stake here, then, is not only the
role of virtues in the good life and the formal coherence of the doctrine –
although these are an important aspect of Cicero's criticism, as we shall
see – but the very notion of what virtue is.

Second, the issue is all the more central in that the Epicureans claim
that the virtues are essential to the good life and that they are inseparable from pleasure. As Epicurus himself says, 'The virtues are naturally

[6] On this aspect of the polemic, see Warren (this volume), and on friendship, Frede (this volume).

linked to the pleasant life and the pleasant life is inseparable from them.'[7]
Epicurean ethics claims to be a moral hedonism, in which the virtues,
although they are indeed means,[8] are also necessary means. Cicero does
not overlook this, and at 1.25 it is precisely Epicurus' inconsistency on that
point that he targets: one cannot say that pleasure is the only intrinsic end
and at the same time that 'right and honourable actions by themselves
produce joy, that is to say, pleasure' (*recta et honesta quae sint ea facere ipsa
per se laetitiam, id est voluptatem*). Such an idea, says Cicero, comes down
to 'overthrowing the whole system' (*totam rationem everti*). However, in
saying this he provides clear recognition of the Epicurean desire to promote a certain form of virtuous life.

There is, I think, a third reason, an indirect and dialectical one, for
the importance attached to the issue of virtues in the first two books of
De Finibus: it involves what is arguably the central concept of the entire
work, namely the *honestum*. In refuting the Epicurean conception of the
virtues, Cicero prepares the ground for later developments in the *De
Finibus* bearing on this point. He thus announces his own conception of
the *honestum*, or at any rate the conception which is, in his opinion, the
most probable.[9] He also starts to stage a *disputatio* in which the Epicurean
position clearly appears as a foil for the other two main doctrines, the
Stoic one, represented and defended by Cato, and that of Antiochus,
defended by Piso. In one version of *Carneadea divisio*, at 2.35, Cicero gives
Epicureanism an explicit place. He there maintains that Epicureanism is
at odds with its own principles, since Epicurus conceives of the principle,
pleasure, as kinetic pleasure, that is, pleasure 'in motion', in the manner of
Aristippus, yet the end that he actually intends is akin rather to the *telos* of
Hieronymus, absence of pain.[10]

Cicero's strategy combines the refutation of Epicureanism with anticipation of issues and controversies that are to follow in the later books of
the *De Finibus*. To refute Epicurus is to lay the groundwork for a defence
of the *honestum* and of *ratio*. It is this anticipatory sort of rebuttal that

---

[7] *Ep. Men.* 132. Text cited below, p. 82. See also *Sent.* 5, *Sent. Vat.* 5.

[8] D.L. 10.138.

[9] I will not here be pronouncing definitively on the conception of the *honestum* that might
be attributed to Cicero as his own, or on its certainly very strong affinity with Antiochus'
Academic-Peripatetic doctrine. See Graver (this volume); Lévy 1992; Prost 2001; Annas in Annas
and Woolf 2001: x–xv.

[10] See Algra 1997: 12 on this precise point, and more generally on Cicero's uses of the *Carneadea divisio* and of ethical divisions. I shall not dwell either on the different kinds of pleasure distinguished
by the Epicureans, or, in particular, on the distinction between katastematic pleasure and pleasure
'in movement'. It is at all events clear that, in Cicero's eyes, setting aside mere plays on words,
pleasure is necessarily 'in movement' (2.75–77).

an analysis of the relevant passages in Books 1 and 2 should allow us to reconstruct.

Torquatus' account in Book 1 (*Fin.* 1.42–54)

Torquatus' account of the virtues is part of his long defence of Epicurean ethics (1.29–72), responding to Cicero's radical attacks at the beginning of the work. Above all, it is important to note that this account is in substantial agreement with orthodox Epicurean doctrine: Torquatus follows in Epicurus' footsteps, and often quotes him. The Epicureanism which Cicero puts into the mouth of his character Torquatus, although we should not attribute it to the historical Torquatus, is on most points in accord with the original doctrine. Cicero's polemical strategy does not involve a falsification of the doctrine, but rather its simplification. He constructs a character – Torquatus – who shows little ability to defend it or to insist on the nuances that an Epicurean more experienced in dialectical skirmishes would not have failed to bring to light.[11] The Torquatus of the *De Finibus* is a fiction, and moreover a fiction that can prove quite disappointing if one wants to see in his remarks a source of information on Epicurean doctrine. Nevertheless, in order to understand Cicero's strategy and his depiction of the Epicurean virtues in the *De Finibus*, it is from Torquatus' formulations that one must start.

Rather than proceed through question and answer, Torquatus prefers to give a long account of the doctrine. He intends thus to progress 'with order and method' (*ratione et via*),[12] declaring that in this he is inspired by Epicurus himself. It is not easy, let us note in passing, to determine with certainty what exactly this method consists in. If we judge by Torquatus' first argument, in 1.29, it could be to do with one of the methodological rules formulated by Epicurus in the *Letter to Herodotus*.[13] It is necessary to start from a firm and well-known principle – in this case, according to Torquatus, the identification of pleasure with the supreme good – relying on sensation or feeling, and laying down that this principle should not itself be subject to investigation or to further proof. Torquatus does indeed insist, at 1.30, on the fact that it is useless to subject this principle to reasoning and discussion,

---

[11] As Inwood 1990 has noticed, Torquatus 'is uncomfortable with close dialectical debate', so that 'Cicero has not really given Epicurus' doctrine a fair chance to establish itself in the mind of the reader'. See also Annas in Annas and Woolf 2001: xvi. On the historical Torquatus and his fidelity to Epicurus' doctrine and terminology, see also Warren, in this volume.

[12] 1.29.

[13] *Ep. Hdt.* 37–38. According to Sedley 1996, Torquatus' speech is governed by a rigorous methodology that can be compared with that of the physical discourse found in the *Letter to Herodotus*.

because it is 'felt' (*sentiri*), in the way that we feel that snow is white or honey sweet – self-evident data, 'none of which needs to be confirmed by refined reasoning' (*quorum nihil oportere exquisitis rationibus confirmare*). As we will see later, it is significant that Cicero attributes to Torquatus, on the authority of the school's founder, the idea that 'sensation',[14] as opposed to reason, constitutes the first principle of moral conduct.

The part of the exposition devoted to the virtues starts on a polemical note, attacking those who place the supreme good in virtue and let themselves be overawed by the grandeur of this word. We probably have here an allusion to Epicurus' provocative saying in which he claims to 'spit on beauty', and on those who admire it, if it does not produce any pleasure.[15] The remark is supposed to apply to those who identify happiness with the virtuous life, but also, probably, to philosophers who resort to rhetorical hyperbole in their praise of the virtues.[16] In addition to the provocation, Torquatus is here confirming that the Epicureans readily admit Cicero's main charge against them, namely that they consider the virtues means towards pleasure. The example chosen by Torquatus, that of medicine, also seems to serve as a *topos* in the Epicurean tradition, as suggested by its similarity to the ethical doxography of Diogenes Laertius (10.138):[17] we choose virtue for the sake of pleasure, just as we choose medical science (*medicorum scientia*) for the sake of the health it brings about. It is not insignificant that 'science' here is ranked as a mere means, but it is even more notable that Torquatus, in going on to refer to the art of navigation, pointedly links the arts, sciences, and thereby the virtues too,

---

[14] Or 'feeling', depending on how one understands *sensus* and *sentiri*. See below, pp. 89–90.

[15] Ath. *Deipn.*, XII, 547a (Us. 512). The reference seems in fact to be to moral beauty.

[16] As suggested by Torquatus' irony about those who get captivated 'by the grandeur of the word' (*splendore nominis*), namely 'virtue' (1.42), and by his allusion to those whose 'eloquence runs riot' (*exsultat oratio*) in praise of the virtues (1.54). This echoes a well-known feature of early Epicureanism, noted above, the rejection of rhetoric (e.g., D.L. 10.118–119). But the jibe may be primarily anti-Stoic, to judge from *Fin.* 4.37, where Cicero himself objects to Cato that the Stoics blind the souls of their interlocutors by the 'brightness' (*splendor*) with which they adorn virtue.

[17] See also Diog. Oen. 33.6 Smith. In fact, however, although this text illustrates the relation of means to end, in it the medical art (here surgery) represents a different category of means from those proposed for virtue. Diogenes assigns to virtue the status of 'productive agent' (ποιητικόν) of pleasure, which is therefore distinct from pleasure itself; but there are three types of productive agent: those that precede their effect (like surgery in relation to pleasure), those with immediate effect (like certain intrinsically pleasant activities), and those that come after their effects, owing to a kind of psychological anticipation (like eulogies at our funerals, whose anticipation we enjoy while still alive). Virtue belongs to the second type, being a productive agent simultaneous with the pleasure it causes. This testimony confirms that the Epicureans were admirably consistent in admitting the instrumental character of virtue – in that respect, Cicero's criticisms merely repeat what they themselves say – but also that they sought to refine the doctrine on this point, by showing that the pursuit of pleasure and virtue are coextensive.

to *utilitas*: what makes the art of sailing commendable is not the art itself, but its usefulness (*utilitate, non arte laudatur*).[18] Neither virtue, nor medicine, nor the art of navigation is an end in itself. Thus Torquatus' speech prepares the ground for Cicero's own polemical arguments, based on the contrast between *utilitas* and *voluptas* on the one hand and the *honestum* on the other. This opposition will in effect underlie the whole of Cicero's critique in Book 2.

Torquatus now proceeds to a systematic review of the virtues, in order to show both that the virtues are means to pleasure,[19] and that Epicurean doctrine recommends their practice: for according to the teachings of Epicurus, a happy life is inconceivable without that practice.[20] However, Torquatus presents the doctrine by adopting the 'standard' framework of the four cardinal virtues: wisdom (*sapientia*, 1.42–46), temperance (*temperantia*, 47–48), courage (*fortitudo*, 49), and justice (*iustitia*, 50–53). Even before we consider Cicero's criticism, the structure of this exposition raises at least two problems: that of its doctrinal attribution, and the linked problem of its compatibility with the role Epicurus assigns to 'prudence' (*phronēsis*).

Let us start with the problem of doctrinal attribution: does Torquatus' exposition carry the hallmarks of Epicureanism, or is it an opportunistic way of responding to the Academics and Stoics on their own ground? As a matter of fact, Torquatus' presentation, in adopting the model of the four cardinal virtues, is unique among all our testimonies for Epicurean ethics. This schema is standard in the Platonic and Stoic traditions, and will be taken up by Piso[21] in Book 5, but it is in no way standard for the Epicurean tradition.[22] It differs notably from the way in which Epicurus presents the virtues in the *Letter to Menoeceus*:

> Of all this the beginning and the greatest good is prudence. Therefore prudence is even more precious than philosophy, and it is the natural source of all the remaining virtues: it teaches the impossibility of living pleasurably without living prudently, honourably and justly, <and the impossibility of living prudently, honourably and justly> without living pleasurably. For the virtues are naturally linked with living pleasurably, and living pleasurably is inseparable from them.[23]

[18] 1.42.   [19] See the end of the section, 1.54.
[20] 1.57; *Ep. Men.* 132; *Sent.* 5; *Sent. Vat.* 5.   [21] *Fin.* 5.67.
[22] For Plato, see *Phd.* 69a–c, *R.* 4.433b–c, *Lg.* 1.631c–d, 12.964b, 965c–d. For an accurate synthesis of Stoic uses of the table of cardinal virtues, and the problem of the relation of *phronēsis* to the other virtues, see Gourinat 2008. On the Stoic material about the virtues Torquatus deals with, see, e.g., D.L. 7.126.
[23] *Ep. Men.* 132 (trans. Long and Sedley): τούτων δὲ πάντων ἀρχὴ καὶ τὸ μέγιστον ἀγαθὸν φρόνησις. διὸ καὶ φιλοσοφίας τιμιώτερον ὑπάρχει φρόνησις, ἐξ ἧς αἱ λοιπαὶ πᾶσαι πεφύκασιν

In this text one does not find any division of virtue into four kinds; the virtues of temperance and courage are not mentioned; and prudence seems to enjoy a special status: it is 'even more precious than philosophy'. To explain these differences in form and substance between Torquatus' account and the text of Epicurus, two possible hypotheses are available.

The first hypothesis lies in assuming that Torquatus, without producing an original theory, is trying to present as Epicurean a widely held picture, in order to convince the Roman public that Epicurean ethics is compatible with current values. This hypothesis, defended in particular by Phillip Mitsis,[24] finds justification in certain rather conventional stances taken by Torquatus, for example on guilty conscience, and on the public shame that must be undergone by anyone who performs an unjust action.[25] This is indeed a doctrine foreign to Epicurus' maxims on law, where the decision to avoid injustice is not dictated by such motives, but by a purely pragmatic avoidance of punishment.[26] This first hypothesis, in so far as it points towards a compromise between the Epicurean position and Roman values, corresponds quite well to the consensual tendency of Torquatus' position. According to this position, there is no conflict between pleasure and virtue, and consequently between pleasure and justice, because 'it is impossible to live pleasurably without living wisely (*sapienter*), honourably (*honeste*) and justly (*iuste*), and impossible to live wisely, honourably and justly without living pleasurably' (1.57).

However, this last quotation, a literal translation of Epicurus' pronouncement on the interdependence of pleasure and the virtues, raises other difficulties, and calls for a different hypothesis. Among these difficulties, note first that justice cannot be admitted without restriction among the characteristic virtues of the sage. Epicurus' maxims on the just (*to dikaion*) do not, or at least do not directly, concern the life of the

---

ἀρεταί, διδάσκουσα ὡς οὐκ ἔστιν ἡδέως ζῆν ἄνευ τοῦ φρονίμως καὶ καλῶς καὶ δικαίως, <οὐδὲ φρονίμως καὶ καλῶς καὶ δικαίως> ἄνευ τοῦ ἡδέως. συμπεφύκασι γὰρ αἱ ἀρεταὶ τῷ ζῆν ἡδέως καὶ τὸ ζῆν ἡδέως τούτων ἐστὶν ἀχώριστον.

[24] Mitsis 1988: 69.   [25] 1.51.

[26] Torquatus sees in legal punishment (*poena legum*) simply one reason among others that we have for avoiding injustice (1.51); likewise in Cicero's polemical reprise (2.53). Contrast Epicur. *Sent.* 34–35. In the case of the wise, it is true, avoidance of injustice can be justified by self-interest, since it enables them to maintain the psychic dispositions required by *ataraxia*. On this see vander Waerdt 1987. Note that the Epicurean Hermarchus, while defending the same doctrine of Epicurus on the fear of legal sanction, introduced a specific fear – perhaps religious or moral – which manifests itself in criminals as a desire to purify the impurity of their actions. He adds that such a fear is in fact irrational or unreasonable (ἄλογος) (ap. Porph. *Abst.* 1.9.4).

sage: Epicurus' reflections on the just and justice are located at a strictly
political or social level, that of the conditions of life in a city. Justice for
Epicurus lies in the agreement men make among themselves not to wrong
each other.[27] General considerations on the need for a contract to gov-
ern common life are, it may be true, not unrelated to the life of the sage.
Thus, later on (1.70) Torquatus will cite the view of certain members of
the school who think that friendship among the wise presupposes a sort
of pact (*foedus*). But even in this case the notion of contract is probably
insufficient to define the mode of sociability characteristic of the wise, that
is to say, the sociability specific to friendship.[28] Generally speaking, if it is
true that justice is counted by Epicurus himself among the virtues necessary for the good life, that is, the life of the sage, it could not be on exactly
the same level as the other virtues,[29] contrary to the impression given by
Torquatus' account. For even if the sage is just, the type of justice which
depends on a simple contract for abstention from mutual harm is applicable at the level, a political one, of relations between citizens; whereas the
mode of life specific to the sage is at a different level, that of friendship.

Another difficulty follows. In his virtual quotation of Epicurus at 1.57
(above, p. 82), Torquatus mentions a list of virtues which is not easily
reducible to the table of cardinal virtues. Courage and temperance are not
explicitly present. We might try to include them under the 'honourable',
as captured by Epicurus' use here of the Greek adverb *kalōs*, but nothing encourages us to do so, this term being a particularly imprecise one.
Besides, the quotation of Epicurus puts the emphasis less on some supposed typology of the virtues than on the mutual entailment of pleasure
and virtue: you cannot have one without the other, regardless of what specific virtues are at issue.

Moreover prudence (*phronēsis*), whereas it is the principal virtue in
Epicurus' eyes,[30] barely finds any place in Torquatus' account. In one sense
however it *is* present, under the heading of *sapientia*. At 1.42–46 Torquatus
extols knowledge, as opposed to the ignorance that breeds fear, the turmoil of passion, or excessive desire. *Sapientia* thus leads to tranquillity, a
term which here captures Epicurus' *ataraxia*, the absence of disturbance.
This probably does represent one aspect of Epicurus' *phronēsis*. Moreover,

[27] See, e.g., *Sent.* 33.
[28] This is probably what is meant by *foedus quoddam* in 1.70: friendship between the wise is a 'kind of'
pact, probably distinct from the covenant of interest underlying civil justice.
[29] This is a matter of debate, see Brown 2009: 191–195. Since the complex and controversial question
of the Epicurean attitude to politics cannot be covered here, Brown's study is recommended for
information on the current state of play.
[30] *Ep. Men.* 132.

the fact that Cicero uses the term *sapientia*, and not *prudentia*, is hardly significant. Although the two terms are not exactly interchangeable in his usage,[31] he does sometimes use *prudentia* in place of *sapientia*, not only here but also in other works when addressing the Epicurean conception of virtue.[32] However, if one judges by his presentation of it in the *Letter to Menoeceus*, Epicurean prudence has another dimension, one that does not appear directly in Torquatus' praise of *sapientia*: the ability to assess the balance of pleasures and pains accurately in the exercise of 'sober reasoning' (*nēphōn logismos*). This assessment leads one in certain cases to give up some pleasures if it turns out that they threaten to cause more pain than satisfaction. For it is immediately after the evocation of this hedonic calculus that Epicurus mentions *phronēsis*. Torquatus does not ignore this aspect of Epicurean prudence, but he deals with it, not in connection with *sapientia*, but when defining *temperantia* (1.47–48). Temperance according to Torquatus consists in maintaining one's resolution or judgement about what to do or not do (*iudicare quid faciendum, non faciendumque*, 1.47).[33] It is not to be confused with that judgement, but is added to it. Nevertheless, the fact remains that it is when temperance is under consideration that the calculation of pleasures enters the Epicurean account.

Epicurean prudence cannot be easily defined, but the two features that can reasonably be assigned to it are those that Torquatus attaches respectively to *sapientia* and *temperantia*. Thus the main Epicurean virtue shows through, in what seem to be its two aspects, at two separate points in the presentation, under two different headings in the table of the cardinal virtues. It is not eliminated, but it is, if nothing else, fragmented. This confirms that the Epicurean doctrine fits that table rather poorly. Such too will be the conclusion of the anti-Epicurean critiques in the *De Officiis*: 'Where, for a start, will prudence find its place?' (*primum ubi prudentiae locus dabitur?*), Cicero asks, and goes on to remark, with regard

---

[31] See Aubert forthcoming, who highlights the different uses of *prudentia* in Cicero. According to her, it is sometimes understood as an essentially practical virtue, closely linked to political experience and foresight (see, e.g., *Div.* 1.111), and defined in contrast to *sapientia* understood as a theoretical virtue. In other instances, *prudentia* is equivalent to this latter. It is, I think, unlikely that Cicero in *De Finibus* is making a real distinction between *prudentia* and *sapientia*, or that he is implicitly ranking the former below the latter, considering that at 5.67, when Piso returns to the fourfold list of cardinal virtues, it is *prudentia*, not *sapientia*, that is used to denote wisdom.

[32] See *Off.* 3.117–118, where Cicero tests the Epicurean doctrine against the table of the four cardinal virtues. Reid 1925 reckons that in our passage of *De Finibus* the terms *sapientia* and *prudentia* are simply synonyms.

[33] Note that this definition bears similarities with the Stoic treatment of temperance as a capacity, closely connected to *phronēsis*, of choice and avoidance: Clem. Al. *Strom.* 2.470 (*SVF* 3.275).

to temperance, that the Epicureans introduce it only with difficulty (*non temperantiam inducunt facillime*).[34]

It is therefore likely – and this is the alternative hypothesis – that Torquatus, without actually modifying the Epicurean doctrine and without wanting to adapt it to an originally alien model, is in fact seeking to place himself in his opponents' territory. The point would be to show the Academics, Peripatetics, and Stoics that *their* virtues are in reality merely means to pleasure.[35] The text gives several indications that point this way: at 1.42 Torquatus' ironic prologue to his account of the virtues refers to 'your virtues' (*vestrae ... virtutes*); at 1.47 the future *dicemus*, to convey what the Epicureans 'will' say about temperance if pressed to do so, suggests a certain distance from the point under discussion; and at 1.54 the virtues are the objects of praise by 'other philosophers' (*ceterum philosophorum*). If these details are significant, and not just accidental, it must be inferred that Torquatus is not making concessions either to the Roman values of his time or to the ethical schemata of opposing schools. More likely he is reflecting a strategy, adopted by certain unidentified Epicureans, of describing the commonly accepted virtues in order to deny them the status of absolute values.

To extend this second hypothesis, we can also assume that Torquatus finds the standard table to be to his advantage, even if there is no question of his adopting it on its own merits. It is a convenient table if one wants to be certain of having made a complete inventory of virtues and thus of having ensured a complete response to the anti-Epicurean critiques. This methodological concern is reflected when Torquatus tackles justice at 1.50: 'It remains to speak of justice, so as not to overlook any virtue' (*iustitia restat, ut dictum de omni virtute sit*). He promised, back at 1.37, to show that 'all the virtues' (*omnium virtutum*) lead to pleasure. If one bears in mind that Torquatus intends to proceed 'with order and method' (1.29), it is natural that he should be concerned with the formal rigour of his account. Note, finally, that Cicero, in the eulogy he will deliver on the four virtues at 2.48 – virtues which are the 'structure of morality', *forma honestatis*,[36] and of which, he says, Torquatus 'mentioned the names' whereas Epicurus ignores them[37] – will see in them the 'complete and perfect' (*expletam et perfectam*) realization of the *honestum*. The list of cardinal

---

[34] *Off.* 3.117–118.   [35] For this interpretation cf. Sedley 1996: 337.

[36] At *Fin.* 5.9 *forma* refers to the division of Peripatetic doctrine into three domains: physics, logic, and ethics. In the expression *forma honestatis* the word *forma* can be understood in an analogous sense.

[37] 2.48.

virtues, for Cicero as for his Epicurean interlocutor, provides a guarantee of completeness.

From these early observations, limited mainly to the Book 1, we can conclude that, in the mouth of Torquatus, Cicero presents a complex and in many ways unclear picture of the Epicurean virtues: we find the principles of the doctrine, but they are transposed into a system which corresponds to the standard table of virtues, and to the *honestum* such as Cicero will define it in Book 2. From a historiographical or doxographical point of view, we must admit that Torquatus' discourse presents more problems than it does solutions. It adds nothing very new to our knowledge of the original doctrine. Nor does it add any information about a possible development in Epicureanism after Epicurus. At most one may note, with regard to justice, a slight realignment in favour of conscience and of public reputation, a tone that contrasts with the maxims of Epicurus on the *dikaion*. Torquatus' presentation also raises epistemological issues that Cicero will be able to exploit in the following pages: the Epicurean criterion of the good life is *sensus*, and one can rightly ask whether such a basis is sufficient for morality.

Cicero's critique (*Fin.* 2.45–77)

For Cicero, Torquatus' position on the virtues is fundamentally incoherent. The first contradiction is between pleasure and virtue. For it is inconsistent to praise virtue while considering pleasure alone to be the end. Virtue by its very essence cannot be a means, as Torquatus wants: it cannot be anything other than the *telos* itself. This argument has been being formulated ever since the prologue to Book 1 (1.25), and it naturally recurs in Book 2, following upon the admission that the *honestum* can rightly be commended for its own sake (*per se ipsum*), regardless of whatever benefits one may draw from it (2.45).

The reason for the Epicureans' mistake on this point is primarily doctrinal: they confuse pleasure and the *telos*, and grant the virtues merit solely for their 'utility'. But it is also due to their use of language: Epicurus does not understand ordinary language (2.48), and Torquatus himself misuses the language of virtue, a language shared by not only the Academics, but also the Peripatetics and the Stoics (2.76) – 'our language', as Cicero calls it – because his doctrine is incompatible with it (2.77). This turns against the Epicureans the reproaches which they address to other schools (2.75), and also establishes that communication is impossible. Whereas Cicero criticizes the Stoics for dressing up in new words ideas that do not differ from those of the Academic tradition, with those who make pleasure the *telos* there is no common language, either in content or in form.[38]

There is also an evident contradiction between doctrine and personal moral conduct. Epicurus' words on his deathbed, which Cicero cites at 2.96, manifest all his nobility of spirit and courage, but also betray the point at which his (hedonistic) words conflict with his actions: 'Listen … to Epicurus' dying words, so that you may understand the conflict between his actions and words' (2.96).

From a strategic point of view, the denunciation of Epicurean inconsistencies is two-pronged: on one level, it contributes to the specific refutation of Epicureanism; on a second level, it is preparing for a much broader dialectical development. In the face of Epicurus' inconsistencies, Cicero claims not to care what Epicurus says or denies, but only 'what it is consistent for someone who places the highest good in pleasure to say' (2.70, *quid ei qui in voluptate summum bonum ponat consentaneum sit dicere*). Now to denounce the contradictions – or mere inconsistencies – of adversaries or interlocutors belongs to the general method of *disputatio*, because the assessment of inconsistencies enables one to classify and distinguish doctrines according to their consistency or their *inconstantia*. Thus at 2.35 Cicero says that schools that make their ends agree with the primary inclinations at least have the merit of consistency, including that of Aristippus, while Epicurus would have been more consistent if he had adopted the latter's position. The following books clearly echo this attack. At 4.39 Cicero blames the Stoics for their inconsistency (*inconstantia*), because they intend to base right conduct and virtue on conformity to nature, while introducing a discontinuity between natural inclination and the highest good.[39] More significantly still, at 5.79 Cicero tells Piso that he does not wonder about the actual power of virtue, but asks himself 'what is said consistently, and what is at odds with itself' (*quid constanter dicitur, quid ipsum a se dissentiat*). Exposing the internal contradictions of Epicureanism allows him to start highlighting *dissensus* in its two forms: external *dissensus*, between different doctrines,[40] and internal *dissensus*, between the propositions that constitute a single doctrine.

---

[38] See e.g. *Fin.* 3.10; 4.3, 56–60; 5.89.

[39] The analogies between the criticism of Epicurus and those of the Stoics, particularly regarding the accusation of incoherence, have been analysed by Lévy 1984. My hope here is to show that we can expand the list of parallels by observing how Books 1 and 2 anticipate not only Book 4, but the entire remainder of the work.

[40] See 5.16.

Such confusion in words, and so great an inconsistency in method, naturally invite one to question the epistemological soundness of Epicurean ethics. The question is very general and not restricted to the problem of the virtues, but it is indeed at this level of generality that it is discussed at the beginning of the work, in Cicero's anti-Epicurean prologue. In a passage which is unfortunately lacunose (2.22), Cicero denounces Epicurus for his incompetence in the argument, his rejection of definitions, and the fact that he 'places the criterion of reality in the senses' (*rerum iudicia in sensibus ponit*). This is a constant theme of anti-Epicurean polemic in Cicero, who for example elsewhere[41] speaks ironically also about the Epicurean rejection and denunciation of dialectic. Epicurus' inconsistencies are linked primarily to his inability to define properly the terms in question, such as pleasure or virtue. This is picked up by Cicero's proposal to agree on definitions, under the double influence of the legal formula *ea res agetur* – agreement on what point is to be judged – and of Plato's *Phaedrus*.[42]

Concerning the identification of sensation as the criterion, we have seen that it touched the heart of the moral controversy. At 1.30 Torquatus said that the principle of action, pleasure, is 'felt' (*sentiri*), as we feel that snow is white or that honey is sweet. In the mouth of Cicero (2.36), this means that 'the senses are sufficient to judge that pleasure is the good and pain the bad'. But this, he says, is to grant the senses more authority than the laws do to a judge in a trial. A judge must decide only on what falls within his jurisdiction. It likewise belongs to sensation to comment on its own specific objects. Cicero then gives examples that include special sensibles (such as sweet and bitter, which belong to taste) and common sensibles (such as near and far, rest and movement, and different shapes). But good and bad belong to neither of these two categories. Sensation is therefore not competent to pronounce on good and bad, which do not fall within its remit.

There is undoubtedly an awkwardness in these texts, which is that the Epicureans distinguished two criteria, *aisthēsis* and *pathos*, of which the first focuses more on knowledge of the objects of experience (sensation in its proper sense), the second on internal states and their practical consequences (to select or reject, to pursue or flee).[43] The Latin *sensus* introduces

[41] *Luc.* 30, 97; Us. 376.
[42] *Phdr.* 237b; *Fin.* 2.3–4. For the importance of the reference to the Platonic dialogue, see Lévy 1984: 122.
[43] See D.L. 10.34. This ambivalence of *sensus* in Cicero, between 'sense' (or 'sensation') and 'feeling' (or 'affection'), is visible in the long list of its meanings given by Merguet 1964: 663: *Gefühl, Sinn, Empfindung, Eindruck, Wahrnehmung, Bewusstsein, Gesinnung, Sinnesart.*

an ambiguity: one might suppose that it is here intended in the sense of
pathos, not *aisthēsis*. This ambiguity is discernible even in the definition
that Cicero himself gives of pleasure, 'a pleasant movement occurring in
sensation' (2.75, *in sensu iucundus motus*). However, the examples given
by Cicero in the two texts mentioned above – the whiteness of snow, the
sweetness of honey (1.30); sweet and bitter, smooth and rough, near and
far, stationary and moving, square and round (2.36) – are undoubtedly
examples of *aisthēsis*. In truth, Cicero does not seem to be concerned
with the distinction that the Epicureans had made between *aisthēsis* and
pathos. He provides a simplified version of the Epicurean doctrine of
criteria, in order to better expose its weaknesses. His argument can be
understood as follows. Sensation (*sensus*) is for the Epicureans the first
criterion of knowledge, yet this criterion does not enable us to appreciate good and bad. Furthermore, pleasure arises *in sensu*; therefore pleasure cannot appreciate good and bad. In other words, the Epicureans
would like *sensus* to be not only a cognitive but also a practical criterion,
but in doing so they take sensation, and with it pleasure, beyond their
competence.

This epistemological weakness of the Epicurean moral principle has the
immediate consequence that reason and its use are undervalued. Cicero
justifies his criticism of the Epicurean overestimation of *sensus* by appealing to the positive role of reason: judging good and bad depends firstly on
'reason (*ratio*), inspired by the knowledge of things divine and human,
which can properly be called wisdom (*sapientia*), along with, secondly, the
virtues, which reason wants to be the mistresses of all things, whereas your
own wish was to make them handmaids and servants of pleasure' (2.37).
This passage, in which Cicero adopts a position diametrically opposed to
that of Epicurus, does not content itself with taking up a metaphor based
on the household (the opposition between the mistress of the house and
her maids): it also has a strong Stoic ring. The term 'handmaids and servants' (*satellites et ministras*), used of the virtues, evokes Cleanthes' famous
polemical allegory, reported at 2.69, where the Epicurean virtues kneel
before the throne of *Voluptas* in the role of 'little maids' (*ancillulas*) with
no other task than to 'serve' (*ministrarent*) her. Moreover, the definition of
wisdom as 'the knowledge of things divine and human' echoes one of the
Stoic definitions of wisdom (*sophia, sapientia*).[44]

---

[44] Cf. Aët. 1, Prooem. 2 (*SVF* 2.35); S.E. *M.* 9.13 (*SVF* 2.36), 123 (*SVF* 2.1017); and in Cicero, cf. *Off.*
1.153, 2.5; *Tusc.* 4.57.

Given Cicero's (scarcely deniable) affinities with Stoic ethics, he cannot but subscribe to a defence of the claims of reason against the arrogance of sensation. Clearly the Stoics, in particular in the more intellectualist aspects of their ethics, are good allies here, when it comes to setting against the Epicureans the idea of an ethics based not on *sensus* but on the *ratio*.

The overlap of the epistemological and the strictly ethical themes becomes clearer still when Cicero grapples with the problem of the definition of morality (*honestum*). The passage at 2.45–46 reflects in the following way the wish to oppose to Epicureanism an ethical model that gives pride of place to both the virtues and reason. The passage begins (2.45) by affirming the primacy of the *honestum* over any other end: regardless of any *utilitas*, morality can be properly commended for itself, *per se ipsum*. The nature of the *honestum* is revealed 'by a judgement shared by all' (*communi omnium iudicio*) and by the deeds of great men. And, Cicero says in effect, it is to their *ratio* that men owe their capacity to behave morally (2.45).

These observations sound like Cicero's way of announcing a major theme of the remaining books of the *De Finibus*, in particular of its refutation of Stoicism: the idea of man's natural inclinations and of the progressive development of the rational faculty.[45] If this is indeed the case, the thought is implicitly the following: the Epicureans refuse to admit that man does not realize his essence in the exercise of the sensory faculty, but by its subordination to *ratio*. Their error is in a sense the opposite of that made by the Stoics, who overlook the continuity and progression of nature in achieving what makes humanity human.[46]

It is therefore on behalf of both *ratio* and the virtues, but also on behalf of nature (2.58) – because the nature of man, when it reaches its highest point of development, is rational – that Cicero can rebut point by point Torquatus' assertions concerning the cardinal virtues: wisdom and justice (2.51–59), temperance and courage (2.60–77). Cicero[47] thus shows at 2.45–46 that the human ability to live according to reason allows a kind of deduction of the cardinal virtues: first justice (2.45), which is based on gradual progression from domestic attachments to civic virtues and a bond with the whole human race; then wisdom (2.46), which stems from the desire to discover the truth; courage (2.46); and finally temperance (2.47), in which order (*ordo*) and measure (*moderatio*) are to be found.

[45] See e.g. *Fin.* 4.34–39, *Off.* 1.11, 105.
[46] 4.39.
[47] Maybe exploiting Panaetius' treatment of the virtues. See Schofield 2012c: 44–45.

Cicero is able to conclude, at 2.48, with the following positive description of the *honestum*: the four virtues are its structure, *forma*, because they are its kinds (*genera*, 2.47).

In retrospect, one can consider significant the fact that in Book 1 Torquatus at the outset addressed the issue of virtue as being the problem of the virtues (plural). He could after all just as easily have started from a portrait of the virtuous man, in the style of the description of the sage found in the *Letter to Menoeceus*.[48] He could have tried to say what virtue is in itself, as a type of psychic disposition. As we have seen, by adopting the outlook defined by the schema of the cardinal virtues, he instead assumes the hypothesis of a complex structure of morality, whether or not he himself endorses it. It is not impossible that here too we are dealing with a strategic choice on Cicero's part. For by assigning such a procedure to Torquatus, he is setting up, from Book 1 onwards, the framework within which he himself will go on to treat virtue. Each of the virtues, instead of being seen as a distinct state or as one moral disposition separable from the others, must be seen as an element within a complex structure, namely the organic whole that unites the plurality of virtues under the single name *honestum*, as Piso will be explaining in Book 5.[49] All this goes to show that, indirectly, the refutation of Epicurean ethics produces a positive effect: it highlights, by means of the contrast, the very structure of morality, the *honestum*.

The rhetorical aspects of this strategy are evident. Brad Inwood has rightly pointed out this aspect of the Book 2 polemic. One of the most effective of these rhetorical aspects is, in my opinion, the game of lexical superimpositions and oppositions. Thus the Epicurean praise of *voluptas* corresponds to the constant search for *utilitas*, such that the pair *voluptas–utilitas* becomes the negative counterpart of *honestas* or *honestum*. In fact, Cicero remarks to Torquatus, showing that morality is 'to be sought for its own sake' is sufficient for 'all your theories to lie in ruins' (2.44). As we saw above, to assimilate *voluptas* to the *telos*, by contrast, amounts to making *utilitas* the criterion of action and the condition under which the virtues can be sought. This thesis is explicitly taken up in the positive portrayal of the *honestum* in Book 2. 'By morality (*honestum*), we understand that which is such that one can rightly commend it for its

[48] *Ep. Men.* 133–135.
[49] *Fin.* 5.58. In another passage, 5.64, the relation of the *honestum* to the virtues is presented rather as one of provenance and correlation: 'Morality (*honestum*), which emanates from the virtues and is attached to them (*quod ex iis oritur and in iis haeret*), is to be sought for its own sake.' On the theme of the close link between the virtues within the *honestum*, see also *Off.* 1.15.

own sake, independently of any utility (*detracta omni utilitate*), reward or profit' (2.45).

Thus in the *De Finibus*, as also in the *Tusculans* and *De Officiis*, the Epicureans implicitly appear as the avowed enemies of the *honestum*. In the *Tusculans* the Epicureans are the philosophers for whom 'virtue has no value in itself, and who say that everything we call honourable (*honestum*) and commendable (*laudabile*) is on the contrary devoid of meaning and dressed up with mere empty words'.[50] If the *De Officiis* differs in lending a positive sense to the notion of *utilitas*, it is careful to contrast this with the false utility that the Epicureans think they see in pleasure and bodily goods.[51] In this treatise, as in the *De Finibus*, the Epicurean position is contrasted with the table of the four cardinal virtues, which are precisely constitutive of the *honestum*.[52] It goes without saying that if we also take into account the social and civic aspect of the *honestum*, as Cicero understands this,[53] the criticism acquires an additional dimension: it denounces not only the Epicureans' subordination of morality to pleasure and their misunderstanding of the very nature of morality, but also a fundamentally individualistic and non-civil mode of life.

The game of lexical oppositions is extended again, after the section of *De Finibus* 2 devoted to the virtues, when Cicero discusses the case of friendship. In 2.78, to denounce the inconsistency of the Epicurean doctrine that combines utility and friendship, Cicero emphasizes the etymological link between *amicitia* and *amor*. To love someone is to love him 'himself and for himself (*ipsum ... propter ipsum*), and to want him to be furnished with the greatest goods 'even if one gains no advantage from those goods' (*etiamsi ad se ex iis nihil redundet*). Thus a friend has a status similar to that of virtue: he is an end in himself rather than a means or instrument. Perhaps, moreover, one should also speak more generally, not of a friend, but of the object of love, because the value system that Cicero opposes to Epicureanism recommends the love of virtue (2.83). Friendship cannot, at all events, be the result of any 'utility calculus' (*utilitatis ratione*),

---

[50] *Tusc.* 5.119.

[51] See *Off.* 3.12, where the conception of utility according to Panaetius, utility linked to the *honestum*, is contrasted with the mere utility that the Epicureans are able to invoke in their praise of pleasure, namely 'a certain appearance of utility' (*specie quadam utilitatis*). On this theme of the opposition between real and apparent utility, the latter of which is 'in conflict' with the *honestum*, see also *Off.* 3.34.

[52] *Off.* 3.117–118.

[53] See Graver (this volume). Also Prost 2003: 100, on Cicero's criticism of Epicureanism's inconsistencies: 'pour Cicéron, la vie en société repose sur l'*honestum*: il y a donc contradiction interne à la conscience entre l'adhésion philosophique (qui exclut la valorisation intrinsèque de l'*honestum*) et l'appartenance au corps social (qui suppose cette valorisation).'

contrary to what Torquatus, following Epicurus, claimed in Book 1. The terms *amicitia* and *utilitas* stand in strong opposition.

The image of the Epicurean virtues as it appears in the first two books of *De Finibus* may seem rather disappointing from a doxographical point of view: in terms of Epicurean testimonia, the crop is, in the last analysis, quite thin. Torquatus' account is largely a relaying of Epicurus' assertions, and when he seems to depart from them it is very difficult to say whether it is a significant modification of the Epicurean doctrine itself. The deviations from the original doctrine seem, rather, to be prompted by the dialectical circumstances and by the imposition of a framework – in particular that of the four cardinal virtues – which seems in reality to be external to Epicureanism.

The main point, however, may perhaps lie elsewhere. The interest of the passages we have studied lies rather in what they contribute to the implementation of a global strategy. This has both a negative and a positive aspect: (a) on the one hand, the refutation of Epicurean ethics and of a certain value system associated with it; (b) on the other hand, the development of themes, and sometimes theses, which will structure the remainder of the work.

Under (a), the refutation of Epicureanism, one thinks of the denunciation, not only of the content of the hedonistic doctrine, but also of its incoherence and contradictions. We should also remember how Cicero uses themes and propositions borrowed from Stoicism, presumably in order to confront the Epicureans with the philosophers most radically opposed to them. Cicero uses Stoicism as a powerful ally when it comes to exposing Epicurean errors.

Under (b), positive strategy, the denunciation of Epicureanism's epistemological weakness serves as counterpoint to an appeal to reason and to the progressive development of human nature – an appeal that will be further developed in the following books, especially 4 and 5. If Epicurus is wrong about the true nature of the *telos*, he is also correspondingly ignorant as to the nature and function of *ratio*. Again, by showing that Epicurus' doctrine is somehow the enemy, or the precise antithesis, of the *honestum*, Cicero is preparing for the debate that will oppose him as 'Cicero' to the Stoics. He thus designs a defence of the *honestum* that will extend it to actions and duties which the Stoics – at least the most radical[54] – make the mistake of separating from the highest good.

---

[54] Cicero's strategy on this point lies in showing that Cato's position, although he in principle admits preferables that fall outside virtue, is actually indistinguishable from that of indifferentists like Ariston, because Cato admits no other goods than virtue. See, for example, *Fin.* 3.12, 5.69.

With Epicureanism there is no possible compromise, and it is precisely in this regard that Cicero's confrontation with its faulty conception of virtue is illuminating. His opposition to Epicureanism, because it takes the form of an antithesis between *voluptas* and *honestum*, reveals true morality through its negative image.[55]

[55] I especially thank David Sedley for his English translation of my text and for his valuable comments. Among participants in the Symposium at Budapest I also thank Margaret Graver, Keimpe Algra, and Malcolm Schofield for their remarks and suggestions.

CHAPTER 4

Epicurus on the importance of friendship in the good life (De Finibus *1.65–70; 2.78–85*)

Dorothea Frede

University of California, Berkeley

1 Philosophers and friendship

Philosophers are often seen as spoil-sports. Instead of leaving intact the 'beautiful sparks of the gods' that enchant our lives, philosophical analyses of these phenomena seem to deprive them of their divine lustre and turn them into problematic or even suspect characters. Ever since Beethoven set Schiller's ode 'An die Freude' to music, that chant continues to uplift billions, totally undisturbed by philosophical quibbles about the nature and value of pleasure. This ode could easily have been extended from *Freude* to *Freundschaft*, had Schiller and Beethoven wanted it so, and perhaps they would have successfully convinced billions that *Freundschaft*, not just *Freude*, is a 'schöner Götterfunke, Tochter aus Elysium' forever.

Friendship, like joy, used to be accepted as one of the unquestionably good things in Greek culture, as witnessed from Homer on. And perhaps this state of innocence might have continued somewhat longer had not Plato, that notorious kill-joy, not only treated pleasure with suspicion but also made friendship the topic of one of his penetrating Socratic investigations. It does not take much reflection to see that the question 'Why do we need friends?' can ruin naïve trust in the preciousness of that relationship. For the very suggestion that friendship is the response to some *need* seems to throw doubt on its status as a good *per se*, because it insinuates that friendship is based on certain types of interests and is therefore an essentially self-centred affair. Once the question is on the table of what it is we *want* from a friend, or what a friend is *good for*, the naïve attitude that friendship is by nature a symmetrical relation and an intrinsic good from youth to old age seems to be undermined forever.

We shall not take a closer look at Socrates' strategies in the *Lysis* that are designed to point up the problematic nature of friendship by questioning what qualifies a friend to be a friend. Suffice it to recall that Socrates at least *prima facie* successfully rules out all options: neither the good, the bad, nor the neither good nor bad, qualify as candidates for real friendship. Regardless of our evaluation of the arguments employed to construct this trilemma, we owe Plato a set of questions that explicitly or implicitly determined future reflections on this issue: who and what is a friend? What kind of relationship is there between friends? What is the purpose of friendship? If the *Lysis* ends without a solution this does not mean that its discussion is fruitless. Quite the contrary: the various twists and turns of the discussion between Socrates and the two young boys, who so far had taken their friendship as a matter of course, were designed to pose the problematic in full relief: should friends be alike or unlike? What need does a good, self-sufficient person have of friends? Is it possible for a bad person to be a true friend? Is there one-sided friendship? And, quite generally, what is it that ties two friends together? For these reasons Plato's *Lysis* clearly represents the major starting-point for later philosophic discussions of friendship.[1] Aristotle's treatises of friendship in the *Eudemian Ethics* and in the *Nicomachean Ethics* show clear traces of that dialogue, as witnessed by the fact that he relies on the same lines borrowed from the poets and highlights the same disagreement among Presocratic philosophers as to whether friendship is an attraction of like to like or unlike to unlike. In addition, Aristotle's distinction between three kinds of friendship: friendship for the sake of benefit, for the sake of pleasure, and for the sake of goodness, clearly reflects the demand in the *Lysis* for an explanation of the basis and the purpose of friendship. Most noteworthy, it emerges that even the best type of friendship, one that seeks the mutual good and treats the friend like another self, remains in a way self-centred:[2] 'The Other' serves as a mirror of one's own self and therefore plays a central role in one's own good life. This should warn us not to expect 'altruism' from a Greek theory of friendship, if that means not just regard for the other's good at a particular occasion and for some special purpose, but a principled disregard of one's own good. Not every true concern for other persons should therefore be identified with altruism. Egoism and altruism are not exclusive alternatives.[3]

We don't know what, if any, effect these philosophical discussions of friendship had on the broader public in antiquity where friendships

---

[1] A unitary interpretation that argues for an innocuous interpretation of the self-centredness of friendship as a joint struggle for wisdom is suggested by Penner and Rowe 2005.

[2] Aristotle famously stipulated that mutuality (*antiphilêsis*), good intentions (*eunoia*), and the awareness thereof (*mê lanthanontes*) on both sides represent the fundamental conditions of any kind of friendship (*EN* 8.2, 1155b27–1156a5).

[3] On this issue cf. Long 2006c: 23–39, 23f.

represented important social functions. Given that friendship nowadays is usually regarded as a purely personal affair, the quest to 'rationalize' its basis may at first sight seem quite off-putting to the philosophically untrained. But reflection shows that friendship should not be filed under 'attitudes that defy rational analyses'. For such an explanation would leave essential ties between human beings in the limbo of an indistinct *je ne sais quoi*. Though we may often feel tempted to leave it at that, it would be odd to claim that reflection on the basis of a friendship has a withering effect on that relation, like a touch on a butterfly's wings. For, apart from obvious cases like that of business friends, the question of why we seek the presence of others does deserve closer analysis. Even the pat answer that human beings by and large don't seem to tolerate solitude for long motivates further reflections on the kind of underlying neediness, that is, on the type of mutual help, enabling, or enhancement, that plays a significant role, if not *the* central motivation in friendships.[4]

2 The Epicureans and friendship

It should therefore come as no surprise that friendship remained a topic that continued to exercise philosophers in antiquity after Plato and Aristotle, as the lists of works in Diogenes Laertius confirms.[5] The Epicureans regarded themselves as a 'society of friends' and deliberately separated themselves from the public community, so therefore had a special incentive to explain the reasons for, and the values of, interrelationships between human beings. This fact also put a special burden of proof on them. For given that pleasure is their highest good and that life's best condition, peace of mind and body, is supposed to be a self-sufficient condition,[6] it seems an uphill fight to justify a more than instrumental role of friendship in the conception of the ideal Epicurean life.[7] That this is a major bone of contention does indeed emerge in Cicero's brief exposition of the Epicurean explanation of the role of friendship in Book 1 of the *De Finibus* and in his equally brief critical rejoinder to that explanation

---

[4] Cf. Cooper 1980, Price 1989: ch. 4.
[5] DL attributes a dialogue *peri philou* to Simmias of Thebes (2.124.32), a treatise *peri philias* to Speusippus (4.4.13), to Xenocrates (4.12.7, two books), to Aristotle (5.22.24, one book), to Theophrastus (5.45.29, three books), and to Cleanthes (7.175.30, one book).
[6] Cf. *Letter to Menoeceus* 130: 'We regard independence (*autarkeia*) as a great good.'
[7] The *Letter to Menoeceus*, e.g., recommends the practice of Epicureanism together with someone like oneself as a bulwark against false fears, and it promises a life among men like a god (DL 10.135). So the protection offered by friends need not be of a physical kind, but may provide mental fortification.

in Book 2. The title of one of Julia Annas' chapters in her monograph *The Morality of Happiness* seems therefore especially applicable to the case of the Epicureans: 'Finding Room for Other-Concern.' As Annas points out there, the ideal of happiness does not *per se* exclude care for others, because it may well be an inclusive conception. But it does become problematic if pleasure and tranquillity are regarded as life's ultimate ends. And given that the Cyrenaics,[8] for all we know, had excluded any value other than instrumental to friendship, the Epicureans faced a two-fold task: to distance themselves from that kind of individualistic hedonism, and to justify a more than instrumental role of friendship in their own conception of the good life as a coherent enterprise.

That the Epicureans put great stock on friendship is witnessed by many of Epicurus' pithy sayings.[9] It might therefore seem strange that no work on friendship is attributed to him in Diogenes Laertius' list. We have to keep in mind, however, that Diogenes asserts that of the over 400 books written by Epicurus he lists only those he regards as the best, a catalogue of no more than forty-one works. Even so, it seems odd that Diogenes mentions a work 'On love' (27.8: *peri erôtos*), but none on friendship.

In order to get some understanding of how friendship fits into the overall conception of the good life of the Epicurean it is apposite to keep in mind, right from the start, that their ideal – *ataraxia* of the mind and *aponia* of the body – though often negatively defined by absence of disturbance, does not call for an inactive life, as has sometimes been claimed by their adversaries. There is therefore no immediate incompatibility between 'static pleasure' and the conception of pleasure as 'unimpeded activity', that was famously suggested by Aristotle in his discussion of pleasure in Book 7 of the *Nicomachean Ethics* and augmented in his explication of pleasure as the crown of perfect activity in Book 10. As G. Striker has pointed out, 'kinetic' and 'static' pleasures should not be treated as mutually exclusive alternatives.[10] In fact, an overall undisturbed life may

---

[8] For an overview of the Cyrenaic position (with reference to further literature) cf. Annas 1993: 227–236. Anniceris reportedly included friendship among the goods to be cherished for mutual goodwill's sake, even if it causes some trouble, because other-concern may bring pleasure. On this view and its problems, cf. Annas 1993: 233–235.

[9] *VS* 52; 78; friendship is called choiceworthy in its own right, even if it originates from benefit, *VS* 23 (for textual difficulties, cf. Annas 1993: 237). For a sympathetic discussion, cf. Mitsis 1988: ch. 3. According to Mitsis, Epicurus is committed to a theory like Mill's because he recognizes a value other than pleasure (104; 111–117). For a defence of the view that friendship for the Epicureans is itself a pleasure, cf. Long 1986. This issue is discussed here only on the basis of the Ciceronian testimony and the question of the overall coherence of the Epicurean conception of pleasure cannot be pursued at all.

[10] Cf. Striker 1993.

be filled with episodes of kinetic pleasures, provided that they are not of a disruptive type. Such episodes could also include joint activities among friends.

But such a basic compatibility of static pleasure with episodes of kinetic pleasure notwithstanding, it is necessary to explain what role, precisely, Epicurus assigns to friendship when he claims that, like the virtues, we cherish friendships for their own sake. Such an explanation requires a closer analysis of their contribution to the happy life. But as has been emphasized in the secondary literature, our evidence on this question is quite slim. The information in the *Letter to Menoeceus* and the fragments is very limited,[11] and Lucretius pays little or no attention to the question of personal relationships.[12] Therefore Cicero is our main evidence – and given his hostility to Epicureanism, his report in the *De Finibus* cannot be expected to be the fairest of witnesses. We should be discriminating on this point however: given Cicero's adherence to the sceptical procedure of presenting both sides, we can expect that even if his exposition of Epicurean doctrine by Torquatus in Book 1 may be all too brief and sometimes stunted, it must in essence be true to that doctrine, while the same may not apply to Cicero's retort to the Epicurean defence in Book 2.

3   Torquatus' defence of the Epicurean position

Given the dearth of information we shall have to go through the text with a fine-toothed comb: In *De Finibus* 1 the discussion of the role of friendship is very short, but intensive, and prefaced by the assurance that it is a topic that is absolutely essential (1.65.17f: *maxime necessarius*) to Epicurean philosophy.[13] Torquatus claims to be responding to his critic, who had objected that if pleasure is the highest good there cannot be room for

---

[11] The letter largely confines itself to the argument that neither the gods nor death are to be feared. In his general recommendation of a life of wisdom as healthy for the soul of young and old, Epicurus does not mention friendship as a possible support. Though he suggests that cooperation with friends might be useful with respect to practising living well and dying well (DL 10.126), he nowhere states that we should seek the presence of friends in the search for sober reasoning and for virtue as the natural outgrowth of prudence, justice, and honour, which have therefore 'grown together' with the pleasant life (132: *sympephykasi hai aretai tôi zên hêdeôs*). That the philosopher is active is mentioned as an aside – at the very end of the letter (135: *en tais praxesi*), unfortunately without specifying what kinds of activities fill his life. Joint exercises with like-minded persons are recommended (*ibid.*), but nothing is said about a need of the wise man himself for such support of his wisdom.

[12] On Lucretius' bitter picture of social conditions, cf. Mitsis 1988: 98.

[13] The Latin text referred to is that of Reynolds 1998; the translation, used with some modifications, is that of R. Woolf, in Annas and Woolf 2001.

friendship at all. Cicero, in his own critical introduction (13–26), had actually raised no such objection, just as he had not objected to the compatibility of Epicurean hedonism with the virtues.[14] So the criticism Torquatus refers to must represent some standard objections to Epicureanism. If the plural (65.19: *adfirmatis*), which naturally does not show up in the English 'you', addresses a group, then it must be the school of the sceptics, unless it is an all encompassing plural addressing the opponents of the Epicureans as a whole – i.e., 'that is what you people always claim'.

Torquatus in Epicurus' name not only energetically rejects the claim that pleasure and friendship are incompatible, but maintains that, on the contrary, of all the things that wisdom (*sapientia*) provides for a happy life there is none greater (*maius*), richer (*uberius*), and more pleasant (*iucundius*) than friendship.[15] As a witness he at first refers not only to the proclamation (*oratio*) of Epicurus to that effect, but also to his way of life, his actions, and his character. This is actually the point which Torquatus starts with, because he holds that the numbers of legendary friendships in the literary tradition compare unfavourably with Epicurus' many close friendships, despite his modest means.[16] This, however, remain the only *ad hominem* argument with respect to Epicurus' personal life; the focus is to be on the question itself (65.3f: *ad rem*).

The question that shall occupy us is, therefore, the very one other commentators have wrestled with, whether the Epicureans can assign a more than *instrumental* role to friendship and justify true concern for others as part of a coherent conception of happiness as a justification of Epicurus' high praise of friendship. That is to say, the onus lies on a proof that friendship is an integral part of, not just a means to, a life of *ataraxia* and *aponia*. One may indeed wonder why there should be much need for friendship anyway, because in principle the *tetrapharmakos* immunizes the Epicurean against the evils of the world. If death is nothing to us, pain is

---

[14] Cicero instead lambasts the derivative character of all three parts of the Epicurean philosophy. Its physics stems from Democritus; and where it diverges from it, the result is *ad peius*. Its method and logic are naïve. Its conception of pleasure as the highest good is derivative and had been anticipated in a more consistent way by Aristippus.

[15] This is an almost literal translation of the *KD* 27: *hôn he sophia paraskeuazetai eis tên tou holou biou makariotêta, poly megiston estin he tês philias ktêsis*. On problems with the meaning of the text, cf. Shackleton Bailey 1926: 367.

[16] As the note in the Cambridge University Press translation states, it may be malicious on Cicero's part to refer to Theseus and Orestes as paradigms of friendship, because they were models of intimate and tried friends, a relationship quite different from that in the circle of the many friends that crowded Epicurus' modest abode. But whether there is malice or not, Epicurus is said to be unique in maintaining so many friendships despite slender means, thus setting an example of the cultivation of friendship which was the pride of the Epicureans.

either intensive and short, or long but mild, unduly strong appetites are curbed, and suicide is a means permitted when life has no charms any more, what need is there for self-protection with the help of friends? This objection ignores the distinction between what is natural and necessary and what is natural and unnecessary: an Epicurean has no more reason to be indifferent to avoidable pains than he has to seek unnecessary pleasures. There is no reason for an Epicurean to expose himself to avoidable dangers. Hence taking precautions against threats and other unpleasant disturbances is as legitimate as against needless pleasures, and they may involve friends.

The most conspicuous feature of Torquatus' *ad rem* discussion is well known: He refers to three different modes of justifying friendship by 'our school', whereby he clearly means three different groups (1.66.6: *Alii* ...; 69.10: *Sunt quidam*; 70.24: *Sunt autem qui...*). The very fact that he does not refer to Epicurus by name suggests that there was no extended explanation and defence of friendship by the Master himself, apart from short but effusive praises of friendship as the greatest gift of wisdom to life, like the one quoted above.[17] A closer look at the positions maintained by the three groups of Epicureans, whose identity is unfortunately not specified any further is therefore necessary. That they must have been sufficiently well known is confirmed by the fact that Cicero in his retort also treats them in the same sequence and (allegedly) systematic way.

Position I (66–68) at first sight does not seem to present a coherent conception of friendship and its value at all. For at the outset Torquatus attributes to its proponents the view that the pleasures experienced by friends are *not* as desirable as those one experiences oneself (66.7f.: *negarent esse per se ipsas tam expetendas quam notras expeteremus*).[18] But at the end of the brief discussion of this position Torquatus comes up with quite a different result: 'We delight in our friends' happiness and suffer at their sorrow, as much as we do our own' (67.26f.). That this is not just a careless *façon de parler* is confirmed by the continuation in the next paragraph: 'Hence the wise will feel the same way about their friends as they do about themselves. They would undertake the same effort to secure their friend's pleasures as to secure their own' (68).

---

[17] Mitsis 1988: 102 n. 9, tends to regard the first position as that of Epicurus, because of Cicero's reference to Epicurus in his retort (2.82), but acknowledges the caution in Cicero's reference (*videbar ab ipso Epicuro dictum cognoscere*). If not the whole then some part of this defence of friendship may go back to Epicurus himself.

[18] For attempts to handle this difficulty in the secondary literature, cf. Mitsis 1988: 112–117: 'Cicero neatly captures the unresolved philosophical tensions that surface in Epicurus' writings.'

The explanation of this inconsistency would be that Torquatus inadvertently has changed horses in his argument, i.e., started with a different position than he ends up with. But Torquatus purports to present a continued and coherent argumentation. For though he admits that the preference for one's own pleasures has been regarded by their opponents as undermining their position on friendship, he nevertheless claims that the proponents of this theory can easily hold their ground. Not only that: in his introduction of the proponents of the second position he addresses them as 'somewhat more timid' than the first group (69.10: *timidiores paulo*). So he was aware that the first group of Epicureans adopted a rather strong position in their treatment of friendship and its relation to pleasure.

A closer inspection of the details is therefore necessary to see what might justify such an unexpected turn.[19] Though Torquatus' conclusion does not literally state the opposite of what he said at the beginning, i.e., that the pleasures of the other *are* to be sought for in their own right as much as one's own (66.8: *expetendas*), he does affirm that we 'rejoice in our friend's joy (*laetamur amicorum laetitia*) as much as in our own and are equally pained by their sorrows' (67.26f.). Moreover, the wise will feel the same way about the other as he does about himself (68.2–4: *eodem modo affectus erga amicum*) and that he should exert the same effort (*eosdem labores*) to secure his friends' pleasures as to secure his own. All this suggest that Torquatus, or rather his source, has deliberately moved away from his initial 'differential treatment' of one's own pleasures and those of others. The argumentation that leads up to that conclusion seems to be based on a succession of steps that supposedly warrant the equal valuation of one's friends' pleasures and pains.

i   66.10–16: Friendship is as inseparable from pleasure as is virtue. Thus, an analogous argument is to be expected to the effect that just as the virtues serve as a means to secure a pleasant life so does friendship. The function of friends seems at first purely external: solitude is a life prone to clandestine attacks (*insidiae*) and full of fears: friends are therefore to be sought as a means of protection. But apart from the immediate protection against danger, the possession of friends also strengthens the soul of the individual and fills it with the expectation of future pleasures.[20] At this point it is unclear whether that effect is due only

---

[19] I leave aside here the discussion of *VS* 23, where Epicurus recommends the same position, at least if Usener's textual emendation of reading *hairetē* instead of *aretē* is accepted. On this problem cf. Erler and Schofield 1999: 668 and the judicious discussion by Brown 2002.

[20] On this issue cf. Schofield 1999, 748–756.

to the expectation of future protection, so that the future pleasure consists only of *ataraxia* and *aponia* of the same kind, i.e., protection against external dangers, or whether the fortification is due to a richer psychological state.

ii 67.16–21: The next step no longer speaks explicitly of a means of defence against danger and fear, but rather contrasts positive and negative psychological states as such: 'Hatred, jealousy, and contempt (*odia, invidia, despicationes*) are the enemies of pleasure, while friendship is the sponsor and author of pleasure – not only in oneself, but also in one's friends.' It is obvious that the concern is no longer, as it is in (i) that negative attitudes on the part of others are a threat to one's security. Instead, the very unpleasantness of experiencing such states of mind is itself at stake. Feelings of hatred, jealousy, and contempt are incompatible with pleasure as peace of mind. The incompatibility of pleasure with such attitudes has already been repeatedly emphasized in the discussion of the benefit of the virtues for the good life (44: 'even when shut up inside the heart they quarrel and fight among themselves. A life of great bitterness is the result'; cf. also 50–51; 58–59). That the emotional states of one's friends are judged under the same perspective here must be due not only to the danger they may represent, but also to the fact that living in an environment that is characterized by such emotions is unpleasant.[21] By contrast, the positive state of mind of one's friends acts as a source of pleasure (*effectrix*) and a promise of more in the future.

What kinds of pleasures are these? Presumably the concern is with both *katastematic* and *kinetic* pleasures, i.e., with the guarantee of a life undisturbed by mental and physical troubles, but also of a life filled with pleasant episodes. These episodes will be pleasant if they contain the opposite of hatred, envy, and contempt, namely acts of love, well-meaning, and mutual respect. If that is what the 'more courageous' Epicureans have in mind, it explains why Torquatus regards the inseparability of friendship and pleasure as the same as in the case of virtue and pleasure – both are equal guarantors of a life spent in an atmosphere of friendly exchange with others. For even an Epicurean sage cannot regard with equanimity a world that resembles a snake-pit rather than a peaceful garden. If kinetic pleasures are involved in

---

[21] Cf. DL 10.117: the wise man overcomes motives such as hatred, envy, and contempt within himself by reasoning, and he never willingly adopts such attitudes again. Nor, one should add, does he willingly encounter them in others.

the preference of pleasant over unpleasant company of friends, their effect will not be limited to the general atmosphere of life. Although Epicurus is not an Aristotelian and therefore does not regard being active as the main element in a happy life, he must consider pleasant exchanges between friends as important elements of happiness. For otherwise the question presents quite a problem: how does an Epicurean actually spend his time? Apart from satisfying the moderate necessary needs that keep body and soul together, does he just revel in *ataraxia* by rehearsing all the reasons why he has nothing to fear? Not only does this sound rather tepid and boring, but it does not agree with Epicurus' own explanation of how to overcome life's unavoidable troubles and pains of the body: by recollections of pleasant encounters and discussions with his friends.

iii 67.21–26: From (ii) the Epicureans conclude that without friendship there is no firm and lasting pleasant state of life. To secure such friendships it is necessary to love one's friends just as one loves oneself, and hence this is the condition created by friendship and it is intimately connected with pleasure. As a consequence one shares one's life's conditions with one's friends, enjoys their joys and sorrows with their sorrows. The question is what justifies the request for such mutuality that seems to turn the friends into 'other selves'. The mention of 'securing the friendship' (67.23: *amicitiam tueri*) suggests that the salient point lies in the genuineness of the friendship. Counterfeit mutual well-meaning will not do. Therefore just as only the real virtues were shown to guarantee the peace of mind of an individual, so only genuine sharing of the emotional attitudes and experiences is now treated as a guarantee of the kind of friendship that is necessary for a pleasant life.

iv 68.1: The consequence is that the wise person – one who understands these inner connections – will feel for a friend just as he does for himself and make every effort to secure his friends' pleasures as he does his own. And for this reason the wise man will also understand that there is the same interconnection between pleasure and friendship as between virtue and friendship: they secure a stable and pleasant life.

The Epicurean saying from *Kyriai Doxai* 16 and 19 that concludes this argument may seem like a relapse into the 'means of protection argument', because it states that just as the Epicurean doctrine gave them the strength to have no fear of everlasting or longlasting evil, so the same doctrine identifies friendship as the firmest protector in the short span of our life. But the protection (*praesidium*) need not be taken in an external sense only: it can mean that the institution of friendship, as interpreted above, will provide a wall against unpleasant disturbances by creating a sympathetic environment. In that sense friendship provides, in fact, a more positive protection than mere liberation from the fear of death or from the threats of a hostile environment, because it maintains internal stability.

But what about the inconsistency of this with the initial denial that the pleasures of others are to be valued as highly in themselves as one's own? I suggest the following reading: taken by themselves (*per se ipsas*) the pleasures of friends are indeed less desirable than one's own. It is only because of the contribution friends make to one's overall pleasant life that their feelings take on the importance attributed to them in the course of the argument. And for that reason, only shared emotions provide the warranty of true friendship.[22] The case of friendship is, then, indeed exactly analogous to that of the virtues. As Torquatus has affirmed repeatedly, the virtues have no value *per se*, but only in so far as they are a source of pleasure (cf. 42.26–31 *et passim*). Only real friends can provide that because they are not secretly divided against each other – in the way that characterizes the soul of an individual beset by vicious desires. Does friendship as understood by the Epicureans remain a self-centred attitude? Or have they adopted an altruistic position, as suggested by Mitsis (at least in respect of Epicurus' *diadochoi*)?[23] As stated earlier, one should be wary of applying the term 'altruism' to ancient philosophy, anyway, if that presupposes a disregard for one's own good in the interest of others. That condition is certainly not fulfilled if the motive of caring for the other's pleasures and pains is the wish to live in a peaceful and pleasant atmosphere, even if no one would feel tempted to call such an attitude egoistical. Position I can therefore be defended as internally consistent, unless it is to satisfy undue conditions.

Position II (69): The treatment of the Epicureans who react against the invective against them 'somewhat more timidly, albeit with sufficient acumen'[24] is much shorter: They are impressed by the consideration that if friendship were to serve only one's own pleasure, the entire relationship

---

[22] *VS* 23 presents the relation as the result of a development: 'All friendship is desirable in itself, though it starts from the need of help.' Perhaps that accounts for occasional evaluations of friendship as a good, as in *VS* 52 where friendship is treated as an enticement towards the happy life, or in *VS* 78 where friendship is compared to an immortal good. The life of the gods is sometimes presented as a life lived in justice and harmony, because it is a life free from all need of toil and labour (see the quotation from Diogenes of Oenoanda in Long and Sedley 1987 and their comments).

[23] Mitsis 1988: 104–112.

[24] The translation in Annas and Woolf 2001 of *satis acuti* by 'with some intelligence' seems too weak.

would seem to limp (69.13: *claudicare*).[25] That is to say, friendship would clearly be a one-sided affair, because the pleasure-seeker would have no reason to reciprocate. Instead, they distinguish two stages of friendship: (a) the incipient stage that arises from acquaintance and familiarity and is determined by the search for one's own pleasure; (b) the advanced stage that consists in a transition to real affection, due to a deepening of intimacy, so that the other is loved for his own sake, even if no benefit accrues to oneself from that association. As a further argument these Epicureans refer to the fact that familiarity breeds attachment to all sorts of things, including animals and even lifeless objects.[26]

At first sight this 'associationist position' reminds one of the fact that Aristotle also grants that a friendship that initially has only pleasure as its aim with increasing familiarity may turn into a true virtue-friendship.[27] But this cannot be what the Epicureans have in mind, as witnessed by the fact that it is mere familiarity and not likeness of character or virtue that causes the change. In fact, no moral value seems to be even thought of as the cause of the growth of affection, because the same condition applies to all kinds of habitual attachments. The only advance from the first to the second stage consists in the fact that in the latter one's own pleasure/utility is no longer the explicit motive. Is this the reason why Cicero calls the proponents 'somewhat more timid', i.e., because they hesitate to assert that pleasure is their ultimate aim? This must certainly be the main explanation, but their timidity also has the effect that it remains unclear what kind of advancement the move from (a) to (b) represents. This comes to the fore when the analogy is drawn within the extension of affection to animals and lifeless objects. For this shows that an *a fortiori* argument is at work here: If it is possible to get fond of virtually anything one habitually associates with, how much easier is it to get fond of people? But this explanation does not explain what an Epicurean should want to explain, i.e., that friendship consists in the love of the others for their own sake and thereby turns them into essential constituents of the good life as such. For in the case of lifeless objects there is no caring for them 'for their own sake'. Nor is there any criterion mentioned for the selection of such attachments, except habit, a factor which depends on contingent

---

[25] This point is obscured in the Annas and Woolf 2001 translation by 'be utterly lame' but also by Rackham's 'be utterly crippled'.

[26] I forgo here the much-debated question whether the Epicurean position should be interpreted as purely psychological or also reflects a theory of cultural history (cf. Mitsis 1988: 106; Long 2006b; Algra 2003).

[27] Cf. *EN* 8.4, 1157a10–12.

circumstances and justifies no attribution of quality to the relation among friends that was postulated by the more daring Epicureans. So the attempt by the more timid Epicureans to make friendship look symmetrical does not lead to a satisfactory explanation, and it certainly does not deserve the epithet 'altruistic'.

Position III (70.24–28): The third group, which is introduced in a very perfunctory way, seems to take the opposite approach to the second: friendship is not due to habituation but is the result of a kind of compact (*foedus*) to love the other no less than oneself. This explanation has the advantage that such friendship clearly does not 'limp', because mutuality is guaranteed from the start. In addition, there must be careful selection at work because it supposedly is a compact between the wise, the *sapientes*. This implies that not everyone is admitted to such a mutual-appreciation society because it is based on mutual benefit from each others' wisdom. But no real explanation is given in the brief justification of the existence of such friendships. For Torquatus merely refers to the alleged fact that such a compact is not only possible but has often been observed. In addition, he asserts that nothing can be found that is more conducive to the good life than such an association. One might therefore look at this alleged third group with some suspicion and attribute its addition to cosmetic reasons, i.e., that a triad always look better than a twosome, were it not for the fact that Cicero includes a rejoinder to the compact-theory in his comments in 2.83.

Apart from the mutuality that is guaranteed by the equal exchange of wisdom and the associated pleasure on the basis of such a compact, the rationale of such a friendship seems rather strange. First of all, it seems questionable how such an association and mutual exchange will profit the self-sufficient *sapientes*. As truly wise persons they should, in principle, not even need others to keep up the convictions on which their *ataraxia* is based (cf. the characteristics of the *sapiens* in 44; 62 *et passim*). In addition and more importantly, the very artificiality of such a *contract* makes it odd to attribute it to the *sapientes*. If they recognize and respect each other's wisdom and regard it as good, they clearly will have no need for a contract but will exchange their insights as a matter of course.[28]

---

[28] In *Fin.* a contract theory is neither mentioned in Torquatus' discussion of justice nor in Cicero's reply. But Epicurus referred to a contract (*synthêkê*) as the basis of justice in order not to harm or be harmed in *KD* 31–35, a conception that was expanded on by Lucretius as a necessary element in the formation of civilization (*DNR* 5.1011–1027) and in the maintenance of public peace (1151–1157). But what applies to justice in society, as a means of ensuring the safety of life and public order in general, does not equally apply to friendships among the wise. The construction of a contract-theory among Epicureans may have in addition been encouraged by *KD* 40, where

There is, of course, the possibility that the reconstruction of this position is the result of a kind of misunderstanding. Some Epicureans may have claimed that in the case of the wise there will be mutuality 'as if by a compact' (*hôsper di' homologias* or *synthêkês*), and the 'as if' somehow got lost in translation. At any rate, though the *sapientes* are often referred to as authorities in Torquatus' speech, as the sources of the most important insights, they are nowhere treated like a separate society that is united by an internal compact. Nor do compacts play any role in the previous discussions, not even in the explanation of justice.[29]

The problem of such a compact notwithstanding, the following rationale of the third group of Epicureans offers itself: their focus on the relation of friendship between the wise is to explain that even for them mutual friendship is no more than a necessary condition for, and not an integral part of, the best life. Given that they are wise they don't have to undergo a development in their attitude like the more daring and the more timid Epicureans of positions I and II: they are aware right from the start of the value of mutuality of friendship for the good life. But does such a contract-friendship, then, commit the sage to an inconsistent set of beliefs, because he must treat both his own and his friend's pleasures as equal goals of his actions?[30] If the ultimate end is the security of one's own pleasant life, then the observance of the other's pleasures to an equal degree can only be a subordinate end, comparable to the distribution of equal shares of gains in a business-transaction. Such observance would be a matter of prudence, not an end in itself. Nothing further is said on this issue in Book I. What follows is just a short summary claiming that all these arguments prove that the Epicurean theory of friendship is not undermined by the identification of the highest good with pleasure, but on the contrary, that proper friendship cannot be found outside that theory. The Epicureans clearly held the view that theirs was the only consistent theory of friendship.

Epicurus mentions 'the securest pledge' (*bebaiotaton pisteuma*) and seems to be thinking of the community of Epicurean friends.

[29] There is a certain analogy in the justification of the value of the virtues, i.e., in the explanation that they are not just mere external causes but necessary conditions of happiness. The evidence is ambiguous, however. Justice is not a mere means of warding off fear of the discovery of misdeeds but also an integral part of peace of mind and therefore intimately tied to pleasure (*Fin* 1.50–53). But there is no mention of justice as a kind of compact between the wise, who, being wise, would have no need of such a compact in the first place.

[30] Cf. Mitsis 1988: 111.

4 Cicero's general critique of the Epicurean conception of friendship (2.78–81)

Cicero's retort is a little longer than Torquatus' exposition and goes beyond it by first introducing quite general objections to the Epicurean position, most of all its utilitarian orientation. Only later does he turn to Torquatus' detailed defence of the Epicurean position (82–85).

The first point in Cicero's criticism is quite general: there can be no friendship if the first person does not love the other for himself (78: *propter ipsum*). The move from friendship to love is justified etymologically: *amare* is derived from *amicitia*.[31] Cicero here insists upon an unselfish basis for friendship: to love someone means to wish that he has an equal share of the good, even if there is no advantage that accrues to oneself. In fact, love should not be based on any rational calculation of advantage (*utilitas*) at all, but should arise spontaneously (78.25f.: *a se oritur et sua sponte nascitur*). This leads to a critique of utility as the incentive to friendship *tout court* (79). Any such 'calculated friendship' will end when the utility in question comes to its end; and in that case to maintain friendship without utility would be quite incoherent. Against such a utilitarian concept of friendship Cicero lines up a barrage of critique: (i) If the Epicurean objects that ending a friendship would be to his disadvantage because of the odium that might arise against him, such odium just confirms the baseness of calculated friendship. (ii) The obligation to keep up a friendship for such reasons would actually make the friend's death desirable. (iii) A friendship might require the sacrifice of property, or perhaps even the risk of one's own life. How will persons fulfil these conditions if they affect their own profit and pleasure? None of these problems apply to the famous cases of self-sacrificing friendships like that between Damon and Phintias and between Orestes and Pylades, cases that seem incompatible with Epicurean utility-friendship.

This invective is supplemented by the kinds of *ad hominem* argument that Cicero had already used against Torquatus' defence of the Epicurean conception of virtue (80): Torquatus himself would, of course, be prepared for such unselfish acts of friendship. But the question is not about his personality, but the consistency of his philosophical convictions (*disciplina*). The same *ad hominem* objection is also raised against Epicurus'

---

[31] The same etymology is mentioned in *De Amicitia* 26 as an argument that friendship must have an older, more beautiful cause, emanating from nature itself that goes beyond the mutual want and interchange whose importance, however, Laelius does not deny.

own attitude towards friendship: Cicero does not doubt that Epicurus was a good, companionable, and humane person (*bonus, comes, humanus*). But what is at issue is not his character (*mores*), but his mind (*ingenium*).[32] In addition, Cicero claims that the evidence of Epicurus' large number of followers should actually not be counted in favour of his position; for all true doctrines are difficult and open only to the few (81: *rarissimum*). Finally, Cicero acknowledges that many Epicureans are true and loyal friends, following duty's requirements (*officio consilia moderantes*). But all that is due to the power of virtue rather than that of pleasure. Epicureans are therefore to be regarded as a living refutation of their own doctrine. While with others their speech is better than their acts, with Epicureans it is the other way round. That Cicero, despite this verbiage, did not overrate the value of his *ad hominem* invectives but regarded them as rhetorical, rather than as substantial, objections is shown by his subsequent turn *ad rem*.

5 Cicero's critique of the three Epicurean accounts of friendship (82–85)

The 'more courageous' Epicureans (1.66–68) get short shrift (2.82.17–23). Cicero reduces their argument to Epicurus' tenet of the inseparability of friendship from pleasure. This is actually the only part of the argument that Cicero attributes to Epicurus himself.[33] The explanation does not address the seeming contradiction in the original presentation by Torquatus of that position, i.e., that though the Epicureans initially attribute less importance to the pleasures of friends, they end up with the claim that pleasures and pains of friends are equal to one's own. Since Cicero does not mention that inconsistency at all, he therefore also does not comment on the presupposition of that conclusion, above all that negative emotions such as hatred, envy, and contempt are incompatible with pleasure in the sense of peace of mind. Instead, he confines himself to the point that, without friendship, life cannot be secure and free from fear, and hence it cannot be lived pleasantly. He therefore attributes only instrumental value to that position on friendship, and claims that it is taken care of by his general refutation of utility-friendship.

---

[32] With respect to the last point Cicero takes a double-edged parting shot: Though he wants to leave it to Greek *levitas* to heap scorn on other people, he does want to claim that Epicurus was not sufficiently sharp – *non satis acutus*.

[33] As the footnote to the Cambridge translation states, there is no such exact saying of Epicurus – but it seems to be in agreement with the general drift of his position.

Concerning the 'more timid' Epicureans (1.69), Cicero not only mentions that they represent a more recent position, different from Epicurus'
own, but also calls their position 'more humane' (2.82.23–30: *humanius*).
What makes the position more humane in his eyes is clearly the fact that
these Epicureans pass from a stage where friendship is sought only for
utility's sake to a stage where familiarity engenders love of friends for
their own sakes, regardless of any expectation of pleasure. But this very
point undermines the position: it agrees with Cicero's own conception of
friendship rather than with the Epicurean tenet that friendship is a means
to pleasure. For an Epicurean it is inconsistent to grant that something
can be morally right that is not connected with pleasure. Cicero clearly
does not take into consideration that friendship on the basis of familiarity
engenders its own pleasure in the eyes of the Epicureans, but he is certainly right that pleasure will no longer present the explicit *purpose* of such
a friendship.

As mentioned above, the response to Position III (1.70) confirms that
the theory of a compact among certain sages to hold their friends in the
same esteem as themselves had certain backers (2.83). Cicero treats this
theory with considerable irony. This is obvious from the fact that he at
first confines his critique to the alleged 'facts': that such a compact not
only is possible, but has been found to work and is highly conducive to the
experience of pleasure. Against such a compact for pleasure's sake Cicero
objects that more would be needed to make such a pact a plausible basis
of friendship: such a contract should also include the agreement to respect
all virtues, without looking for a reward (83.7–9). This objection indicates
that Cicero regards only the virtues as a safe warrant of compacts. Though
the Epicureans on their side regard the virtues as essential conditions of
the happy life, as argued in Book 1, they attribute value to them only in so
far as they lead to pleasure as their reward. And this is clearly the butt of
Cicero's objections.

Is this an objection against the viability of such a contract in Cicero's
eyes? The end of that paragraph indicates that his point is rather that
such a contract does not have friendship but utility as its ultimate aim
(83.9–14): For, as he objects, the ultimate motive of friendship remains
advantage and gain, instead of the kind of affection that would make it
desirable in its own right and for its own sake. But if utility is friendship's ultimate aim then it would be only logical to prefer landed property
and whole islands to friends. Cicero is clearly unwilling to grant to the
Epicureans that for them friendship can be anything but an instrumental
good, because he ignores the fact that they treat positive attitudes towards

friends as an important aspect of friendship. This blind spot is also notice-able in his peroration (84–85) that consists, once again, in a lengthy *ad hominem* argument that is designed to show that Torquatus himself does not really live by his Epicurean convictions with respect to friendship; if he did, then he would seek friendship because of its utility only.

Utility is here spelled out exclusively in terms of material goods and external protection, as witnessed by Cicero's objection that these ends are provided for by the laws, ordinary friendships, and especially affluent means, because liberality will secure the goodwill of many. Hence there would be no need for a friendship like that between Orestes and Pylades. This, no doubt, ironic statement is meant to indicate that the latter is the only type of friendship that Cicero regards as worth its name – and that he expects Torquatus to concur. He adds the further point that it is impos-sible to share one's deeper thoughts, both light and heavy (*iocosa seria*, 85.1–2), with anyone, in the case of mediocre friendships of the Epicurean type. Thus, although Cicero professes not to deny all usefulness of that type of friendship, he does hold that by the Epicurean principles of util-ity, friendship cannot compete with the advantages of vast wealth. Cicero, by contrast, wants to be cherished for his own sake, not for his property. What 'cherishing' someone for his own sake means is not explained any further; Cicero seems to go here on the assumption that such friendships arise spontaneously (78; 83). That such spontaneity is not without a cause, albeit not a material cause, is not discussed here; on that point one has to consult the *De Amicitia*.[34]

6 Concluding critical remarks

It does not take much to show that Cicero's final assessment is quite unfair to the Epicurean position. For it treats neither vast wealth nor 'util-ity' of the material kind as the basis of friendship. Why, then, should an Epicurean not value friendship *sua caritate*, (85.4) as an integral part of the good life? Given their ideal of a quiet, unperturbed life, the Epicureans are at somewhat of a disadvantage when it comes to giving a full account of what friendship will do for them. Pyladean and Damonian types of friendship do not really fit their recommended life-style, because heroic

---

[34] In that work, dedicated to Atticus, Cicero's friend and an adherent of Epicureanism, Cicero leaves no doubt that real friendship is not based on need and advantage, but on the natural tie that exists between the virtuous (esp. 29ff.) and the natural tie between all creatures of a like nature (79–81). It is unclear whether by the sages in Greece' who treat friendship mainly under the perspective of self-interest he has certain Epicureans in mind (45–47).

deeds are deemed undesirable. Nor does their intellectual life sound like
an exciting enterprise that would intrigue a philosopher's philosopher,
more Platonico aut Aristotelico, because Epicurus did not cherish science
for science's sake. His recommendation of constant study of philosophy
as well as 'sober reasoning and the searching out the motives for all choice
and avoidance' (*Ad Men.* 132) is geared toward soul-searching rather than
to intellectual endeavours aiming at truth as such. Instead of inciting the
scientific curiosity of his adherents, Epicurus treats the avoidance of disturbance of the spirit as philosophy's ultimate aim (*KD* 11–13). Nor does
he recommend any other active exciting engagements to his adherents.
Politics as a field of occupation is ruled out (at least under the circumstances then prevailing), so that there is nothing of great interest to share
in that field either.

Given the limited scope of Epicurean recipes for the art of living, it is
difficult to envisage what an Epicurean will do with himself all day long,
apart from reconsidering the conditions of the *tetrapharmakos* and planning his life carefully to avoid the pursuit of unnecessary desires, so that
they do not undermine *ataraxia* (*Men.* 132). What applies to individual
Epicureans *mutatis mutandis* also applies to a group of Epicurean friends.
What pursuits did they engage in when they spent their time together,
apart from submitting to the kind of pedagogical treatment administered
by the wise to the not yet wise, or mutually reinforcing their Epicurean
convictions?

Before deciding to assign a low grade to the quality of the Epicurean
life, it should be kept in mind, however, that such negative judgement
to quite some degree is due to a lack of information. If we are ignorant
with respect to the Epicurean lifestyle, that is because most of the primary
sources confine themselves to recipes of how to become an Epicurean,
or of how to stay one if one is in a somewhat precarious condition, but
they contain very little information concerning what it means to *be* an
Epicurean in the fullest sense.[35] The secondary sources offer little information of that sort because they are usually critical of the Epicurean position. But there are at least some indications that it is wrong to present the
Epicureans as a community of friends whose greatest enjoyment consisted
in doing as little as possible, apart from rejoicing in the very frugality of
their pleasures (*SV* 41). In the *Tusculan Disputations* Cicero mentions that
Epicurus commended a variety of different types of pleasure, including

---

[35] On this issue cf. Long 2006b. There would probably have been more information had the four volume 'On Lives' that is mentioned in DL 10.28 survived (on its content cf. Erler 1999, 669–674).

the pleasures of taste, sex, and listening to music (3.41). The kinds of activities an Epicurean shared with his friends may therefore well include all sorts of cultural engagements and need not be limited to the explicit pleasures of good food, etc., which Epicurus approves of, at least if they are easy to get.[36]

Even so, it is hard to see how this careful picking and choosing would constitute a form of life that friends could consistently share with each other in the way suggested, for instance, by Aristotle. Hence it is not only the paucity of information that causes us difficulty. It is harder for Epicureans than it is for other philosophers to explain what friends *are* to each other, except that they join in what we might call 'the small pleasures of every day-life', like taking walks together, engaging in conversation, reading together, playing checkers, taking part in sports, and performing or listening to music together.[37] This would mean that everyday life consists in a variety of kinetic pleasures, both physical and mental. None may be individually necessary, but given that all human beings aim for sensible occupations, to have a variety of them is necessary. And all of them, if pursued in moderation, are natural. The unavailability of this or that pleasure does not constitute a disturbing disruption of one's *ataraxia*; so forgoing them does not make the sage or even any ordinary Epicurean vulnerable to chance and frustration, as some people have suggested.[38] Hence, apart from jointly doing their Epicurean exercises, friends will spend their time together sharing the variations of natural but non-necessary pleasures that are suitable for everyday-life. Such sharing may, of course, be of a more or less demanding type, depending on the kind. You may enjoy playing chess, have a philosophic discussion, play table tennis, or just have dinner together. Where the pleasure presupposes a partner – which it often does – its pursuit either constitutes or presupposes a kind of mutuality.

The real problem with such a view of life can be summed up in the following objection: even if there is mutuality in spending one's life together in occupations that require a partner or several partners, the mutuality

---

[36] I leave open the question whether Cooper is right when he includes such delights under the rubric of 'pleasures necessary for happiness' (Cooper 1999a: 498–508), or whether these are just natural but unnecessary varieties of pleasure.

[37] Epicurus famously claimed that the pleasure of remembering the conversations with his friends far outweighed the pains on his deathbed (DL 10.22; Cicero *Fin.* 2.96).

[38] Cf. the emphasis on tensions within Epicurean self-sufficiency and the need for friends in Mitsis 1988: 126–128. Mitsis goes on to the assumption that betrayal and disappointment in friendship constitute a severe handicap for an Epicurean's happiness. This would be true if for Epicurus particular friendships were the all in all, but not if he regards a particular failure as negligible. This possibility is not ruled out by the fact that *VS* 28 requires the running of risks for friends, and in *VS* 56–57 that one should feel the torture of a friend more than one's own and even be ready to die for him.

seems to remain quite superficial if the desire for the pleasure is not to be frustrated. Partners, to some extent, would therefore be replaceable. If A can't come for tennis today, B will do as well, unless he is a bad player. So there is no real reason to care deeply for a particular *person*, except that he/she should be in the condition and mood to share the activity in question. Moreover, the Epicurean, for the sake of *ataraxia*, must not worry too much about the availability of this or that particular person. In fact, if people are not to worry about their own death, why should they worry too much about that of another person?[39]

Given our ignorance about the details of the Epicurean life, there is no point in lining up further objections against the meaningfulness of personal friendships in such a life. Hence it is difficult for us to picture the interactions between particular persons on the basis of the general explanation concerning the nature of friendship in the Epicurean conception of happiness as such.[40] If the picture just drawn of the communal life in an Epicurean society of friends looks quite tepid to us, this is due to the fact that it deliberately excludes joint activities that provide excitement in the pursuit of high aspirations.[41] An Epicurean should avoid such excitement and aspirations. Needless to say, such considerations tend to make *ataraxia* as the ideal conception of the good life unattractive in our eyes. Whether we are well advised in regarding excitement and high aspirations as essential elements of our lives, and in treating them as the salt of friendship, must remain moot questions.

If we leave such demands aside, however, it has to be admitted that the types of kinetic friendships accepted by the Epicureans should well be familiar to us: playing tennis or bridge, hiking together, or having discussions constitute the basis of many of our own so-called friendships. And, as far as these occupations go, in each case one person can without great loss be replaced by another. Sharing deeper convictions may be another matter, unless such sharing is treated as a mere pleasant pastime. Thus we may come to the conclusion that the Epicurean life-style is very much like

---

[39] So Cooper 1999a: 510. I am not convinced that Epicurus was really so much misunderstood that others did not see more in Epicurean friendships than can reasonably be seen, as long as it is just based on habituation. And given that one should not attach too much value to the existence of a personal friend, lest his death might cause great distress, friendships should, on principle, not be too intense.

[40] On the two-fold nature of friendship in Epicureanism, cf. Algra 2003.

[41] There is something to Cicero's final plea against Torquatus that humans are made for higher ends than pleasure and the avoidance of pain, if we disregard some of the examples of super-heroic acts from Greek and Roman history and rather think of the development and application of our best abilities (2.111–119).

our everyday life. And such was indeed its purpose: to recommend the kind of life to its adherents that allowed them to live a life that was satisfactory to all those who kept their desires and aspirations in check.

What is problematic about such a self-imposed restraint from a philosophical point of view is the 'quietism' implied in the ideal of *ataraxia*, because it looks very much like an antidote against worries in troubled times. Coming to terms with the world's deep troubles by downplaying their importance seems only a second best in comparison with making a valiant attempt to solve them. And that seems to have been the real reason behind Cicero's relentless polemics against Epicureanism that manifests itself in his critique of their conception of friendship and his *ad hominem* arguments against Torquatus: how can anyone with a sufficient amount of self-respect even admit that all he cares for is his own pleasure and tranquillity?

That picture of Epicurean quietism, in all fairness, needs some correction. Epicurus clearly held that it was beyond a philosopher's power to solve the difficulties of the world. For that very reason he confined himself to a society of friends to ensure that at least within its limits human beings would learn how to live a peaceful and in that sense fulfilling life. Recruiting adherents and leaving his message to posterity are, after all, acts of friendship, and it is to be assumed that Epicurus regarded his legacy in just this light. Doing something for the salvation of the world at large may look much more impressive. For that very reason it is often not only unrealistic but also futile.[42] Doing something for a limited number of people who will thereby be truly benefited sounds much more modest, but its effect should not be underrated. The long lasting effect of Epicurean philosophy over many centuries speaks for itself. And Diogenes of Oenoanda, Epicurus' very late, but to this day most visible, spokesman, did try to preserve just that legacy in the name of friendship, writ large in stone, explicitly for the benefit of posterity.[43]

---

[42] The comparison of the fate of Cicero with that of his Epicurean friend Atticus is often invoked in that connection; Cicero's worst enemy cannot withhold his respect in view of his final heroic effort, as witnessed in his *Philippics*, the speeches that cost him his life.

[43] Cf. Long 1986 as in 2006a: 193, with reference to frg. 2 col. 4.

CHAPTER 5

Honor and the honorable
Cato's discourse in De Finibus 3

Margaret Graver
Dartmouth College

The longest of Cicero's extant works, the *De Finibus Bonorum et Malorum* is certainly not lacking in expansiveness. Yet nothing could be more succinct than the one-sentence summation of Stoic ethics offered by Cato early in Book 3:

> This is the claim that sums up not only the philosophical doctrine I am explaining but our lives and fortunes as well: that only what is honorable should be accounted good in our eyes.[1]

As an account of what Book 3 is doing these words merit serious reflection on at least three fronts. We should reflect, first of all, on the character of the speaker: placed in the mouth of the dead Cato at the height of Caesar's domination, must not a reference to "our lives and fortunes" be a political statement; and if so, of what kind? Also, we need to inquire sooner or later into the attitude of the putative hearer – that is, Cicero himself; for although his self-assigned role in *De Finibus* is in opposition to Cato's postulate, he is elsewhere more favorable, even calling it the "the truest way to speak about happiness."[2] We are thus left with a puzzle regarding his overall attitude toward Stoic ethics. But even if this were resolved, we would still need to know about the *content* of Cato's utterance: what he means by "the honorable" (that is, by the Latin word *honestum*), what basis he can offer for his claim that this "honorable" is the sole human good, and how instances of "the honorable" may be identified in lived experience. This last set of issues seems to me especially interesting and important, and so for the purposes of this study I shall limit myself to them. For this notion of the honorable is, as Cato indicates here, the keynote of the Stoic discourse in *De Finibus* 3; not coincidentally, it is also the key to Ciceronian ethics overall.

---

[1] *Fin.* 3.26. Unless otherwise noted I supply my own translations for all ancient sources, for the text of *De Finibus* following Reynolds 1998.
[2] *Tusc.* 5.82; compare *Paradoxa pref.* 5; *Att.* 10.4.4.

The problem is in part linguistic. *Honestum*, the word I translate as "honorable," is transparently intended as an equivalent for Greek καλόν: Cato's claim is meant to be the one that is expressed in Greek Stoicism as μόνον τὸ καλὸν ἀγαθόν.[3] In view of its origins, though, *honestum* would seem to be a narrower term than τὸ καλόν. Where the Greek word connotes visual beauty and attractiveness as well as praiseworthiness and general merit, *honestum* is more specifically the adjectival form of *honos*, the respect paid to rank, or, frequently, a public accolade or elected magistracy. Since the etymological connection must have been immediately evident to Latin speakers, one cannot but wonder about the extent to which it is functional in Cicero's usage. English translations of *De Finibus* have tended to replace *honestum* and the related noun *honestas* with "morality" or "moral worth," as if Cicero used them solely as a way of referring to virtuous conduct. But even a brief survey of cases will show that a reference to the expected perceptions of others is usually to be found in Cicero's use of these words and is sometimes functional in his argumentation. His word *honestum* can certainly be used to refer to virtuous conduct, but it is at the same time a descriptive term reminding his readers of the esteem in which virtuous conduct is held.

Resolution of the linguistic issue brings us face to face with the philosophical significance of honorableness (if I may use so ungainly a term) as a core value in ethics. When we speak of what is honorable, rather than of what is in fact honored, we view some course of action prospectively, as the agent himself might consider it when deciding whether to proceed. That is, we identify a particular type of motivation. The distinctness of such motivations is recognized already by Plato in the *Republic*, when he makes honor (τιμή) the chief concern of the spirited part of the psyche and thus an end in itself for those who are most engaged in the political life of their communities.[4] Aristotle too gives τιμή a prominent role in his ethics when he makes it the particular concern of the large-minded person and an important element in friendship.[5] Honor, he says, is the correct assessment of virtuous conduct; as such, it is the prize or reward of virtue.[6]

---

[3] The equivalence between *honestum* and καλόν is not new with Cicero; it is found among Latin writers as early as Terence, *Hecyra* 151, and Lucilius, frg. 1288 Marx. (I wish to thank Mathieu Jacotot, who supplied these references from a paper he delivered at the colloquium "Acculturation culturale des concepts et motivation terminologique à Rome," École normale supérieure de Lyon, Oct. 26, 2007.)

[4] The orientation of the spirited part to honor is most clearly stated in *Rep.* 9.581a–e but is also stated earlier, at 5.475a. On the role of the honor-loving *thumos* in the *Republic* see Cooper 1984; Brennan 2012.

[5] For the objectives of the magnanimous see *NE* 4.3, 1123b1–24; for honor in friendship, 1159a12–27, 1163b1–19.

[6] *NE* 1123b35–36, 1163b5.

It is not difficult to reason out some of the considerations which might induce Plato and Aristotle to take an interest in motivations concerned with honor. The honor motive is responsive to considerations of veridicality in a way that the analogous pleasure motive is not: pleasures are gratifying whether or not they are deserved, but praise and honor are more appreciated when one believes them to be sincere and based on a proper estimation of one's merits. At the same time, Plato in particular is quick to point out that a sensitivity to praise and blame does not in itself amount to integrity; rather, the concern for honor is edifying just in so far as it is guided and governed by reason. In Book 6 of the *Republic*, a nature endowed at birth with deep insight and various virtues is nearly always corrupted by sophists and by the assembly, whose noisy shouts of approbation impart to him their own debased opinion of what actions are honorable.[7] The implication is that motives related to honor cannot properly guide action unless one has developed some internal standard which can, as it were, assess the external assessment. What is required is a properly grounded notion of the honorable.

It is by this route that Cicero's lifelong interest in public honor arrives in time at what we intuitively call morality or the moral point of view. As with all Cicero's writings, the *De Finibus* is conditioned by its author's career in public service and by the ceaseless competition for status among politically active members of the elite. For one whose career was founded not on military achievements or a prestigious *gens* but on a reputation for probity and talent, it was a matter of professional sense to appeal frequently to considerations of individual merit – *dignitas, nobilitas, honestas, quod decet* – and recognition for merit: *laus, gloria, decus, honor*.[8] Quite apart from his personal investment in the ideology implied by such terms, it was in his interest to control their application.[9] In this connection it is striking how often he touches on the concept of *gloria*, or, as he frequently says, *vera gloria*, in the personal letters and in all five of the major

---

[7] *Rep.* 6.490a–93b.

[8] The ideology is laid out in Cicero's *Pro Sestio*, 138–139. For the importance of this ideology to the Roman elite see Knoche 1934; more broadly Barton 2001; for its emotional dimensions Kaster 2005: 28–65, though this last is more specifically concerned with shame. More generally on Ciceronian ideas of political virtue see Mitchell 1991: 12–62, Atkins 2000, Schofield 2009.

[9] Rather too much has been made of Cicero's emotional need for public recognition, the keynote in Sullivan 1941 and a platitude of the biographers since Plutarch. An orientation toward external approbation was a practical necessity for a man in his position and hardly unusual among his peers. But Cicero did also admit to an emotional dimension; in an early letter, he speaks of it as a personal weakness that he is *non* ἀφιλόδοξον (*Att.* 2.17.2; Sullivan 1941: 385).

ethical treatises.[10] In particular, the *De Officiis*, written in the aftermath of Caesar's assassination, repeatedly turns to language of honor and glory as a way of expressing Cicero's continued commitment to Republican ideals.[11] The lost *De Gloria*, written at about the same time, must have done the same.[12]

But an approach that considers only Cicero's personal and political agenda cannot do justice to the depth and subtlety of his reflections on honorable conduct in the more abstract and theoretical treatises of 45 BC. The vagaries of his career in politics provided an occasion for him to articulate a position; the content of that position, however, came almost entirely from his reading in Greek philosophy. His tendency to frame current events through the lens of Greek ethical theory can be illustrated even from the letters, where the Greek καλόν repeatedly finds its way into his text when values other than expediency are at stake.[13] It is even more evident in the *De Finibus* and its companion piece, the *Tusculan Disputations*. In these works the *honestum* is first and foremost a Stoic concept, defined in language derived from Stoicism and defended with arguments that match closely with known fragments of Chrysippus' treatise *On the Fine* (Περὶ τοῦ Καλοῦ).[14] Though not himself an adherent of Stoicism, Cicero recognizes that the school of Chrysippus offers the rigorous understanding of this term that he needs if he is to put forward a substantive notion of moral behavior as a value in public life. The inadequacy

[10] In *De Re Publica* especially at 6.8 and 6.23; in *De Legibus* at 1.37–38; among the letters note especially *Fam.* 15.4.13; *Att.* 13.28.2. See also Sullivan 1941.

[11] See further Long 1995a; Dyck 1996: 32–33, 355.

[12] The *De Gloria* was written in July of 44 when Cicero was obsessed with Brutus (*Att.* 15.27.2). As Shackleton Bailey notes, it must have been either the *De Officiis* or the *De Gloria* that Cicero believed had brought about the change in the younger Quintus' political views in *Att.* 16.5.2. Note also his caution about having the *De Gloria* read aloud (*Att.* 16.2.6; 16.3.1), and see further Long (1995a) 223–224; Dyck 1996: 32, 412.

[13] The term appears in Greek as early as *Att.* 2.19.1 (July 59), where Cicero in risking Clodius' threats is "clinging to τὸ καλόν"; again in *Att.* 8.8.2 (Feb. 49), where Pompey's departure for Brundisium "bids farewell to τὸ καλόν"; and significantly in *Fam.* 15.17.3 (Jan. 45), where Pansa's concern for others "demonstrates to all that τὸ καλόν is δι'αὐτὸ αἱρετόν". For a detailed study of philosophical language in the correspondence see Griffin 1995; on *Fam.* 15.17 and related correspondence with Cassius, Griffin 1995: 343–345; Shackleton Bailey 1977: 377–379.

[14] It is significant that arguments from that work presented as contiguous by Plutarch, *St. Rep.* 1039c, appear in the same order in both *Fin.* 3.27–28 and *Tusc.* 5.43–40; there are close correspondences as well with the citation of it in D.L. 7.100–101. (See further nn. 38 and 39 below.) Cicero in *Tusc.* 5.19 shows that he knows *De Honesto* as a Stoic title and associates it with such arguments. Arnim 1903–1924, vol. III: 9 attributes to *On the Fine* the position mentioned in *Fin.* 4.68 as argued *diligentissime* by Chrysippus against Aristo. The Chrysippan provenance of the material is important even on the alternative assumption that Cicero knows of Chrysippus' work only through an intermediary.

of the prephilosophical notions expressed in the inherited honor code was glaringly obvious to him from his own experience. Stoic thought seemed to offer a corrective to those notions, both in that it refuses to compromise on the ascendancy of honorable conduct and in that it establishes a meaningful standard for what honorable conduct might consist in. His long-term engagement with Stoic ethics is thus a working out of his own most pressing concerns.

Central to his inquiry is his version of the Stoics' best-case account of moral development. In Cato's speech in *De Finibus* 3.16–22 he restates in Latin the account he knows from reading and discussion, giving it a distinct emphasis on the role of self-awareness in rational beings. Since it is in our nature to value certain features of our bodies and certain of our mental faculties for their own sake, we have at least the opportunity to apply the same appreciative capacity to patterns of behavior over time. Above all, we can and should come to appreciate patterns of behavior that exhibit a kind of internal logic and coherence. When we do this, Cato argues, we are exercising a properly grounded conception of honorable conduct. That is, we exercise a correct conception of behavior that should be called καλόν – for at this crucial point Cicero, thinking simultaneously in Greek, draws in notions of symmetry and concord, *ordo et concordia*, that are implied by the Greek word (at least in Stoic contexts) but not directly by the Latin equivalent. The result is a Greek-inspired account which yet communicates its intent clearly to Latin speakers, indeed with particular clarity because of the need to make explicit what is lost in translation. As an Academic skeptic, Cicero does not formally endorse this account, but it is, finally, the best account he has to give; it is contested in the remainder of *De Finibus* but retires, like Cato, undefeated. And it is the same specifically Stoic conception of the *honestum* that comes to the fore again in the *Tusculan Disputations* and *De Officiis*.

In what follows, I consider first the semantics of *honestum* and the related noun *honestas* within Cicero's usage. Then in section 2, I trace out his assumptions about the nature of honorableness as a property of conduct that is theoretically distinguishable from virtue itself, though coinstantiated with it. Section 3 turns more directly to the argument of *De Finibus* 3 and in particular to the reasoning in 3.27–29 by which Cato attempts to prove that only what is honorable is good. My concern with this reasoning is not whether its arguments succeed: in the context of *De Finibus*, no argument can be both constructive and successful. The point of interest is the assumptions on which these Chrysippan arguments are based and the way Cicero uses them to bring out shared intuitions about the connections between praise, pride, merit, and value. Shared assumptions alone are not sufficient, however, to supply us with a clearly defined and accurate concept of honorable conduct. In sections 4 and 5, I consider our prospects for developing such a concept. Section 4 traces out the origins of the mistaken notion of glory that Cicero holds responsible for most of the political turmoil of his lifetime. Then section 5 studies in some detail the process by which, according to the crucial first segment of Cato's discourse, humans as rational beings are able without external assistance to work out an adequate conception of the honorable. That process, I argue, depends crucially on our innate capacity to perceive and value certain formal properties of our mental life, of skills that we acquire, and ultimately of lives conceived as well-coordinated wholes.

1   *Id quod honestum est*

Before Cato ever comes on the scene, Cicero provides his readers with a definition for what he means by "the honorable." This is in the refutation of Epicurus in *De Finibus* 2.45.

> By "the honorable", we understand that which is of such a kind that even with all utility set aside, with no rewards or emoluments, it can rightly be praised for its own sake. What it is like cannot be understood from the definition I have just given – though that is of some assistance – nearly as well as by the shared view of all and by the endeavors and deeds of the best sort of people, who perform many of their actions for this reason alone: that it is seemly, that it is right, that it is honorable, even if they see that no advantage will follow.

The term *honestum* is here explained strictly in terms of merited praise: it is "that which is of such a kind that ... it can be rightly praised for its own sake" (*per se ipsum*). What makes something *honestum*, in the proper sense of the word, is the approbation of a reliable observer. We note also that *honestum* has primary application to certain kinds of conduct, since the best way to understand it is by what "the best sort of people" have in mind when they undertake some action. The definition itself may be of Stoic origin, for it bears a general resemblance to the Stoic definitions for καλόν that are recorded in Diogenes Laertius, as "that which makes those who have it praiseworthy," or "what is worthy of praise."[15] It is probably

---

[15] D.L. 7.100. Note also the strong resemblance of the definition to the account of the *honestum* Cicero gives later in *De Officiis*, in an explicitly Stoic context: *quod etiamsi nobilitatum non sit, tamen honestum sit, quodque vere dicimus, etiamsi a nullo laudetur, natura esse laudabile.*

relevant, too, that Cicero has just aligned himself with Chrysippus' refutation of hedonism. It is of paramount importance, however, that the statement made here is presented as Cicero's own view and in explication of the word used by Latin speakers.

Also in Book 2, at 2.48–49, Cicero criticizes as counterintuitive Epicurus' view that *honestas* is chosen only for the sake of pleasure. Epicurus understands the honorable to refer only to that which is glorious by popular repute; it is this that one pursues instrumentally, as a safeguard to tranquility. For Cicero, this view fails entirely to grasp what it means to call something honorable. What is praised by the crowd is sometimes "ugly" (*turpe*), the very opposite of *honestum*, and even when the crowd does praise what is in fact honorable, it is not the praise of many that makes it so but a quality inherent to itself: it is "intrinsically right and praiseworthy" (*per se rectum atque laudabile*). Even if people did not know about some honorable act or failed to speak of it, it would still be praiseworthy "by its own beauty and appearance" (*sua tamen pulchritudine esset specieque laudabile*).

These statements make a clear connection between Cicero's use of *honestum* or *honestas* to render τὸ καλόν and the etymological and usual sense of these words in Latin as that which merits public marks of esteem. They suggest, too, that he associates the Latin adjective, like its Greek counterpart, with visual or quasi-visual observation.[16] When we study Cicero's actual usage of these words, however, in the remainder of the *De Finibus* and in his other writings of this period, we may well be inclined to question whether a notion of external assessment is always present in them. The substantive adjective *honestum*, the phrase *quod honestum est*, and the noun *honestas* occur very frequently in the ethical writings, and it often seems as though these expressions are just another way of saying "virtue" or "virtuous conduct". It is in these instances that a translator is most likely to render these terms by "moral worth" or the like, draining them of any specific notion of external assessment. Indeed there is more than one passage where Cicero goes so far as to partition *omne quod est honestum* into the four cardinal virtues of prudence, justice, temperance, and courage.[17] But the suspicion that *honestum* means neither more nor less

---

[16] The Latin adjective can also mean "handsome" (examples in *OLD* s.v. 4a), although this usage is far less prevalent than the visual sense of καλός in Greek. Cicero was aware of it, and will occasionally pair *honestus* with *pulcher* to bring out the quasi-visual sense, as at *Tusc.* 5.67: *omnia quae pulchra, honesta, praeclara sunt.* For the visual sense of *turpe*, see *OLD* s.v. 1 and 2.

[17] *Off.* 1.15 is a particularly striking instance, but the same move is made in *Fin.* 2.48: *formam honestatis quae tota quattuor his virtutibus ... continetur*; and 5.58 (for Antiochus): *prudens, temperata,*

than "virtue" arises in other passages as well,[18] and above all in those many instances where *quod honestum est* stands for τὸ καλόν in that familiar axiom of Stoic ethics, μόνον τὸ καλὸν ἀγαθόν.

The tendency of translators simply to equate "the honorable" with "virtue" or "morality" may seem to derive justification also from *De Finibus* 3.14, where Cicero remarks in his own voice that *honestum* and several similar expressions are valid and helpful ways of talking about *virtus*:

> If only virtue, only that which you name the honorable, the right, the praiseworthy, the seemly – for what it is like will be better known if designated by several terms all indicating the same thing – if only that, I repeat, is the good, then what else will there be for you to pursue?

At first glance it appears that Cicero here tells us directly that *honestum, rectum, laudabile,* and *decorum* all have the same meaning as *virtus*: they "indicate the same thing" (*idem declarantibus*). This must at least describe the way he is conscious of using these words in serious ethical writing, for he repeats the observation early in the *Tusculan Disputations*, saying that these five terms all "embrace the same thing."[19]

But we should be careful here. To say that two terms "indicate the same thing" need not say that they have the same meaning, any more than "the President of the United States" and "Barack Obama" have the same meaning. Indeed, if *honestum, rectum, laudabile,* and *decorum* all had the same meaning as *virtus*, they would be of no use for telling anyone what virtue is like. Rather these terms are alternative descriptions, additional ways of referring to virtuous conduct by mentioning properties that only virtuous conduct has. Cicero's account of the matter resembles that of the Greek Stoics quoted in Diogenes Laertius 7.100, when they observe that τὸ ἀγαθόν and τὸ καλόν "have the same power" (ἰσοδυναμεῖν); that is, that they are equivalent expressions. They are equivalent in that both refer to the same thing.

We can make things easier for ourselves by distinguishing in our minds between a referential *honestum* and a descriptive *honestum*. Referential *honestum* functions simply as a way of referring to virtuous conduct, just

---

fortis, iusta ratio, reliquaeque virtutes at actiones virtutibus congruentes, quae uno verbo complexi omnia honesta dicimus. The linguistic habit is not his alone; compare D.L. 7.100: εἴδη δ' εἶναι τοῦ καλοῦ τέτταρα, δίκαιον, ἀνδρεῖον, κόσμιον, ἐπιστημονικόν· ἐν γὰρ τοῖσδε τὰς καλὰς πράξεις συντελεῖσθαι.

[18] For instance in *Fin.* 5.66, where Piso remarks that the *honestum* "is either virtue itself or a deed done by virtue" (*aut ipsa virtus est aut res gesta virtute*).

[19] *Tusc.* 2.30: *illud, quod recte amplexantur isti, quod honestum, quod rectum, quod decorum appellamus, quod idem interdum virtutis nomine amplectimur.*

as τὸ καλόν often does in philosophical Greek. In effect, Cicero's expression *quod est honestum* spells out the demonstrative force of the definite article in τὸ καλόν: it is "that which is honorable" just as τὸ καλόν is "that which is καλόν."[20] But neither for *honestum* nor, I suspect, for τὸ καλόν does this referential habit make any alteration in the descriptive content of the adjective. If *quod est honestum* conveys the notion "virtue" it is only because of the unstated further assumption that virtue is the one thing to which a descriptive word meaning "rightly praised" can be applied. Cicero could at any point make the equivalence explicit, as he does when he speaks of living "honorably; that is, with virtue" (*honeste, id est cum virtute*; *Fin.* 3.29).

2   *Honestum ipsum quasi virtutis lumen*

This more careful reading of terms puts us in a position to inquire more closely into the relationship between virtue and the honorable. Take for instance what Cato says right at the opening of the dialogue section of Book 3. The Stoic spokesman is insisting, as he does throughout, on the substantive difference between his own ethics and the modified Aristotelianism of the Peripatetics and Antiochus. If even one external object is counted as a good, the Stoic end ceases to have any meaning at all.

> For when you say that anything other than what is honorable is choice-worthy and count that as one of your goods, you have extinguished the honorable itself, which is as it were the radiance of virtue, and you have overthrown virtue entirely.
>
> (*Fin.* 3.10)

In the first part of the sentence, the expression "what is honorable" functions in the way we have seen: it refers to what Cato thinks should be regarded as the good, namely to virtuous conduct. As part of the same utterance, though, we hear that the Peripatetic notion of value will not only extinguish "the honorable itself, which is as it were the radiance of virtue" (*honestum ipsum quasi virtutis lumen*) but will also overthrow virtue.[21] At that point the honorable is named alongside virtuous conduct, as

---

[20] Compare Seneca's rendering of τὸ ὄνας *quod est* in *Ep.* 58.

[21] Compare *Fin.* 5.83, where Cicero, arguing for Stoic consistency against Antiochus, twice speaks of *virtus* and *honestum* as distinct: *in virtute enim sola et in ipso honesto ... nec virtus, ut placet illis, nec honestum crescat.*

something closely associated with virtue yet still distinct from it. Virtue is virtue, and the *honestum* is the radiance of virtue.

But what is the radiance of virtue? *Prima facie* the expression suggests that "the honorable itself" is some sort of property which virtue always has and by which it can be recognized. The Antiochean Piso, speaking in his Stoic mode in *De Finibus* 5.64, says similarly that not only is virtue to be chosen for its own sake, but so also is "that thing, the honorable, which arises from the virtues and inheres in them" (*honestum illud, quod ex iis oritur et in iis haeret*). Here too the use of *honestum* is not simply referential: Piso is *not* saying "not only virtue but also virtue." Rather "the honorable" identifies a property that inheres in all the virtues, and only in them, "honorableness" as it were. A plausible interpretation is that it is a concomitant property; that is, an additional property that is always present in a person when virtue is present, and only then, but which is theoretically different from virtue – different in the account, as Aristotle would say, but not in substance.

The metaphysics would then resemble what some Greek Stoics said about the property of fineness or beauty; that is, κάλλος, the noun related to καλός. Beauty of body is a matter of symmetry among the limbs or proportionality of each limb to the whole, and likewise beauty of mind is, according to Chrysippus, "some sort of symmetry among the parts of the mind" (συμμετρίαν τέ τινα τοιῶνδέ τινων μερῶν); that is, among the judgments which are "the components of reason" (μέρη, δι' ὧν ὁ ἐν αὐτῇ λόγος συνέστηκε).[22] Thus beauty is a property of psyche, just as the virtues are. But beauty might not itself be a virtue, at least not in the same sense as the cardinal virtues, for it is not clearly a form of knowledge. The Stobaean author classes it as one of the "non-intellectual virtues" along with health, strength, and soundness, virtues which do not consist in theorems and are not skills.[23] The relation between such properties and the cardinal virtues is described by Panaetius' pupil Hecaton as being like the relation between the strength of an arch and the arch itself. For Hecaton, good qualities like psychic health and strength "follow upon" (ἀκολουθεῖν) and "co-extend" (παρεκτείνεσθαι) with the knowledge-virtues.[24] The

---

[22] Galen *PHP* 5.2.47–49 = *SVF* 3.471a, quoting from Chrysippus, *On Emotions* Book 4. For a more direct analogy to beauty of body in Stoicism compare Stob. 2.7.5b4 (63W, *SVF* 3.278): "Just as beauty of body is a symmetry of its constituent parts in relation to each other and to the whole, so also is psychic beauty a symmetry of reason and its parts in relation to the whole of it and to each other."

[23] Stob. 2.7.5b4 (62W). The term "non-intellectual virtue" (ἀρετὴ ἀθεώρητος) appears in D.L. 7.90.

[24] D.L. 7.90–91.

expression "follow upon" is admittedly rather vague: as a rule, B follows upon A when A necessitates B, but this is without further stipulation as to the relation between A and B. But the inclusion of "co-extend" and the arch comparison suggest that Hecaton did think of this group of psychic properties as concomitants that emerge in the virtuous mind while still being theoretically different from virtue.[25] And if Hecaton spoke of such concomitants it is likely that other Stoics did so as well.

Cicero was evidently familiar with such discussions, since he captures the gist of the metaphysical point in his own explanation of psychic beauty in a rather technical passage in *Tusculan Disputations* 4.30. There, summarizing a Stoic source, he describes a series of psychic properties called "health," "beauty," "strength," and "quickness" and explains their relation to the cardinal virtues. For some Stoic authors, Cicero says, the property called "health" ("when the judgments and beliefs are in harmony") is just the same thing as the virtue of temperance, while others prefer to say "that it is obedient to the dictates of temperance and that it follows upon it (*eam subsequentem*) and has no independent aspect." Similarly psychic beauty (*pulchritudo*) is evenness and consistency in the opinions and judgments, "either following upon virtue or containing the very force of virtue" (*virtutem subsequens aut virtutis vim ipsam continens*). This is to say that, even if psychic beauty is not merely the same thing as virtue, it is still the case that every virtuous psyche is also a beautiful psyche.[26]

More surprisingly, Cicero also employs the language of "following" and concomitants in speaking about *gloria* or merited acclaim. In Book 1 of the *Tusculan Disputations*, he remarks twice that *gloria* is a sort of concomitant to virtue: "glory follows virtue of necessity, even if it is not the object of your endeavor" (1.91); and later "even though there is no inherent reason why one should pursue glory, still it follows virtue like a shadow" (1.109). *Tusculan Disputations* 3.3 gives the same view in more detail. There glory is contrasted with mere reputation (*fama*) in that it is "the regular accompaniment to right action," comparable to a reflection or echo. Although it should not be pursued for its own sake, it comes

---

[25] The arch analogy works best if we consider the arrangement into an arch to be itself a *property* of the group of stones.

[26] The point of the phrase *vim ipsam continens* is not entirely clear to me. In my 2002 translation I was influenced by *ipsam temperantiam esse* in 4.30 to write "identical with." I now think it more likely that Cicero or his source has in mind coreferentiality of the term (cf. παρεκτείνεσθαι in Hecaton above) rather than identity, even though this weakens the parallel with psychic health. I would like to thank Tad Brennan for discussing this issue with me.

along even if not pursued, and good men need not reject it.[27] *Honestas* and *vera gloria* are alike, then, in the regularity of their association with virtuous conduct: one is the radiance of virtue, and the other is virtue's shadow. The difference between them is that *honestas* is that quality of action that merits esteem, while *gloria* is marks of recognition that are actually bestowed. Both relate to an external assessment of virtuous conduct, but honorableness is inherent in such conduct, while glory merely results from it.

3   *Beata vita honestate cernitur*

If virtue and honorableness are distinct properties, then Cato's Stoic claim, "only the honorable is good," says something significantly different from "only virtue is good." It need not be different in extension, since honorableness and virtue might be coinstantiated (as indeed they are), but the conduct to which it applies is thought of in a different way, as what merits approval from right-minded observers, rather than under some other description such as other-concern or a harmonious state of mind. We can see how this difference comes into play in the argumentation Cato uses to support his contention. In particular, we see it in two arguments presented in paragraphs 27 and 28 of *De Finibus* 3.

The first argument demonstrates Cato's preference for the Stoics' "brief and pointed syllogisms" over the ornamental phrases and lofty sentiments of a more oratorical presentation. Cato at first pares the case in favor of the Stoics down to the following:

P1: Everything that is good is praiseworthy.
P2: Everything that is praiseworthy is honorable.
C: Therefore, everything that is good is honorable.

He then comments that although the argument is logically valid, the first premise is likely to be challenged. And indeed Cicero will challenge that premise *in propria persona* in Book 4, where he aligns himself with the Academic and Peripatetic opponents of Stoicism.[28] Anticipating

---

[27] This claim in *Tusc.* 3 may have some bearing on a rather complicated discussion in *Fin.* 3.57, which reports on a controversy between Carneades and his Stoic rivals in Athens. Under pressure from Carneades, Cato says, Stoics after Chrysippus and Diogenes gave up on the view which he himself approves, that good repute (εὐδοξία) is entirely indifferent to happiness; instead, these later Stoics accepted it as an intrinsic good. While Cicero makes Cato endorse the hard-line Stoic view, we can assume that the position argued by Carneades in favor of good repute would have had considerable weight with one who considered himself a Carneadean skeptic.

[28] He will, nonetheless, repeat the same argument in expanded form in *Tusc.* 5.45.

this critique, Cato follows up his own argument with the following defense of P1:

> But it would be absurd to say that anything is good which is not choice-worthy (*expetendum*), or anything choiceworthy which is not pleasing, or if that, not also lovable, and hence also commendable; thus also praise-worthy; but this is honorable. Thus it is established that what is good is also honorable.

This second portion of the argument has a known antecedent in a fragment of Chrysippus' Περὶ τοῦ Καλοῦ preserved by Plutarch. Chrysippus writes, "What is good is choiceworthy (αἱρετόν); what is choiceworthy is pleasing; what is pleasing is praiseworthy; what is praiseworthy is καλόν."[29] Like the version Cicero gives to Cato, the Chrysippan argument works by connecting the good with the choices of agents and those choices with what the person choosing approves and thus considers worthy of praise; from there, it is an easy step to the καλόν. In this, the descriptive sense of καλόν, and likewise of *honestum*, plays an important role: the last step is automatic precisely because the final term carries the meaning "that which is praiseworthy in action."

For one who works with the precise understanding of choice that was worked out within the Stoic school, the argument would immediately be convincing. Within the Stoic theory of action, the objects toward which choice is directed are really predicates; for instance not riches but "to have riches," not a cup of cold water but "that I should drink when thirsty."[30] Moreover if one is talking about "choosing" something, as opposed to merely "taking" it, then the predicate involved is a rather elaborate one which incorporates something about the manner in which something is to happen.[31] Choosing to drink implies choosing to drink in a certain way, sensibly for instance.[32] The adverbial term indicates what it is about the predicate that appeals to one's rational nature. Rational beings do not choose to drink without further specification, but only sensibly; that is, only when they judge that drinking is advisable under the circumstances.

---

[29] Plut., *St. Rep.* 1039c.
[30] The first example is from Cicero, *Tusc.* 4.21, the general account in Stob. 2.7.9 (86W); discussion in Inwood 1985: 42–101.
[31] For the distinction between things that are "to be chosen" and things that are merely "to be taken" (*sumenda*, ληπτά) see Stob. 2.7.50 (75W). It was well known to Cicero, who refers to it in *Fin.* 4.39. *Sumenda* is Cicero's rendering of ληπτά in *Acad. Post.* 1.37.
[32] The link between the choiceworthy and adverbial formulations is spelled out in Plutarch, *De Communibus Notionibus* 1070a–b. Plutarch's examples have a sarcastic ring ("sensibly extending a finger, sensible endurance of torture, reasonably throwing oneself over a cliff"), but the manner in which they are formulated undoubtedly mirrors his Stoic source.

In the same way, one might choose to undergo some specific pain or hardship when one believes that doing so means acting prudently or well. For a Stoic to say that an object is choiceworthy, then, is to say that it is a predicate the agent can fulfill, where doing so will be to behave in what he or she thinks is the right manner. Moreover the agent's belief that acting thus means acting well must be true: what is choiceworthy is not just what someone chooses but what merits choice. Narrowly interpreted, then, the Chrysippan syllogism has no difficulty at all linking what is choiceworthy to what is praiseworthy. Given the Stoics' specialized way of speaking about choice, some sort of virtuous conduct is already implied when one says that something is choiceworthy.

On the other hand, a philosopher who specifically rejects the Stoics' distinction between what is choiceworthy and what is merely "to be taken" will not be at all convinced by the argument. Such are the Academic and Peripatetic philosophers whose position Cicero represents in Book 4. These philosophers insist, contrary to the Stoics, that some goods are chosen *simpliciter*, without adverbial elaboration. These would be goods like pleasure, health, and abundance of resources, that are in accordance with our nature and yet are not praiseworthy. Speaking for these philosophers, Cicero in 4.48–50 objects vehemently to P1 above, that everything that is good is praiseworthy, and likewise to the version that states that everything that is choiceworthy is praiseworthy. Very few philosophers would grant this, he says in 4.49. Aristotle, Xenocrates, and other philosophers of their persuasion certainly will not, for they consider health, strength, wealth, glory, and many other things to be good, but not praiseworthy. Consequently, the argument is inefficacious, "a leaden dagger."[33]

This line of thought is indeed present already in Aristotle in *Nicomachean Ethics* 1.12, although it is by no means clear whether Cicero had any specific knowledge of that work.[34] In that passage, Aristotle considers whether eudaimonia is something praiseworthy (ἐπαινετόν) or instead something prized (τιμητόν); that is, something intrinsically valuable.[35] Aristotle favors

---

[33] In 4.50 Cicero objects also to the *sorites* form of the argument. But the *sorites* can hardly be the main issue, since the speaker of Book 4 does not trouble to reproduce the sequence exactly but instead abbreviates it considerably: where Cato moves from *expetendum* to *placens* to *diligendum* to *probandum* and so to *laudabile*, the objector steps directly from *optabile* to *expetendum* to *laudabile*.

[34] The connection is noted by Wright 1991: 138. For the question whether Cicero could have read the *Nicomachean Ethics*, see Barnes 1997: 44–50, 57–59.

[35] Τιμητόν can mean either "prized" or "honorable," depending on whether one thinks of τιμή concretely, as a prize or price, or more abstractly as esteem. Since Aristotle does not assume an easy slide from τιμητόν to ἐπαινετόν, only the meaning "prized" is applicable here. So W. D. Ross in the Oxford translation (Barnes 1984). Irwin 1985 favors "honorable," but explains the semantics in his glossary (408–409).

the latter, arguing that there is nothing beyond eudaimonia that we could refer to in praising it. In addition, he reports that the hedonist Eudoxus makes use of that same distinction to support his view that pleasure is beyond praise and thus beyond all other goods. Although Aristotle does not endorse Eudoxus' view of the highest good, he does agree with him that eudaimonia is not something to be praised; rather it is something for which one is to be congratulated. It follows that virtue does not by itself suffice for happiness: we praise virtue, but happiness is something greater and better. Both Aristotle and Eudoxus thus maintain a firm divide between the perspective of external assessment – what other people might admire when they see it in us – and internal assessment, what we value for ourselves.

This is just the kind of philosophical thinking the Stoic argument tries to break down. In asking the interlocutor to concede that what one chooses is also what one finds pleasing and for that reason also commends in others, Chrysippus appeals to what he believes are widely shared intuitions about what is valuable in various forms of behavior. Even non-philosophers might be expected to agree that the conduct we decline to praise in others is conduct we disapprove of and would not want to adopt for ourselves; conversely, if we do praise someone's behavior we must value that sort of behavior in everyone including ourselves. In rehearsing the connections between honor, praise, and what is lovable and pleasing, the Stoic brings these preconceptions to light.[36] Thus while the argument may be most convincing to those who are already versed in Stoic use of terms, it may also be intended to gain a hearing with a broader audience whose intuitions run in this direction. Cicero, for all that he favors the Academic/Peripatetic position within the structure of *De Finibus*, shares these intuitions as well. The criticism he expresses in his own voice as the speaker of Book 4 are seriously meant, but the appeal to the honor motive has been too prominent in his own career and writings to be dismissed out of hand. The Stoics' claim has not been proven here, but neither has it been shown to be false.

In terms of its reasoning, Cato's second argument in *De Finibus* 3.28 is again a weak one. The argument works upon intuitions concerning the sort of life one can take pride in. Again, honor and glory are key terms.

---

[36] This strategy of drawing out an audience's prior ethical beliefs to demonstrate the appeal of a seemingly counterintuitive claim is sometimes called the "dialectical" method in ethics: see Irwin (1998) 156–159.

Next I ask you, who could take pride in (*gloriari*) a miserable life, or in a life that is not happy? Only, then, in a life that is happy. From this it follows that a happy life is worthy of pride-taking, if I may call it that. But if a life were not honorable, one could not rightly take pride. Thus it is established that the happy life is an honorable life. And since he whose lot it is to be praised for legitimate cause has something marking him out for renown and glory, so that because of these, which are of such magnitude, he can be legitimately said to be happy, the same thing may be said, very correctly, about the life of such a man. Hence, if a happy life is recognized by honorableness, then that which is honorable should be considered the only good.

This is no great demonstration of Stoic logic, for the steps are jumbled and hard to follow, and at least one needed premise is missing.[37] Cato apparently intends to establish, first, that the *beata vita* is necessarily an honorable life; and second, that honorable conduct always yields happiness; i.e., that every honorable life is happy. From this it is supposed to follow that only what is honorable is good, and along the way that perceptions of what is honorable can be a means of recognizing a happy life. This convoluted reasoning contrasts markedly with the straightforward version of this argument we have from Chrysippus: "What is good is something to rejoice in; something to rejoice in is something to take pride in; something to take pride in is fine."[38] Cicero's refutation in Book 4 duly criticizes Cato's version as "hardly a syllogism at all," and when this line of thought is taken up again in *Tusculan Disputation* 5, the argumentation is revised in the interest of cogency.[39]

---

[37] I parse it out roughly as follows:

P1: No one can take pride in a life that is not happy.
P2: *(missing) But there is some life in which one can take pride.*
C1: The happy life is such that one can take pride in it *(from P1 + P2)*.
P3: One could not take pride in a life if it were not an honorable life.
C2: The happy life is an honorable life *(from C1 + P3)*.
P4: An honorable person has some observable characteristic that marks him out for renown and glory, and because of these he is properly considered happy.
P5: What can be said about the person can also be said about the life.
C3: A happy life is recognized by the fact that it is honorable *(from P4 + P5); and thus every honorable life is happy.*
C4: What is honorable is the only good *(from C2 + C3)*.

[38] From *On the Fine* quoted by Plutarch in *St. Rep.* 1039c: καὶ πάλιν 'τἀγαθὸν χαρτόν, τὸ δὲ χαρτὸν σεμνόν, τὸ δὲ σεμνὸν καλόν'. The continuation of the passage makes it clear that the χαρτόν is specifically an action one can rejoice in having performed, such as temperately abstaining from a prostitute. The relevance of the Chrysippan argument to *Fin.* 3.28 is noted already in Hutchinson 1909: 114.

[39] The argument is given first in *Tusc.* 5.43 as an expanded version of what we have from Chrysippus; it is developed further in *Tusc.* 5.47–50, at 5.49 supplying the premise that seems to be missing from

For all its shortcomings, though, the pride-taking argument of *De Finibus* 3 still aims to produce a favorable impression on its readers. Though less tidy than either the Chrysippan version or Cicero's own later versions, the version given to Cato is also more expansive and engaging. For the primary audience of *De Finibus*, the mention of "renown" (*decus*) and "glory" (*gloria*) serves as a reminder of powerful preconceptions that support the conclusion at an intuitive level. An intriguing element not found in the more formal versions is the remark that a person who is praised for legitimate cause "has something marking him out for renown and glory" (*insigne quiddam ad decus et ad gloriam*). This would seem to be an application of the "radiance of virtue" idea. The word *insigne* indicates an observable characteristic, a "mark" (*signum*) belonging to honorable conduct or to the person who displays such conduct. This mark is recognized on its own account: people tend to realize when praise is warranted, even if they cannot quite say why. Honorableness thus serves as a means of discovering the good, for it is in some sense perceptible, while happiness itself is not.

The thought will surface again in *De Finibus* 3.36–38, where Cato asserts, with remarkable optimism, that people in general, regardless of their upbringing but especially if raised in good families, are invariably delighted by exceptional instances of virtuous conduct and repelled by exceptional cases of vice.[40] It is, he says, a very easy and quick way of defending his thesis (*perfacilis et perexpedita defensio*). His strategy in this resembles the *consensus omnium* arguments Cicero uses in *De Natura Deorum* and elsewhere: views that all people share arise from innate tendencies of the human mind.[41] It is hardly conclusive proof, however, since intuitions supposed to be shared by all humankind are at best difficult to verify, and since large numbers of people may also go badly astray in their moral assessments.

Fin. 3.28 (above, n. 37): *Atque hoc sic etiam concluditur: nec in misera vita quicquam est praedicabile aut gloriandum nec in ea, quae nec misera sit nec beata. Et est in aliqua vita praedicabile aliquid et gloriandum ac prae se ferendum.* Compare also *Tusc.* 5.67, expanding Chrysippus' notion of the χαρτόν: *Hinc omnia quae pulchra, honesta, praeclara sunt ... plena gaudiorum sunt. Ex perpetuis autem plenisque gaudiis cum perspicuum sit vitam beatam existere, sequitur ut ea existat ex honestate.*

[40] Cato says at first *quis autem tam agrestibus institutis vivit* but then *quis autem honesta in familia institutus et educatus ingenue*, implying that a proper upbringing is necessary for the maintenance of the preconception. *Tusc.* 5.66 is similar both in wording and in context.

[41] Cic., *ND* 1.30, 36–38; 2.5, 2.12, but the argument is said to be weak in *ND* 1.62; 3.11; see also *Tusc.* 1.29–32. These *consensus omnium* arguments are related in thought to the appeal to innate tendencies in ethics as seen earlier in Cicero's work (*Rep.* 1.1–3, 1.39–41, *Leg.* 1.16–33, 37–38).

4 *Veram illam honestatem expetens*

Although neither of the arguments in *De Finibus* 3.27–28 manages to prove
the Stoics' entire case in short order, as Cato hopes, the two of them together
do succeed in fixing our attention on a set of shared assumptions about
the relation between being honored and gaining something of value. Even
untrained minds have some instinctive understanding of these matters, sufficient to generate appropriate reactions to egregious instances of virtue and
vice. Outstanding moral heroes do meet with general approbation, outstanding wickedness with general loathing. When our obligations are extra-
ordinarily clear cut, as they are in *De Finibus* 3.36, we would much prefer,
independently of reward, to obtain our objectives by fair means rather than
foul.[42] The point is expressed more forcefully in *Tusc.* 2.58–60: we have by
nature a powerful yearning toward the honorable, and whenever we catch
sight of "some gleam of its radiance" (*si quasi lumen aliquod aspeximus*),
we are strongly motivated to pursue it. But all of this could come about
through quite a broad and vaguely understood notion of the sorts of behavior that count as honorable. In more complicated situations, where there are
conflicting obligations to consider and fine distinctions to be drawn, a more
precise notion will be required. In particular, only a fully defined and accurate conception of the honorable could guide a person through the moral
intricacies of a political career. It is therefore of considerable importance to
understand how a mind in the course of formation comes to possess a concept of the honorable and to appreciate its significance.

Here we encounter something of a puzzle. Honorableness is inherently
a relational notion: it has reference to an evaluation of conduct by some
real or imagined observer. How then is it possible to develop an accurate
notion of what conduct is truly honorable? For concepts are developed
through experience, and the external evaluations we experience in our
lives are only those of our existing communities. It is hard to see how any
stable and reliable conception could be arrived at by the usual means; that
is, by internalizing the behavioral standards promoted by an imperfect
society. At best, it seems, one would be like the beast-keeper in Book 6 of
Plato's *Republic*, who learns only "the moods and the pleasures of the mot-
ley multitude in the assembly."[43]

---

[42] Again Irwin 1998: 162–164 is helpful on this form of argument.

[43] *Rep.* 6.493b–d, in the ringing translation by Paul Shorey (1930). Although the material treated
in this section shows primarily Stoic influence, Plato's concern with the moral formation of political leaders in *Republic* 6 has contributed as well. For Cicero's knowledge of Plato's work see
Long 1995b.

That Cicero is aware of this difficulty is evident already in the first book of *De Legibus* and even more so in the *Tusculan Disputations*. In both works Cicero takes it upon himself to explain the origins of human error and corruption in a world governed by benevolent Nature. Although exhibiting certain innate tendencies that favor the development of the virtues, young people invariably fall into error, either (1) through the influence of caregivers, educators, poets, and the general population, or (2) through the misleading appearance of objects themselves. This is recognizably the Stoics' twofold cause of epistemic corruption (διαστροφή) as known to us from other sources.[44] But Cicero gives us a more nuanced account than can be recovered for the early Stoics, with a much stronger emphasis on the role of honor and glory and a specific application to the education of political leaders.

As Cicero explains the matter, the more elusive second cause comes about through the immature mind's confusing one object for another which closely resembles it or which co-occurs with it. Pleasure in *De Legibus* 1 "has something in it similar to what is good by nature" and so is misconstrued as something healthful; pain "is seen to accompany" (*videtur sequi*) destructions of our nature. Likewise there is a resemblance between *gloria* and *honestas*, "which is the reason why those held in honor are regarded as fortunate and those in disgrace as unfortunate."[45] The preface to *Tusculan Disputations* 3 goes further. Glory now dominates the account: it is the principal objective of society's leaders, "the noblest among us," who interpret it as consisting in "public office, military commands, and the glory of popularity." Their desire for these things expresses a natural inclination toward genuine *honestas*, which is "the one chief aim of their nature."[46] But they misconstrue.

[44] The earliest and most general Stoic account of epistemic corruption is in Cleanthes' hymn (*SVF* 2.537), lines 22–31. The "twofold cause" appears in D.L. 7.89: "The rational animal is corrupted sometimes by the persuasiveness of things from without, sometimes through the teaching of our associates." The point is expanded in Galen, *PHP* 5.5.14 (quoting Chrysippus' *On Emotions*; cf. 5.4.5–17); 5.5.14–21 (= Posidonius fr. 169E EK); and the late but apparently knowledgeable account in Calcidius, *On the Timaeus of Plato* 165–166 (= *SVF* 3.229). The Stoic background is discussed in more detail in Graver (2007) 149–163; on Cicero's handling of it see further Graver (2012). Note that the explanation is not for error in general but for the prevalence of certain types of error, namely misevaluations of money, fame, and pleasure.
[45] *Leg.* 1.31–32. Compare also *Fin.* 5.69, for Antiochus, prefiguring the imagery of *Tusc.* 3.3: "The wise pursue right actions clear-sightedly, as it were, under nature's guidance, but people who are imperfect but have some aptitude for excellence are often motivated by glory, which has some semblance and similitude of the honorable. What joy would they feel if they had full view of the honorable itself – complete and perfect, the most eminent of all things and most to be praised – considering how much they are pleased by the shadowed opinion of it." But Piso emphasizes the resemblance rather than the error.
[46] *Tusc.* 3.3; the passage is treated in more detail in Graver 2002.

Glory is in fact an especially confusing analytical problem for these noble natures to sort out. There are two ways to understand glory. Real glory, which is "approval sounded without bias by those who know how to judge excellence of character," is a regular accompaniment to right actions and thus a reliable indicator of virtue.[47] But there is also mere popular acclaim, which "pretends to imitate" the first kind of glory, but which lacks the solid epistemic basis of the other and so frequently praises misdeeds and faults. Figuratively, true glory is a solid and clearly modeled image of virtue itself, whereas popular acclaim is only a distorted shadow of real glory. It is when the image – either image – is mistaken for its original that this most insidious form of epistemic corruption occurs.

Who or what is responsible for this corruption? The noble natures who are misled by it have not gone astray by choice (*voluntate*), for their desire was always for some sort of excellence. Nonetheless the errors in which they are involved are their own errors; it is not merely a matter of their being infected by the false values of their culture. The common people have indeed made the mistake of praising some wrong actions as if they were right actions, but the doers of those actions have erred at a deeper and more dangerous level, in that they have wrongly assessed the external assessment itself. They have treated an unreliable sort of approbation as if it were reliable, and have transferred to it the yearning that they properly feel toward the honorable itself. Even if the actions for which they receive praise are appropriate actions, ones that truly promote the interests of the state, they would still be in error in so far as they undertake such actions for the sake of the glory that attends them. To be motivated in this way is to miss completely the inherent quality that makes an action praiseworthy in the first place. One comes to think of the *honestum* merely as "that which is praised by the most people" (*Tusc.* 2.63). This is the importance of Cicero's insisting, as he does in the *Tusculan Disputations* and in letters as early as 50, that while glory need not be repudiated, there is no need ever to pursue it for its own sake.[48]

---

[47] *Tusc.* 3.3–4. For glory as a concomitant of right action compare Stob., *Ecl.* 2.7.11i (103.6–7 W): "the deserving of a reward, that being the prize for virtue which does good"; Calcidius 165–166 = *SVF* 3.229: "the testimony to virtue." Some early Stoics must also have made the distinction between glory (i.e., properly merited praise, τιμή) and mere reputation (δόξα), for the terms are defined differently in Stobaeus, *Ecl.* 2.7.7e (83W), 2.7.5l (73W), 11i (103W). Cleanthes wrote separate treatises on each (D.L. 7.175).

[48] *Tusc.* 1.91, 3.3; among the letters esp. *Fam.* 15.4.13, to Cato concerning the proposed *supplicatio: Testis est consulatus meus, in quo sicut in reliqua vita fateor me studiose secutum ex quibus vera gloria nasci posset, ipsam quidem gloriam per se numquam putavi expetendam.* See further Sullivan (1941): 387.

The corruption brought about by the misguided pursuit of glory represents a deep and pervasive strain of Stoic influence in Cicero's ethical thought. We hear it again in *De Officiis* 1.65, now referring more pointedly to the errors of statesmen:

> But the true and wise greatness of mind judges that the thing it is by nature most eager to pursue, namely the honorable, consists in deeds, not in glory, and prefers to be a leader rather than to seem to be one. For one who depends on the errors of the untutored multitude ought not to be accounted a great man. The most exalted minds are also most easily motivated toward unjust acts through desire for glory. That is a dangerous matter, because there is hardly anyone who performs the labors and braves the dangers without then expecting to receive glory as payment, so to speak, for his endeavors.

Elsewhere in *De Officiis*, the same errors are attributed specifically to Julius Caesar and others of his persuasion:

> This point was recently made clear by the outrageous conduct of Caesar, who perverted every divine and human law for the sake of that domination which he had contrived for himself through mistaken belief. In this regard it is problematic that it is the greatest minds, the most luminous talents, that most exhibit the desire for honor, authority, power, and glory.
>
> (*Off.* 1.26)

Concerning Caesar's desire for absolute power he writes,

> If anyone thinks that this kind of desire is honorable, he is insane; he is giving approval to the demise of laws and of freedom. He regards the suppression of these – which is in fact an abomination – as a glorious thing.
>
> (*Off.* 3.83)

At this point the theme is very much his own, regardless of philosophical influences. It expresses all too well what he had observed firsthand during the dissolution of the Republic, as talented individuals threw themselves into an increasingly high-stakes competition for status and supremacy. Yet the philosophical provenance of his remark is discernible even here, in his analysis of the dictator's motives. What moves his Caesar to pursue his abominable program of domination is not that he sets his sights on expediency alone; rather it is that he believes, wrongly but sincerely, that in gaining domination he gains "a glorious thing." Corrupt as it may be, his desire is still directed at what he conceives of as honorable, exactly as with the noble natures of *Tusculan Disputations* 3.3. The problem is that he harbors a misguided notion of what the honorable consists in.

5   *Illud hominis per se laudandum et expetendum bonum*

The example of Caesar serves to bring out the pressing importance of developing a properly grounded conception of the *honestum*. If it is not possible for human beings to arrive at a correct understanding of what honorable conduct is, Cicero's condemnation of Caesar will be unfair, and indeed his entire project in ethics will be left without foundation. The problem could be stated as a challenge to philosophers to demonstrate that a meaningful conception of the honorable is at least available for discussion, even if the role of that conception in the human good remains open. Alternatively, it could be stated as a question about human development, whether a child in the course of maturation has any reasonable opportunity to work out a proper conception of the *honestum* without relying on cultural transmission. Even if that opportunity is not realized in any given case – even if there is often conspicuous failure, as there was with Caesar – it is still essential that some philosophers should be able to demonstrate how it belongs to human potential.

This demonstration is worked out most fully, though still with gaps and areas of uncertainty, in the first part of Cato's speech in *De Finibus* 3. There we find the development of a proper concept of the honorable, *honeste facta ipsumque honestum*, treated as part of the process of coming to understand the good.[49] We begin to possess and also to understand the good only when we begin to exhibit an order and harmony in all our actions; and, moreover, to realize that we are doing so; and at the same time to esteem that order more highly than anything else. But to see an action as an element in a rationally ordered system and to esteem it for that reason is precisely what it is to see that action as honorable.

According to the account entrusted to Cato, our ability to conceive of the good and likewise of the honorable is grounded in the most basic tendencies of human nature. These tendencies are described at the very beginning of the developmental narrative from 3.16 to 3.18. Against the Epicureans, who hold that the human being has an instinctive impulse toward pleasure, Cato maintains that the innate inclination is toward whatever preserves one's own "constitution" (*status*). The capacity for

---

[49] The passage has been treated in more or less detail in most recent studies on the ethical foundations of Stoicism, including White 1979, Striker 1983 and 1991, Brunschwig 1986, Engberg-Pedersen 1990, Annas 1993: 169–79, Inwood and Donini 1999, Gill 2006: 129–165, and the works listed in n. 55. Specifically on the formation of the concept of the good in Stoicism see Inwood 2005: 271–301 and Frede 1999. Frede in particular comments on the role played by the καλόν as what is admirable and attractive.

appetition implies a basic level of self-perception (*sensum sui*, 3.16): one could not extend a hand to take food if one did not have some kind of awareness of hunger and of the functions of hand and mouth. Hence our orientation toward our own nature is necessarily prior to any experience of pleasure from the satisfaction of our desires. Moreover, this constitution includes both body and mind. For just as we prefer for our limbs to be sound and in their proper configuration even if this makes no difference in their function, so also we favor the *cognitiones* or "grasps" (καταλήψεις) of single facts and the skills (*artes*), interrelated groups of cognitions concerned with some single area of endeavor.

All this is also maintained by Cicero as a speaker for the Peripatetics in *De Finibus* 4.16–18 and by Piso in 5.24–43. But Cato is also given a further point which seems intended to bring out the distinctiveness of the Stoic view as against the Peripatetics and Antiocheans. In his account, but not in theirs, our most basic instincts enable us to appreciate features of our constitution in two different ways: we may favor them *propter se* (sometimes *per se*), that is "for their own sake," or we may favor them merely for their utility. The difference becomes apparent first as concerns certain of our mental faculties:

> But our understandings of situations, which may be called "grasps" or καταλήψεις, we regard as worth acquiring for their own sake, because they have something in them that as it were embraces and contains the truth. This can be inferred in small children, when we observe that they are delighted when they reason something out by themselves, even if they gain nothing by it. The skills, too, we think should be acquired for their own sake, both because there is something in them that is worth taking up and because they are made up of cognitions and have something in them that is rationally and systematically arranged.

Among the capacities and activities of the mind, there must be some that we are merely aware of and feel some ownership of without attaching much importance to them: seeing a wall, perhaps, or learning something by rote. For it is in contrast to such uninteresting items that the "grasps" strike us as especially worthwhile. The child who delights in figuring something out for herself is not thrilled merely that she has had a thought, as though every flicker of consciousness were something to get excited about; and neither is she rejoicing only in the acquisition of some new piece of information, useful as that might be. It is rather that the use of her reasoning powers triggers in her a special sort of appreciation, different in kind and intensity from the attitude she might take toward other aspects of psychic functioning. So also with the skills. Out of all the things we think worth doing in a day, there are only some that we find worth-while *propter se*, because of the kind of activity they are. At some level, of course, we have an investment in all our activities, simply because they are our own, or because they enable us to achieve various ends. But we feel differently about the ones that qualify as skills.

That we have in fact two levels of appreciation for the various features of our constitution is made explicit in 3.18, when Cato touches briefly on the attitudes people naturally take toward the parts of their own bod-ies. After a rather abrupt transition – perhaps an instance of that stylistic awkwardness for which he apologizes in the following paragraph – he dis-tinguishes carefully between a mere utilitarian appreciation and a second attitude which has a more aesthetic dimension.[50]

> As for our limbs (that is, the parts of our bodies), some appear to have been bestowed on us by nature because of their utility (*propter eorum usum*), such as the hands, legs, feet, and the internal organs, the extent of whose utility is still a subject for debate among physicians; but others seem not to have been bestowed for any utility but rather for ornament, as it were; for instance, the tail of the peacock, the iridescent plumage of pigeons, and the nipples and beards of men.

Neither a man's beard nor his nipples contribute anything to his physical survival, any more than the tail of the peacock enables the bird to find food. If a man appreciates having these parts nonetheless, it can only be for aesthetic reasons, because of the way they contribute to the symmetry and attractiveness of the body as a whole.[51] This accords with the attitude posited in 3.17 toward our overall bodily configuration: "there is no one

---

[50] The last sentence of *Fin.* 3.18 is transposed in Wright 1991 to 3.63 and is bracketed in Reynolds 1998; Jonathan Powell is cited in Reynolds' note as suggesting transposition to 3.11. Annas and Woolf 2001 follow Reynolds. But the received text should be preserved, as it is in Moreschini 2005: there is no paleographic reason to suspect disruption in the text at this point, and the point made here is neither needed nor particularly relevant in either of the other passages. The flow of ideas in the received text is certainly halting and elliptical, but this is true in other passages as well, notably 3.32 (which is likewise bracketed by Reynolds and transposed by Wright) and 3.35. I take it that Cicero's apology (in Cato's voice) in 3.19 for the *ieiunitas* or lack of fullness in his exposition refers to this very awkwardness in what he has written, passing it off as Cato's preference for the Stoics' clipped style of exposition (cf. *Paradoxa Stoicorum, praef.* 2; *Fin.* 4.5–7). The real explanation is probably that Cicero is excerpting from a longer treatment of the subject in Greek. For the record, though, it may be observed that reading *etiam membrorum*, rather than *iam membrorum*, would improve the flow of text considerably. Cato would then say that *even* in the body (i.e., *as well as* in the mind), our appreciation is at more than one level.

[51] *Fin.* 3.17. The comparison to doves and peacocks indicates that *ad quendam ornatum* is to be taken seriously; it is not merely a way of saying that these parts serve no useful function. A simi-lar thought may lie behind the remark of Chrysippus (in Plut., *St. Rep.* 1044d), that "the peacock exists for the tail, not the tail for the peacock."

who would not prefer if given the choice to have all parts of the body well fitted and whole, even with no difference in use, rather than diminutive or twisted." What is described is a *propter se* appreciation which recognizes and favors an emergent property of the body, namely the symmetry of one's overall body shape and the proportionality of each limb to the whole. Both in the mind and in the body, then, we have a natural tendency to prize some elements for reasons other than what they contribute to our survival.

As the account progresses, it will be the *propter se* valuation we attach to certain mental events that will become the basis of the developing capacity for moral evaluation. Let us therefore return for a moment to what is said in 3.17 about the characteristics that make some, but not all, mental processes seem special and important in their own right. We find something on this in what is said about acts of cognition, that they "have something in them that as it were embraces and contains the truth." This "something" must be something about the mental event itself, the way this new realization seems to be bound up in the very structure of one's thinking process. Somewhat clearer is what Cato says about the attitude one takes toward the skills. When we find something in the skills that is worth taking up (*dignum assumpsione*) for its own sake and not merely because of the products, it is for two reasons: because they consist of "grasps," and because they are "rationally and systematically arranged" (*ratione constitutum et via*, 3.18).[52] Someone who wants to learn to knit, to drive a car, or to play the violin is recognizing that a whole assemblage of items of knowledge and acquired responses can be systematically coordinated and directed toward some single product or performance. We perceive the way the components of the skill fit together exactly as they need to to produce the result, with no wasted motion, no irrelevant bits of knowledge, and we find this both admirable and worth having for its own sake.

Cato's main contention is that a proper concept of honorable conduct both can and should develop from these same universal tendencies. The preference for systematic coordination of elements that we show when we seek to acquire a skill is indicative of the attitude we can take, are naturally suited to take, and should take, toward a similarly orderly arrangement among all our actions over time. It belongs to our human nature to realize the possibility of such an arrangement and to adopt an attitude toward it which is analogous to the *per se* appreciation we have for cognitions and

---

[52] Compare the Greek definition quoted in Sextus, *AM* 7.227, 11.182: "a system of accurate cognitions trained together toward some good end."

skills, but at a new level that registers the difference between what is partial and what is complete.

> Once pursuit and avoidance are discovered, there follows in order appropriate pursuit, then long-term appropriate pursuit, then at last consistently appropriate pursuit in agreement with nature. And it is in this that one first begins to locate and understand what it is that can properly be called the good. For the human being's first orientation is toward those things that accord with nature; but once one gains an understanding or conception (which they call an ἔννοια) and sees the order and, so to speak, the harmony among one's actions, one values that much more than all those things one loved at first. Thus by cognition and reasoning one realizes that one should consider the good to reside in this – that highest human good, which is praiseworthy and choiceworthy for its own sake. And since it is in what the Greeks call *homologia* – I'll use the word "agreement" if you don't mind – since it is in this that the good to which everything should be referred resides, honorable actions and the honorable itself – which alone is considered a good – is the only thing that is choiceworthy in its own capacity and worth, even though it arises later.
>
> (*Fin.* 3.20–21)

This new attitude is one of honoring. In it, we become as it were the observers of our own behavior – of what it could be, even if it is not yet – and we approve that behavior by the standards that rational beings have, standards of consistency, fit, coherence, completeness. To take this attitude is to recognize something as praiseworthy and choiceworthy in itself, *per se laudandum et expetendum*, and by its own intrinsic quality and worth, *vi sua et dignitate*. It is in fact to conceive of the human good in the way that a human being ought to think about goodness.

We should try to get clear as to what that orderly arrangement is and what it means to recognize and honor it. From what Cato says in 3.20–21, it seems that each individual action is an instance of "selecting" (*selectio*) among options that present themselves. For convenience, we can call these options "objects"; technically they ought to be predicates to be satisfied, not bread but "that I should eat the bread" and so on. Because only some objects are such as to preserve our constitution, regularities will emerge over time. In some cases this comes about quite easily (I regularly choose to eat bread rather than grass); in others more discrimination is required, when there are conflicting options all of which accord in some way with one's constitution (I can eat the bread *or* give it to my child *or* save it for tomorrow). Even in the most complex situations, though, there is only a limited range of options that are actually appropriate for me;

that is, that accord as well as possible, both for the short term and for the long term, with all salient considerations: all parts of myself, the needs of all those who are connected to me, and my physical environment. If I choose thoughtfully, I might hit upon these appropriate selections more often than not, guided only by my self-perception and my own reasoning powers. But if it *is* more often than not, then self-perception should also enable me to discover various properties that characterize some significant subset of my actions taken as a group. I begin to see them fitting together in the way that the components of a skill fit together, and I naturally regard that orderly arrangement with the same special attitude as I take toward skills.

This awareness of a systematic coordination among my actions need not be a matter of stepping back to conduct some kind of internal review of all my actions throughout life. It might be just an element in what I believe myself to be doing in any given moment, an adverbial component that appears in many of the action-guiding predicates I select. My awareness of putting the broccoli in the grocery cart includes an awareness of doing so in a certain manner; viz., as part of a program of healthy living. And I may choose that action with an emphasis on the adverbial component, the one that applies to a range of activities and brings them into relation with one another. In this way the pattern will tend to reinforce itself.

This is not yet virtue, for I might similarly be aware of putting my paycheck in the bank in a wrongful but consistent manner, as part of a program of keeping my entire income for myself. Even this latter awareness illustrates the fundamental commitment I have as a rational being to systematic behavior. In this case, though, the pattern can only be among a subset of my actions; it can't be rendered consistent with other priorities I inevitably exhibit in my behavior, e.g., my sympathy for homeless teens. Thus it could never be extended to encompass all the decisions I make. But selections that truly are appropriate can, in theory, fit together into a pattern that is extended on and on until there is absolute logical consistency in everything I do. Actions undertaken as part of that sort of life are what Cato means by honorable actions, and the psychic condition that acts in that way is virtue.

Notice that on this way of thinking people ought to be able to recognize and honor virtuous action even before they become virtuous themselves, just as they see skills as worth acquiring even before acquiring them. Our appreciation for what is honorable is an appreciation for patterning among multiple elements; and one's ability to recognize a pattern does not depend on that pattern's being complete. We can look at a tattered Oriental rug and appreciate the beauty of the design it once had, and we could do the same if the rug were half-finished on the loom. A nine-fingered man could see himself as an incomplete ten-fingered man even if he had never seen another person's hands. In the same way we ought to be able to conceive of a fully consistent and orderly pattern among our actions even before bringing that pattern into existence. Basic aesthetic notions of unity, symmetry, and completeness, such as are developed through our experience of visual or auditory patterns, can be brought to bear on the flawed and incomplete pattern that encompasses our existing lives and can enable us to conceive of what those lives might become.

Those basic aesthetic notions are also, in their own way, notions of the honorable. A connection between our appreciation of visual symmetry or musical harmony and our admiration for some kinds of action is easily established in Greek, where καλόν conveys the notion of symmetry or proportionality wherever it is applied.[53] In Latin this is much less evident, for *honestum* lacks the idea of symmetry: it can be applied to the visual appearance of things, but in token of their being admirable, not of their being well proportioned.[54] Cicero's readers have to make do without this verbal connection and simply realize for themselves that there is something about the "order and harmony in the performance of actions" (*rerum agendarum ordinem et concordiam*) that has a special sort of appeal, an appeal that is not of a class with the strictly utilitarian interest we have in a foot or a kidney, but that is of a class with our appreciation for the overall configuration of the body.

There are certainly further questions to be asked about the human good in Stoicism; in particular, whether the account of goodness for rational creatures depends upon further postulates about the rational structure of the cosmos, and what role the apprehension of such cosmic regularities might play in the formation of each person's concept of the good.[55] But these questions are not easily addressed in the context of Cato's speech, for Cicero does little to bring them into focus. His concern here is more specifically with the connection between goodness as understood by Stoics and a rationally grounded notion of the honorable. He does hope to make it clear why Stoics believe that virtuous knowledge, that is, consistency with oneself and with the natural order, is the one thing human nature finds choiceworthy for its own sake. He will allow them the opportunity

---

[53] See especially D.L. 7.100, along with Long 1991.
[54] Above, n. 16.
[55] He does have Cato say more on the second question in *Fin.* 3.73. On these issues see Cooper 1996, Long 1996: 152–155, Schofield 2003: 241–246, Annas 2007a, Boeri 2009.

to prove by reason and argument that this is so. But even if that effort fails (as of course he knows it will), Book 3 will still have performed an essential function: it will have provided, on behalf of the Stoics, a compelling account of how tendencies that appear to be universal in human beings can give rise to a well-grounded and reliable conception of honorable conduct.[56]

[56] I wish to thank the Symposium participants for a stimulating discussion of this paper, and Thomas Bénatouïl for additional suggestions afterward. I am indebted also to Brad Inwood, who made numerous invaluable comments on the revision, and to a helpful set of notes from an anonymous reader for Cambridge University Press.

CHAPTER 6

The voice of nature

Brad Inwood
Yale University

When nature is regarded as criterial of important aspects of ethics, as it was by the main Hellenistic schools of philosophy and indeed by Cicero himself, we need to consider carefully what we can learn from nature and *how* we can learn it. Sometimes this involves active investigation of facts in the natural world. As the late Jacques Brunschwig (1986) emphasized, it often seems as though philosophers in the ancient world would go right up to the cradle and peer in at the pre-rational, uncorrupted infant lying there, in order to gain insight into what nature has to tell us. Brunschwig cited *De Finibus* 5.55 for the explicit mention of the cradle, but this or a very similar point is made repeatedly in that work and elsewhere. Of course, just how closely or critically ancient philosophers actually looked when undertaking those cradle-peeking expeditions is an interestingly open question. There are also, to be sure, important questions about how in the Hellenistic period this particular approach to naturalism came to dominate the debate among Stoics, Epicureans, and others, but it won't be possible to explore those background issues here.

There are, however, a couple of remarkable things to note about the famous passage from Book 5. First, the speaker, Piso, claims that this is the procedure of 'all the ancient philosophers, especially our people' (*omnes veteres philosophi, maxime nostri*). By 'our people' he may mean Academics generally, the Old Academy as he understood it, in particular, or even Peripatetics (on whose views he is said to be exceptionally well informed and to whom he seems unusually sympathetic, 5.8).[1] Are we to

I wish to thank Symposium participants (including Dorothea Frede, Margaret Graver, and Teun Tieleman) for a great deal of helpful critical comment. I am especially grateful to Gábor Betegh, Thomas Bénatouïl, and Charles Brittain for providing invaluable written comments at various stages of this chapter's development. Predictably, I have not taken all the good advice offered; for that and for the chapter's remaining defects I have only myself to blame.

[1] The ambiguous nature of Piso's speech is reflected in Görler's (somewhat exaggerated) claim that it is 'eine zusammenhängende Darlegung … der peripatetischen Lehre' (Görler 1989: 247). I do not

gather, then, that the procedure that we now most commonly associate with Epicurean and Stoic[2] philosophers was ever practised 'especially' by the 'Old Academy'? Second, the whole process of looking into the cradle is supposed to be very easy (*facile est cernere ... videmus igitur*); reading the intentions of nature from infant behaviour is apparently dead simple. Would that it were so. Simple inspection of uncorrupted babies or other pre-cultural animals has not, in the end, proven to be enough to settle the question about what nature is telling us. It turns out that more is needed.

But cradle-peeking itself is not, even on Cicero's view, the only way to learn what nature has in store for us.[3] Sometimes, in Cicero, nature talks to us, indeed even shouts at us, to indicate what she intends.[4] Since just peeking into the cradle may not be sufficient, direct declarations from nature would clearly provide welcome assistance, both in determining the appropriate way to interpret the non-verbal observations of the cradle and in settling what nature 'wants' when cradle-behaviour is not directly pertinent, as perhaps it is not when we are considering distinctively adult behaviour patterns. But it can only provide this assistance if its 'voice' is clearly audible and straightforward to interpret. And even if this

---

intend to endorse this view; the role of Staseas of Naples in Piso's account is a complicated question which I cannot address fully here. I say something about it in Inwood 2014: chapter 3.

[2] It is generally agreed that the appeal to the cradle in order to establish what is natural for humans was originally an Epicurean move (though no doubt with antecedents among some members of the Academy, not least Eudoxus, and Aristotle). Their interest in newborns as particularly strong evidence for what is natural follows from their strong rejection of civic acculturation (*paideia*) as being contrary to our natural inclinations and values. The Stoic adoption of the cradle argument, no doubt in response to the Epicureans, might at first seem to lack this motivation, since they regarded the kind of social organization represented by the *polis* as natural – hence they need not be radically critical of the city and its institutions. But here the Cynic roots of Stoicism are pertinent. Although all humans are naturally inclined to virtue they are all, also, inevitably corrupted by the influence of companions (*katēchēsis tōn sunontōn*) as well as by the persuasiveness of the objects of our experience (D.L. 7.89). The double impact of external objects and social influence begins very young, in Chrysippus' opinion: the (mis-)handling of newborns by midwives is blamed for our mistaken attachment to pleasure (see Calcidius 165 = *SVF* 3.229; see also Galen at *SVF* 3.229a). The Stoics were, for their own reasons, as suspicious of early acculturation as the Epicureans were.

[3] This is not surprising, if only because for the Stoics the relevant aspects of nature extend beyond the individual animal to embrace a providential cosmic nature as well (D.L. 7.89). But by and large the nature of the whole, as Chrysippus apparently called it, is not invoked in the *De Finibus*, which tends to restrict itself to arguing at a level which might in principle be common to all the schools involved in the debate (Epicurean, Stoic, and Academic/Peripatetic).

[4] I cheerfully accept the emendation at *Fin.* 5.55, *voluntatem* for *voluptatem*, as far as I know universally approved since Lambinus made it. Even if the manuscript reading were correct, the general sense would be the same: nature's 'pleasure' would have to be interpreted as the state of affairs which does or would please her and so would indicate the way she likes things to be. The notion that nature has a 'will' is common enough in ancient thought, though often merely metaphorical, no doubt: a partial list of the evidence would include Aristotle *Politics* 1255b3, *GA* 731a12, 757a25, 778a4–5, *HA* 542a20, *Met.* 354b32, *PA* 682a6; Theophrastus *De Causis Plantarum* 1.21.2 end, *Hist. Pl.*

level of clarity is achieved it won't necessarily settle substantive philosophical disputes unless we can agree that what nature wants matters to us in the appropriate way.

Although I will begin with a longish detour, eventually the focus of my attention will be *De Finibus* 3.62, where Cato invokes the 'voice of nature' to support his claim about the naturalness of the inclination to protect one's off-spring, a key point in the doctrine (certainly not unique to Stoics[5]) that social bonds and social commitments have intrinsic rather than merely instrumental value to human beings and so play an indispensable role in the flourishing and happy (i.e., *eudaimōn*) life, properly understood; this issue was a major point of debate with the Epicureans and the first two books of the *De Finibus* have already primed the reader for its significant role in Cato's Stoic account. We should also keep in view a few other places (I doubt I have found them all[6]) where Cicero or one of his characters purports to lend an ear directly to nature's utterances. The metaphor of nature talking is not a surprising one, but its force and the way it is used by Cicero may, I hope, tell us something about the relationship between ethics and natural teleology in Stoicism and perhaps in Hellenistic philosophy more generally.

Several important aspects of the argument at 3.62 and the paragraphs which follow are best understood in light of the kind of argument about *oikeiōsis* towards oneself which is found earlier in the book, and which itself

---

1.10.2.11; Philo *Post.* 5, *Spec.* 3.136, 3.176; Epictetus 2.20.15; Galen *De usu partium* 3.296.2K; Marcus 5.1.3.2; Alexander *Mantissa* p. 163.17.

[5] At *De Finibus* 4.17 Cicero claims that the Academy was the first to make the claim that the love for offspring by their parents was nature's gift. Though the view was clearly shared by many, boasting rights about priority for the doctrine may have been contested.

[6] Where else, then, does nature speak in some such way? At *De Finibus* 1.71 Torquatus expresses typical Epicurean gratitude to the founder who listened to nature's voice and relied on it to help establish his salvific doctrines. At *De Finibus* 1.30 Torquatus refers to the unspoiled *judgement* of nature (*natura ... iudicante*), a similar personification of nature, though explicit reference to nature talking to us is absent. Julia Annas (note *ad loc.* in Annas and Woolf 2001: 13) takes this 'judgement' to be the equivalent of the cradle-peeking at *Fin.* 5.55, but while the point may be the same the metaphor is clearly different. As Thomas Bénatouïl observes, *Fin.* 3.11 makes important claims about nature as a teacher, though without the metaphor of speaking. At *Fin.* 4.55 nature joins human experience (*sensus cuiusque*) and truth itself to cry aloud that Zeno has his value theory all wrong. At *Tusculan Disputations* 1.29–35, part of the discussion of the soul's immortality, there is a sustained contrast between what one knows merely by nature and what can be learned by other means, such as physical theory (1.29) and institutional reinforcement (1.30); here widely held views, the *consensio omnium gentium*, are nature's law (1.30), and general human concern for what happens after death is equivalent to a judgement by nature on the question of the immortality of the soul (1.31–34). These considerations culminate at 1.35, where the *consensus omnium* is glossed as the *naturae vox* and is treated as firm authority. I do not intend to undertake a full study of the metaphor for its own sake (though that would be interesting and helpful, I'm sure); rather, my hope is to use reflection on the notion in order to come to a better understanding of how the Stoics (and Cicero's Cato in particular) use nature as an authority.

can best be understood in light of other relevant ancient texts.[7] In that connection, it quickly becomes apparent that mere observation of infants can hardly be taken to be a decisive move in any argument about ethics (if only because mere observation of what newborns do underdetermines assessments of their natures).[8] Simply pointing at the behaviour of babies doesn't decisively settle the significance of what they are doing, let alone what that means for normative ethics. A baby snuggling towards the breast could be pursuing pleasure or self-preservation – or both, although all the ancient participants in this debate seem to have thought that one of these interpretations must be explanatorily dominant, so that a choice had to be made. If a decisive interpretation is what we want, then additional information, argument and perhaps even supplementary observations of other animals are needed. Hence Chrysippus' teleological argument, summarized at D.L. 7.85–86, is designed to force a non-hedonistic interpretation of infant behaviour[9] and a similar argument is used by Hierocles in his *ēthikē stoicheiōsis*, column 6. Both Stoics aim to constrain, if not determine, the interpretation of observed behaviour by relying on assumptions about the purposive and adaptive character of nature.

In Chrysippus' case, the argument goes roughly like this. Once Nature has created an animal it must do one of three things: make it dear to itself, make it indifferent to itself, or make it hostile to itself. (That it should do nothing at all, which is distinct from making it indifferent to itself, is not considered. Nature is a restless creator.)[10] Only the first is compatible with background assumptions about Nature's character and motivations. In Hierocles' case there is perhaps less overt personification of nature, but the teleological assumption at work is comparably clear. An animal aware of itself must either be pleased, neutral, or displeased at the self of which it

<hr/>

[7] The suggestion that we understand the naturalness of social connections on the model of the self-directed attachment often referred to as 'personal' *oikeiōsis* is supported by the claim made towards the end of *Fin.* 3.66, where attention is drawn to the similarity between the way we naturally (i.e., before we explicitly learn their purpose) use our body parts and the way we are attached to natural social groupings. See more below.

[8] Simple observation of animals and human newborns is bound to underdetermine the correct account of *what* they are doing. See Inwood 1985: 192–194 and Brunschwig 1986: 117, 129–130, 135.

[9] Brunschwig 1986: 122 points out that Epicurus' own 'proof' that pleasure is the good comes not from infant behaviour but rather from adult *pathē*; the cradle argument is a kind of backup tactic (indicating that 'the adult is justified in accepting the force of his feelings'), though, as his subsequent discussion shows, matters become more complicated later in the tradition.

[10] The analysis of Chrysippus' argument, as summarized at D.L. 7.85–86, is complicated and contestable. I am still convinced that the broad outlines of the account I gave in ch. 6 of Inwood 1985 are roughly right, though I am now more wary about homogenizing the argument of this text and the accounts of *oikeiōsis* in Hierocles, Seneca, and Cicero.

is aware. The decisive rejection of displeasure and neutrality towards one-self is based on the claim that nature would have made its arrangements for the animal in vain (*hōs matēn ta toiauta kamousa pro geneseōs*, 6.41) if a newborn animal did not immediately feel pleasure at the awareness it has of itself.

Hierocles and Chrysippus, then, use arguments of similar form (an apparently exhaustive trilemma of possibilities) in which the decisive element (which suffices to eliminate two of the possibilities) is an assumption of some form of natural teleology. Nature is assumed to be in control and not to be self-undermining.[11] If nature is assumed to have made animals and not to be self-undermining, then any interpretive possibility which would entail that nature undermines her own efforts can be ruled out.

We want to distinguish two assumptions here. One is that nature actually *does* something, is a maker or creator; the other is that nature is a benevolent and relevantly all-powerful force. We do not have to assume that nature is all-powerful or benevolent to make this argument work; but we are required to think of nature as some kind of agent rather than a mere redescription for the aggregate result of the relevant processes. If we suppose nature to be some sort of force without any measure of agency, then it might be constrained by a requirement not to violate the law of non-contradiction, but not necessarily by a requirement not to do something pointless or self-undermining. Agents are expected to avoid undermining themselves on pain of being judged ineffective, irrational, or perhaps not agents at all. A weak or malevolent agent could create something too feeble to stand up to threats from other entities or something designed to inflict pain, perhaps even on itself. But an agent which, to the degree possible, undermines its own objectives, is (on this argument) an impossibility, so much so that Chrysippus and Hierocles are prepared to exclude two out of three interpretations of otherwise ambiguous animal behaviour on that basis.[12]

---

[11] The conviction that nature is not self-undermining is also a critical background assumption, though without the trilemmatic structure of argument, in Epictetus *Diss.* 1.6 (see especially 3–7) and 2.23. Since a systematically unused capacity would be a flaw in the economy of nature, the existence of a capacity entails that it is meant to be used. Epictetus and other Stoics, then, can argue both from the functional goal to the necessity of the capacities to carry out that goal and from the capacities to the existence of the goal as something meant to be achieved. Similarly *DND* 2.58. See also *Fin.* 2.39–41 for an example of the inference from apparent fitness of body and mind to the natural goals of human beings.

[12] I focus on these minimal constraints imposed by the notion of agency in order to emphasize that the basic argument here does not rely on assumptions about nature as a whole being benevolent

Hierocles' articulation of this argument uses terminology reminiscent of Aristotle's teleological assumptions. What must be avoided, he thinks, is that nature should turn out to be labouring in vain (*matēn*); the Aristotelian dictum[13] that nature does nothing in vain is the universal major premise behind the argument here (which Hierocles obligingly calls a *sullogismos*, though its formal structure would be Stoic rather than Aristotelian). If vain labours are ruled out, the assumption must be that there is a point, if not a conscious purpose, to the creative activity of nature. This minimal teleological requirement (MTR) is shared not just by Aristotle and the Stoics, but also by Platonists.[14]

Let's consider briefly the two trilemmatic arguments in light of the MTR. In the summary of Chrysippus' argument (D.L. 7.85) we are told: 'for it is not likely that nature would make an animal alienated from itself, nor having made the animal, to give it neither affinity to itself nor alienation from itself. Therefore the remaining possibility is to say that having constituted the animal she gave it an affinity to itself.' Agency is asserted; nature makes or constitutes an animal. And some minimal constraint of reasonableness or plausibility is invoked with the word 'likely' (*eikos*). Chrysippus assumes that the unlikely or implausible will not occur when there is an effective agent in control of the process. The assumption that self-alienation would be self-undermining (and so unreasonable) is taken to be unproblematic, but nothing is said to support the claim (which is less clearly true) that neutrality of motivation with regard to oneself is self-undermining. We are certainly invited to agree that it would be folly for nature to make an animal which is indifferent to itself and no doubt it is easy to accept that assumption; but it is much less compelling than the claim that self-alienation is directly self-defeating.

So it is perhaps not a surprise that this point is addressed in the corresponding argument advanced by Hierocles. He says (as far as we can reconstruct the text at 6.27–49):

> At any rate, one must certainly pause to consider three possibilities. Either the animal is well disposed to the representation that it has of itself or it is ill disposed to it or it is neutral with regard to it ... And nature would be subject to criticism for having laboured in vain before the animal's birth if

and globally powerful in the way that Stoic cosmic Nature is understood to be. A more or less global, benevolent Nature (on the model of the Craftsman of the *Timaeus*) would have to meet a higher standard of coordination between species and would of course not have malevolent motivations. The Stoics did, of course, also adopt this higher standard for Nature, but the argument at this stage does not rely on that richer conception of agency.

[13] See the note on 6.41 of Hierocles in Long and Bastianini 1992: 439.

[14] Hence we are not surprised to see it assumed in the 'Antiochean' books of the *De Finibus*: 2, 4, 5.

the animal is not going to be well disposed to itself as soon as it is born. That is why, in my view, no one, not even a fool like Margites, would say that an animal at birth is hostile to itself and to the representation of itself – and indeed it isn't neutral either. For simply failing to be well disposed, no less than actually being ill disposed, conduces to the destruction of the animal and to contempt for its nature.

Whereas the summary of Chrysippus left us to imagine why mere indifference to oneself might amount to a self-destructive disposition (and so be grounds for the charge against nature of self-undermining agency), Hierocles at least hints at a connection (of course, for all we know Chrysippus did so too in his own, no doubt excruciatingly full version). Contempt for one's own nature (*katagnōsis tēs phuseōs*) is where affective neutrality about oneself ends up, or so it is claimed. Even this attempt to fill in the connection between affective neutrality and self-undermining is incomplete and frustrating. But it is not, in fact, very difficult to fill in the blanks of assumption in the argument. A self-hostile animal might be thought likely to take action against itself (hurling itself over a cliff or otherwise directly harming itself), and so to imagine nature creating that sort of animal really would be to postulate that nature is a self-undermining agent. But if we merely assume that the environment for any newly made animal is inevitably dangerous to it, then indifference to oneself will lead reliably to the same end. Our hypothetical newly made animal cares not a fig for itself, and up comes a hungry predator. Or the new animal feels hunger and cold but bizarrely (in our view) doesn't seem to mind and so sits around passively as it starves and freezes. The physical suffering of its own nature is merely something it notes with equanimity and so no compensatory or evasive action ensues. In such cases doom will be swift and so the creative efforts of nature will be in vain, pointless.

There is no reason to think that the line of thought hinted at by Hierocles was absent from Chrysippus' argument. In fact, such arguments and hypothetical scenarios must have been obvious to anyone, at the very least to anyone familiar with Plato's *Protagoras*. For in the Great Myth of that dialogue the title character sets out in narrative form just what would happen as animals of various kinds are endowed with different sets of characteristics as they are generated and sent up to the earth to live their lives, and the myth crucially underlines the significance of the hostile environment in which all animals find themselves. This is especially clear when Epimetheus, in effect the eponymous hero of self-undermining creative agency, fails to equip humans with appropriate defensive gear (though they are not deprived of an inclination to self-preservation and the basic dispositions which accompany it). The environment is clearly hostile; without the right equipment humans are simply eaten by the competition. And they, at least, try to fight back, having a strong desire to save themselves. One can only imagine how quickly they would perish if they lacked the self-preservatory drive as well as the equipment necessary to defend themselves. The myth of the *Protagoras*, then, confirms (what common-sense observation would suggest anyway) that animals are imagined as being born into a hostile natural environment, one in which being under-equipped to save oneself means certain death. There is no doubt that a failure to try (owing to indifference) would lead to the same outcome. Hierocles is right – disinterest in and so contempt for oneself are just as self-undermining as self-loathing. The trilemmatic argument holds up nicely.

Hierocles' trilemmatic argument is designed to make nature speak clearly on the question of animal self-perception. Chrysippus' argument seems to have had a focus more immediately germane to the *De Finibus*, for it was addressed directly to the issue with which we began: how are we to determine what it is that nature is telling us in a case where mere observation of natural behaviour is insufficient? Epicureans claim to see hedonism confirmed, and mere counter-observation won't suffice as a response. The trilemmatic argument aims to settle the matter. But to do so it requires, as we have seen, quite significant background assumptions about nature, assumptions that Epicureans are disinclined to share with the other major schools. So it is that in the *De Finibus* cradle inspection is invoked on behalf of Epicurean hedonism at 1.30[15] (alluded to again perhaps at 1.71) and independently on behalf of Stoicism at 3.16 and the Old Academy at 5.55. But on this point there seems to be no active debate in the *De Finibus* itself. There is no direct rebuttal of the Epicurean move by Cicero in Book 2 nor any but the most passing dismissal by Cato in Book 3. Cicero, as author, could surely have invoked something like Chrysippus' argument on either of those occasions. His failure to do so is, for now at least, bound to remain one of the puzzles about Cicero's authorial strategy.[16]

---

[15] See above n. 6 on *Fin.* 1.30, where Torquatus twice refers to nature's judgement about what is naturally valuable.

[16] At *De Finibus* 5.28–30 the trilemmatic argument is used to support the claim that self-love underlies the natural drives and motivations of all animals. This forms part of the very general Peripatetic argument about nature: even plants participate in the basic naturalistic structures which ground the drive for actualization that culminates in humans as the motivation for virtue. Self-love is also deployed in Cato's Stoic account in *De Finibus* 3, though, as Ákos Brunner has persuasively argued in his doctoral dissertation (Brunner 2011), this is apparently not a reliably Stoic feature

But nature is invoked not only with regard to cradle observations and the arguments which can be deployed to disambiguate those observations. At 1.71 Torquatus doesn't just revive cradle observations (*infantes pueri, mutae etiam bestiae*); he also strengthens them with direct invocations of nature. These babies and beasts practically speak to us *magistra ac duce natura*. The construal of this text is difficult, and I suggest that the point about nature's guidance here is not that nature helps them to babble things out which we interpret as supporting Epicurean claims. Rather, it is we the intepreters who are helped by nature's guidance to understand the mute beasts and burbling babies. Observing them, but guided by nature, we learn that 'nothing is favourable except pleasure, nothing harsh except pain' (*nihil esse prosperum nisi voluptatem, nihil asperum nisi dolorem*). The way that nature guides the observer to interpret them in a pro-Epicurean manner needs further analysis – presumably it is not because of the same sort of assumptions about nature that guide and shape the Stoic trilemmatic argument. But the remarks which immediately follow about Epicurus ought, I think, to confirm that nature here is helping the interpreter rather than the subject of observation.[17] Torquatus asks whether we should not be grateful to him who 'heard the voice, as it were, of nature and understood it so reliably and profoundly that he could lead all people of sound mind along the road to a life which is peaceful, calm, restful and happy' (*hac exaudita quasi voce naturae sic eam firme graviterque comprenderet ut omnes bene sanos in viam placatae tranquillae quietae beatae vitae deduceret*). It is because Epicurus heard the voice of nature clearly that he was able to understand her so well and thus to be the heroic guide to the happy Epicurean life.

By contrast, it is noteworthy that in the early stages of Cato's account in Book 3 nature has nothing to say on behalf of the Stoic theory of cradle observation. No doubt if Cato had been made responsible for the rebuttal of Epicureanism he would have followed Chrysippus' lead more closely, but Cicero kept that job for his own character in Book 2[18] and gave Cato

---

of his account, being rather a feature of Cicero's general strategy for the *De Finibus* as a whole. I have learned a great deal about how to approach the question of Cicero's authorial strategy from Brunner's thesis, from Charles Brittain's contribution to the Symposium, and from Schofield 2008.

[17] Interestingly, there is Aristotelian precedent for the notion that the natural world can help the interpreter to understand the phenomena by making some things too obvious to miss. For example, at *Metaphysics* 984a18–19 the plain facts (*auto to pragma*) show the way to the natural philosopher and make them investigate properly; at 984b9–11 it is the truth which has this effect.

[18] And in Book 2 Cicero does not adopt this anti-hedonist strategy, relying for the most part on something rather less sophisticated and interesting. See *inter alia* Inwood 1990. It is worth noting that the character Cicero does engage with the issue of neonatal self-love at *Fin.* 2.33–34, in a manner that anticipates the Antiochean use of self-love seen also in Books 4 and 5. He does so even

the chance to develop the Stoic theory *not* as a response to Epicureanism but in its own terms. For better or worse, neonatal observation is left to speak for itself in the early paragraphs of Book 3.

But nature does speak for Stoicism, and it does so on a very important issue, one which is perhaps just as contentious for them as the cradle argument is. And that is the issue of the natural basis of social bonding. The relationship between *oikeiōsis* as a foundation for one's commitment to the good in one's own life and *oikeiōsis* as a foundation for social bonding and one's responsibilities to others is a bit murky at times, and I am aware of having contributed my own bit of mud to the waters some years ago.[19] But this much, at least, is clear. Stoics looked to facts about human nature not just in order to reject hedonism and shore up the claim that virtue is the only good, but also to support the claim that humans are a *naturally* social species and that this natural sociability generates normative claims on us with regard to our relationships with others. Just what those claims are and how they fare in the inevitable competition with other demands on us is, of course, a matter for debate and argument even within the school. It is also unclear (and in the end perhaps not very important) how consistently the language and conceptual apparatus of *oikeiōsis* were used in articulating the theory.

The main thrust of the argument is certainly that the value of those bonds for human happiness is intrinsic rather than instrumental and it is clear that invocations of nature play a key role in argument to that effect.[20] Before getting back to *De Finibus* 3 on this, it is worthwhile to remind ourselves of the way this issue was addressed in the myth of the *Protagoras*. That is because Protagoras' understanding of human nature as expressed in the myth is clearly teleological, as we have seen, and clearly obeys the MTR. At the same time, though, we are given a clear picture of a state of

---

while rejecting the relevance of non-rational animals as analogues for human values (*bestiarum vero nullum iudicium puto* at *Fin.* 2.33), which seems to be an opportunistic line of argument against Epicureanism.

[19] Inwood 1983.

[20] This may be the best place to invoke *De Officiis* 1.11–12, where Cicero brings together two of the themes at stake in *Fin.* 3: the natural basis of self-preservatory inclinations and procreative desires in all animals. Humans share those drives, and their rationality contributes improved instrumentality in pursuit of those desires by giving us access to causal analysis. Yet Cicero says in 1.12 that it is 'by the same force of reason' that nature links human to human (*hominem conciliat homini*), gives humans our distinctively strong love for our offspring, inclines us to social life and even sacrifice of our own lives for the group. This seems to be an assertion that it is only instrumental reason which marks us off from the beasts and that all of the distinctively human bonding behaviours we observe and live by are grounded in an instrumentally rational elaboration of inclinations shared among all other animals. This instrumental rationality is natural to us, since reason is our distinctive trait; but there is nothing intrinsic and distinctive about human sociality; we have the same motivations as

human society in which there are no natural bonds between people sufficient to ensure social cohesion and survival. When our relatively naked
ancestors were sent up to the earth by Epimetheus without the tools for
individual survival (no claws, no teeth, no armour, and not much mus-
cular power relative to other animals), they of course tried to ensure survival for themselves by joining together into mutual-defence groups. That
is no doubt confirmation that as individuals they had and recognized a
natural self-preservatory inclination, but they also lacked the dispositions
and inclinations for social behaviour which would make true social cohesion possible. So whenever they banded together, their societies fell apart
and the carnivores had a feast. It was only when Zeus intervened, having
Hermes install mutual respect and a sense of justice (*aidōs* and *dikē*) in
humans, that the vicious cycle was broken and the species became stable.

The moral of the story is not completely clear, but it seems to me that
sociability among humans is meant to be thought of as having instrumental value – we need it severally to avoid being eaten by the carnivores out
there. And we did not have it 'by nature', that is, given by Epimetheus as
we were being born. In fact, *aidōs* and *dikē* are clearly described as components of a craft (the *politikē technē* sent by Zeus). Yet these pro-social inclinations and skills are, in this story, actually god-given, something which
the later Stoic and Platonic tradition would regard as an indication of a
natural status. Zeus himself makes us capable of stable and reciprocally
beneficial social relations, even though the main reason for doing so is to
compensate for the failure of Epimetheus to endow us with other attributes which might protect our lives from the ravages of the wild beasts
all around us. A mixed message, then, with aspects which would appeal
to a naturalist in the Democritean/Epicurean tradition and some which
a Stoic might embrace. Our divinely given capacity for social bonding
serves an instrumental purpose.

Cato's account of Stoic ethics moves on from broad ethical theory
to specifically social issues, just as friendship forms the last phase of the
Epicurean account offered by Torquatus in Book 1. In Book 3 the transition from the discussion of suicide (3.60–61) is not particularly smooth,
though suicide itself is introduced as an example of a topic of practical
deliberation to be carried out in light of our responsibilities (*officia*) –
none of which involves duties or commitments that we have to other
people such as friends or family. If social or familial relations have any

---

animals, but reason makes us better at acting on those motivations, especially in complex or difficult situations. Note that there is no argument in favour of these claims here (nor does nature do
any shouting); these are unadorned claims, though important ones.

weight at all in such deliberations, they must be concealed under the general label of 'things which are according to nature', but they are not mentioned overtly or even alluded to here.

3.62, then, comes as a somewhat abrupt transition, rather than a natural extension of the immediately preceding previous topic.[21] We are to understand, says Cato, that it is a result of nature's doing[22] that children are loved by their parents. The fact that children are loved by parents is the starting-point (*initium*) from which we trace out[23] the shared society of the whole human race. The basis for this line of inference (that it is nature's doing that parents love their children) is then given. First, the configuration of the relevant bodily parts shows that nature applied her rationality to the issue of procreation. Fitness of form to function is taken to be proof of rational planning and it is taken to be obvious that nature is the possessor of such rationality.

This is step 1, the demonstration that nature must have *intended* that procreation occur. This being so, the MTR can now be invoked. 'And the following things cannot be mutually consistent, that nature should want there to be procreation and that she should not ensure that the offspring be loved' (*Fin.* 3.62). The MTR bans self-undermining activity on the part of a purposive agent (indeed, it bans a *self*-undermining state of affairs whenever there is a purpose, whether or not there is a real, individual agent). Observations of animal behaviour are then invoked in support of the claim that nature works this way (*vis naturae*); the effort expended on the birthing and rearing of offspring is clear evidence on the matter. And it is this point which is redescribed as the 'voice of nature' which we can hear pronouncing on the matter: *naturae ipsius vocem videmur audire*.

The voice of nature, then, is what we (metaphorically) hear when we observe non-rational animals and assess their behaviour against the background of MTR. In this way the argument here is not unlike what we saw in Hierocles and in Chrysippus. But there are significant differences. It is important to the argument that the animals observed against the

---

[21] Hence the transitional *autem* is not surprising. The backward reference of *pertinere ad rem* is not completely clear (Woolf, in fact, suppresses it completely when he translates, 'Now the Stoics consider it important to realize'). Charles Brittain points out that the likely reference is to the entire theme of the distinctions among indifferent things that has been running since 3.50, including the topic of *kathēkonta* brought in at 3.58, of which the topic of suicide in 3.61 is an example. Granted that this is the intended structure of Cato's exposition, the connections are neither transparent nor well articulated.

[22] *naturā fieri*, which does not, however, entail agency as the construction with *ab* and ablative would do.

[23] *persequor*, *Oxford Latin Dictionary* s.v. 7.

background of MTR not be themselves rational, for if they are rational the intention might be construed not as a fact of nature but as part of the instrumentalist reasoning undertaken by a rational agent. And since human parents are by stipulation at the age of reason, human parenting is not, as it were, an eligible subject of observation here. Application of the MTR to their observed behaviour could just as easily prove that human parents are sensible enough to work for their children's survival for purely instrumental reasons (we would all like to be fed and cared for in our old age). Human children, into whose cradle we are elsewhere urged to peek, are not a problem in this respect, since they are taken to be relevantly similar at birth to brute beasts.

The voice of nature cries out, then, that irrational animals naturally love and care for their offspring; but it cannot directly shout out that conclusion for humans. Hence a distinct inferential step is needed, and Cato invites us to join him in making it. The key assumption needed is that humans are relevantly similar to animals in this regard, that our parental love is *no different than* that of animals. If this were assumed, then it would be uneconomical to suppose that our species owes its capacity for parental love to any other source than animals do – so ours is natural too. But that assumption is, if not outright distasteful to sentimental human parents, manifestly question-begging.[24] Since that would be an unsatisfactory move, Cato sensibly does not pursue that line of persuasion, and instead offers up an analogy (which is, unfortunately, also of dubious value): 'Therefore, just as it is clear that we avoid pain by nature so too is it obvious that we are driven by nature[25] to love those to whom we have given birth. And *this* is the origin[26] of the fact that the shared affinity of human beings with each other is *natural*' (3.62–63).

---

[24] An anonymous reader suggests that simple economy of explanation would warrant postulating that humans take the same affective stance towards their offspring that non-rational animals take towards theirs, with the result that Cato could legitimately assume here that humans naturally love their offspring. (This would help Cato's case considerably, since he has already claimed that it is the love human parents feel for their offspring which lays the foundation for general human concern for other humans and hence for society.) But since humans of reproductive age are rational, their nature is, in important respects, different from that of non-rational animals. And since their nature is different in some respects, it would be contentious simply to assume that the ways in which it is different from animal nature do not include the kind of affective relation in question. Hence it would be question-begging simply to assume that because non-rational animals love their offspring so too must human parents.

[25] *a natura ipsa*, an expression of agency. But does it go with *apparet* or with *impelli*? I follow Martha, Woolf, and others in taking it hyperbatically with *impelli*, though the translation is my own.

[26] *Ex hoc nascitur*. One might ask what the reference of 'this' is supposed to be in Cicero's account. It seems quite clear that the neuter pronoun refers to the immediately preceding clause: *ut eos quos genuerimus amemus impelli*, the fact that we are driven to love our offspring. And that must be

If the shared affinity of humans with each other is natural, as this argument purports to show, then so-called social *oikeiōsis* is established and the rest of the argument and exposition on social and political issues can proceed smoothly. But the job now is to assess how good this argument is. In place of an explicit assertion that our reproductive and parental nature is relevantly similar to that of animals, we are given ... what? The 'therefore' at *De Finibus* 3.62 seems to be completely cosmetic (there is no ground for inference here, so unless the reader already shares the key Stoic assumptions this just guides him or her onwards in the account without providing any additional basis for rational assent). And the comparison is at best merely illustrative. Worse yet, the comparand is misguided: by nature we avoid pain. Who thinks that the avoidance of pain is a basic and natural fact about animals? Epicureans. For Stoics, it is not a basic behaviour but rather a consequence of avoiding things which threaten our survival; it is natural, but derivatively so. Pain is not avoided for its own sake but only as an indication of destructive forces to be avoided for the sake of self-preservation.[27] Perhaps Cato is just being ecumenical here, using an endoxic premise in his analogical argument. But if so, it would be a rare case of such intellectual outreach in Book 3. More likely, in my view, Cato is just offering us a desperate argument; he is flailing his philosophical arms in hopes of landing a telling blow.

All is not lost for the Stoic, of course, since there are no shadows of question-begging or shoddy argumentation falling across Cato's first argument (from the teleological analysis of reproductive body parts). And if that argument is solid, it can serve all by itself to establish its (admittedly limited) conclusion, which is that nature wants us to use those organs for their evident purpose. The shape and fitness to function of our body parts when viewed in the light of the MTR confirm that nature wants us humans to sire and bear children. And she can hardly want that if she does not want them to live. (Otherwise, why bother?) And obviously they won't live unless we take care of them. But this is where we hit the limits of what can be concluded from this argument on its own.[28] For why

right, since earlier in 3.62 Cato has claimed that parental love for children is the starting-point for the development of human society (*a quo initio profectam ... societatem*).

[27] For this suggestion, compare *De Legibus* 1.31: pain is thought to be a great evil not just because it is harsh but also because it is an indicator that our nature is being undermined (or worse: *naturae interitus videtur sequi*).

[28] This is indeed the limit of the argument that follows from the straightforward teleological interpretation of the reproductive organs through the MTR. But it does not follow from this that nature wants us to *love* our children. Cato's claim that it is natural that we humans should love them is not a supplementary or merely illustrative observation; Cato explicitly makes our *love* for

should we have to feel tenderly towards our offspring in order to take care of them? No doubt we could argue that an autonomous and internal cause of care-giving is simply more efficient than the alternative. But must it be actual affection and a sense of belonging, of the sort which when generalized will then incline us to care for other humans whose survival does not depend solely upon us? No, there is no reason why that kind of caring should be the way that nature makes sure that we feed our babies. (Why not make nursing and cuddling as intensely pleasurable as sexual intercourse, if that is all nature wants to achieve? Why do we have to *like* the source of pleasure in either case, from a narrowly teleological point of view?)

Doubts about the solidity of this starting-point (parental love for their children) are disturbing, of course. But there is, as Gábor Betegh pointed out to me, an even more disturbing weakness. If parental love for off-spring is meant to correlate with social bonds within the species (by some mechanism or other, not specified), and if animal parents of all species love their offspring, then it ought to be the case that all animal species are social. But they are not. Hence there must be some further factor beyond parental love for offspring which is required for species-level social bond-ing. And Cato says nothing about what that additional factor, common to all social species, might be. The gap in the analysis permits doubts about the naturalistic foundations of human social bonds to persist.

Perhaps one reason why Cato goes on with the arguments in his next paragraph (3.63) is just that there are real grounds to doubt the power of the arguments so far. The arguments which follow are again based on comparative analogies. His conclusion is that humans are naturally fit for social groups, and the comparisons which he uses to drive the *a fortiori* argument (note *multo coniunctius*) are from two different domains. Some body parts (such as the eyes and ears) exist for their own sake (*tamquam sibi nata*), others (such as arms and legs) also to assist those parts (*etiam ceterorum membrorum usum adiuvant*);[29] similarly, some animals (the big

our offspring rather than our natural inclination to care for them the basis for the general *societas* of the human race. Since it is the key premise linking nature's intentions to our bond with our fellow humans (and not a supplementary observation superfluous to the main point, as has sometimes been thought) it ought to be established by an argument linking it to nature in the relevant way. But it is precisely that connection which is missing in Cato's speech.

[29] Strictly speaking Cato merely notes that the arms and legs are for the sake of the other body parts, rather than singling out the cognitive parts just mentioned. But in the context, and given Cato's emphasis at *Fin.* 3.17 on the fundamental nature of the human drive for cognition, it is hard to avoid concluding that Cato believes that the arms and legs exist in part to serve the cognitive parts (eyes and ears) while those cognitive parts exist for their own sake.

and aggressive species, by and large) exist for their own sake, others for the sake of those dominant beasts.

What this suggests, however, is *not* that to some degree each human being is also for the sake of the whole of humanity – which seems to be the conclusion Cato wants to draw. (That, after all, is the kind of natural sociability which makes social virtues and collectively oriented behaviour an intrinsic rather than an instrumental value.) Sadly, what both of these comparisons suggest, if pressed closely, is that some people (the weak, no doubt) exist for the sake of others, while these others (who are socially dominant, no doubt) exist for their own sakes.

That cannot really be what Cato means to conclude from these comparisons. I suppose, and I hope that this suggestion will be taken in the spirit of exegetical charity, that instead he expects these comparisons to establish a negative claim only. He wants to deny the ultimate atomism of human life, the notion that each individual is completely independent and separate as a centre of consciousness and motivation: this is in fact how he put the point at the beginning of 3.63: 'one human being does not seem to be alien from another' (*hominem ab homine* ... **non alienum videri**). There is *some* kind of reciprocity and mutual dependence in all natural systems, whether it be the body of a single human being, a symbiotic ecological unit of fauna, or human societies. It isn't clear why he claims that human societies are even more tightly joined than these other examples; perhaps we can guess why if we suppose that the comparison of *multo coniunctius* is meant to apply only to the animal groupings, and that the others mentioned are examples of inter-species collaboration and interdependence – we might well suppose that a similar interdependence within our natural kind is even stronger. (But it is very hard to suppose that social bonds of mutual cooperation and interdependence are stronger than those among the body parts of a single animal.)

Starting with 3.64 this inflection of the voice of nature is muted. Cato continues to argue for the naturalness of social bonds within our species as a whole, but it is now on a different basis. In 3.64 we are asked to accept the Stoic claim that the cosmos is a cosmopolis – a thesis in Stoic physics, so there is a reason to conclude that *by nature* we have reason to put our social group ahead of individual interests in cases of conflict, though only on the assumption that Stoic cosmological theories[30] are true and

---

[30] As we know from elsewhere (see Vogt 2008 and Schofield 1991), the basis on which this cosmological argument is supposed to work is a recognition that rationality is shared not just among all humans, but among gods and men; indeed, that the cosmos itself is a rational being which we have reason to

pertinent to human values.[31] In 3.65–66 the naturalness of other-regarding behaviour is defended on the basis of observed human behaviour in *current* social settings. This cannot serve to establish the desired conclusion without begging the question of why it is that we behave this way. Self-serving personal calculation, rule utilitarianism, and ideologically inculcated bad faith are all competing explanations for such apparently altruistic behaviours. And hence on their own these expressions of confidence in the naturalness of other-regarding have little probative force.

Even the acute observation in 3.65 that no one would want to live alone even amidst the greatest pleasures, and the rosily optimistic claim that we are all naturally inclined to teach others, do not demonstrate that human social bonding is an end in itself rather than being generally pursued for instrumental reasons. There may be some force in the comparison with other animals (3.66): just as bulls naturally protect calves from predators, so great heroes (such as Heracles and Dionysus) naturally serve mankind – though even here question-begging may be suspected. And a counterargument comes readily to mind. It is precisely in this regard that Heracles and Dionysus are least human and most godlike (hence their deification).

More promising is the claim that our belief in the tutelary concern of the gods for men would be irrational if we did not think humans worthy of their care. And if the gods care for us, surely our own care for ourselves is natural in so far as we emulate the gods. But this is, again, an argument dependent on theological and cosmological commitments which the Stoics embrace – the voice of nature in quite a distinct register. It is hard to know just what to make of the claim in 3.66 that our natural bonding with other humans is prior to institutional expressions of that bond (even though we are unaware of those inclinations). It seems to have

include in our sphere of shared concern. If the basis for shared interests is rationality, then it is not clear that the cosmological perspective adds much; the part–whole relationship may be just as important. But the exact way the cosmological considerations are supposed to work is left unclear by Cato.

[31] This is the kind of support for the philosophical (not exclusively Stoic) claims made about naturally pro-social behaviour in *De Legibus* 1.22–32. Our basic nature is fixed first by our relationship to the divine, whose purposes our natures reflect and whose characteristics they in part share. The purpose for which the gods design humans is to be superior to the other animals, and it is we who, on our own initiative, use our reason to enhance that superiority (1.27). There is a powerful emphasis on the species-level similarity of humans with each other as the foundation of justice (1.28–32). It is from this that Cicero concludes (*sequitur igitur*) that we are made by nature to know and share justice, unjust behaviour being a deviation from our naturally intended state. This is a complicated set of arguments, only loosely connected with each other; they clearly rely at some level on MTR for their effectiveness but the emphasis here on our difference from other animals is so strong that it is difficult to see how one could use this run of argument (even if were said explicitly by Cicero to be Stoic) to shed light on the arguments in *Fin.* 3 – though they certainly argue for the same conclusions.

force only on the assumption that the social institutions of law and justice cannot be groundless, so that if we have them they must serve some purpose grounded in our nature. This line of thought would fail to persuade an Epicurean, who would agree that the institutions of law and justice are not groundless (for they promote personal safety) but has no reason to grant that they are based on facts about our intrinsic nature.

The last gasp of nature's cry comes in 3.67, where it is observed that *just as* humans have a natural bond of justice with other humans they have none with animals. This may be no more than a reassertion of Stoic anthropocentrism, but a bit of imagination may help to construct an actual argument on the point at issue. Animals care for other members of their species, at least their own offspring (though social animals go further than that), and that must be natural. Humans care for others of their own species as well. And part of the naturalness of animal behaviour is their indifference and even hostility to other species. Humans, if they cared for other animal species, would have to do so for reasons unrelated to their naturalistic similarity to the beasts. Hence our radical indifference to any species but our own permits us to retain the parallelism between humans and animals – what is natural is a closed, intra-species bond. Rabbits care for rabbits, wolves for wolves, humans for humans. The parallel could be threatened if humans cared for all (or even very many other) living things indifferently, for in that case our motivation for loving our own kind would cease to be similar to the natural motivation shared with animals (our love of bunny rabbits and kittens might be misguided sentimentality, and so too our concern for other humans might be an artefact of our culture). Along the same lines, if *homo homini lupus* (unlike real wolves, I hasten to add) then this behaviour is marked as unnatural precisely because it is unlike the norm in nature.

At this point Cato has shot his bolt. The claim that human beings have a natural and intrinsic attachment to other humans is presumed to have been successful. As he says at the beginning of 3.68, we are born to protect and preserve other humans and this claim is the basis for further analysis of social practices: this is why we should go into politics if we can and why we should marry and raise children (3.68), views about the best human way of life long held by Stoics, though also shared by other branches of the Socratic philosophical family tree. It is also why sharing of benefits and advantages is mandated[32] and this is the further motivation for the

---

[32] 3.69, *ut conservetur omnis homini erga hominem societas.*

institution of *amicitia*[33] and of law[34]– to the degree that fairness (*aequitas*) and advantage (*utilitas*) are necessarily convergent. All of these familiar social practices are grounded in the arguments and assertions about natural human bonding. Beginning in 3.62, nature has been holding forth in varied accents on this point, and its voice has a long and loud echo in the chapters which follow.

It is worth stepping back at this point to assess. What Cato is arguing in favour of (at least until 3.64) is by no means a distinctively Stoic position. Stoics and Platonists, as well as Peripatetics and Antiocheans (if they are a distinguishable group), all hold that the intrinsic value of social bonds, pro-social deference, even self-sacrificing behaviour of various sorts for the common good, are rooted in nature, rather than being explicable as instrumentally rational in the Epicurean mode. This is clearly reflected in Books 4 and 5 of the *De Finibus*. What is of particular interest in Book 3, then, is not this broadly shared commitment, but rather the particular way nature-as-an-agent is invoked to ground it. For it is nature's teleological agenda, as expressed in the MTR, which is the best candidate for being a distinctively and interestingly Stoic move in the complex dialectic about naturalism in ethics.[35] The question we might best ask at this point is the deeper and harder one. Supposing that we establish to our satisfaction that nature does make us with the relevant built-in teleological aims (self-preservation and intrinsic attachment to social bonds), why even then should *we* as individual agents be motivated to assign intrinsic value to social bonds and all that follows from those bonds? Why, in the eyes of Cato and other Stoics, should nature's will for us – no matter how loudly she shouts it out and no matter how manifest her intentions to cradle-peekers – settle the issue of how we ought to behave and feel? In short, what, in our own terms, is the normative force of naturalistic motivation of the ancient kind? That is one of the most unclear and contentious questions that arises in the study of ancient ethics, and it is also one of the central unresolved issues for the interpretation of Cicero's *De Finibus*, coming back in different forms in each of the three dialogues that make

---

[33] 3.70, note *amicitiam adhibendam esse … quia sit ex eo genere quae prosunt*.

[34] 3.71, *ius*.

[35] Book 4 is, of course, largely critical of the distinctively Stoic aspects of Cato's speech, while in Book 5 Piso develops a parallel positive account of ethical theory, also based on naturalistic starting-points. The dialectic of Book 5 is too big a topic to broach here and I hope to address it elsewhere (see Inwood 2014: ch. 3); it is worth, however, noting briefly that in broad outline it is more Peripatetic in tone and content than the critique found in Book 4, this more Aristotelian character being reflected in the emphasis on natural drives for activity and in the inclusion of plants, not just animals, in the discussion of what is according to nature.

up the work. I had hoped, when I embarked on this project, that I would find some clue to this much more important question in the second half of Book 3, but I have not done so. All that Cato gives us – and it is not a trivial thing– is a set of arguments of varying force for the claim that various pro-social values are intrinsically and non-instrumentally binding on us and the most important of these has to do with the centrality of the telelogical assumptions underlying Stoic (and also Peripatetic, Platonist, and Antiochean) views about human nature. In the end, when we listen carefully to the voice of nature we can hear, loud and clear, *what* we are supposed to believe on the issue, but not, ultimately, *why* we should ourselves believe it and act on it.

CHAPTER 7

Sententia explosa
Criticism of Stoic ethics in De Finibus 4

Anna Maria Ioppolo
Università di Roma La Sapienza

I

In Book 4 of the *De Finibus* Cicero criticizes Stoic ethics, considered to be the same as Peripatetic ethics, differing only verbally. We find a polemical attack which the Stoic Cato in Book 3 attributes to Carneades:

> Your beloved Carneades, however, with his exceptional proficiency in dialectic and his powerful eloquence, brought the matter to a real head (*rem in summum discrimen adduxit*). He would tirelessly contend that on the whole issue known as 'the problem of good and evil' there was no dispute between the Stoics and the Peripatetics other than a verbal one.[1]

That the difference between Stoic and Peripatetic ethics is nothing but a dispute about terminology is an opinion also shared in the second century BC by other schools who are rivals to the Stoa, as is shown by the ironic epithet ὀνοματομάχοι applied to the Stoics by the Peripatetic Critolaus with regard to their doctrine of εὐπάθειαι.[2]

Whether this argument was first adopted by Carneades for dialectical purposes, as some scholars would have it,[3] or by Critolaus, as others prefer,[4] and whether subsequently taken up again with renewed vigour by Antiochus of Ascalon, as indicated by Cicero, it is important to bear in mind that the same objection, albeit argued in a different way and from different assumptions, had been put forward previously in the Stoa by

I would like to thank Julia Annas for her English translation and also all those scholars who made observations and suggestions that helped me improve this paper.

[1] *Fin.* 3.41: *Carneades tuus egregia quadam exercitatione in dialecticis summaque eloquentia rem in summum discrimen adduxit, propterea quod pugnare non destitit in omni hac quaestione, quae de bonis et malis appelletur, non esse rerum Stoicis cum Peripateticis controversiam, sed nominum.* The English translation of *De Finibus* I adopt is that of Annas and Woolf 2001. Cf. also *Tusc. Disp.* 5.120, on which see Giusta 1964–1967: I: 148.

[2] See Hahm 2007: 67, who observes that Critolaus accuses the Stoics of 'semantic quibbling', and refers to Clement of Alexandria, *Stromateis*, 2.7.33.1–2 (cf. *Critolaus* fr. 24).

[3] As Görler 1994: 956, explains, Carneades referred only to the Peripatetics because the Academics of his time did not profess any doctrines.

[4] Cf. White, S. 2002: 90, Hahm 2007: 67.

Aristo of Chios, who held that 'to define (λέγειν) something as a preferred indifferent is the same as considering it a good, different practically in name alone'.[5] The fact that Cicero claims that Carneades had 'brought the matter to a real head', not that he was the author of the argument, presupposes awareness that the argument had already been used earlier.[6] Rather than accusing Zeno of making a simple play on words, Aristo's objection to Zeno's concept of φύσει προηγμένον was directed towards insisting on doctrinal consistency. On the one hand Aristo's reasoning identified a genuine difficulty intrinsic to the doctrine of preferred indifferents, on the other it rigorously applied the implications of the central thesis of Stoic ethics: he aimed, in fact, to defend the doctrine's basic principle, which was also shared by Zeno in that both originated from Socratic-Cynic ethics, which rejected corporeal and external values and acknowledged value only in moral behaviour. Hence Aristo's objection had to be given serious consideration by the Stoa, since if not demolished it risked making the entire Stoic system of ethics collapse with it. And it is precisely on this aspect – that is, the destructive potential of Aristo's argument towards the internal consistency of Stoic ethics – that Carneades had played in order to embarrass the Stoa.

Not only in Book 4 of the *De Finibus* but also in other works Cicero refers to Aristo's doctrine as a *sententia explosa*, and stresses that after Chrysippus nobody else paid it any attention. But even if it is true that Aristo's doctrine is now a *sententia explosa*, the fact that Carneades takes up its arguments to attack Stoic ethics deserves some explanation. First of all, it presupposes that the nucleus of the argument contesting the status of the preferred indifferents has not actually been *refuted*, and so, as concerns its polemical force at least, Aristo's doctrine would not be, as Cicero[7] or his source claims, a *sententia explosa*.

I personally share the widely held opinion that the criticism of Stoic ethics in Book 4 stems from Antiochus, whose spokesman Cicero is.[8] As has also been pointed out, it is difficult to establish how far Cicero

---

[5] Cf. SE *M* 11.61–67 (*SVF* 1.361).

[6] The fact that Cato, spokesman for Stoic ethics, attributes the argument to Carneades can be explained by the awkwardness felt by the Stoics in confronting Aristo's criticisms. This does not exclude, as Schofield 2012b: 238 holds, that, 'it is important for him [Cato] to emphasize that the point at issue is one only a sharp and accomplished dialectician was capable of raising. The mention of the great Carneades is precisely fit for the purpose.'

[7] Cf. *Fin.* 2.43 (*SVF* 1.364), 5.23; *Tusc. Disp.* 5.85ff.; *De Off* 1.6 (*SVF* 1.363).

[8] Cf. Madvig 1876 [1839]. Gill (2006): 169, points out that the criticism of the Stoics in *Fin.* 4 is fully consistent with Piso's perspective in *Fin.* 5.6–8.14.75. 81, which can reasonably be attributed to Antiochus. According to Dillon 1977: 62, the relationship between Cicero and Antiochus in Book 4 can be understood 'if the reader always bears in mind that the stylistic form of these works is due to Cicero's adaptation, as he says himself (*Fin.* 1.6, *Ep. ad Att.* 12.52) and so only the technical terms …

reproduces the thought of his sources faithfully rather than making use of it for his own ends.[9] In any case Cicero in Book 5 criticizes Antiochus himself, accusing him of inconsistency in upholding the thesis that virtue is sufficient for happiness and at the same time holding that bodily and external goods contribute, though to a lesser degree, to its achievement.[10] In this chapter I will not be discussing the problem of whether, and, if so, how far Cicero the author distances himself from Antiochus' positions, since establishing the use Cicero the author makes of the character 'Cicero' is irrelevant for the analysis of the philosophical argument I propose to discuss. I will highlight the way that Antiochus' criticism of Stoic ethics in Book 4 lets us establish that Chrysippus' position is nearer to that of Aristo than the verdict of *sententia explosa* implies. To do this I will attempt to reconstruct Chrysippus' argumentative strategy in the debate with Aristo, both on the basis of the report of Antiochus in Book 4 and in comparison with other independent parallel sources. I will try to show how this strategy differs from the response of the Stoics who are his direct successors. These, in emphasizing the concept of choice in the definition of the *telos* in an attempt to neutralize their opponents' criticisms, introduce an element of weakness into the theory, which further exposes Stoic ethics to these criticisms. Further, even if it is true that Aristo's doctrine is *explosa*, Stoic ethics in its post-Chrysippean developments nonetheless

can be claimed for Antiochus'. With regard to Antiochus' arguments, Hahm 2007: 97, has put forward the hypothesis that Antiochus' strategy consists in taking over Critolaus' thesis without citing the author. 'In laying out his own version of Peripatetic ethics, he [Antiochus] adopted Critolaus' creative arguments, but avoided giving him credit.' Earlier, Giusta 1964–1967: 1: 100, had upheld the much more radical opinion that the arguments used by Cicero in Book 4 to attack Stoic doctrine are taken from Peripatetic ethics and hence are free from 'any contamination with Antiochus' thought'. Giusta 1990: 29, complains about the tendency of historians to attribute to Antiochus passages in which he is not explicitly quoted, referring as an example to Mette's collection (see Mette 1986: 9–63). Donini 1982: 73, more cautiously warns against the risk of making a new myth of Antiochus (as happened to Posidonius), given that reconstructing his philosophy is rendered difficult by the shortage of textual fragments. A full account of Antiochus' philosophy can now be found in Sedley (ed.) 2012: 334–346, which reports in an Appendix the testimonia and fragments, collected by Sedley, which refer explicitly to Antiochus.

[9] Inwood 2012: 189, notes, 'But even the most explicit Ciceronian evidence for Antiochus is in need of very careful handling … More worrisome, perhaps, is the fact that Cicero is himself a very learned man, with his own views on philosophical matters, and that his aim throughout is philosophical rather than merely historical or doxographical. His own intelligence, learning and goals must have had an impact on his "reports" of Antiochean doctrine, even when we cannot be at all sure what that impact may have been.' Cf. also Görler 2012: 378: 'Aufgrund der engen Parallelität zu de *Fin*. 5 gehört dazu auch die antistoische Argumentation in *de fin* 4. Hier ist behutsame Interpretation geboten, denn Cicero hat nicht einfach übersetzt. Er hat eigene philosophische Intentionen und benutzt Antiochos fur seine eigenen Ziele.' Cf. also Görler 1974: 199–200. Algra 1997:128, attributes to Cicero some autonomy with respect to his sources, as is shown by his diverse uses of the *divisio Carneadea* according to the different contexts in which it is placed.

[10] Cf. *Fin*. 5.75–86.

fails to escape the charge of being either inconsistent or false. In the first part I will dwell on two problematic issues, the doctrine of οἰκείωσις and the definition of the final end, which, in my opinion, make it clear that the exposition of ethics in Book 3 does not correspond exactly to Chrysippus' position, but also contains further doctrinal developments from the works of Diogenes of Babylon and Antipater of Tarsus.

In the preface to Book 3 Cicero underlines the difficulty for Stoic ethics in facing and solving the problem raised by Aristo, in order to legitimize the thesis, upheld by Antiochus, of substantial identity between Stoic and Peripatetic ethics. Cato rejects this charge, declaring that it is groundless and claiming that the moral value of the good is unique and that virtue and happiness are the same:

> Unless it is maintained that what is moral is the only good, there is no way of establishing that it is virtue that brings about a happy life.[11]

Cicero then retorts that this basic principle, on which is founded the difference between Stoic and Peripatetic ethics, unites Stoic ethics with those of Pyrrho and Aristo, as shown by the use of the same impressive words (*verborum gloria*).[12] The Stoic response to this objection consists in linking the concept of virtue with that of selection:

> It is the essence of virtue that one makes choices among the things that are in accordance with nature. These philosophers make everything equal and collapse all distinctions between alternatives. Hence no selection is possible, and virtue itself is abolished.[13]

Cato then expounds the Stoic doctrine of natural familiarization (οἰκείωσις), which in his opinion constitutes the basis of Stoic ethics. As soon as it is born, a living being comes into contact with the external world and feels some sensations: it perceives its being as its own and directs its efforts to preserving it. Because the first thing which a living being perceives, and towards which it directs its primary instinct is its own constitution, the first thing to which it is familiarized consists in preserving it. It thus comes about that prior to being affected by pleasure or pain it is driven to seek what preserves it and to avoid what harms it; then

[11] *Fin.* 3.11.
[12] *Dicuntur ista, Cato, magnifice, inquam, sed videsne verborum gloriam tibi cum Pyrrhone et cum Aristone, qui omnia exaequant, esse communem?* Cf. also *Fin.* 4.60, where Cicero upholds the identity of the concepts of Stoic and Academic-Peripatetic ethics, underlining the *verborum magnificentia et gloria* of Zeno.
[13] 3.12: *cum enim virtutis hoc proprium sit, earum rerum, quae secundum naturam sint, habere delectum, qui omnia sic exaequaverunt, ut in utramque partem ita paria redderent, uti nulla selectione uterentur, hi virtutem ipsam sustulerunt.*

it avoids things that are harmful and seeks out those that are good for its health. As *logos* develops, the person goes from seeking primary natural things to virtue and to wisdom, which become dearer to him than the objects of the primary instinct by means of which it has been achieved.[14] A development then begins in which the individual succeeds in valuing something else, the good, as a far higher value. In the performance of appropriate actions, and then of selecting things according to nature and rejecting those contrary to it, there first comes about *selectio cum officio*, which is achieved when it is continuous. When the *selectio* is gradually transformed into selection which is consistent with itself and conforms to nature, then for the first time what can truly be called *good* starts to come about and to be understood.[15] The individual then reaches *homologia* when he understands that preferred things no longer play any role in the ὁμολογούμενος βίος; but the passage from *selectio cum officio* to *selectio constans* is a complete conversion, since, as Cato underlines, right action is not to be found in the primary natural things.[16] The development thus sketched is in agreement with Diogenes of Babylon's formulation of the end, εὐλογιστεῖν ἐν τῇ τῶν κατὰ φύσιν ἐκλογῇ καὶ ἀπεκλογῇ, and in particular with the second of Antipater's formulae, πᾶν κατ᾽ αὐτὸν ποιεῖν διηνεκῶς καὶ ἀπαραβάτως πρὸς τὸ τυγχάνειν τῶν προηγουμένων δὲ τὰ κατὰ φύσιν,[17] in which the adverbs διηνεκῶς and ἀπαραβάτως correspond precisely to the mode of the *selectio* Cato talks of, which must be *constans consentaneaque naturae*.

We learn in any case from Diogenes Laertius that in the work Περὶ τελῶν Chrysippus set out the doctrine of οἰκείωσις in a form not exactly corresponding with Cicero's exposition. Chrysippus does not in fact have recourse to the cradle argument to explain the doctrine, but uses a deductive argument founded on the behaviour of nature faced by its products, demonstrating by elimination that nature, unable to alienate the individual from itself and its own constitution, distances it from what harms it and familiarizes it to what is good for it.[18] The fact that a living being rejects what harms it and embraces what is proper to it is a conclusion rationally deduced from the premise that nature has so constructed it as to be familiarized to itself and to its self-preservation.

---

[14] Cf. *Fin.* 3.23 and Diogenes Laertius 7.85 (*SVF* 3.178).

[15] *Fin.* 3.20.

[16] *Ibid.* 22: *propterea quod non inest in primis naturae conciliationibus honesta actio.*

[17] Cf. Stob. *Ecl.* 2.76, 9–3 (*Diogenes of Babylon, SVF* 3.44 and *Antipater of Tarsus, SVF* 3.57).

[18] Here I follow Jacques Brunschwig's interpretation of the doctrine of οἰκείωσις (see Brunschwig 1986: 128), to which I shall return.

Although Diogenes Laertius' account contains only a few brief literal quotations from Chrysippus' work Περὶ τελῶν, it still allows us to establish that Nature operates in such a way that ὁρμή, with the addition of *logos*, is transformed and becomes an integral part of moral development.[19] It seems that for Chrysippus the behaviour of babies was not, as it was for the Peripatetics and the Epicureans, a point of departure for investigating the end, but a detail hard to elaborate consistently with the principle that pleasure, health and the other preferred indifferents do not have moral value. Rather, in the process of οἰκείωσις sketched by Cato the unchanging and continuous choice of natural things plays a central role in the individual's moral development, enough to justify the charge that Antiochus will make against Stoic ethics in Book 4, namely how the Stoics can possibly justify the claim that wisdom makes us abandon the things that nature has familiarized us to from the start.[20]

In paragraph 30 Cato, after having illustrated the principles of Stoic ethics, holds that he has shown that it is possible to uphold the thesis *solum bonum esse quod honestum sit* without falling into Aristo's indifferentism. However, to confirm this thesis it is absolutely necessary for him to reaffirm the distance separating the orthodox Stoic position from both Aristo's ethical rigorism and Peripatetic ethics. He thus introduces a classification of ends which distinguishes sharply between those who have placed the final good in the mind from those who separate the final good from virtue, thus underlining the singularity of the Stoic position with respect to that of the other philosophical schools.

> Any philosopher, of whatever kind, who locates the supreme good in the mind and in virtue, is to be preferred. It is, however, an absurd philosophical position to declare that the ultimate good is to live knowledgeably; or that all things are indifferent, and the wise person will be happy in not ranking anything above anything else to the slightest degree. Absurd too is the supposed view of the Academy that the final good and supreme duty of the wise person is to resist appearances and resolutely withhold assent to them.[21]

---

[19] Cf. Diogenes Laertius 7.86: τοῦ δὲ λόγου τοῖς λογικοῖς κατὰ τελειοτέραν προστασίαν δεδομένου τὸ κατὰ λόγον ζῆν ὀρθῶς γίνεσθαι τούτοις κατὰ φύσιν· τεχνίτης γὰρ οὗτος ἐπιγίνεται τῆς ὁρμῆς.

[20] Cf. 4.26 and following.

[21] 3.30–31: *his tamen omnibus eos antepono, cuicuimodi (cuius modi Lévy 1992: 351 n. 50) sunt, qui summum bonum in animo atque in virtute posuerunt. Sed sunt tamen perabsurdi et ii, qui cum scientia vivere ultimum bonum, et qui nullam rerum differentiam esse dixerunt, atque ita sapientem beatum fore, nihil aliud alii momento ullo anteponentem, <et qui>, ut quidam Academici constituisse dicuntur, extremum bonorum et summum munus esse sapientis obsistere visis adsensusque suos firme sustinere.*

Here, the *divisio* in unequivocal terms gives preference to those who, although mistaken, have located the final good in the mind to those who have detached the final good from virtue, even if the latter have made the worse mistake of considering virtue incomplete without attaching an addition such as pleasure, absence of pain or the natural advantages. We have here, then, a classification which derives from the Stoa, in that it takes a perspective which privileges theories of the end which have located the final good in the mind, theories whose principal inspiration plausibly goes back to Chrysippus.[22] We know in fact that Chrysippus was particularly given to studying the moral doctrines of the other philosophical schools, and had reduced the possible options about the end to three only, depending on whether they located the end in *honestas*, in pleasure or in the combination of both.[23] He naturally held that the only correct doctrine was the Stoic one which identified the end with moral virtue; however, he considered that the only real contest was between virtue and pleasure,[24] arguing indeed that, if pleasure is followed as the end, all the virtues are destroyed, including justice.[25] Although it is true that the *Carneadea divisio* was very familiar to Cicero, who may have adapted it in this case also to his own ends,[26] the fact remains that Chrysippus had already, before

---

[22] I agree with Algra 1997, according to whom the use of the *divisio* to establish the Stoic conception of the *telos'* preferability to that of all other existing theories derives from Cicero. Still, it is necessary, in my view, to bear in mind that the formulation of the problem is traced back here to Chrysippus, even if Carneades may be Cicero's nearest source here. On the fact that the *Carneadea divisio* is not an extension of the *Chrysippea divisio*, but rather a refutation of it, cf. Lévy 1980: 246, who holds that Cicero uses a *divisio* combined from both the Stoic and Carneadean ones (see Lévy 1992: 350–351).

[23] Cicero, *Lucullus*, 138: *Testatur saepe Chrysippus tres solas esse sententias quae defendi possint de finibus bonorum: circumcidit et amputat multitudinem: aut enim honestatem esse finem aut voluptatem aut utrumque; nam qui summum bonum dicant id esse, si vacemus omni molestia, eos invidiosum nomen voluptatis fugere, sed in vicinitate versari, quod facere eos etiam, qui illud idem cum honestate coniungerent, nec multo secus eos, qui ad honestatem prima naturae commoda adiungerent: ita tres relinqui sententias, quas putet probabiliter posse defendi.*

[24] *Fin.* 2.44: *ita ceterorum sententiis semotis relinquitur non mihi cum Torquato, sed virtuti cum voluptate certatio. quam quidem certationem homo et acutus et diligens, Chrysippus, non contemnit totumque discrimen summi boni in earum comparatione positum putat.* The argument rests on the fact that the end for every living being is located in the aspect in which it excels, or in the soul: *ibid.* 4.28 (*SVF* 3.20): *Chrysippus autem exponens differentias animantium ait alias earum corpore excellere, alias autem animo, non nullas valere utraque re; deinde disputat, quod cuiusque generis animantium statui deceat extremum.* Since excellence for humans lies in the mind, the final good has to consist in the soul's activity, i.e., virtue.

[25] *Lucullus* 140 (*SVF* 3.21): *Unum igitur par quod depugnet relicum est, voluptas cum honestate. De quo Chrysippo fuit, quantum ego sentio, non magna contentio. Alteram si sequare, multa ruunt et maxime communitas cum hominum genere, caritas amicitia iustitia, reliquae virtutes, quarum esse nulla potest, nisi erit gratuita. Nam quae voluptate quasi mercede aliqua ad officium impellitur, ea non est virtus, sed fallax imitatio simulatioque virtutis.*

[26] Cf. Algra 1997: 127–129; cf. also, Annas 2007a: 207. The *divisio* is explicitly attributed to Carneades and endorsed by Antiochus; cf. *Fin.* 5.6–20.

Carneades, worked out a classification of ends. On the other hand, the *Carneadea divisio* did not take into consideration those philosophers who did not set up a relationship between the primary impulse and the end, but considered them marginal, while in the classification of ends at *Fin.* 3.31 a central role is played by these so-called indifferentists. Besides, two significant elements indicate that Chrysippus is the inspiration for this classification. First, and more especially, the indifferentists are included among those who locate the end in *honestas* like the Stoics themselves, and hence are for this reason ranked above all the others; and it is well known that Chrysippus shared with Aristo the principle that the moral good is absolute. But it is also well known that he rejected Aristo's moral radicalism, and this chimes with the harsh comment expressed in the comparison with the indifferentists, namely that unlike the Stoics they understand the end *vitiose*. Secondly, the classification puts the position of the Academic sceptics among the refuted theories too, because of their suspension of judgement. The assimilation of the Academic sceptics' position to the doctrines of Erillus and Aristo is established by the outcome at which both arrive: by negating differences between things, they render life impossible. Here, then, we have a version of the *apraxia* argument, a cornerstone of the debate between Stoics and sceptical Academics at the time of Chrysippus. This is also especially significant because the indifferentists are assimilated to the Academic sceptics only here, that is, where the Stoic *telos* is claimed to be preferable to all the others, while in other Ciceronian passages the indifferentists are bracketed with Pyrrho.[27] Hence it is most plausible that the censure of the sceptical Academics derives from a Stoic like Chrysippus rather than from a sceptical Academic like Carneades! Even more so because Cato's words at the end of the discussion of the ends, 'the usual procedure is to respond at length to each of these latter positions in turn' (*his singulis copiose responderi solet*)[28] do not contradict the hypothesis that the author of the classification is Chrysippus, who devoted many arguments to refuting Aristo's doctrine.[29] Cato's conclusion, that 'what is evident (*perspicua*) requires no lengthy explication', authoritatively closes down the issue of demonstrating that the ethical theory,

---

[27] Annas 2007a:198, holds that here Cato 'rejects the Academic view, which here perhaps replaces Pyrrho, taken to be irrelevant'. In my view the appeal to the sceptical Academy's position is not equivalent to, and does not replace, the reference to Pyrrho, to whom Erillus and Aristo are often assimilated, but has more important implications, as I shall try to highlight below.

[28] 3.28: *sed quae perspicua sunt longa esse non debent.*

[29] However, this does not exclude, as Algra 2007: 127 claims, that 'even these "marginal" views are claimed by Cicero to figure prominently in contemporary ethical discussions (*his singulis copiose responderi solet*)'.

both of the indifferentists and of the sceptical Academics, cannot be sustained.[30] At this point Cato can briefly summarize why the theories of the indifferentists have been discarded, putting stress on the fact that virtue consists in the capacity to choose natural things as opposed to their contraries, since,

> if one does away with the notion of choosing between what is in accordance with nature and what is against, then that highly sought after and hallowed virtue of practical reason will be completely abolished.[31]

With this he reaffirms that the only doctrine to be followed is the Stoic one, which locates the highest good in living in agreement and harmony with nature, and explains that agreement with nature is achieved in 'living applying one's knowledge of the natural order, selecting what accords with nature and rejecting what is contrary.'[32] The definitive response to all this is therefore contained in the Stoic *telos* formula which blends together Chrysippus' and Diogenes' formulations. But this formulation, as we shall see, opens the way to the refutation in Book 4 of Stoic ethics, which is there geared to the concept of selection.[33]

So a highly relevant problem opens up. The *telos* formula of Chrysippus, transmitted by Diogenes Laertius, does not include any reference to selection of natural things, but explains that the end is living in accordance with experience of natural events. However, at *Fin.* 3.31 Cato assumes that Chrysippus' formula, completed by Diogenes' corollary, is just a different way of expressing Zeno's formula *id est convenienter congruenterque naturae vivere*. Here is an interpretation which cannot be unreservedly accepted, since it is based on equivalence not only between the two formulae of Chrysippus and Diogenes, but also between these and Zeno's original formula – equivalences which should be proved if we are to accept them. This appears evident immediately from the criticism levelled against Stoic ethics in Book 4 of the *De Finibus*.

---

[30] 3.31: *sed quae perspicua sunt longa esse non debent.* Referring to this passage Algra 2007: 129 observes, 'Cicero here clinches the issue very much in an *ex cathedra* manner.'

[31] *Fin.* 3.31: *si selectio nulla sit ab iis rebus quae contra naturam sint, earum rerum quae sint secundum naturam, <fore ut> tollatur omnis ea, quae quaeratur laudeturque, prudentia.*

[32] *Relinquitur ut summum bonum sit vivere scientiam adhibentem earum rerum, quae natura eveniant, seligentem quae secundum naturam et quae contra naturam sint reicientem, id est convenienter congruenterque naturae vivere.*

[33] Cf. 4.46: *non enim in selectione virtus ponenda erat.*

2

Cicero, spokesman for Antiochus, starts off from the *telos* formula to assert the thesis that there is substantial agreement between the doctrines of the Old Academy, the Stoa and the Peripatos. The Old Academics, Speusippus, Xenocrates and his pupil Polemo, as well as Aristotle and the Peripatetic Theophrastus, taught the same doctrine as Plato: Zeno had no reason to depart from the teaching of his master Polemo,[34] as he had nothing new to say on the doctrine of the highest good. Polemo in fact had already stated very clearly (*planissime*) that the highest good consisted of living in agreement with nature.

> His predecessors, most obviously Polemo, declared that the supreme good was to live in accordance with nature. The Stoics interpret this formula in three ways. Firstly, they say it means 'to live applying one's knowledge of the natural order'. Zeno himself, they say, held this to be the highest good; it explicates the phrase 'to live in harmony with nature'.[35]

It is well known from ancient sources that Zeno's *telos* formula was interpreted in various ways by his successors, so much so that every one put forward a different interpretation of it.[36] But even if the *telos* formulae of his successors merely had the aim of clarifying the basic idea underlying Zeno's formula, not of solving a difficulty intrinsic to it, we do not yet understand why each of them provided a different version of it. Even given that Diogenes' *telos* formula was certainly not offered as a deviation from Chrysippus', rather an extension of it,[37] it still forms an interpretation of it. Above all Chrysippus asserts that the end consists in 'living in agreement with the experience of natural events', φύσει συμβαίνοντα; is this

---

[34] 4.3 (Speusippus fr. 27 Isnardi Parente; Xenocrates fr. 153 Isnardi Parente 2nd edn; Polemo fr. 7 Gigante): *Existimo igitur, inquam, Cato, veteres illos Platonis auditores, Speusippum, Aristotelem, Xenocratem, deinde eorum Polemonem, Theophrastum, satis et copiose et eleganter habuisse constitutam disciplinam, ut non esset causa Zenoni, cum Polemonem audisset, cur et ab eo ipso et a superioribus dissideret.*

[35] 4.44 (Polemo 129 Gigante): *Cum enim superiores, e quibus planissime Polemo, secundum naturam vivere summum bonum esse dixissent, his verbis tria significari Stoici dicunt, unum eius modi, vivere adhibentem scientiam earum rerum quae natura evenirent. Hunc ipsum Zenonis aiunt esse finem declarantem illud, quod a te dictum est, convenienter naturae vivere.* Annas in Annas and Woolf (2001): 95 n. 15, rightly observes, 'there are problems in Cicero's rendering of three Stoic definitions of happiness: (1) living in harmony (or in agreement) with nature is ascribed to Zeno, but the explication here is in other sources ascribed to Chrysippus (with "experience" instead of "knowledge").' Moreover, in *Fin.* 2.34 the Stoic end is located in *consentire naturae*.

[36] Diogenes Laertius 7.89 (*SVF* 1.555, 3.4).

[37] This is the explanation provided by Long and Sedley 1987 I: 407, followed by Lévy 1992: 408–409. In my opinion, the different interpretations of Zeno's formula are in any case a sign of a difficulty. Cf. also Bett 1997: 95.

just a different way of expressing the concept of 'agreement with nature', with respect to the formula of his predecessors Zeno and Cleanthes?[38] We cannot neglect the point that the term *nature* in ancient Stoicism is not univocal, at least given the various specifications of the concept attributed by Diogenes Laertius to the heads of the Stoa who succeeded Zeno.[39] However, Zeno was the first to fail to clarify the concept sufficiently, if we trust his debate with Polemo on natural things and to the discussions of this problem between the individual representatives of the school.[40] Is the subject human nature or universal nature, or both? And is 'living in accordance with experience of natural events' equivalent to, 'selecting and rejecting things according to nature'? It is therefore imperative to establish what Chrysippus means by ἐμπειρία.[41] Again: if Chrysippus intended to take selection of natural things into consideration in his formula of the *telos*, why wouldn't he have expressed it clearly?

So if, as Antiochus claims,[42] a school's unity is measured by its agreement on the formula of the end, since 'anyone who disagrees on the highest good is in disagreement with the whole philosophical system', then the assimilation, under the formula *congruenter naturae vivere*, of all the Stoics' *telos* formulations, from Zeno to Antipater, together with that of the Old Academy and the Peripatetics, cannot fail to arouse suspicion.[43]

---

[38] The formula reported by Cicero is inexact because it also replaces the term ἐμπειρία used by Chrysippus with that of *scientia*, which is not equivalent.

[39] Cf. Diogenes Laertius 7.89 (*SVF* 1.555, 3.4).

[40] On the different meanings of nature in the formulae of the Stoic *telos*, see Ioppolo 1980: 142–170, with related bibliography.

[41] Long 1967: 64, explains that the συμβαίνοντα are not distinct from φύσις, but represent φύσις split up into particular processes, which are then natural events. Experience of such events gives a human understanding of κοινὴ φύσις. This explanation does not, however, justify equivalence between Chrysippus' formula of the end and that of Diogenes of Babylon, since understanding κοινὴ φύσις does not necessarily include, and is not exhausted by, rational choice of natural things. For a possible explanation of the meaning of ἐμπειρία in Chrysippus, see the useful testimony reported in *PHerc.* 1020 (ed. H. von Arnim (1890) *Hermes* 25: 473ff.), fr. 1 n (*SVF* 2.131) which I will discuss below.

[42] Cf. 5.14: *qui autem de summo bono dissentit de tota philosophiae ratione dissentit.* 4.14: *Nunc videamus, quaeso, de summo bono, quod continet philosophiam, quid tandem attulerit, quam ob rem ab inventoribus tamquam a parentibus dissentiret*; cf. also *Luc.* 129.

[43] It is significant that in *Fin.* 4.14–15 three different meanings of the formula *secundum naturam vivere* are presented. I will focus only on the first, as the other two meanings do not affect the problem I wish to deal with. It should suffice to point out that the second meaning refers to Archedemus' formula, though incomplete (cf. Giusta 1964–1967: I: 305–306), and that the third, *omnibus aut maximis rebus iis, quae secundum naturam sint, fruentem vivere*, is not even Stoic, and Cicero is fully aware of this (cf. again Annas in Annas and Woolf 2001: 96 n. 15). The fact that Cicero twice relies on a Stoic source (*his verbis tria significari Stoici dicunt … ut ab ipsis Stoicis scriptum videmus*) is considered unimportant by Görler 2004a: 207, because *ut ab ipsis Stoicis scriptum videmus* is a formula to which Cicero has recourse when he has no precise source. In any case, if there had been a source, this would have had to be a Stoic later than Antipater, as has been rightly pointed out by

The formula is directed to support Antiochus' thesis that the difference between the ethics of the Old Academy and that of the Stoics is merely terminological and not one of content.[44] Here emerges the intention which characterizes Antiochus' philosophical position, that of assimilating the positions of different philosophers. The objective Antiochus pursues is that of showing that the Stoics, after having included natural things in their formulation of the final end, then abandon them, considering them indifferent, when it comes to pursuing the highest good. Obviously the disagreement turns on the meaning of the term *nature*, which, as is clear, is not understood in the same sense by everyone who makes use of it.

This is immediately evident from the account of the doctrine of οἰκείωσις which Cicero depicts shortly afterwards. He reproaches the Stoa for conceiving an end for a being who is a *dimidiatus homo*, and attacks the concept of nature attaching to this. If nature has given us self-preservation as our first impulse,[45] the preservation must be with regard to the entire person. Since the highest good consists in satisfying natural impulse, and natural impulse is directed to obtaining primary natural things, the end must consist in obtaining the most and most important natural things.[46] 'This, then, is what the ancients held to be our end. It is living in accordance with nature. I put it at some length, they more concisely.'[47]

Thus Cicero asks the Stoics to explain how it is that, starting out from the same principles as the Ancients, they end by setting the highest good in living morally, *honeste vivere*, or in living in harmony and in accordance with nature (*id est enim vel e virtute vel naturae congruenter vivere*).[48]

This way of conceiving the end, Cicero objects, involves abandoning the body. This is a surprising conclusion, because it contradicts the opening thesis that there is substantial identity between the Stoic, Academic and Peripatetic positions. If the end consists in living morally, and living

von Arnim and Giusta (who however thinks of Arius Didymus as the hypothetical author of the *Vetusta Placita* of ethics) *against* Pohlenz, who thinks of Chrysippus!

[44] 3.10: *Vide, ne magis, inquam, tuum fuerit, cum re idem tibi, quod mihi, videretur, non nova te rebus nomina inponere. Ratio enim nostra consentit, pugnat oratio.*

[45] 4.25: *Sed primum positum sit nosmet ipsos commendatos esse nobis primamque ex natura hanc habere appetitionem, ut conservemus nosmet ipsos.*

[46] *Ibid.*: *Quem, si prima vera sunt, ita constitui necesse est: earum rerum, quae sint secundum naturam, quam plurima et quam maxima adipisci.*

[47] 4.26: *Hunc igitur finem illi tenuerunt, quodque ego pluribus verbis, illi brevius secundum naturam vivere, hoc iis bonorum videbatur extremum.* This is, according to Antiochus, the end shared by the Ancients and the Stoics.

[48] *Ibid.*: *quonam modo ab isdem principiis profecti efficiatis, ut honeste vivere – id est enim vel e virtute vel naturae congruenter vivere – summum bonum sit, et quonam modo aut quo loco corpus subito deserueritis omniaque ea, quae, secundum naturam cum sint, absint a nostra potestate, ipsum denique officium. Quaero igitur, quo modo hae tantae commendationes a natura profectae subito a sapientia relictae sint.*

morally, according to the Stoics, takes only the mind into consideration, Antiochus should allow that the formula *secundum naturam vivere*, on which he had based agreement between the Stoics and the *Veteres*,[49] cannot mean the same thing for both of them. Antiochus' strategy is, instead, to accuse the Stoics of contradicting themselves.

The Stoics claim that a living being's first impulse is towards what preserves its constitution, and so to things that are healthy for it, but when they wish to reach the highest good they completely abandon the natural principles from which they started, as though a human were nothing but a mind.[50] Their mistake is thus inferring the good of a living being, endowed with both mind and body, only from the mind.[51] Cicero has recourse to an example to show the gravity of their mistake: 'Construct any kind of animal you like, even one without a body as we just imagined, and it will still have mental attributes parallel to the bodily ones.'[52]

This mind would thus desire health, absence of pain, etc., because it would have mental attributes analogous to those of the body. The example is well chosen to damage the psychological monism of Chrysippus, who conceived mind and body as an inseparable unit, the mind being corporeal. He extended the parallel between mind and body right into their details,[53] using εὐτονία and ἀτονία to refer equally to the good and bad constitution of body and mind.[54] For Chrysippus the human mind is responsible for both forming the body and for all its vital functions, and what differentiates the human mind from that of all other living things is reason.[55] Λόγος is not a faculty alongside the others, but is the functioning of the mind as a whole, in which there are no irrational elements opposing one another;[56] for this reason the leading part (ἡγεμονικόν) is identified with διάνοια and with λογισμός.[57] Λόγος develops gradually

---

[49] Cf. 4.14 (above, n. 42).

[50] Antiochus attributes this position to Zeno in Cicero, *Luc.* 139: *Zeno, quasi corporis simus expertes, animum solum complectitur.*

[51] 4.25: *Sumus igitur homines. Ex animo constamus et corpore, quae sunt cuiusdam modi, nosque oportet, ut prima appetitio naturalis postulat, haec diligere constituereque ex his finem illum summi boni atque ultimi.* For an analysis of Antiochus' anthropology, cf. Lévy 1992: 420.

[52] 4.28: *Cuiuscumque enim modi constitueris, necesse est, etiamsi id sine corpore sit, ut fingimus, tamen esse in animo quaedam similia eorum quae sunt in corpore.*

[53] Cf. Cicero, *Tusc. Disp.* 4.30 (*SVF* 3.279).

[54] Cf. Galen, *de Hipp. et Plat. decr.* 5. 2. 22–24 (*SVF* 3.471).

[55] Cf. Iamblichus, *de An.* apud Stob . *Ecl.* 1.367.17 (*SVF* 2.826), Galen, *de Hipp. et Plat. decr.* 4.2. (*SVF* 3.462): τὸ ὅλον γὰρ εἶναι τὸ τῶν ἀνθρώπων ἡγεμονικὸν λογικόν. For a precise reconstruction of the soul–body relationship in ancient Stoicism, see. Long 1982: 34–37.

[56] Cf. Plutarch, *De Virt. Mor.* 7.446F (*SVF* 3.459); Chalcidius, *ad Timaeum* 220 (*SVF* 2.879).

[57] Cf. Stob. 2.65, 1 (*SVF* 3.306); Diogenes Laertius 7.110 (*SVF* 2.828); Aet. *Plac.* 4.21 (*SVF* 2.836).

in humans and in the adult individual supervenes like a craftsman of impulse.[58]

That the target of Antiochus' polemic is Chrysippus' doctrine transpires also from the reference to the classification of living beings which forms the basis of the *divisio Chrysippea* of ends.[59] Chrysippus divided living beings according to their excellence of body or mind or of both, and on the basis of this established the highest good for each of them. But in identifying the highest good with virtue exclusively he failed to take account of human nature as a whole. In fact, 'He regarded the human species as one that excels mentally, but from his definition of the supreme good you would have thought that human beings had nothing but mind, not just that they excelled in it.'[60]

And to confirm the absurdity of this position identifying the highest good with virtue and hence conceiving of a human as an exclusively mental being, Cicero puts forward the only condition which would make it possible, one which, in my opinion, deserves special attention: the condition is 'that such a mind had nothing connected with its mind that was in accordance with nature, such as health, for example'.[61]

3

Debate over preferred indifferents was the key theme of the polemic under way between Chrysippus and Aristo, a polemic which had health as its favoured target;[62] this debate tended to weaken the difference between the orthodox Stoic position and that of the indifferentists, as we shall shortly see. Furthermore, health is closely associated with self-preservation, which constitutes the object of a living being's primary impulse right from birth.[63] Cicero identifies Chrysippus' inconsistency precisely in

---

[58] Cf. Diogenes Laertius 7.86 (*SVF* 3.178).

[59] The *Chrysippea divisio* is presented more fully by Cicero at *Luc*.138. Cf. also the argument following in *Luc*.140: *Audi contra illos qui nomen honestatis a se ne intellegi quidem dicant, nisi forte quod gloriosum sit in volgus, id honestum velimus dicere: fontem omnium bonorum in corpore esse, hanc normam, hanc regulam, hanc praescriptionem esse naturae, a qua qui aberravisset, eum numquam quid in vita sequeretur habiturum.* As Algra 1997: 137 observes, from Chrysippus' point of view the opponents' argument objects 'that nature indicates that the source of all things that are good is in the body, and that whoever stays away from this norm will never have any objective to follow in life'.

[60] 4.28: *Cum autem hominem in eo genere posuisset, ut ei tribueret animi excellentiam, summum bonum id constituit, non ut excelleret animus, sed ut nihil esse praeter animum videretur.* Cf.4.33–34.

[61] 4.28: *Ut ea mens nihil haberet in se, quod esset secundum naturam, ut valetudo est.*

[62] For the importance attributed by Aristo to health, cf. Plutarch, *De Virt. Mor.* 440F (*SVF* 1.375), and Ioppolo 1980: 152–162, 212–224.

[63] Diogenes Laertius 7.85 (*SVF* 3.178): τὴν δὲ πρώτην ὁρμήν φασι τὸ ζῷον ἴσχειν ἐπὶ τὸ τηρεῖν ἑαυτό, οἰκειούσης τῆς φύσεως ἀπ' ἀρχῆς.

his inability to draw the necessary consequences from the doctrine of οἰκείωσις. If the mind is corporeal, as the Stoics claim, and conformity with nature is the criterion to start from to establish the end, it is impossible not to take account of health, which among natural things is closely linked to self-preservation.[64] The mind 'is not some strange immaterial entity, but is itself a species of body. It is not therefore satisfied with virtue alone, but also desires freedom from pain.'[65] Cicero thus accuses the Stoics of establishing natural things as the object of our primary impulse only to abandon them in specifying the end, veering off towards a monism of virtue. 'We must agree that there is a certain natural desire for things that are in accordance with nature. If so, then all such things should be formed into some kind of whole.'[66]

To rectify the Stoics' mistake and avoid the contradiction, it would be necessary to assume a different doctrine of οἰκείωσις, that is: right from birth a human seeks to preserve his best part, that is to say, the mind. This is, however, just a hypothesis which, even if accepted, would not equally resolve the contradiction into which Stoic ethics falls. In fact, if this were the case, it would be human nature alone which was capable of abandoning the human, forgetting the body, locating the highest good not in the person as a whole but in a part of it.[67]

But the Stoic doctrine of Book 3 does not locate, as the object of the living being's primary impulse, preservation of its best part, as Antiochus contends. Nor does it conclude that the end is to live according to virtue because the primary impulse is directed towards preserving its best

---

[64] The reference to health is important also in view of the psycho-physical unity of body and mind, referred to a little earlier in 4.28 and reaffirmed in 4.36. Voelke 1973: 65, observes, 'Quant' au stoïcisme, il ne connait que l'analogie de proportion. Selon cette doctrine, dire que le bien est un concept analogique, c'est dire que, par exemple, il est à l'âme ce que la santé est au corps … Le corps est pour les stoïciens une matière pourvue d'une certaine qualité et l'âme est elle-même un corps: s'élever de l'un à l'autre, c'est rester dans le même "genre de l'être".'

[65] 4.36: *cum praesertim ipse quoque animus non inane nescio quid sit – neque enim id possum intellegere – sed in quodam genere corporis, ut ne is quidem virtute una contentus sit, sed appetat vacuitatem doloris.* Gill 2006: 169, observes that here Antiochus is actively distorting Stoic ethics: 'The model ascribed to Stoicism is that in which the human personality consists of distinct parts (body and soul or mind or reason), one of which is the essential or genuinely valuable part. By contrast … reason in Stoicism is precisely *not* a distinct part, but a function or capacity which, in adult humans, has the power to inform *all* the functions of the human being as a psycho-physical unit.'

[66] 4.32: *Atqui si, ut convenire debet inter nos, est quaedam appetitio naturalis ea, quae secundum naturam sunt, appetens, eorum omnium est aliqua summa facienda.* But the *appetitio naturalis* referred to here does not coincide with Chrysippus' ὁρμή; cf. Plutarch, *de Stoic repug.* 11.1037F (*SVF* 3.175) and n. 99 below.

[67] 4.32: *Quo modo igitur evenit, ut hominis natura sola esset, quae hominem relinqueret, quae obliviscaretur corporis, quae summum bonum non in toto homine, sed in parte hominis poneret?* 33: *Tale enim visum est ultimum Stoicorum.*

part, that is, the mind. However, Cicero seems to be aware of this when he poses the question, 'but why best if there is no other part that is good?'[68] This objection contradicts the one just set out, which does presuppose that the Stoics wish to achieve the end based on what humans excel in. So the claim that if the Stoics wish to be consistent they should change their point of view on natural principles and say that every living being is from birth directed towards preserving its best part, is not so much a misunderstanding as an attempt to make the Stoic position more vulnerable.[69]

Over the years various hypotheses have been put forward by scholars (from Hirzel to Lörcher, from Pohlenz to White, to name but a few) on the relationship between Books 3 and 4. Some have wondered whether the criticism of Book 4 is actually directed at Book 3, or rather whether on the contrary Book 4 preceded Book 3, which would then contain responses to the objections.[70] Evidence in favour of the priority of Book 4, according to Hirzel, would be the unjustified charge levelled against the Stoics of failing to explain how a human gets from a state purely in conformity with nature to one that is moral, making one follow the other with a leap in kind. However, this criticism, which might appear inappropriate if referring to Book 3, could more simply be ascribed to the fact that Antiochus does not accept the justification of human ethical development proposed by the Stoics, so might be derived from a genuine misunderstanding. An important point in favour of this hypothesis is that a doctrine of οἰκείωσις according to which a human tries from birth to preserve what is best in him has not been expressed in that form in Book 3, but is a logical implication which Antiochus draws from Stoic premises – and precisely from the fact that the Stoics, having first located natural things as the object of primary impulse, then later consider them preferred indifferents with respect to achieving the end and virtue.

> They determine that natural desire – what they call ὁρμή – and appropriate action, and even virtue itself are all things that are in accordance with nature. Yet when they wish to arrive at the supreme good, they skip

---

[68] 4.34: *Quo modo autem optimum, si bonum praeterea nullum est?*

[69] Lévy 1992: 453, interprets this differently, and advances the hypothesis that, in spite of everything, Cicero leaves a kind of way out for the Stoics by suggesting that they should modify the basic principle of their ethics and state that humans do not respond to the same type of οἰκείωσις as all other living beings; on 453. n. 25 he observes that in *Fin.* 4.27–29 this possibility is refuted because it represents the 'indifferentist' reading of Stoicism (to which, however, a formal consistency is accorded). But see 4.33–35, where there is confirmation that this type of οἰκείωσις is not sustainable.

[70] Hirzel 1877–1883: 621, comments: 'Was Cicero von ihnen fordert, das hat der Stoiker des dritten Buch schon geleistet.'

over everything else and leave us with two tasks instead of one – to 'adopt' some things and 'seek' others, rather than including both of them under a single end.[71]

The Stoics, while ascribing to virtue a value which is incommensurable with respect to everything else, have attributed value to natural things, and have moreover admitted that these should be accepted if they do not produce conflict with virtue. With this they have agreed that natural things are goods in a sense, even if lesser goods in relation to virtue, warranting their opponents' criticism that their difference with Academic and Peripatetic ethics is merely terminological. Antiochus insists on the strong naturalistic assumption that the Stoics reject, namely that the highest good must be what results from everything in accordance with nature, because nature proceeds by addition without change in kind.[72] This is why he accuses Stoic ethics of inconsistency rather than falsity, as is underlined by the words which conclude the criticism directed at the Stoic concept of nature: 'Hence to live in harmony with nature will be to abandon nature.'[73] Antiochus bases himself on the assumption that goods and virtue belong on the same scale of values, distinguished not on the basis of kind but solely on the basis of difference in quantitative value.[74] It is not by chance that in the *De Natura Deorum* the Stoic Balbus declares himself surprised to find that a philosopher of Antiochus' calibre confuses difference in degree with difference of kind.[75] On the contrary, it is just for this reason,

---

[71] 4.39: *Naturalem enim appetitionem, quam vocant* ὁρμήν, *itemque officium, ipsam etiam virtutem tuentem volunt esse earum rerum quae secundum naturam sunt. Cum autem ad summum bonum volunt pervenire, transiliunt omnia et duo nobis opera pro uno relinquunt, ut alia sumamus, alia expetamus, potius quam uno fine utrumque concluderent.*

[72] As Lévy 1992: 438 rightly observes, the expressions *explere summam, facere summam* with which Cicero shows that life in accordance with nature must be the outcome of all things in accordance with nature corresponds perfectly with a vision of nature which proceeds by addition and without a change in kind like that of Cicero's in Book 3. The Stoics do not adequately consider what the course of nature is: the development by addition from the senses up to reason, as occurs in the example of the vine, in which nature would first endow the vine with senses and then reason, and would finish by transforming it into its vinegrower. Cf. 4.38–39, 41. The vine example is taken up again by Antiochus in 5.39–40, although for a different purpose (cf. Gill 2006: 169).

[73] 4.41: *Ergo id est convenienter naturae vivere, a natura discedere*; cf. also 4.39: *ut mirari satis istorum inconstantiam non possum.* An analogous argument is developed by Plutarch, *De Comm. Not.* 4.1060c–d. In Book 5 Cicero contests the accusation of inconsistency directed at Stoic ethics; he defends the Stoic thesis of the self-sufficiency of happiness, based on the premise that only the moral good is good, not because he holds that the thesis is true, but because he is displaying the logical consistency of Stoicism: 5.79: *Non quaero iam quid verumne sit; illud dico, ea quae dicat (Zeno Stoicus) praeclare inter se cohaerere;* 83: *non enim quaero quid verum, sed quid cuique dicendum sit;* cf. also 5.85.

[74] As Donini 1982: 76 points out: 'Ovviamente, l'idea di una gradazione nella vita felice e il far posto ai beni del corpo accanto alla virtù nell'ideale della vita è quanto di più ripugnante possa darsi per uno stoico.'

[75] *De Natura Deorum*, 1.16: *Egone – inquit ille – miror Antiochum, hominem in primis acutum, non vidisse interesse plurimum inter Stoicos, qui honesta a commodis non nomine, sed genere toto diiungerent,*

that they introduce a gap in the scale of value, that Antiochus reproaches the Stoics for contradicting their starting-point and hence being forced to share Aristo's rigorist position, affirming the absolute indifference of everything not virtue or vice – that is, indifference towards natural goods, with all the consequences implied by this solution.[76] The controversy thus turns on the meaning to be ascribed to nature, as is polemically pointed out by Cicero: 'If our whole nature were nothing but reason, then let the highest good lie in virtue alone.'[77]

This is the final point and at the same time the distinctive feature which, according to Antiochus, unites Chrysippus' position with that of the unorthodox Stoics, as is shown at 4.25. Here the mistaken interpretation of the end 'living according to nature' in the sense of 'living according to virtue' refers back to Chrysippus' classification of ends and his theory of the mind.

4

To demonstrate that the Stoic position is untenable, in fact, Cicero takes up again the criticism that Cato in *Fin.* Book 3.31 levelled at the position of all those who locate the end in *honeste vivere*, but do so *vitiose* – but with two important differences: (1) the Stoics themselves are encompassed in the mistake for which they rebuked the indifferentists, and (2) there is no further mention of the sceptical Academics, who are replaced by Pyrrho. Their doctrines are not all equally open to criticism, but are set on a hierarchical scale according to the gravity of the error; the objection that unites them is that they have all failed to identify a sound principle of action, since they have placed no link between natural inclination and the end which could give a content to virtue. Unlike Pyrrho, who, 'having posited virtue, leaves nothing at all to seek after', Aristo is not so

---

et Peripateticos, qui honesta commiscerent cum commodis, ut ea inter se magnitudine et quasi gradibus, non genere, different. Haec enim est non verborum parva, sed rerum permagna dissensio. Cicero also in *Luc.* 132 dissociates himself from Antiochus' viewpoint: *est enim inter eos non de terminis sed de tota possessione contentio*; Cf. *Luc.* 137, 143, and Barnes 1989: 79ff.

[76] 4.40: *At enim iam dicitis virtutem non posse constitui, si ea, quae extra virtutem sint, ad beate viven-dum pertineant. quod totum contra est. Introduci enim virtus nullo modo potest, nisi omnia, quae leget quaeque reiciet, unam referentur ad summam. Nam si +omnino nos+ neglegemus, in Ariston ea vitia incidemus et peccata obliviscemurque quae virtuti ipsi principia dederimus; sin eanon neglegemus neque tamen ad finem summi boni referemus, non multum ab Erilli levitate aberrabimus. Duarum enim vitarum nobis erunt instituta capienda. Facit enim ille duo seiuncta ultima bonorum, quae ut essent vera, coniungi debuerunt; nunc ita separantur, ut disiuncta sint, quo nihil potest esse perversius.*

[77] 4.41: *Quid ergo aliud intellegetur nisi ut ne quae pars naturae neglegatur? In qua si nihil est praeter rationem, sit in una virtute finis bonorum.*

bold as to leave nothing, but introduces impulses moving the wise person to desire something: whatever enters one's head (*quodcumque in mentem incideret*) and whatever may occur to one (*quodcumque tamquam occurreret*).[78] What moves the impulse are the *occurrentia*, but Cicero pretends not to understand what Aristo means: *ille enim occurrentia nescio quae comminiscebatur*. Cicero's failure to understand raises some suspicion, because it comes from criticism by an Academic,[79] who is not disposed to concede that it is possible to set up a criterion of action unconnected to natural inclination. However, he claims that the Stoics, though superior to Aristo, because they have set up natural things as a starting-point for appropriate action, not what is accidental, fall back into Aristo's position when they disconnect natural principles from the highest good.[80]

Since Cicero does not provide sufficient material for an in-depth study of the affinities and divergences between the Stoics and Aristo, it is useful to recall the testimony of Sextus Empiricus. At *M* 11 Sextus presents a tripartite division of the concept of the indifferent, which includes a meaning well adapted to Aristo's *occurrentia*, one which no other source reports. This is especially interesting because in the following paragraphs (64–67) Sextus relates Aristo's attack to the Stoic concept of φύσει προηγμένον – again the only source to give us information about it. The hypothesis that the two testimonies are in some way connected precisely with regard to Aristo's philosophy is quite plausible.

---

[78] 4.43: *Itaque mihi videntur omnes quidem illi errasse, qui finem bonorum esse dixerunt honeste vivere, sed alius alio magis. Pyrrho scilicet maxime, qui virtute constituta nihil omnino, quod appetendum sit, relinquat, deinde Aristo, qui nihil relinquere non est ausus, introduxit autem, quibus commotus sapiens appeteret aliquid. Quodcumque in mentem incideret, et quodcumque tamquam occurreret. Is hoc melior quam Pyrrho, quod aliquod genus appetendi dedit, deterior quam ceteri, quod penitus a natura recessit.* Madvig 1876 [1839]: 543 *ad loc.* points out that the emendation to the text from the manuscripts' *quod cuique in mentem incideret* to *quodcumque in mentem incideret* and the additional *quodcumque occurreret* are confirmed by the reading at 47 (*quodcumque in mentem veniat aut quodcumque occurrat*). I omit the discussion of the philosophical assumptions of Pyrrho's position, which Cicero does not go into, and I have already dealt with in Ioppolo 1980: 176–183, and 2012a: 197–222.

[79] Given the state of the sources, we cannot establish whether the author of the criticism of the criterion of action is Chrysippus or Carneades. Since the criticism consists in claiming that Aristo's position has little clarity, rather than in discussing it, the most likely hypothesis in my view is that the author may be Carneades, since the sources inform us that Chrysippus had discussed the content of Aristo's doctrine. However, it is significant that in Chrysippus' formula of the *telos* there is mention of τὰ φύσει συμβαίνοντα. The συμβαίνοντα might correspond to the Latin *occurrentia*. This opens up the possibility that there was a debate between Chrysippus and Aristo on the role of the συμβαίνοντα. It is not possible to discuss here this hypothesis, raised many years ago by Dyroff 1897: 120 n.1, but in my view it deserves consideration.

[80] 4.43: *hi [sc. Stoici] autem ponunt illi quidem prima naturae, sed ea seiungunt a finibus et a summa bonorum; quae cum praeponunt, ut sit aliqua rerum selectio, naturam videntur sequi; cum autem negant ea quicquam ad beatam vitam pertinere, rursus naturam reliquunt.*

The Stoics hold that the indifferent is spoken of in three ways: in one way, it is that towards which there occurs neither impulse nor repulsion – for example the fact that the number of stars or hairs on one's head is odd or even; in another way it is that towards which impulse and repulsion do occur, but not more towards one thing than another, as in the case of two drachmae indistinguishable both in markings and in brightness, when one has to select one of them; for there does occur an impulse towards selecting one of them, but not more towards one than the other. They call indifferent in the third and final way that which contributes neither to happiness nor to unhappiness.[81]

The indifferents, which the Stoic sources define as that towards which impulse and repulsion do occur, are the natural things.[82] In Sextus' testimony the second meaning of indifferent, 'that towards which impulse and repulsion do occur, but not more towards one thing than another' fits Aristo's *occurrentia* well, in that, unlike the orthodox Stoics, Aristo considers things between virtue and vice absolutely indifferent, but, unlike Pyrrho, does not deny that the wise man is affected by them.[83] For an action to be produced, representation and impulse are necessary; faced by the representation of two indistinguishable drachmae, an impulse is determined to take one of the two, but the external object is not such as to arouse interest in selecting one or the other, because the two drachmae are absolutely equivalent. This does not mean that the wise person is not affected by them in some way, as happens in the case of what is καθάπαξ ἀδιάφορον, but rather that neither of the two drachmae possesses selective value, ἐκλεκτικὴ ἀξία, that is, neither of the two has anything in itself preferred urging one to take it rather than the other. But for the Stoics also the value of natural things is incommensurable with that of good. Cato clearly asserts this when he distinguishes the 'value' of intermediate things even terminologically from valuing the good.[84] The difference

[81] Sextus Empiricus, *M* 11.59–60 (*SVF* 3.122): τὸ ἀδιάφορον δ'οἴονται λέγεσθαι τριχῶς, καθ'ἕνα μὲν τρόπον πρὸς ὃ μήτε ὁρμὴ μήτε ἀφορμὴ γίγνεται, οἷόν ἐστι τὸ περιττοὺς ἢ ἀρτίους εἶναι τοὺς ἀστέρας ἢ τὰς ἐπὶ τῇ κεφαλῇ τρίχας, καθ'ἕτερον δὲ πρὸς ὃ ὁρμὴ μὲν καὶ ἀφορμὴ γίγνεται, οὐ μᾶλλον δὲ πρὸς τόδε ἢ τόδε, οἷον ἐπὶ δυοῖν δραχμῶν ἀπαραλλάκτων τῷ τε χαρακτῆρι καὶ τῇ λαμπρότητι, ὅταν δέῃ τὴν ἑτέραν αὐτῶν αἱρεῖσθαι· ὁρμὴ μὲν γὰρ γίγνεται πρὸς τὸ ἕτερον αὐτῶν, οὐ μᾶλλον δὲ πρὸς τόδε ἢ τόδε. Cf. Stob. *Ecl.* 2.79.1 (*SVF* 3.118), *Ecl.* 2.82.5 (*SVF* 3.121), Diogenes Laertius 7.104 (*SVF* 3.119), in which the indifferents are divided into two categories, καθάπαξ ἀδιάφορα (cf. Cicero, *Acad.* 1.36, *in quibus nihil omnino esse momenti*) and ὁρμῆς καὶ ἀφορμῆς κινητικά (cf. Cicero, *Fin.* 3.50).
[82] Cf. Stob. *Ecl.* 2.82.7 (*SVF* 3.121), Diogenes Laertius 7.104 (*SVF* 3.119).
[83] Cf. Cicero, *Luc.* 130: *Pyrrho autem ea ne sentire quidem sapientem, quae apatheia nominatur.*
[84] *Fin.* 3.34: *nam cum aestimatio, quae axia dicitur, neque in bonis numerata sit nec rursus in malis, quantumcumque eo addideris, in suo genere manebit.* **Alia est igitur propria aestimatio virtutis, quae genere, non crescendo valet.** The difference between the value of the good and that of natural

between the value of the good and of virtue, and that of natural things, is one of quality, not quantity; while the ἀξία proper to the good has absolute value, that of natural things admits differences of degree. As Cato explains in *Fin.* 3.34, the value of the good *genere non crescendo valet*. This difference of value between the good and natural things is shown also in the way in which each of them moves impulse. 'What is worth choosing (αἱρετόν) differs from what is worth selecting (ληπτόν); what is worth choosing moves ὁρμή completely (τὸ ὁρμῆς αὐτοτελῶς κινητικόν).'[85] But if it is proper only to the good to move impulse completely, while natural things move it only in incomplete form, the attitude of Aristo's sage faced by the Stoic preferred indifferents can be justified by the second meaning of *indifferent* reported by Sextus.

Sextus himself informs us that Aristo attacks the Stoic φύσει προηγμένον by taking the example of health and illness.[86] They are indifferents which from the viewpoint of inclination appear to have a well-defined value such that the former is preferred to the latter; but if it is necessary for all the healthy people to serve a tyrant and hence die, while all the ill people are able to avoid this service and survive, the sage will in this circumstance prefer to be ill rather than healthy. The main point that Aristo claims is that there is no natural and necessary connection between preferred things and the fact of being selected in particular circumstances: 'because neither are the so-called preferred things to be preferred absolutely (πάντως) nor are those to be rejected necessarily (κατ' ἀνάγκην) to be rejected.'[87] But for the orthodox Stoics also there is no natural and necessary connection between natural things and

---

things is underlined very clearly also at 3.53, where the *praepositum* is defined as *quod sit indifferens cum aestimatione mediocri.*

[85] Stob. *Ecl.* 2.75.1 (*SVF* 3.131): διαφέρειν δὲ λέγουσιν αἱρετὸν καὶ ληπτόν· αἱρετὸν μὲν γὰρ εἶναι τὸ ὁρμῆς αὐτοτελοῦς κινητικόν ... ὅσῳ δὲ διαφέρει τὸν αἱρετὸν τοῦ ληπτοῦ, τοσοῦτῳ ... τὸ ἀγαθὸν τοῦ ἀξίαν ἔχοντος. I accept the proposal of Long (1977): 85, to change αὐτοτελοῦς into αὐτοτελῶς. 'The absence of the term αὐτοτελῶς from ὁρμή when this faculty is described as "movable" by "natural advantages" implies that an agent is capable of refraining from selecting these, even when he is roused by them.' Cf. Cicero, *Fin.* 3.34: *hoc autem ipsum bonum non accessione neque crescendo aut cum ceteris comparando, sed propria vi sua et sentimus et appellamus bonum.*

[86] Thus it is likely that at *M* 11.77, where we read that Aristotle set up health as the highest good, we should accept the correction of the received text *Aristotle* to *Aristo* proposed by Spinelli 2012: 281–288.

[87] Cf. Sextus Empiricus, *M* 11.65: ἴσον γάρ ἐστι τὸ προηγμένον αὐτὴν λέγειν ἀδιάφορον τῷ ἀγαθὸν ἀξιοῦν, καὶ σχεδὸν ὀνόματι μόνον διαφέρον· καθόλου γὰρ τὰ μεταξὺ ἀρετῆς καὶ κακίας ἀδιάφορα μὴ ἔχειν μηδεμίαν παραλλαγήν, μηδὲ τινὰ μὲν εἶναι φύσει προηγμένα, τινὰ δὲ ἀποπροηγμένα, ἀλλὰ παρὰ τὰς διαφόρους τῶν καιρῶν περιστάσεις μήτε τὰ λεγόμενα προῆχθαι πάντως γίνεσθαι προηγμένα, μήτε τὰ λεγόμενα ἀποπροῆχθαι κατ' ἀνάγκην ὑπάρχειν ἀποπροηγμένα.

selection, since only the good is by nature and necessity that which is
worthy of choice (αἱρετόν, *expetendum*). Seen from the viewpoint of the
mechanism of action, the question of selection implies that a preferred
indifferent, health for example, is not able to move an impulse completely, because it possesses no intrinsic value. From the moral point of
view, the fact that 'moral action is not included among our original natural attachments',[88] as Cato asserts while expounding the Stoic doctrine
of *oikeiōsis*, shows how the transition from *selectio cum officio* to *selectio
constans* can only be explained through a total conversion.

So the criticism directed at Aristo by Chrysippus in *Fin.* 4.68 reveals
that the controversy between the two philosophers centred on the practical consequences of refusing to admit the 'preferability' of natural things
rather than on a philosophical examination of doctrinal principles.

> In declaring what is moral to be the only good, you do away with con-
> cern for one's health, care of one's household, public service, the conduct of
> business and the duties of life. Ultimately morality itself, which you regard
> as everything, must be abandoned. Chrysippus took great pains to make
> these very points against Aristo.[89]

Chrysippus' response to Aristo's attack against the φύσει προηγμένον
does not involve the thesis 'the moral is the only good', but is limited to
reminding Aristo that if ἀποπροηγμένα are accepted, given that for Aristo
they can be accepted just as much as the προηγμένα, presenting no difference, he runs the risk of destroying any care for health, family, state – in
brief, life itself is destroyed and implicitly also the possibility of achieving
morality.[90] The consequences of Aristo's ethical radicalism, which abol-
ishes every difference between enjoying excellent health and being very
ill, translate into abolishing virtue itself, which no longer has either a

---

[88] *Fin.* 3.22: *propterea quod non inest in primis naturae conciliationibus honesta actio.* However, the
Stoic definition of καθῆκον as an action for which 'after it is performed a rational justification can
be given' implies that the moral value of the action is closely linked to the rational justification
which the agent can give for it. It is significant, in fact, that among the examples of κατορθώματα
provided by the Stoics no rules of conduct are ever given – that is, the content of the action is
never made determinate, and only each action's mode is simply indicated, that is, its moral aspect.
Cf. *SVF* 3.494.498.501. This explains how every κατόρθωμα is a καθῆκον, but not every καθῆκον a
κατόρθωμα. On this argument, see Ioppolo 2000: 15–36.

[89] 4.68: *Cum enim quod honestum sit, id solum bonum esse confirmatur, tollitur cura valitudinis, diligen-
tia rei familiaris, administratio rei publicae, ordo gerendorum negotiorum, officia vitae, ipsum denique
illud honestum, in quo uno vultis esse omnia, deserendum est. Quae diligentissime contra dicuntur a
Chrysippo.*

[90] Zeno's statement in 4.56 can also be understood in the same sense as Chrysippus' objection to
Aristo; Zeno holds that for the tyrant Dionysius it is better to die, whereas for Plato it is better to
live – Plato has hope of becoming wise.

starting-point or a foothold.[91] Thus it seems that the controversy between Chrysippus and Aristo hinges on the problem of justifying rational action, a frequent problem in the debates among Hellenistic schools in the third century BC. In short, Chrysippus rebukes Aristo for not knowing how to specify a criterion adequate to guide rational action.[92]

A confirmation of this hypothesis comes from Book 3. Cato objects that if Aristo's thesis were accepted,

> the whole of life would be thrown into chaos (*confunderetur omnis vita*), wisdom would have no role or function, since there would be no difference whatsoever between any of the things that pertain to the conduct of life (*cum inter res eas, quae ad vitam degendam pertinerent, nihil omnino interesset*) and so no method of selecting could properly be applied (*neque ullum dilectum adhiberi oporteret*).[93]

Chrysippus' objection is that the action of Aristo's sage, which has as its ultimate consequence the actual destruction of life, is an arbitrary and unmotivated action which cannot be rationally justified. This is an objection connected to the *apraxia* charge which Chrysippus also made against Arcesilaus.[94] Cicero offers us a confirmation of this when, in the *Lucullus*, he puts Aristo's position alongside that of Pyrrho because both of them reach the same consequences at the level of conduct, that is the impossibility of 'getting moving', Aristo holding that the sage is not moved one way or the other with respect to intermediate things and Pyrrho holding that the sage is not even affected by things.[95] Furthermore, Aristo's criterion of conduct, which describes the mechanics of action and explains its rationality, gets its full meaning if it is an attempt to rebut objections

---

[91] 2.43: *Quae quod Aristoni et Pyrrhoni omnino visa sunt pro nihilo, ut inter optime valere et gravissime aegrotare nihil prorsus dicerent interesse, recte iam pridem contra eos desitum est disputari. Dum enim in una virtute sic omnia esse voluerunt, ut eam rerum selectione exspoliarent nec ei quicquam aut unde oriretur darent, aut ubi niteretur, virtutem ipsam, quam amplexabantur, sustulerunt.*

[92] As confirmation that the controversy between Chrysippus and Aristo was based on the justification of a criterion of action, cf. Plutarch, *De Stoic. Rep.* 23.1045D-F, where he tells us that Chrysippus faced and discussed the problem of selection between two similar indifferent things, taking two drachmae as his example. Cf. Ioppolo 2012a: 197–222.

[93] 3.50: *Deinceps explicatur differentia rerum, quam si non ullam esse diceremus, confunderetur omnis vita, ut ab Aristone, neque ullum sapientiae munus aut opus inveniretur, cum inter res eas, quae ad vitam degendam pertinerent, nihil omnino interesset, neque ullum dilectum adhiberi oporteret.*

[94] This constitutes confirmation of the fact that the classification of ends in *Fin.* 3.31, where the positions of Aristo and Pyrrho are put alongside that of *quidam Academici*, depends on Chrysippus. See above, p. 172.

[95] Cicero, *Luc.* 130: *Aristonem, qui cum Zenonis fuisset auditor, re probavit ea quae ille verbis, nihil esse bonum nisi virtutem, nec malum nisi quod virtuti esset contrarium; in mediis ea momenta, quae Zeno voluit, nulla esse censuit. Huic summum bonum est in his rebus neutram in partem moveri, quae adiaphoria ab ipso dicitur.* (= SVF 1.362) *Pyrrho autem ea nec sentire quidem sapientem, quae apatheia nominatur.*

connected to the charge of inactivity. Not only is action possible for someone who locates the end in *adiaphoria*,[96] it is neither absurd nor unmotivated, because, given the absolute value of virtue, all other objects intermediate between virtue and vice have relative value, value of circumstances relevant only to expert specification from time to time. Aristo justifies the selection of an ἀποπροηγμένον like illness rather than health by basing it on a criterion going back to Socrates,[97] shared by all Stoics, which defines the *ousia* of the indifferent as that of which it is possible to make good or bad use, establishing what is distinctive of the good in the variability of good or bad use.[98] Health, like life, is not a value if what is in play is the achievement of the good and virtue; the result is that death is not the most serious evil, because life is not the highest good, just as Socrates claimed in the *Apology*.[99] For Chrysippus, too, virtue does not consist in 'selecting' and rejecting natural things, as these have no value with regard to achieving the end; it is the use of them which determines their value.[100] Chrysippus shares with Aristo this basic principle of Stoic ethics, derived from Socratic ethics. The fact that virtue requires an area of action does not mean that the material to which it applies has moral value; morality consists in the correctness of the *logos* from which is derived the capacity to use things rightly, and hence their selection. Thus Chrysippus could not level against Aristo a criticism which applied to his own doctrine.

So the point in contention in the debate between Chrysippus and Aristo is not the content of virtue, but the primary instinct of self-preservation; Chrysippus rebukes Aristo for having so neglected it as to threaten survival,

---

[96] Cf. *Fin.* 4.43–47.

[97] Cf. Xenophon, *Mem.* 4.2, 31–33, where the argument is laid out that being healthy is not always a good Cf. Plato, *Laches* 195c–d, where the doctor has knowledge of health and disease, but not whether it is better for the patient to live or die.

[98] Diogenes Laertius 7.103 (*SVF* 3.117): ὡς γὰρ ἴδιον θερμοῦ τοῦ θερμαίνειν, οὐ τὸ ψύχειν, οὕτω καὶ ἀγαθοῦ τὸ ὠφελεῖν, οὐ τὸ βλάπτειν. οὐ μᾶλλον δὲ ὠφελεῖν ἢ βλάπτειν ὁ πλοῦτος καὶ ὑγίεια· οὐκ ἄρα ἀγαθὸν οὔτε πλοῦτος οὔτε ὑγίεια· ἔτι τέ φασιν· ᾧ ἔστιν εὖ καὶ κακῶς χρῆσθαι, τοῦτο οὐκ ἔστιν ἀγαθόν· πλούτῳ καὶ ὑγιείᾳ εὖ καὶ κακῶς χρῆσθαι· οὐκ ἄρα ἀγαθὸν πλοῦτος καὶ ὑγίεια.

[99] Cf. Plato, *Apol.* 42a.

[100] Cf. Diogenes Laertius 7.102 (*SVF* 3.117). The term 'selection', ἐκλογή, does not appear in the fragments explicitly ascribed to Chrysippus, with the exception of Epict. *Diss.* 2.6.9 (*SVF* 3.191). The passage is controversial and has been discussed by many commentators and from many points of view, because of the problem whether the notion of ἐκλογή can have been used as early as Chrysippus and also the presence of the theory of ὑπεξαίρεσις. For my part I agree with von Arnim (*ad loc.*) that only the last phrase from καὶ γάρ is a literal quotation from Chrysippus. The language is typical of Epictetus; we need only peruse Schenkl's index.

as is testified by the iconic subject of the debate, health. The role of ὁρμή in the individual's moral development has to be established. For Chrysippus a living being right from birth is attracted by itself and its constitution; therefore this impulse is directed towards the things which advance its constitution and hence survival. Denying a difference with a natural basis among intermediate things means denying the impulse towards self-preservation which gets us to recognize things that preserve us and reject those that damage us. What sharply distinguishes the two philosophers' positions is the fact that for Chrysippus ὁρμή with *logos* supervening becomes an integral part of moral development,[101] while for Aristo there is no continuity, rather a break, between ὁρμή and *logos*. Aristo, in denying to ὁρμή the ability to specify a norm of conduct, raises doubt that what is natural as conforming to impulse can harmonize with *logos* and so become morally valuable.[102] He objects to Chrysippus that if conforming to nature is the moral good, 'conformity to nature' cannot be the measure of value for the intermediate objects, only the criterion of a life according to virtue. Chrysippus' response appeals to concrete facts; he argues that if the condition for acting morally is keeping oneself alive because this is part of universal reason's plan,[103] health must be preferred to illness and so should be selected, *sumenda*, even if not sought for its own sake, *expetenda*.[104] In this way affirmation of conformity to nature

---

[101] Cf. Diogenes Laertius 7. Chrysippus' definition of ὁρμή reported by Plutarch is also significant: *De Stoic. Rep.* 11.1037F (*SVF* 3.175) τοῦ ἀνθρώπου λόγος ... προστακτικὸς αὐτῷ τοῦ ποιεῖν.

[102] Another subject of dispute between Chrysippus and Aristo is the role of pleasure in human development in its capacity of attracting impulse. If it turns out to be the capacity of so setting impulse in motion as to make an indifferent preferable, Aristo objects that pleasure not only cannot be included among preferable indifferents, according to Zeno's doctrine, but is the object most able to move ὁρμή. This also explains Aristo's refusal to accept the doctrine of οἰκείωσις. On this problem see Galen, *De Hipp et Plat. Decr.* 7.2.6–8, p. 436 de Lacy (*SVF* 3.256) and Ioppolo (2012b): 43–68.

[103] Cf. Aristo in Seneca, *Ep.* 94.7: *omnia fortiter excipienda quae mundi necessitas imperat.*

[104] On these terminological distinctions, which opponents insist on considering as purely artifical terms, cf. Plutarch, *De Comm. Not.* 1070 (*SVF* 3.123), Cicero *Fin.* 4.56: *Postea tuus illePoenulus ... verba versare coepit et primum rebus iis, quas nos bonas ducimus, concessit, ut haberentur aestimabiles et ad naturam accommodatae, faterique coepit sapienti, hoc est summe beato, commodius tamen esse si ea quoque habeat, quae bona non audet appellare, naturae accomodata esse concedit;* 57: *Hic loquebatur aliter atque omnes, sentiebat idem quod ceteri. Nec vero minoris aestimanda ducebat ea quae ipse bona negaret esse, quam illi, qui ea bona esse dicebant;* 5.89: *bonum appello quicquid secundum naturam est, quod contra malum, nec ego solus, sed tu etiam, Chrysippe, in foro, domi; in schola desinis. Quid ergo? Aliter homines, aliter philosophos loqui putas oportere?* Piso finishes his final criticism of Stoic ethics in 5.92–93 opposing the Stoics' artificial terms, which Cicero himself does not tolerate: cf. *Fin.* 4.21–23 and Lörcher 1911: 126.

as the point of departure, the ἀρχή of appropriate action, and the ὕλη, the material, of ἀρετή, can be justified.[105]

5

Cicero refers briefly to Chrysippus' response to Aristo,[106] without discussing it. He does not distinguish between the position of Chrysippus and that of his Stoic successors, who in their debate with their Academic opponents identified virtue with rational selection of natural things, placing virtuous action not in the correct use of indifferent things but in their correct selection. What emerges from this account is that Chrysipppus' doctrine cannot be considered *explosa* in the same way as Aristo's, given that Chrysippus introduced a reason for preference among the things intermediate between virtue and vice.[107] Cicero continues, though, to have recourse to a dualistic conception of human nature, one appropriate to Academic and Peripatetic ethics, refusing to take Stoic psychological monism seriously and making reference to a different theory of οἰκείωσις. The heart of the criticism is that the Stoics, in describing human ethical development as though its summit were quite independent of the final end of a human being at the start of its development, have completely misunderstood nature.[108] If the primary impulse is towards self-preservation and search for the primary natural principles, then to be consistent the final end requires that healthy things to which nature has appropriated us should also be included in it, becoming valuable as good. On the contrary, all those who have located the end in *honeste vivere* alone should be rejected for 'remaining with philosophers who actually denied that their supreme goods derived from nature', as is shown by their use of the same arguments and the same opinions (*uti isdem argumentis, quibus illi uterentur, isdemque sententiis*).[109] And so if it is true that Aristo's theory is now a

---

[105] Plutarch, *De Comm. Not.* 23.1069E (*SVF* 3.491): πόθεν οὖν, φησίν, ἄρξωμαι καί τινα λάβω τοῦ καθήκοντος ἀρχὴν καὶ ὕλην τῆς ἀρετῆς ἀφεὶς τὴν φύσιν καὶ τὸ κατὰ φύσιν; Cf. also *Fin.* 3.60: *cum ab his [sc. principiis naturalibus] omnia proficiscantur officia.* The κατὰ φύσιν are ληπτά in so far as they are ὁρμῆς κινητικά; cf. Stob. *Ecl.* 2.82.20 (*SVF* 3.142).

[106] That Cicero in 4.68 is making a polemical and partial use of Chrysippus' argument is clear from its premise, as he argues as though Chrysippus did not agree with the thesis 'what is moral is the only good.'

[107] Cf. *Fin.* 4.47.   [108] Cf. White 1979: 149.

[109] 4.45 (Polem. fr. 128 Gigante): *Mihi autem aequius videbatur Zenonem cum Polemone disceptantem, a quo quae essent principia naturae acceperat, a communibus initiis progredientem videre ubi primum insisteret et unde causa controversiae nasceretur, non stantem cum iis, qui ne dicerent quidem sua summa bona esse a natura profecta, uti isdem argumentis, quibus illi uterentur, isdemque sententiis.* Cf. Annas in Annas and Woolf 2001: 104 n. 24, according to whom *qui ne dicerent quidem sua summa bona esse a natura profecta* must be identified with Pyrrho.

sentientia explosa, neither can anyone's theory be accepted who locates the end in *honeste vivere*.[110]

It is significant that before demolishing the Stoic position and definitively setting it aside as a doctrine that cannot be accepted, Cicero emphasizes that he also disapproves of this aspect of it (*minime vero illud probo*): 'It was wrong of you to have located virtue in an act of selection, since it means that the ultimate good will itself be in pursuit of some further thing.'[111] So if Chrysippus' response to Aristo's indifferentism is what has just been out-lined, Chrysippus did not make virtue consist in the *selectio* of natural things. However, the fact that Cicero includes 'selection' as if it were a supplementary argument to the criticism just put forward is confirmation that if the Stoics introduced the concept of selection, it is to respond to an objection, rather than to put forward their own doctrine of the end. Chrysippus limited him-self to challenging Aristo on the absurdity of the practical consequences that flow from refusing to admit the preferability of natural things, but leaving the formula of the *telos* indeterminate with regard to the content of action.[112] Succeeding Stoics, Diogenes of Babylon and Antipater of Tarsus, under pres-sure from Carneades' criticisms,[113] had to make precise the role of natural things in the individual's moral development, and had resort to a triparti-tion of the meaning of ἀξία.[114] The first meaning is what has value in itself, to which Cato refers in *Fin.* 3.20 as 'whatever is either itself in accordance

[110] 4.43: *Itaque mihi videntur omnes quidem illi errasse, qui finem bonorum esse dixerunt honeste vivere, sed alius alio magis ...*; 47: *ut Aristonis esset explosa sententia ... sic errare Zenonem.*

[111] 4.46.

[112] Even the polemic about using the term with which to refer to preferable things is a sign that Chrysippus focussed the controversy with Aristo on how to give rules for daily conduct: cf. Plutarch, *De Stoic. Rep.* 30.1048A (*SVF* 3.137). That there was a Stoic reaction to the arguments raised by Aristo against the φύσει προηγμένον, minimizing the importance of the term, emerges also from *Fin.* 3.52: Cicero, after having introduced the προηγμένον as a new term coined by Zeno, adds: *re enim intellecta in verborum usu faciles esse debemus.*

[113] 4.39: *Naturalem enim appetitionem, quam vocant ὁρμήν, itemque officium, ipsam etiam virtutem volunt esse earum rerum, quae secundum naturam sunt. Cum autem ad summum bonum volunt pervenire, transiliunt omnia et duo nobis opera pro uno relinquunt, ut alia sumamus, alia expeta-mus, potius quam uno fine utrumque concluderent.* As Annas (in Annas and Woolf 2001: 201–202) observes: 'The Stoics are forced to defend their theory in a way which defends their divergence from the set of six options, without falling into the camp of the non-starters ... the claim that rational development involves a radical re-evaluation of everything that we have hitherto been attracted to, while still regarding that attraction as natural.'

[114] Stob. *Ecl.* 2.83.10–84.17 (*SVF* 3.124–125) reports three meanings of ἀξία, which go back to Diogenes of Babylon and Antipater of Tarsus, who are explicitly named. As Görler 1984: 445–468 points out, this tripartition of the concept of ἀξία refers exclusively to the range of what is κατὰ φύσιν. He observes (108 n. 12) that the first meaning of ἀξία as δόσις and καθ'αὑτό is not also applicable to the moral good (disagreeing with what many scholars such as Rieth, Long and Forschner hold), since in the context of the same passage (cf. Stob. *Ecl.* 2.84,9= *SVF* 3.125) there is confirmation that these two meanings of ἀξία can only refer to προηγμένα.

with nature, or brings about something that is'.[115] The second meaning is a value which is not intrinsic to things, but which can be specified only by the expert. The third is comparative value, which Antipater calls ἐκλεκτικὴ ἀξία,[116] according to which, 'given certain things (or certain circumstances) we select some things rather than others, for example, health rather than illness', etc. This third meaning is the value characteristic of natural things, which is intrinsic to the things themselves if it has to motivate selection, that is, allow for a preference. This is a kind of value which drives towards selection or rejection, but which is not such as to contribute in any way to the good life.[117] Natural things are thus *sumenda*, ληπτά, because they make a contribution to the κατὰ φύσιν βίος, but not *expetenda*, αἱρετά, since what is worthy of choice is only the good, given that it is proper only to the good to make a contribution to the ὁμολογούμενος βίος.[118] This meaning of ἀξία, however, risks making a crack in the Stoic claim that 'value' and happiness are sharply kept apart, and as a result suggests the possibility of measuring the value of indifferents in relation to the contribution they make to achieving the end.[119]

The Stoic formulae of the τέλος from Zeno to Chrysippus contain no reference to natural things, the κατὰ φύσιν. This is not without significance, because the original formula, 'living in accordance with nature' leaves open the possibility that only the καλόν, that is, moral good, is 'according to nature', while in Diogenes' formula of the end there appears the concept of ἐκλογή, tightly linked to the κατὰ φύσιν. Chrysippus' τέλος formula, 'living in accordance with experience of natural events' is thus not precisely equivalent to that of Diogenes of Babylon, 'acting rationally in selection of natural things and rejection of their opposites', as Cicero claims.[120] Nor can this argument be considered a satisfactory

---

[115] *Fin.* 3.20: *Aestimabile esse dicunt – sic enim, ut opinor, appellemus – id quod aut ipsum secundum naturam sit aut tale quid efficiat, ut selectione dignum propterea sit, quod aliquod pondus habeat dignum aestimatione, quam illi* ἀξίαν *vocant.*

[116] Stob. *Ecl.* 2.83.10 (Antip. Tars. *SVF* 3.52): καθ' ἣν διδόντων τῶν πραγμάτων τάδε τινὰ μᾶλλον ἀντὶ τῶνδε αἱρούμεθα.

[117] Stob. *Ecl.* 2.79.1 (*SVF* 3.118); Cicero, *Fin.* 3.50 (*SVF* 3.129): *cum inter res eas, quae ad vitam degendam pertinerent, nihil omnino interesset, neque ullum dilectum adhiberi oporteret.*

[118] Diog. Laert. 7.105 (*SVF* 3.126): ἀξίαν δὲ τὴν μὲν λέγουσιν σύμβλησιν πρὸς τὸν ὁμολογούμενον βίον, ἥτις ἐστὶ περὶ πᾶν ἀγαθόν.

[119] At *Fin.* 5.90 Piso defends Peripatetic ethics from the charge of inconsistency, referring to the Stoic definition of *praeposita, ut satis magno aestimanda sit* (cf. also Stob. *Ecl.* 2.84.14–18, *SVF* 3.133, 128, who distinguishes preferable things on the basis of quantity of ἀξία: τῶν δ'ἀξίαν ἐχόντων τὰ μὲν ἔχειν πολλὴν ἀξίαν, τὰ δὲ βραχεῖα): Piso shows how, if attention is paid to the substance and not the words, Stoic and Peripatetic ethics do not differ.

[120] Diogenes Laertius 7.88 (Diog. Babyl. fr. 45 *SVF* 3): ὁ μὲν οὖν Διογένης τέλος φησὶ ῥητῶς τὸ εὐλογιστεῖν ἐν τῇ τῶν κατὰ φύσιν ἐκλογῇ. Cf. *Fin.* 3.31 and 2.34, in which the same formula is repeated.

justification: if Diogenes' formula of the end did not constitute an explanation of *homologia* with nature, his having introduced selection of natural things into the formula of the end would represent a deviation from orthodox doctrine.[121] The modification of Chrysippus' τέλος formula on the part of Diogenes undoubtedly brings to our attention selection and rejection of natural things which acquire an intrinsic value if selection is to make sense.[122] We need to take into account the internal dialectic among the philosophical schools, and their need to elaborate new arguments to tackle objections, as is illustrated by the Academic criticism of Stoic ethics in Book 4.[123]

That the meaning of Chrysippus' formula of the end does not imply selection and rejection of natural things is also suggested by Chrysippus' definition of philosophy reported in *PHerc.* 1020:

> In the first place, philosophy is both the exercise of the correctness of reason and science, or a particular kind of investigation concerning logos, sufficient if, being within the parts of reason and their ordering, we are going to use it with experience, ἐμπείρως. By reason I mean that which belongs by nature to all rational beings.[124]

The ability to make use of reason flows from the fact that one is part of this reason and of its σύνταξις. This corresponds to Chrysippus' explanation of the end reported by Diogenes Laertius, κατ᾽ ἐμπειρίαν τῶν φύσει

---

[121] Cf. Barney 2003: 306.

[122] The formula is an attempted response to Carneades' arguments. Cf. Cicero, *Luc.* 131: *Introducebat etiam Carneades, non quo probaret, sed ut opponeret Stoicis, summum bonum esse frui rebus eis, quas primas natura conciliavisset*; Cf. also *Fin.* 2.42, 5.20.

[123] I agree with Barney 2003: 317, that the Stoics do not give us, 'a reasonably good picture of how Stoic deliberation should proceed ... either every action is a "selection" or it is not; either the Sage selects the indifferents for himself or he does so in some more agent-neutral way.' She identifies two strategies used by the Stoics, one which places happiness not in the possession of external goods but in the correct exercise of reason, the other which takes there to be continuity between 'natural' conduct and virtuous activity. She holds that despite Chrysippus' reference to the indifferents as the ὕλη of virtue, he has still not clarified the relation between use and selection of indifferents. In my view, if the present analysis of *De Finibus* is plausible, there is enough material for the hypothesis that it was only after Chrysippus that the Stoics identified virtuous activity with rational selection of indifferents.

[124] *PHerc.* 1020 col. 1n Arnim =*SVF* 2.131, p. 41 (ed. G. Ranocchia, http://www.pherc.eu/Appendix .pdf modified at lines 16–17): πρῶτον μὲν γάρ ἐστιν ἡ φιλοσοφία, εἴτε ἐπιτήδευσις λόγου ὀρ[θό]τητος ε[ἴ]τ᾽ἐπιστήμη, ἢ[τις] ἴδια περὶ λόγον π[ρ]αγ[μ]ατεία ἱκα[νὴ εἰ, ἐντὸς ὄντες τῶν το[ῦ λόγου μορίων καὶ τῆς συν[τ]άξε[ως αὐ]τῶν, χρησόμεθα ἐμπ[ε]ίρως αὐτῷ· λόγον δὲ λέγω τὸν κα[τὰ] φ[ύσ]ιν π[ᾶσ]ι τ[οῖς λογικοῖς ὑπάρχοντα. Ranocchia's text supersedes Arnim's because he deciphers the papyrus with technical aids unavailable in Arnim's day. At lines 16–17 Arnim's reading is incompatible with the traces of the papyrus, but Ranocchia's restoration ἡ [ἐν] ἰδία περὶ λόγον π[ρ]αγ[μ]ατεία is problematic as well, since the text remains extremely uncertain. The alternative reading ἢ [τις] ἴδια περὶ λόγον π[ρ]αγ[μ]ατεία ἱκα[νὴ εἰ, suggested to me by David Sedley, seems to me more convincing.

συμβαινόντων ζῆν, which identifies human nature with that of the universe;[125] living according to nature means understanding human rationality and that of the universe, and the place that humans occupy in it. Individual *logos* therefore reflects the structure and organization of universal nature, to whose law it conforms in understanding it. A person who knows this law knows what advantages it gives to them and to the system of the whole. But if this is so, Chrysippus has, with his formula of the end, left the content of moral action undetermined, since he locates virtuous action in correct use of intermediate things and in their selection. This requires that health, wealth, etc. have no value independent of their use, while selection requires bestowing on them their own intrinsic value. It is Cicero in Book 3 who equates the formulae of Zeno, Chrysippus, Diogenes and Antipater, leading us to believe that they have the same meaning.[126] Chrysippus' Stoic successors, in fact, under pressure from Carneades,[127] introduced natural things into the formula of the end, making room for the possibility that living in conformity with nature might be equivalent to including the primary natural things in the highest good also. In this way they rendered plausible Antiochus' claim that the difference between Stoic ethics and Academic and Peripatetic ethics is a merely verbal one. However, at the beginning of Book 3 Cato states that what is distinctive of Stoic virtue is exercising selection among natural things, excluding their all being on the same level, *unlike Aristo*.[128] It is no chance

---

[125] Cf. Diogenes Laertius 7.88 (*SVF* 3.4): μέρη γάρ εἰσιν αἱ ἡμέτεραι φύσεις τῆς τοῦ ὅλου. Diog. Laert. 7.98 (SVF 3.4): φύσιν δὲ Χρύσιππος μὲν ἐξακούει, ᾗ ἀκολούθως δεῖ ζῆν τήν τε κοινὴν καὶ ἰδίως τὴν ἀνθρωπίνην. White 1979: 176, believes that Chrysippus' thesis, according to which following human nature and that of the universe as a whole is the same thing, provoked, among other consequences, Antiochus' misunderstanding of Stoic ethics, as is shown by his doctrine of οἰκείωσις in Book 5 of the *De Finibus*. This is a misunderstanding which has continued among some commentators up to the present day (principally Pohlenz): 'It then became easy to think of Stoicism as a doctrine that emphasized reason simply because it was the distinguishing feature of mankind and to lose sight of the fact that the original importance of reason for the Stoics lay in the fact that, as they thought, it is by means of reason that we apprehend order in ourselves and in the universe.'

[126] With regard to the hypothesis that the Stoic ethical doctrine illustrated in *Fin.* 3.6–22 represents the Stoic position in the second century BC, see Hahm 2007: 64 n. 29.

[127] Plutarch, *De Comm. Not.* 27.1072F (Antip. Tars. *SVF* 3.59) emphasizes that Carneades expressed harsh criticisms of Antipater's doctrine of the *telos*: ἐκεῖνον [sc. Ἀντίπατρον] γὰρ ὑπὸ Καρνεάδου πιεζόμενον εἰς ταῦτα καταδύεσθαι τὰς εὑρησιλογίας. On the substantial identity between the *telos* formulae of Diogenes of Babylon and Antipater cf. Stob. *Ecl.* 2.76.9–13 (Diog. Babyl. SVF 3.44 and Antip. Tars. *SVF* 3.57): Διογένης δὲ εὐλογιστεῖν ἐν τῇ τῶν κατὰ φύσιν ἐκλογῇ καὶ ἀπεκλογῇ ... Ἀντίπατρος ζῆν ἐκλεγομένους μὲν τὰ κατὰ φύσιν, ἀπεκεγλομένους δὲ τὰ παρὰ φύσιν.

[128] 3.12: *cum enim virtutis hoc proprium sit, earum rerum quae secundum naturam sint, habere delectum, qui omnia sic exaequaverunt, ut in utrumque partem ita paria redderent uti nulla selectione uterentur, hi virtutem ipsam sustulerunt.*

happening that the formula of the end attributed to Diogenes of Babylon, εὐλογιστεῖν ἐν τῇ τῶν κατὰ φύσιν ἐκλογῇ καὶ ἀπεκλογῇ, and – in agreement with all the Stoics up to Antipater – Cicero's *vivere scientiam adhibentem earum rerum quae natura eveniant, seligentem quae secundum naturam et quae contra naturam sint reicientem, id est convenienter congruenterque naturae vivere*, is exactly the opposite of Aristo's τὸ ἀδιαφόρως ἔχοντα ζῆν πρὸς τὰ μεταξὺ ἀρετῆς καὶ κακίας.[129] To avoid the dilemma set by Antiochus – either the highest good is absolute indifference, or primary natural things must be included in the end – they introduced the concept of selection into their formula of the end, which according to Antiochus is actually embracing the position of the *Veteres*. With this they avoided having the verdict of *sententia explosa*, which had been levelled against Aristo's indifferentism, turned against their own doctrine by Antiochus, but they were unable to evade the objection that the Stoic doctrine of the end is not consistent with its starting-point.

---

[129] Diog. Laert. 7.160 (*SVF* 1.351): τέλος ἔφησεν εἶναι τὸ ἀδιαφόρως ἔχοντα ζῆν πρὸς τὰ μεταξὺ ἀρετῆς καὶ κακίας, μηδὲ ἡντινοῦν ἐν αὐτοῖς παραλλαγὴν ἀπολείποντα, ἀλλ᾽ ἐπίσης ἐπὶ πάντων ἔχοντα· εἶναι γὰρ ὅμοιον τὸν σοφὸν τῷ ἀγαθῷ ὑποκριτῇ ὅς ἄν τε Θερσίτου ἄν τε Ἀγαμέμνονος πρόσωπον ἀναλάβῃ ἑκάτερον ὑποκρίνεται προσηκόντως.

CHAPTER 8

Structure, standards and Stoic moral progress in De Finibus 4

Thomas Bénatouïl

Université de Lille, CNRS, UMR 8163–STL – Savoirs Textes Langage

In this chapter, I would like to salvage Book 4 of *De Finibus* from its long-established reputation as badly written and failing to refute Stoicism. I suggest we read this book on its own terms, by taking stock of its avowed aims and structure, instead of aligning it with Piso's Antiochean discourse in Book 5, as most commentators have done. I will in particular insist on the methodological organisation of Book 4, by which I mean that arguments are grouped according to their type or style (rhetorical or dialectical) and not according to the topic or problem they address. This will allow me to account for many of Book 4's puzzling features in terms of its method of refutation, instead of blaming them on Cicero's carelessness as a writer. This will also lead me to uncover different, albeit not inconsistent, lines of arguments about the Stoic theory of moral progress, some explicit and uncompromisingly critical, others implicit and anticipating the end of Book 5 (where Stoicism is defended against Antiochus) and even Cicero's later attempts, in the *Tusculans*, at blending Stoicism and Platonism.

Some obvious problems and established solutions

The first problem one encounters when reading Book 4 is that it contains a lot of repetitions. On the face of it, the main objections against Stoicism are not numerous and are stated again and again. They are roughly the following:

I received very helpful comments from the participants of the Budapest Symposium in July 2010 and from the audience of the Séminaire de philosophie hellénistique et romaine in Paris in June 2011. I am especially grateful to Carlos Lévy, who read the very first version of this paper and to whom I owe more than I can say, to Margaret Graver who thoroughly discussed it with me twice, in Budapest and in Nancy, and to Brad Inwood who sent me useful remarks on the penultimate version.

- Stoicism borrowed the doctrine of the Ancient Academy, modified it with no good reasons, and disguised it under a new vocabulary (3, 19–23, 56–61, 78).[1]
- Stoicism is incoherent in basing ethics on our first natural instincts while reducing the *telos* to virtue, which is only one good among all those constituting human happiness (25–39, 47–48, 70–73, 78).
- If everything between virtue and vice is neither good nor bad, ethics cannot guide our actions (40–43, 46, 68–69).
- Equality of vices is an absurd doctrine (21, 64–66, 74–77).

When, around the middle of the book, Cicero says 'let us now consider what remains' (44: *nunc reliqua videamus*), we expect new arguments but all the objections until the end have more or less already been stated, except for the criticism of Stoic syllogisms (48–55).

A second problem appears if one reads Book 4 in connection with Book 3, as one should since they are parts of the same dialogue. The first three objections I just listed are already clearly stated at 3.10–14: either Stoicism is in fact the same as Peripatetic ethics with a different and useless language or it boils down to Aristo's doctrine that everything is indifferent except virtue and vice, and cannot guide our life. Cato's presentation of Stoic ethics aims in no small measure at answering this objection,[2] but his precise answers (3.12, 21–23, 30–31, 41–43, 50) do not seem to be taken into account in Book 4, as perhaps suggested by his reaction to Cicero's opening remarks (2).[3] Furthermore, the Stoic doctrines mentioned in Book 4 represent only a fraction of those presented in Book 3: identity between what is good (*bonum*) and what is moral (*honestum*) and rejection of bodily and external goods (3.27–39), definition of 'things prefered' (*ta proegmena*) and their relations with what is good (3.45–48), equality of vices (3.48 and 69) and some Stoic paradoxes (3.75).

---

[1] I just use paragraph numbers between parenthesis to refer to passages in Book 4. When I add a book number, the reference is to another book in *De Finibus*.

[2] As noted by Annas 2007a: 197.

[3] 2: *Cur igitur easdem res, inquam, Peripateticis dicentibus verbum nullum est, quod non intellegatur? Easdemne res? inquit, an parum disserui non verbis Stoicos a Peripateticis, sed universa re et tota sententia dissidere? Atqui, inquam, Cato, si istud obtinueris, traducas me ad te totum licebit. Putabam equidem satis, inquit, me dixisse.* See also the last lines of Book 4, at 80, where Cato says that next time they meet to discuss, he will only ask *ut audias me quae a te dicta sunt refellentem.* Cato then repeats what he already said at least twice (3.10 and 40–43) about Stoicism disagreeing entirely with the doctrines of the Ancient Academy. This could be a sign that the matter is far from being settled, in Cicero's mind, and the character Cicero's answer (*scrupulum, inquam, abeunti; sed videbimus*) could be taken as a proleptic allusion to the end of Book 5, to which I will come back at the end of this chapter.

The discrepancy between Books 3 and 4 was already emphasised by Hirzel (1877–1883: II: 620), followed by other *Quellenforscher* like Lörcher (1911: 120–121) and Thiaucourt (1885: 91–102).[4] They give several arguments to show that Cicero's refutation either fails to address Cato's presentation or is already answered by it. Their solution to this discrepancy is that the Greek source of Book 3 is a late, albeit quite orthodox, Stoic treatise answering Carneades' objections to Stoicism (3.41),[5] whereas the source of Book 4 is a treatise from Antiochus of Ascalon attacking an earlier, Chrysippean, version of Stoic ethics.[6] Cicero's references in Book 4 to Cato's presentation would thus be rhetorical tricks.[7] Books 4 and 5 and perhaps also Book 2 would come from the same source, presumably Antiochus' *On Ends*.

There are many objections to be made against this interpretation, even on its own terms.[8] The most important is probably the discrepancy between Book 2 and Book 4 (to which I will come back presently): given that Cicero mentions recent Epicureans (1.15), just as Cato mentions Stoics posterior to Chrysippus in Book 3, and supposing that Cicero copied Books 2 and 4 in Antiochus' *On Ends*, why wouldn't he make Book 4 answer Book 3 just as he made Book 2 answer Book 1?

The *Quellenforschung* interpretation may however seem completely discredited, since the assumptions about Cicero's philosophical writing on which it rests have been refuted for a long time.[9] Be that as it may, its main conclusions still stand on other grounds as far as *De Finibus* 4 is concerned. Scholars have transferred the discrepancy between Books 3 and 4 at the philosophical level: most of them claim that Book 4 does not really refute Stoicism, because it wrongly attributes to it the same doctrine

---

[4] See also the references to other concurring *Quellenforscher* (like Philippson and Pohlenz) about Book 4 given by Giusta 1964–1967: I: 316. For another example of such discrepancies between the presentation of a Stoic doctrine and its refutation by Cicero (as a character), see Schofield 1986: 62–63.

[5] Hirzel 1877–1883: II: 592 offered Hecato as a probable source.

[6] Madvig 1839, LXII–LXIV, already stated that Antiochus is the source of Book 4.

[7] See for example 4.24, 29, 48, 73 with Hirzel 1877–1883: II: 620 or Thiaucourt 1885: 97.

[8] Antiochus is in fact not named once in Books 3 and 4, and Hirzel 1877–1883: II: 628 and Lörcher 1911: 120 make their case by using so-called 'signs' refering to Book 5 (where Antiochus is named at 8, 14, 16 and 81), such as the mention of Piso's arguments against the Stoics at 4.73 or the similarity between Cicero's general objection againt Stoicism in 4.2 and 14 (or 44) and the criticism of Stoicism found at 5.22. Another well-known similarity is the use of the *cultura vitium* analogy at 4.37–39 and 5.38–40. However, Book 4's main argument about the Stoics and the Peripatetics agreeing *de re* and disagreeing only *de nomine* is attributed to Carneades by Cato at 3.41. See also *Leg.* 1.53 and *Tusc.* 5.120 with Lévy 1984: 124 and 1992: 391–394, who, following Giusta 1964–1967: I: 82 and 223–224, rightly insists that the attack against Stoicism as a stolen doctrine was not invented by Antiochus. There is thus much room for doubt about the source of Book 4.

[9] See Boyancé 1936, Striker 1995, Mansfeld 1999: 13–16.

of human first impulses and ensuing development as Antiochus', namely the alleged account of *oikeiōsis* offered by the Ancient Academy. But the evidence these scholars offer as proof of the difference between Stoic and Antiochean *oikeiōsis* comes mainly from Book 3:[10] it is the much studied testimony about the Stoic conception of moral development from first impulses to virtue, at *Fin.* 3.16–22. This reading of Book 4 is clearly reminiscent of Thiaucourt's argument about Book 3 anticipating Book 4's objections.

Another recent line of interpretation, inaugurated to my knowledge by Carlos Lévy, has emphasised how Cicero's arguments against Stoic (and Epicurean) ethics are largely based upon Carneades' classification of ethical doctrines (*Carneadea divisio*) used by Antiochus (5.16–20), which illuminate the general strategy of Book 4 (and Book 2).[11] I do not intend to challenge this interpretation, but I shall set it aside, because I think it leads us again, albeit on far better grounds, to align Book 4 with Book 5 and overlook many other important features of Book 4, which I shall try to read on its own terms. The central role of the *Carneadea divisio* in Book 4 is borne out by its conclusion: 'your Stoic school seems weighed down above all by one particular flaw (*uno vitio maxime*), namely that of believing that they can uphold two opposing views' (4.78, tr. R. Woolf). The following dilemma is the same as the one which will be deduced from Carneades' division in Book 5. Still, if I may use about Book 4 an argument made in Book 4, we should not reduce the many objections it offers to the *vitium maximum*: there are other *vitia* if there is a greatest one. What are they and how are they organised? Can they account for Book 4's apparent shortcomings?

Book 4's explicit strategy and structure

Books 2 and 4 compared

At least one of these shortcomings appears also in Book 2. Just as Cato's speech is an answer to objections which are put forward again by Cicero in Book 4, Torquatus' speech is an answer to objections made by Cicero at 1.15–26 and further developed in Book 2. So this must be a conscious

---

[10] See Goldschmidt 1953: 131–132, White 1979: 164–165, Striker 1996: 269 and 288, Annas and Woolf 2001: 99–100 (nn. 20–21 of R. Woolf's translation), Gill 2006: 167–173.

[11] See Lévy 1984 and 1992: 387–418. A similar interpretation of Book 4 is also suggested in Striker 1996: 197 (first published as Striker 1993) and has been recently re-elaborated and strengthened from a different perspective by Annas 2007a: 199–204.

choice on the part of the author, Cicero: the openings of the dialogues in Books 1 and 3 are proleptic, they announce Books 2 and 4 respectively, so much so that Torquatus' and Cato's speeches are sandwiched between objections from Cicero.

This is probably intended to avoid writing an ethical encyclopedia or a treatise masquerading as a dialogue. Due to their complexity, his rhetorical preferences and the Academic method of *disputatio in utramque partem*,[12] Cicero chose to present the Hellenistic ethical doctrines in long speeches and refute them afterwards with another long speech. Still, in order to dramatise each presentation and connect it tightly to its refutation, he cast and even partly structured each presentation as a defence. This is very clear with Book 3, as already said. But why not write the refutation in Book 4 as a precise answer to Cato's defence? This is indeed more or less what happens in Book 2.

We find some repetitions in Book 2 about the problem raised by the definition of pleasure, but they are not as striking as in Book 4. Book 2 follows Book 1's overall structure, so much so that all the main themes in Book 1 (pleasure, virtue, friendship) are reviewed and criticised in Book 2. There is no similar parallelism or dialogue between Books 3 and 4. As a matter of fact, Book 2 is itself largely a dialogue, because Cicero (the character) refuses at first to make a long speech like a teacher (*schola*), and claims to refute Epicureanism in the Socratic manner, also typical of Arcesilaus (2.1–3). So he first asks questions to Torquatus (2.6–17). When asked by Torquatus to adopt *perpetua oratio* (2.17), he stops asking questions but his speech remains quite dialectical: he quotes Epicurus often, refers back to what Torquatus said and follows more or less the order of his speech. Cicero sometimes even plays the Epicurean part in the dialogue and makes objection to himself, guessing what Epicurus or Torquatus would answer to his objections (see 2.70, 75, 87, 90, 93).[13]

There are similar attempts by Cicero to allow the Stoics to answer his objections (19, 29, 62–63, 77), and I shall examine some of them presently, but they are not as conspicuous or systematic. Clearly, Book 4 does not adopt the Socratic or dialectical method of refutation used in Book 2. Why? The answer is given in the preface to the second dialogue, where

---

[12] See Schofield 2008: 64–70.
[13] This is reminiscent of Socrates' discussion with Callicles in the *Gorgias*, after the latter stops answering the former's questions. There are several echoes of the *Gorgias* in the *De Finibus*, the most obvious one being that both works consist of three 'successive' dialogues between the same person (Socrates/Cicero) and three different interlocutors with different and at first sight increasingly stronger positions about the best life.

Cicero draws Brutus' attention to the fact that the Stoics are a different type of adversaries (3.2–3):

> We were forceful enough in our debate with Torquatus. But a still fiercer struggle with the Stoics is at hand. The topic of pleasure militates against really sharp or profound discussion. Those who defend pleasure are not well versed in argument, and those opposing it are confronting a case that is not hard to refute. Even Epicurus himself said that pleasure is not a matter for argument, since the criterion for judging pleasure is located in the senses … So the debate we held on either side (*in utramque partem disputatio*) was a simple one. There was nothing involved or abstruse in Torquatus' exposition, and my own speech, so I believe, was perfectly lucid. The Stoics, on the other hand, as you well know, have a way of arguing which is more subtle and thorny (*subtile vel spinosum potius*), even for the Greek reader, and thus far more so for us Romans who have to find a new vocabulary and invent new terms to match new concepts.
>
> (Tr. R. Woolf, slightly modified)

Torquatus and Epicurus were not refuted dialectically out of respect for their arguments but in order to teach them a lesson in a method they did not know and that their topic of choice, pleasure, does not really require. The debate was thus easy to follow, with two parallel discourses made of matching arguments and objections.[14] The same strategy will not work with the Stoics, because they are fierce and meticulous dialecticians.[15] Cicero opposes Torquatus' style or method to the Stoics' and thus implies and warns Brutus that his discourse against them will not be *perlucida*, unlike his refutation of Epicurus. We have here a first justification for the sometimes tedious progression of Book 4 and for its lack of correspondence with Book 3:[16] it is not a sign that Stoicism is mistreated by Cicero but, on the contrary, a necessary consequence of the dialectical rigour of this school, which will not be defeated by small and patronising Socratic objections leading the naive interlocutor to see for himself his blatant

---

[14] See Inwood 1990 about the strategy and standards of Book 2.

[15] *Spinosum* does not mean 'obscure' (Woolf). 'Crabbed' (King) is better, but the meaning is 'thorny', 'tricky', 'biting'. This feature of Stoic arguments will be criticised in Book 4.79, but it is here presented as an obstacle for those willing to attack them, and thus as a strength. On *spinosum* applied to the Stoics in Cicero, usually with a derogatory meaning, see Aubert 2006: 898, who offers a useful study of Cicero's vocabulary in his accounts of Stoic rhetoric and dialectic.

[16] Interestingly, Schofield 1986: 62–63 finds similar discrepancies between the Stoic defence of divination by Quintus and its refutation by Cicero in the *De Divinatione*. He concludes that the criticism of divination may not be the purpose of the dialogue, which proves to be 'a multilayered work of surprising obliqueness and complexity'. I will draw analogous conclusions about *De Finibus* 4 in the last part of this chapter.

contradictions. The debate with the Stoics cannot be a *simplex disputatio in utramque partem*. Refuting the Stoics is a different ballgame.

The general strategy of Book 4

How should Stoicism be refuted then? Cicero explains his strategy at 4.3, which needs to be quoted in full in Latin and in Raphael Woolf's translation, although I will ultimately not endorse it:

> Existimo igitur, inquam, Cato, veteres illos Platonis auditores, Speusippum, Aristotelem, Xenocratem, deinde eorum, Polemonem, Theophrastum, satis et copiose et eleganter habuisse constitutam disciplinam, ut non esset causa Zenoni, cum Polemonem audisset, cur et ab eo ipso et a superioribus dissideret. quorum fuit haec institutio, in qua animadvertas velim quid mutandum putes nec expectes dum ad omnia dicam, quae a te dicta sunt, universa enim illorum ratione cum tota vestra confligendum puto.

> Here, then, Cato, is my view: Plato's original disciples, namely Speusippus, Aristotle and Xenocrates, and then their pupils Polemo and Theophrastus, put together a system of thought full of richness and refinement. So there was no reason at all for Zeno, as a pupil of Polemo, to dissent from Polemo and his predecessors. I shall set out this system below. If you think that any of my exposition needs correction, then draw my attention to it and do not wait until I have made a complete reply to your own treatment. I suspect that every point of this system will need to be brought into opposition with every point of yours.

After introducing the system of the Ancient Academy, Cicero apparently says he will refute each and every point of Cato's presentation. There would thus be a big gap between what Cicero announces and what he does in Book 4, as indicated above. We could argue that Cicero's last sentence refers only to the presentation of the Academic doctrine (4–23), where Cicero indeed compares *each* aspect of the Academic system with its Stoic counterpart (or lack of it). But this is impossible, because Cicero announces a *complete* answer to Cato: such an answer is clearly not given in paragraphs 4–23, and Cicero's sentence must therefore refer to a longer section of Book 4.[17] Moreover, I doubt that *universa* and *tota ratio* in the last sentence refer to a 'point by point' exhaustive confrontation between

---

[17] This is confirmed by 24, which starts with a sentence similar to the first half of the one under scrutiny: *Sed ut proprius ad ea, Cato, accedam quae a te dicta sunt, pressius agamus eaque quae modo dixisti cum iis conferamus quae tuis antepono.* Cicero does not claim here that he will answer *everything* Cato said, so this passage does not contradict the interpretation I am presently going to offer of 4.3. See also 4.73 *sub fine*.

the two doctrines. They rather indicate a comparison of the first doctrine *taken as a whole* with the other *taken as a whole*. This is what happens in most of Book 4 after the presentation of the Academic system, where the comparison is admittedly more detailed, as already noted.

But, if this is true, why does Cicero announce he is going to refute everything Cato said?[18] I suspect he might be doing exactly the contrary, as Martha well understood in his translation. Cicero means in fact that Cato should 'not wait for the possibility that I answer [*dicam* is subjunctive] everything you said'.[19] I would thus correct the second part of Raphael Woolf's translation in the following manner:

> I shall set out their system below. Draw my attention to what you think needs to be changed in it, and do not expect from me a complete reply to your own treatment, since I think that their teachings as a whole need to be brought into opposition with your entire view.

This fits the context – the end of the sentence as I understand it, and the method followed in Book 4 – perfectly.

The explicit structure of Book 4

How does Cicero then proceed? He presents the doctrine of the Ancient Academy in the following order: nature as a source of human virtues, the division of philosophy in three parts (4), politics (5–6), rhetoric (6–7), logic (8–10), physics (11–13). Cicero compares the Academic treatment of each topic with the Stoic one. The part of ethics dealing with the end of goods is voluntarily postponed (5, 8). It is presented afterwards (14–19), before Cicero asks (as announced in 14) why Zeno disagreed with the Ancient Academy, and shows he had no good reason (19–23).

Cicero offers then (24) to leave behind common doctrines between the two schools and compare more closely (*pressius*) the doctrines Cato explained and their Academic (superior) counterpart. Cato agrees to have a 'subtler' (*subtilius*) debate, because he thinks the preceding arguments were 'popular' (*popularia*) or 'commonplace' as Raphael Woolf translates. There follows a long series of arguments comparing both schools and refuting Stoicism, which ends in 44:

---

[18] *Omnia* clearly does not suggest a global refutation but a detailed or, at least, exhaustive one.

[19] See *Ver.* 2.2.125 for an identical construction used to make a similar argument: *Nolite exspectare dum omnis obeam oratione mea civitates: hoc uno complector omnia, neminem isto praetore senatorem fieri potuisse nisi qui isti pecuniam dedisset.* Cicero says that he will not or cannot go through each and every (*omnia*) step of Verres' pillage of Sicilian cities; his solution in this case is to give only two typical examples. I thank Carlos Lévy for referring me to this passage.

Up to this point, Cato, I have been explaining why Zeno had no good reason to depart from the teaching of his predecessors (*cur Zenoni non fuisset quam ob rem a superiorum auctoritate discederet*). Now let me deal with the remaining issues (*nunc reliqua videamus*), unless you wish to make a reply to what I have already.

(tr. R. Woolf)

This is a clear reference back to 14 or 19,[20] which closes one part of the speech and apparently opens up a new one.[21] The presentation of the 'remaining' arguments goes on until 78, where Cicero comes to the end of his speech (*iam enim concludatur oratio*) and states 'the one major problem' (*uno vitio maximi*) hampering the Stoic doctrine: he summarises his central argument about the failed attempts by the Stoics to create a doctrine different from the Academic one and enrolls Panetius on his side (79).

We thus have the following *explicit* structure for Cicero's speech:

Introduction about method (3)

1 Comparison between the two doctrines (4–43)
   a The parts of philosophy other than ethics (5–13)
   b The Academic end of goods (14–18)
   c Why did Zeno secede? He had no good reasons (19–43)
      i 'popular' arguments (19–23)
      ii 'more precise' analysis (24–43)
2 'Remaining' arguments (44–78)
  Conclusion (78–79)

After what I said about the repetitions of Book 4, we should not be surprised to see that its natural divisions – with the exception of (a)/(b) – are not drawn according to subject-matters, unlike the first three (out of four) sections of Book 2.[22] The distinction at 23 between 'popular'

---

[20] 14: *Nunc videamus, quaeso, de summo bono, quod continet philosophiam, quid tandem attulerit quam ob rem inventoribus tamquam a parentibus dissentiret. 19: Quae exposita scire cupio quae cause sit cur Zeno ab hac antiqua constitutione desciverit, quidnam horum ab eo non sit probatum.*

[21] Unlike the one at 23, this turning-point at 43 is missed in studies of Book 4's structure, probably because they look for thematic sections instead of carving the text at its natural joints, but also because of the very elusive purpose of this last section. Martha's 'argument analytique' offers the following sections: 3–13, 14–18, 19–23, 24–48, 49–55, 56–77 (see Martha 1928: ii, p. 53 in his translation in the Budé series). MacKendrick 1989: 140–142 distinguishes a *Narratio* (3–23), a *Refutatio I* (24–55) and a *Refutatio II* (56–77). Annas 2007a: 199 also seems to overlook 43 when she indicates that 'From 41 onwards, we find an attempt to show that the Stoics have a problem in holding both that virtue is the only good and that we can rationally discriminate among primary natural advantages'. But in her notes to Raphael Woolf's translation, she observes that 'a break in exposition' happens at 43 (Annas and Woolf 2001: 104).

[22] 2.6–35 is about pleasure, 36–77 about *honestum* and virtue, 78–85 about friendship. As mentioned earlier, this division is taken from Torquatus' speech: 1.29–42 is about pleasure, 43–54 is about

and 'more refined' arguments is quite significant, since it could neatly account for some of the repetitions mentioned earlier. One could object that the distinction between *popularia* and *elegentiora* (or *subtilia*) at 24 is Cato's (see also 3.26). Cicero however introduced himself the idea of a 'more precise' treatment (24: *pressius agamus*), accepts Cato's distinction and repeats it later (4.74); he refuses only to forego his first popular arguments.

Sections (i) and (ii) could therefore be intended to deal with the same topics and problems, but with different *types* of argument. This is all the more plausible, given that this way of proceeding is quite typical of Cicero's philosophical dialogues. As argued by Ruch (1969), the two speeches of the *Lucullus* have a similar structure: Lucullus starts with rhetorical and general arguments followed by a thorough refutation of the New Academy, whereas Cicero starts with technical arguments and then offers to leave them aside for a more general, albeit no less philosophical, presentation of the Academic position.[23] The same structure appears in Books 3 and 4 of the *Tusculans*.[24] This pattern can be explained by the *disputatio in utramque partem*, which forces the speaker to adapt his style or method to the opponent he is trying to answer, and above all by the double aim of Cicero's philosophical works: to present precisely and completely the various Greek doctrines, but also to make them as persuasive and appealing as possible to his Roman readers.[25]

Sections (i) and (ii) represent however only one third of Book 4, the structure of which cannot be reduced to the double pattern found in the *Lucullus* or *Tusculans*. Still, the hypothesis of a methodological, rather than topical, organisation of the whole book is worth exploring, since it could account for its many repetitions and its lack of correspondence with Book 3.

---

virtues, 65–70 is about friendship. The third section, 55–64, has several topics, some of which are treated in the last section of Book 2, for example the distinction between bodily and psychic pleasure and the importance of time in the latter (1.55–57, 2.87–89, 2.104–110).

[23] See *Luc.* 45: *Sed progediamur longius et ita agamus ut nihil nobis adsentati esse videamur; quaeque ab his dicuntur persequamur ut nihil in praeteritis relinquamus;* and *Luc.* 99: *Sed ut omnes istos aculeos et totum tortuosum genus disputandi relinquamus oestendamusque qui simus, iam explicata tota Carneadia sententia Antiochi ista conruent universa.*

[24] *Tusc.* 3.13–21 argues *Stoicorum more*, i. e., dialectically, and 3.22–60 argues *latius* for the same (Stoic) point about passions. An identical structure is found in *Tusc.* 4.11–32 and 33–81. I thank Margaret Graver for pointing this out to me.

[25] See Ruch 1969: 311 and 326–329, who quotes *Ad Att.* 13.19.5 or *De Div.* 2.2. I thank Carlos Lévy for pointing out Ruch's paper to me. See also Schofield 2008: 68–69, who refers to *Tusc.* 1.7, 2.6–7 or *De Or.* 3.80. In all these passages, Cicero insists on combining philosophical rigour and rhetorical elegance.

Book 4's methods of refutation

The standards of the refutation

To understand better the purpose of each section of the refutation, it
might prove useful to go back to its first section, where the doctrine of
the Ancient Academy is summarised (5–18). Its function is not just that,
for two reasons. First, if Cicero only needed to introduce the specific
doctrines he wants to oppose to Stoic ethics, he would have restricted
himself to the ethics of the Ancient Academy. Second and more important, the refutation of Stoicism already starts in this section, as mentioned
earlier.

Since he leaves aside for later the most important topic, the end of
goods (5), Cicero starts his presentation of the doctrine of the *antiqui* with
politics and then goes on with logic and physics. For each section, Cicero
emphasises the thorough treatment the Ancient Academics gave it and the
lack of any significant progress made by the Stoics. A striking feature is
that Cicero emphasises the methods and style of the *antiqui* rather than
their specific doctrines. He just lists the topics of their political works (5),
whereas he expatiates upon the rhetorical qualities of these works and the
Stoics' failure to emulate them (6–8). About physics, important positions
about cosmology and theology are mentioned (14), but Cicero gives pride
of place to the goals of physics (13) and the number and variety of empirical studies of natural phenomena conducted by the *antiqui* (15). This
emphasis suggests that Cicero is at the same time presenting a 'perfect'
doctrine and setting up the standards or criteria provided by this philosophical model for the ensuing refutation.

Cicero insists first that a good doctrine should be formulated in such a
way as to persuade and move us to act in accordance with it. This gives us
the main criteria of the *popularia* section, which exposes the inadequacy
of Stoic philosophy 'in the life of city, in the law-courts or in the Senate'
(tr. R. Woolf, 21: *in urbem, in forum, in curiam*), because it holds paradoxical positions, which are either impossible to state seriously in public,
since they contradict shared values, or vain because they have no practical
consequences. Note that these 'rhetorical' arguments, although they seem
quite rapidly disposed of, are not to be dismissed as irrelevant (as Cato
does at 24): they are repeated later (52–53, 72–73) and are without any
doubt very important to Cicero, as shown by the fact that he develops
them repeatedly in his rhetorical works.[26] They address not only the Stoics'

---

[26] See *De Or.* 1.89, 2.157–160, 3.65–66 and *Brut.* 118–120.

vocabulary, but their philosophical method or style as a whole,[27] their inability to convince people to change their behaviour and the paradoxical nature of their positions, which make them unfit, like the Epicurean ones (2.74) but for opposite reasons, to be used publicly or, at least, in front of an assembly by a statesman.

As for logic, after mentioning their studies of the art of definition and division (8), Cicero attributes the following epistemological procedure to the Ancient Academics:

> Their system of deductive argument begins from propositions that are evident, and proceeds methodically through to the right conclusion in each individual case. What a large variety of methods of deductive argument they set out and how different each are from captious dialectical questions![28]

The procedure starting with obvious facts in order to reach conclusions through good reasoning is indeed the one adopted by Cicero once he is done with 'popular' arguments. Cicero argues at length that the Stoic notion of the end is logically incompatible with the claims about human nature Stoicism is supposed to share with the Ancient Academy,[29] and he makes explicit references to dialectic (55) and to inconclusive arguments (48). One of the Stoic arguments proving that *bonum* is identical to *honestum* is even said to be 'utterly inconclusive' (50: *minime consectarium*) and is thus treated as one of the *captiosi interrogationes* identified by the *antiqui* in the passage just quoted.[30]

Another epistemological teaching of the Ancient Academics listed by Cicero in the following sentence is to keep the senses and reason together instead of using them separately from each other: this standard is clearly applied in all those arguments where the Stoic doctrines are blamed for leading to the inconceivable idea of a pure mind with no body or nothing natural in it.[31]

---

[27] See Aubert 2008.

[28] 8–9 (tr. R. Woolf, slightly modified): *Iam argumenti ratione conclusi caput esse faciunt ea quae perspicua dicunt, deinde ordinem sequuntur, tum quid verum sit in singulis extrema conclusio est. Quanta autem ab illis varietas argumentorum ratione concludentium eorumque cum captiosis interrogationibus dissimilitudo!*

[29] 26: *quonam modo ab isdem principiis profecti efficiatis ut honeste vivere summum bonum sit*; 39: *ut mirari satis istorum inconstantiam non possim.*

[30] This is borne out by the fact that, just before, Cicero blames the Stoics for using the *sorites* despite holding it to be *vitiosius* (50). The Stoics blur the difference between good and sophistic arguments established for example by Aristotle in the *Analytics* and *Sophistic refutations*.

[31] See 29: *Sed id ne cogitari quidem potest quale sit, ut non repugnet ipsum sibi.* Cf. 36 for a refined version of this argument, where Cicero blames also the opposite option which defines the end *tamquam de inanimo aliquo loquantur* and thus makes no use of reason. See also 42, where Cicero compares the Stoics to some philosophers who started their research from the senses, but discovered

To the objection that Chrysippus developed dialectic a great deal, Cicero answers then (10) that he nevertheless neglected important aspects of it: Cicero introduces a distinction between the *ars inveniendi* and the *ars disserendi* and claims the Stoics dealt only with the second, while the Peripatetics cultivated both. This charge is already made at the beginning of Cicero's *Topics*,[32] but it is here supplemented with an interesting philosophical rationale: thanks to their study of *loci*, these *thesauri* from which arguments can be extracted, the followers of the Ancient Academy can improvise arguments instead of always following what they were taught or their written handbooks. The implication is that the Stoics cannot,[33] as will be shown repeatedly in Book 4, where they are accused tirelessly of either plagiarising the Ancient Academy or seceding for no good reasons (3, 19–23, 56–61, 78). Not only are the Stoics repeating their founder's arguments like parrots, but his very arguments and doctrines are themselves copies of Polemo's or fall into absurdities when they try to innovate. Judged according to the standards of intellectual independence (10 : *esse in disputando suus*), Stoicism is a complete failure.

The Ancient Academy is thus used by Cicero not only as offering a set of coherent and true positions to which Stoic doctrines can be compared, but first and foremost as embodying and having stated a number of criteria, rules and goals defining what philosophy in general should be and against which Stoic ethics is measured and found wanting in Book 4. This is particularly clear with the epistemological standards, namely logical deduction from *perspicua* and combination of reason with the senses, which the Stoics acknowledge as valid but do not follow in their ethics according to Cicero. But how can physics be taken as providing such standards?

In the next paragraphs of the first section (11–12), Cicero acknowledges that the Stoics did not reduce physics to an instrument, unlike the Epicureans, and expatiates upon its intrinsic moral merits, but also upon the pleasure it produces. He then lists a few cosmological doctrines about

divine things and 'relinquished the senses'. I shall come back later to this passage, which reveals a strong concern with Platonism and is crucial to understanding the purpose of Book 4.

[32] *Topica* 6. Cf. *De Or.* 2.157. On this division and the charge againt the Stoics about *inventio*, see Reinhardt 2003: 189–198 and Aubert 2008: 77–84.

[33] This is a criticism found elsewhere in Cicero: the dogmatic schools are tied to the authority of their founder and cannot depart from his *dogmata*, whereas the Academics are characterised by their intellectual freedom: see *Luc.* 8 and Bénatouïl 2007: 16–19. These 'Academics' are the followers of Arcesilaus and Carneades rather than the Ancient Academics and Peripatetics, but this is not a problem: there were some common threads in Academic attacks against Stoicism, from Polemo to Antiochus.

which the Stoics followed or disagreed with the Peripatetics, but soon comes to what he calls *materia rerum*, the empirical content of physics, and opposes the Stoics' lack of it to the various and numerous data collected by the Peripatetics[34] about animals, plants, natural phenomena and their causes: 'In numerous wide-ranging cases they explain and demonstrate how and why natural phenomena occur. From this great store-house they can draw on a wealth of highly convincing arguments to account for every aspect of nature' (13). This prepares and justifies Cicero's accusation that the Stoics ignore the various parts and specific development of human nature, so much so that their ethics is untrue to nature.[35]

Mapping the standards with the sections
In the presentation of the doctrines of the Ancient Academy, Cicero is therefore clearly putting forward the methods and standards he is going to use to assess Stoicism in Book 4. The order of presentation of these standards[36] could also shed light on the structure of his refutation. It might not be casual that rhetorical standards are introduced first and applied to Stoicism in the first 'popular' section of the refutation. Could a similar match hold for the 'more precise' and 'remaining' sections? Since rhetorical arguments are used again in the former section, as already mentioned above, it would be preposterous to define these two sections by the application of only one type of argument, but both sections might be taken to be organised around one central, albeit not unique, methodological issue closely tied to one of the standard, as the first 'popular' section is.

If we go back to the presentation of the Ancient Academics' method of proof (8 quoted above), we can distinguish two steps in the production of true knowledge: establishing the *perspicua* and deducing valid conclusions from them. Logic *per se* is only concerned with the second step. The idea just quoted that strong 'arguments' should be based on the results of inquiries into natural phenomena (13) obviously explains how the first step works: the *perspicua* which provide starting-points for good arguments are obtained inductively from a thorough observation of nature.

---

[34] As the previous objections about rhetoric and logic, this point is made elsewhere in Cicero, in this case at *Nat. d.* 2.124–125 where Balbus acknowledges that most of his biological examples are borrowed from Aristotle and Theophrastus.

[35] 37: *Itaque mihi non satis videmini considerare, quod iter sit naturae quaeque progressio.* 54: *In prima igitur constitutione Zeno tuus a natura recessit.* 55: *Sensus enim cuiusque et natura rerum atque ipsa veritas clamabat quodam modo non posse adduci ut inter eas res quas Zeno exaequaret nihil interesset.* Cf. 56 and 68, to which I shall come back presently.

[36] Note the different order in 5.9–11: physics, logic, ethics.

This distinction between two steps, one empirical and the other logical, is confirmed by the requirement to use both the senses and reason in knowledge (9) and happens to be very illuminating to understand the 'more precise' and 'remaining' sections.

Although the 'more precise' section is heavily concerned with nature, since one of its main topics is the relationships between body and mind in human development (25–28, 32–38, 42), Cicero does not refute the Stoic view of human nature by means of empirical observations (made by himself or by the Ancient Academics). At 37–39, Cicero suggests that the Stoic view of human development does not fit nature, but he then opposes a thought experiment to this view.[37] Moreover, Cicero shifts back to a 'logical' refutation when he draws the conclusion of this argument and applies it to the Stoics.[38] The central criteria of the 'more precise' section is indeed logical consistency. Symetrically, although there are several references to dialectic in the 'remaining' section (48, 50, 55), they are generally not meant to blame the Stoics for their inconsistency but, on the contrary, to emphasise that their arguments are logically valid but nevertheless unacceptable, either because their premises are not shared by any of their adversaries (50) or because their conclusions are so absurd that their premises must be false (55, 67). In both cases, the gist of the objection is not logical but exposes the Stoics' starting-points as not being *perspicua*: they are empirically false.

Both sections are thus concerned with the Stoic views about human nature and the good and with the consistency of Stoic ethics, but each section approaches these nagging problems from a distinctive angle, which does not account for all the arguments of the section but provides an overall method or purpose for it. Let us make these two angles clearer.

In the more precise or 'logical' section, Cicero relies on a 'common' definition of human nature (as consisting of body and mind) to criticise the Stoic view of human development as inconsistent *in itself*. After offering to be 'more precise' in his refutation, Cicero adds: 'Let us grant those points on which you are in agreement with the ancients, and restrict our discussion to the controversial areas, if that is alright with you.'[39] The following arguments indeed show how the Stoics cannot deduce their main doctrines from the conception of human nature they supposedly share

[37] 38: *licet … fingere aliquid docenti causa.* This is the famous example of the vine, about which see below and Prost 2001: 248.
[38] 39: *ut mirari satis istorum inconstantiam non possim.*
[39] 24 (tr. R. Woolf): *Quae sunt igitur communia vobis cum antiquis, iis sic utamur quasi concessis; quae in controversia veniunt de iis, si placet, disseramus.*

with the Ancient Academy (26–27). More precisely, Cicero emphasises that the assumptions of the Ancient Academy about human nature are obvious, namely agreed upon by everyone,[40] including the Stoics, who are then shown to contradict these *perspicua* and therefore *themselves*. The main criterion is thus logical consistency or sometimes conceivability.[41]

If correct, this interpretation undermines or, at least, qualifies the traditional Antiochean reading of Book 4. Cicero is probably using Antiochus' arguments at various points (see especially 29–32), but it should be noted that Cicero takes care to go beyond simply blaming the Stoics for disagreeing with the Ancient Academy, as he did at 19–20 or will do again at 56–63. He tries to make his argument independent from the assumption that the Stoics agree with the *antiqui* on human nature,[42] and argues in detail that the Stoics cannot but contradict *themselves* as long as they maintain that only what is *honestum* is good.[43]

In the last 'remaining' section, the approach is quite different. Cicero summarises the 'more precise' arguments by blaming Zeno for not explaining where exactly and why he modified Polemo's doctrine, but then acknowledges that Zeno in fact started from principles which were not Polemo's:

> Now Zeno agreed with Polemo about what the principles of nature were. It seems to me it would have been fairer, then, in his dispute with Polemo, for Zeno to have begun with these shared principles and then to have indicated where he took a stand and where the cause of the controversy arose. Instead, he lined himself up with philosophers who actually denied that

[40] See 32: *Quid de quo nulla dissensio est? Nemo enim est, qui aliter dixerit.* 33: *Quo modo autem, quod ipsi etiam fatentur constatque inter omnis.* 36: *Cum enim constet inter omnes.* 37: *quia virtus, ut omnes fatemur...*

[41] At 27–28, Cicero argues that a pure mind without any natural states or resources is an impossible thing and at 36, he says that he does not know what a pure empty mind can be. In both passages, the hypothesis is not rejected because of its logical inconsistency or because empirical observation proves there are no pure minds, but because it is impossible to understand (*intellegere*) the hypothesis. As already noted, the implicit standard seems here to be the Academic epistemological method of always combining reason and the senses, as suggested by Cicero's requirement (in both passages) that the mind be conceived by analogy with the body or as a type of body (even when supposing it could exist separately from any organic body).

[42] Note how Cicero uses paired conditional arguments starting from opposing assumptions: if this is true about nature, it follows necessary that ... if that is true, then ... (35, 40, 41). This shows that his argument is not always dependent upon a specific conception of human nature, but explores chiefly what is consistent or not with various assumptions about it.

[43] A similar method is at work in Plutarch's *De Comm. Not.*, where the Stoics are shown to contradict themselves on various points because they contradict common notions they explicitly or implicitly accept: see Bénatouïl 2004. I surmise this method was used by Carneades and borrowed from him by Antiochus.

their supreme goods derived from nature, and he employed the same arguments and the same doctrines that they did.[44]

In the following paragraphs, Cicero attacks these Stoic principles, like the
identity of *bonum* and *honestum*, and refutes the arguments used by the
Stoics to prove them. There are many repetitions, because these principles have already been mentioned, but from a different point of view: they
were mocked as useless in public debates or as incompatible with the doctrine of *prima naturae* shared by the Stoics and the Ancient Academy,
whereas they are now criticised as such and as disagreeing with nature.

The central standard is not logical any more, as shown by Cicero's
emphasis on comparing doctrines *de re*:

> Now every dispute tends to resolve around either facts or terms. Ignorance
> of facts or misuse of terms will lead to one or other form of dispute. Where
> neither is the case, we must make every effort to employ the most familiar
> and appropriate terminology, namely that which reveals the facts. There
> can be no doubt that the ancients had a more suitable terminology, assum-
> ing they were right about the facts.[45]

This distinction clearly puts forward facts or things themselves as the best
yardstick of any controversy, since even if it is *de nomine*, the criteria to
apply words is not only usage but also their ability to make things clear.[46]
Zeno's and his masters' doctrines should be compared as to their practical import: the attitude they advocate towards pain or health rather than
the names they give to them (58–60), the change they can foster in our
life (52).

Last but not least, in the final scrutiny of the Stoic paradoxes and the
comparisons used to justify them (64–72, 74–77), Cicero insists on testing
the Stoic analogies (*similitudines*) against the relevant ethical phenomena[47]

---

[44] 45 (tr. R. Woolf, slightly modified): *Mihi autem aequius videbatur Zenonem cum Polemone disceptantem, a quo quae essent principia naturae acceperat, a communibus initiis progredientem videre
ubi primum et unde causa controversiae nasceretur, non, stantem cum iis qui ne dicerent quidem sua
summa bone esse a natura profecta, uti isdem argumentis quibus illi uterentur isdemque sententiis.*

[45] 57 (tr. R. Woolf): *cumque omnis controversia aut de re soleat aut de nomine esse, utraque earum
nascitur, si aut res ignoratur aut erratur in nomine. quorum si neutrum est, opera danda est, ut verbis
utamur quam usitatissimis et quam maxime aptis, id est rem declarantibus. num igitur dubium est,
quin, si in re ipsa nihil peccatur a superioribus, verbis illi commodius utantur?*

[46] On this important topic in Cicero, see Görler 1974: 198–205, Lévy 1984: 121–126, Schofield 2002
and Aubert 2006: 788–794. Lévy and Aubert refer Cicero's position and polemics against Zeno's
use of language to the *Cratylus*. As far as the formulation of the objection in 57 is concerned,
forensic rhetoric and more specifically *stasis* theory is probably also a significant background, as
suggested by *De Inv.* 1.10: *Omnis res, quae habet in se positam in dictione ac disceptatione aliquam
controversiam, aut facti aut nominis aut generis aut actionis continet quaestionem.*

[47] 64: *dissimillimas proferebas.* 65: *ista non similia sunt.* 76: *Ecce aliud simile dissimile.*

or blaming the Stoics for ignoring relevant features of the practical situation they assess.[48] The methodological principle of his analysis is made clear in the following lines:

> Well now: should the evident clarify the doubtful or be refuted by it? This at any rate is evident, that some vices are worse than others. Whether or not what you call the supreme good admits of any increase is open to doubt. But you Stoics try to overturn the evident with the doubtful, when you should be illuminating the doubtful with the evident.[49]

We have here a final explicit reference to the logical method of the Ancient Academics based on *perspicua* (8). This time, the Stoics are not blamed for making incorrect deductions from the *perspicua*, but for denying or ignoring the *perspicua* themselves. After dealing with the Stoics' logical inconsistencies in (most of) the 'more precise' section, Cicero exposes their wrong or wild principles in (most of) the 'remaining' section.

This explains, I hope, the structure and logic of Book 4 on its own terms, and accounts for its many repetitions as due to its method rather than to Cicero's awkward pasting of sources. However, the problem of the discrepancy between Books 3 and 4 still needs to be tackled.

Book 4 between Books 3 and 5

Refuting the Stoic theory of moral progress as natural

As I noted at the beginning, the Stoic theory of moral progress is the topic on which many interpreters of Book 4 have focused their blame,[50] wondering 'why the crucial turn taken by the account in Book 3 at c. 20 ff should be almost completely ignored both in the criticism of Stoicism in Book 4 and in the directly competing account in Book V' (White 1979 164). Is this really the case? I shall obviously leave aside Book 5, not only because it falls outside my scope, but also because it is one of my contentions that Book 4 and Piso's speech should not be assumed to represent the same Antiochean point of view.

At first sight, even when Book 4 seems to refer back to Book 3, it misses the mark. At 3.23, Cato uses the famous *commendatio* analogy to explain

[48] 76: *Hoc non videre, cuius generis onus navis vehat, id ad gubernatoris artem nihil pertinere!* 77: *quasi nihil inter res quoque ipsas, in quibus peccatur, intersit.*

[49] 67 (tr. R. Woolf): *utrum igitur tandem perspicuisne dubia aperiuntur, an dubiis perspicua tolluntur? atqui hoc perspicuum est, vitia alia [in] aliis esse maiora, illud dubium, ad id, quod summum bonum dicitis, ecquaenam possit fieri accessio. vos autem cum perspicuis dubia debeatis illustrare, dubiis perspicua conamini tollere.*

[50] See note 10, p. 201 above.

the Stoic position about moral progress: it often happens that A recommends to his dear friend B another person C (whom A knows but B does not know), and that B eventually ends up being more friendly with C than with A. Thus, 'it is hardly surprising that, at first, wisdom [= C] is recommended to us [= B] by the first natural [tendencies = A], but that, later, wisdom [C] becomes dearer to us [B] than those things [A] which led us to it' (3.23). When Cicero again uses this analogy at 4.26, he says something very different: 'How is it that so many of the things originally recommended by nature are suddenly forsaken by wisdom?'[51] In Cicero's phrasing, natural things [= C] are directly recommended to us – or perhaps even to wisdom – [= B] by nature [= A], and there is thus no logical reason for wisdom to abandon them: the *commendatio* analogy is reversed and thus blocked. The 'complete reshaping of motives and emotions' (Gill 2006: 173) that takes place in the Stoic view of human development seems indeed to be overlooked by (the character) Cicero in Book 4.

Why is that so? Nicholas White (1979: 164–165) offered three possible but ultimately insufficient (in his opinion) solutions: 'guile and the desire to make the Stoics look unoriginal and inept', 'genuine misunderstanding' or the fact that 'Panetius may well have adopted a doctrine quite like the one that Antiochus is criticising'. I think we can offer another and more generous explanation, as suggested by Carlos Lévy in his answer to Victor Goldschmidt's (1953: 131) reproach (identical to White's) that Cicero forgets in Book 4 the crucial Stoic idea of transition (*passage*) evidenced by Book 3: 'Notre opinion est qu'il y a de sa part refus plutôt que méconnaissance.'[52] Lévy's main argument is Cicero's use in Book 4 of the *Carneadea divisio*, which was more or less designed to refute Stoicism.[53]

There is indeed other evidence for Cicero's conscious rejection of the Stoic position as false. At 4.37, the Stoics are blamed for not observing how nature proceeds (*naturae progressio*). Humans are said to be different from corn, where the first step of growth is erased by the final blooming.[54] We have here a concise but clear acknowledgement of the specificity of moral

[51] 4.26 (tr. R. Woolf): *Quaero igitur quo modo hae tantae [= corpus omniaque ea quae, secundum naturam cum sint, absint a nostra potestate] commendationes a natura profectae subito a sapientia relictae sint.*

[52] Lévy 1984: 119.

[53] The two principles of the division, that wisdom is an art and has what is natural as its object (5.16–17) are indeed put into question by Cato (3.24–25) but seem to be adopted by Cicero in his refutation (4, 16–17, 41). See Striker 1996: 304–315 and Lévy 1992: 354–355.

[54] 4.37: *non enim, quod facit in frugibus, ut, cum ad spicam perduxerit ab herba, relinquat et pro nihilo habeat herbam, idem facit in homine, cum eum ad rationis habitum perduxit.* About this passage, see Prost 2001: 247–248.

progress in Stoicism. This is followed by the well-known vine analogy, which purports to provide a correct, albeit hypothetical, model illuminating what happens in the case of man, namely that the later and superior part (mind) takes care of the earlier lower part (body). Could Cicero give us here a hint that the *antiqui* might not be as faithful to nature as Antiochus claims, since they need an imaginary illustration (a vine taking care of itself), whereas the Stoics have a perfectly natural model (the growth of corn) for the 'complete reshaping' of human nature they posit? I very much doubt it. Even when he defends Stoicism against the Ancient Academy at 5.83–85 or in *Tusc.* 5.21–32, Cicero never revises the charge made at 4.25–26 or 78: the superior consistency attributed to Stoicism by Cicero is between the Stoic definitions of the good and of happiness, not between the Stoic definitions of the good (or happiness) and the Stoic conception of our first impulses. Cicero simply does not believe that nature herself can lead us to relinquish our first impulses and care only about virtue.

From Zeno back to Plato: moral progress as a break from the senses

But does the fact that Cicero refuses to accept the Stoic *commendatio* mean that he thinks Stoicism is a lost case as far as ethics is concerned, and that Carneades and Antiochus are entirely right in their criticism? Not necessarily. This can be at least suspected when one reads 4.42, a passage Nicholas White (1978: 164) already singled out as registering the 'crucial turn taken by the Stoic account, but only in the most cursory way':

> There are philosophers who began with the senses but then saw a grander or more divine vision, whereupon they abandoned the senses. So, too, the Stoics moved on from original desire to the beautiful vision of virtue, and cast aside all that they saw apart from virtue. But they forgot that in its entirety the nature of what is desirable has a very wide scope, from starting-points to final ends. And they failed to realise that they were undermining the foundations of those beautiful objects of their admiration.[55]

There is in fact much more to this passage, since it is impossible not to read the first sentence as an allusion to Plato, which could extend to some of his first disciples.[56] Woldemar Görler (1990: 97) believes that we have

---

[55] 4.42 (tr. R. Woolf): *ut quidam philosophi, cum a sensibus profecti maiora quaedam et diviniora vidissent, sensus reliquerunt, sic isti, cum ex appetitione rerum virtutis pulchritudinem aspexissent, omnia, quae praeter virtutem ipsam viderant, abiecerunt obliti naturam omnem appetendarum rerum ita late patere, ut a principiis permanaret ad fines, neque intellegunt se rerum illarum pulchrarum atque admirabilium fundamenta subducere.*

[56] Cf. *Varro* 30 about the epistemological teachings of the Ancient Academy (according to Antiochus): *quamquam oriretur a sensibus tamen non esse iudicium veritatis in sensibus: mentem*

here a voluntarily veiled mocking of Plato by Antiochus. If this is correct, Antiochus would assimilate Stoic ethics to Plato's epistemology in order to blame the Stoics for not following Plato's followers in ethics. Is this really plausible?[57] I am not denying that, in Book 4, the epistemology attributed to the Ancient Academy is not Plato's: this is clearly established by 4.9 and 39, where the separation of reason from the senses is refused. But comparing the Stoic method to Plato's when you are blaming the Stoics for not adopting Plato's disciples' views – how could this not be a self-defeating argument?

I surmise that Antiochus is not behind this analogy, which is later borne out by 5.84, where the Peripatetics and Piso are said by Cicero to be unable to follow Socrates and Plato in their 'noble discourse' (*honesta oratio*), whereas Zeno can. Cicero gives us here (at 4.42) a clue that Zeno's inconsistency is not as certain as Antiochus claims and that the *fundamenta* of virtue can be found elsewhere than in our nature *taken as a whole*. The defence or solution Cicero hints at is, however, not the 'Stoic' doctrine from 3.20–22 we modern readers expect. What 4.42 suggests instead is that Zeno's move from natural things to virtue is analogous to the Platonist break from the senses and pursuit of a higher form of knowledge (and reality).[58] Cicero already quoted Plato against Epicurus on this very point: 'the eyes are our keenest sense, but we cannot see wisdom with them. What blazing passion wisdom would have aroused for herself if we could.'[59] Stoics and Platonists can be compared because they value virtue as if they were *seeing* it, which leads them to forget everything else.[60]

---

volebant esse iudicem, and 33: *Aristotele primus species quas paulo ante dixit labefactavit, quas mirifice Plato erat amplexatus, ut in iis quiddam divinum diceret.*

[57] It might be if, as some believe, Antiochus approved Aristotle for criticising Plato's theory of Forms. But I do not think *Varro* 33 warrants this interpretation. See Karamanolis 2006: 61–63 and Bonazzi 2012: 316–323.

[58] The most obvious example is probably the prisoner's escape from the cave and her ensuing contemplation of real things in *Republic* 7, but other Platonic texts could be equally relevant, such as philosophy as a preparation to death in the *Phaedo*, the flight of the philosopher's mind from the city to nature as a whole in the digression of the *Theaetetus*, and the ascent towards Beauty in the *Symposium*.

[59] 2.52 (tr. R. Woolf) quoting *Phdr.* 250d: *oculorum est in nobis sensus acerrimus quibus sapientiam non cernimus. Quam illa ardentis amores excitaret sui.* I surmise there is a common, albeit very discrete, Platonic thread in Cicero's three interventions as a character in the *De Finibus*, namely Book 2, Book 4 and the end of Book 5. About his overall strategy and his subtle use of his double status as author and one of the characters, see Charles Brittain's chapter in this volume.

[60] See 4.37: *aciem animorum nostrorum virtutis splendore praestringitis*, and 4.29, where Chrysippus answers the charge of neglecting the body by saying that *obscurari quaedam nec apparere, quia valde parva sint*. The Stoics 'leave aside' objects which are valued by our first natural impulses, because they are made invisible by the much brighter light of virtue (cf. 3.45). This must be contrasted sharply with Antiochus' position. Piso explains that, at first, nature is *quidem mirabiliter occulta* and our *prima commendatio* to ourselves is *incerta et obscura* (5.41). It is only later that we begin to know ourselves and how we differ from other beings. Moral development according to Antiochus

This analogy seems to be an anticipation of the original blend of Stoicism and Platonism, with the leading role granted to the latter, offered in the *Tusculans*, written just after the *De Finibus*.[61] The connection between both books is made retrospectively explicit at *Tusc.* 5.31–34.[62] In *Tusc.* 5, Cicero defends the sufficiency of virtue for happiness and argues against various philosophers, like Epicurus or Theophrastus or the Ancient Academics, who hold that virtue is not the only good *and* that the sage is always happy: this is absolutely inconsistent (*Tusc.* 5.21–31). At this point, Cicero's interlocutor or disciple warns Cicero that he risks being inconsistent with what he said in Book 4 of *De Finibus*. In his answer, Cicero does not qualify his refutation of Stoicism, as noted by Malcolm Schofield (2008: 83): he invokes the freedom of the Academics, which allows them to 'say whatever strikes our mind as probable' (*Tusc.* 5.33). He nevertheless also refers to his argument against Piso at the end of Book 5, saying that he is not inquiring whether Zeno's view is true but whether it is consistent, and that Brutus should see if it is consistent for himself to hold that the wise man is always happy. But Cicero then offers (for those, like his disciple or Brutus, who follow authority rather than consistency) to save Zeno's doctrine from the lack of pedigree of its author by refering it back to Plato and quoting the *Gorgias* as a proof that Socrates held happiness to depend only upon virtue (*Tusc* 5.34–35).

This move is very similar to the implicit point made by the analogy at 4.42,[63] and above all to a later and much more explicit passage of Book 4, where Cicero has the Ancient Academics raised from the dead ask Cato

---

is thus about uncovering our nature, as shown by Gill 2006: 171, whereas the process seems opposite for the Stoics, since moral progress obscures what was important to us at first.

[61] One should perhaps also mention the *De Officiis*. See especially *De Off.* 1.14: *quam similitudinem natura ratioque ab oculis ad animum transferens multo etiam magis pulchritudinem, constantiam, ordinem in consiliis factisque conservandam putat.* This passage, which is followed by a quotation of Plato about seeing wisdom, echoes quite precisely *Fin.* 3.21, 4.42 *and* the *Symposium*. If this passage comes from Panetius, it means that Cicero's (not Antiochus') blending of Platonism and Stoicism was anticipated by the successors of Chrysippus. It may indeed not be casual that Panetius is mentioned at the very end of Book 4 as not following earlier Stoics as far as argumentation, style and admiration for the *antiqui* are concerned (79, see also 23): like 4.42, this passage hints at the possibilty of a synthesis between both schools and paves the way to the *De Officiis* as another 'solution' to the final dilemma (Stoicism or Antiochus) of the *De Finibus*.

[62] On this passage of the *Tusculans* and, more generally, on Cicero's attempt in this work to solve the dilemma(s) of the *De Finibus*, see Lévy 1992: 445–467 and 485–494, and Schofield 2012b: 246–249.

[63] This is confirmed by the next paragraphs, where Cicero explains his position by starting from 'commun nature' (*Tusc.* 5.37–39). He describes the *scala naturae* and introduces man as superior but as comparable only to god (cf. *diviniora* at 4.42), since the human mind comes from divine thought and, provided it is cured from the errors which blind it, can reach *absoluta ratio* or virtue (cf. *omnia quae praeter virtutem ipsam viderant abiecerunt* at 4.42). This is a Platonised version of the Stoic *scala naturae*, which inserts a sharp gap between the human mind and lower natural beings or tendencies, as noted by Lévy 1992: 488–489.

why he did not choose them rather than the Stoics (4.61).[64] Cato refuses to answer this 'rhetorical' question and asks Cicero to do it himself. He obliges and imagines Cato specifying what the Stoics discovered and the Ancient Academics missed (62–63). On the face of it, it is very difficult to believe that this answer is not ironical and meant to attribute to Cato absurd and offensive objections to *antiqui illi quasi barbati*, which are moreover compared to the roman *maiores*.[65]

However, Cicero will eventually use very similar arguments at 5.79–84 against Piso and the Peripatetics. At 4.62–63, Cicero, speaking for Cato, first blames the Ancient Academics for not knowing that there is no good but what is *honestum*.[66] At 5.80, Cicero also harshly blames Piso for not seeing that natural things are not goods. The second of Cicero's arguments at 4.62–63 objects to attributing a better life to a healthy and rich virtuous man than to a poor, sick, virtuous man. This argument is put forward again with the examples of Q. Metellus and Regulus at 5.82–83, where Cicero makes the same radical answer on behalf of the Stoics, with no irony this time: *Nihilo beatiorem esse Metellum quam Regulum.*

Cicero's answer on behalf of Cato to the Ancient Academics' charges is therefore not as ironical as it seems, and should be read as proleptic, like 4.42 about the parallelism between Platonism and Stoicism. Cato still has a few things to teach the Ancient Academics, or rather to *Antiochus'* Ancient Academics. Despite his following a mere nobody from Citium, Cato might be more faithful to Plato than Polemo, Theophrastus or Aristotle. At various points in Book 4, Cicero hints at his coming subversion of the idea that Zeno stole his doctrine from the Academy: yes, he did, as far as ethics is concerned, if 'the Academy' is taken to mean 'Plato' himself.[67]

---

[64] Note the emphasis on Plato in this paragraph (61): first, the Ancient Academics are introduced as Plato's heirs and then the authority of Plato is again opposed to Zeno's, who has none. See Görler 1974: 162–163 about the appeal to *auctoritas* in this passage.

[65] See Lévy 1992: 440 about this analogy.

[66] Note, in this answer (62–63), the insistence on the fact that the Stoics *saw* things (i.e., virtue or wisdom) the Ancient Academics did not manage to grasp: *quas res illi propter antiquitatem parum vidissent, eas a Stoicis esse perspectas, eisdemque de rebus hos cum acutius disservisse, tum sensisse gravius et fortius.*

[67] See Lévy 1992: 339–340 and 493. Cicero's idea is obviously not that Plato and Zeno have the same ethical doctrine, but that the latter leads back to the former, which then allows us to interpret Stoicism correctly, namely to get rid of its naturalism (i.e., the *commendatio* conception of moral progress: see above, p. 216) and to view its picture of virtue as an ideal. I would thus dispute Julia Annas' claim that Cicero ignores Plato in the *De Finibus* because his antinaturalism 'does not fit into Hellenistic ethical debate at all' (Annas in Annas and Woolf 2001: xxii). I agree Cicero chose the three doctrines treated in *De Finibus* from this point of view, but I think he also sketches in this work (and more clearly in *Tusculans*) a criticism of Hellenistic naturalism inspired by Plato.

CHAPTER 9

Antiochus' theory of oikeiōsis

Christopher Gill

University of Exeter

A core element in Book 5 of Cicero's *De Finibus* (*Fin.*) is the long exposition of Antiochus' theory of ethical development (5.24–74). Like some
other accounts of ethical development in this period, including the Stoic
version, this is presented as a natural process of self-extension or 'familiar-
isation' (*oikeiōsis*). The aim of this discussion is to probe the question of
the underlying rationale and philosophical cogency of this theory, especially when taken in comparison with the other treatment of *oikeiōsis* in
this work, the Stoic version presented in Book 3 (3.16–22, 62–68). I also
explore the question how Cicero understands the distinctive features and
the merits or demerits of the two accounts of *oikeiōsis*, as far as we can tell
from his presentation in *De Finibus*.

I begin by reviewing the main themes of Antiochus' account of development, as presented in *Fin.* 5,[1] and consider what seem to be the origins
and underlying rationale of the account. I also discuss what Antiochus
himself, or readers sympathetic to his position, might regard as the strong
points of the account, by contrast with the Stoic one. Then I consider how
far Antiochus' account of *oikeiōsis*, if closely examined, does actually support his distinctive position on the good, drawing comparisons with Stoic
theory in this respect. Finally, I discuss whether we can gauge Cicero's
overall attitude to the debate between Stoic and Antiochean thinking on
the nature of the human good or goal of life which dominates *Fin.* 3–5.

This chapter represents a substantially revised version of the paper given at the Symposium
Hellenisticum at Budapest. I am most grateful for a very stimulating discussion on that occasion,
as well as for perceptive written comments by Brad Inwood and Malcolm Schofield on a later draft.
I would like especially to thank Thomas Bénatouïl for an exceptionally detailed and helpful set of
comments.

[1] Although spoken by Piso, the account is explicitly and repeatedly presented as reflecting the teachings of Antiochus; see, e.g., 5.6–8, 14, 75, 81 (all references not otherwise specified are to books
and chapters of *Fin.*). On the form of the debate, the use of characters as spokesmen, and Cicero's
authorial shaping, see section 5 below.

1   Main themes of the Antiochean account

I begin by offering a straightforward summary of the main themes of the
account of ethical development given by Piso (the Antiochean spokesman) in *Fin.* 5.24–76, designed to provide a basis for further analysis.

The account begins with three recurrent motifs: that self-love is a universal and primary motive in all life-forms; that this motive, while present
from the start, develops with time and growing self-awareness; and that the
highest good for each creature consists in realising the best possible state
of its own nature (5.24). Although this applies to all life-forms, including
plants, the good for any one creature varies with its specific nature. This
claim is supported by arguments for the thesis that self-love is a primary
motive or desire, which is universal in all life-forms and which underlies
other kinds of desire (5.27–33). Human nature is presented as a combination of more or less valuable parts, the body and the (more valuable) psyche or personality (*animus*) of which the most important part is intellect
or mind (*mens*). Corresponding to these parts are good qualities of body,
psyche and mind; psychological qualities are subdivided into non-volitional
and volitional ones (that is, virtues), the latter being presented as more valuable (5.34–36). On this basis, Piso argues that human self-love is naturally
expressed in wanting all our parts to be as perfect as possible, which is identical with achieving the highest good (5.37). Hence, the proper functioning
of these parts will be desirable in itself (*per se appetenda*), and will have more
desirability in so far as those parts and their functions have greater value
(*dignitas*). Thus, the virtues are more valuable than other psychological or
mental qualities and mental qualities are more valuable in turn than bodily
ones. This valuation is supported by a brief spectrum of natural kinds, in
which the superior value of the virtues is explained by their being functions
of reason (*ratio*), which is divine, by contrast with other qualities, especially
bodily ones, that are common to other animals, including pigs.[2]

The discussion outlined so far might seem to contain a rather uneasy
mixture of emphases, combining the ideas that we value features that are
distinctive to *our* specific nature and that we value features that are *intrinsically*, or by some objective criterion, valuable. However, if this tension
is sensed by the author of the theory, or his spokesman, it is resolved in
favour of the latter theme by a double thought experiment.[3] The idea proposed is that of a vine which has inherent in it the art of viticulture, and

---

[2] 5.38: thus, virtue is defined as 'perfection of reason' (*rationis absolutio*).
[3] This resolution is also indicated in this passage (5.38): 'our most desirable components are those
which possess the highest worth. Hence, the most desirable virtue will be that which belongs to

which also has the vine-keeper's human, especially rational, functions. It is maintained that, in such a case, the vine itself would place greater value on the higher qualities, rather than those of its original or distinctive nature (5.39–40) However, this does not mean that the original, merely physical, functions which are characteristic of the vine are not also valued, though at a lower level.[4] By analogy, in the case of humans, the highest good (*summum bonum*) should be conceived inclusively, as 'the combination of full bodily integrity with the perfection of reason' (*summum ... cumulatur ex integritate corporis et ex mentis ratione perfecta*, 5.40), and not defined solely by reference to the highest functions. Although the expression of our nature is said to have an inherently motivating force, it is only gradually that human beings, and other animals, develop more than a vague and indistinct understanding of what our nature is. Thus, although human children exhibit seeds or sparks (*semina* or *scintillas*) or 'images' (*simulacra*) of the virtues, these only become full virtues with the formation and exercise of reason.[5]

This last point is presented as concluding the first part of the account, centred on the idea that self-love (the desire to realise our nature) constitutes our primary desire. The focus now falls on the claim, which is still closely related to the first idea, that there is an inherent attraction in exercising the various functions of our nature, especially the higher and more advanced ones (5.46). This claim is unfolded in a series of linked or overlapping points, centred increasingly on showing that we are naturally disposed to see virtue or the right (*honestum*) as inherently desirable, and, by implication, that this valuation is explained most effectively by the kind of analysis of ethical development offered here.[6] Piso maintains, first, that we are inclined to give our bodies the best possible form and appearance, and to place an inherent value on this form even if there is no practical utility in doing so (5.46–47). Second, it is claimed, in a rather rambling and digressive section, that we are also naturally disposed, from childhood onwards, to use our minds to gain knowledge, even if this does not serve

---

the best part of us, a part desired for its own sake'; (*maxime esse expetenda ex nostris quae plurimum habent dignitatis, ut optimae cuiusque partis quae per se expetatur virtus sit expetenda maxime*). Text cited throughout is Reynolds 1998 and translation Annas and Woolf 2001 (sometimes modified).

[4] The same thought experiment is used in *Fin.* 4.38–39 to make a related point: that the vine's superadded reason would take care of the vine as a whole not just of itself, in criticism of the (alleged) Stoic over-valuation of virtue at the expense of other goods.

[5] *Fin.* 5.41–43. The question whether pleasure does or does not constitute one of the good qualities of our nature is set aside as making no substantive difference to the claim being maintained: that the realisation of the best state of our nature is the supreme object of our desires (5.45).

[6] Rather than by the Stoic account of *oikeiōsis*, which also claims to explain this valuation (see *Fin.* 3.16–22 and section 4 below).

any immediate practical function (5.48–54).[7] Third, all animals, as well as all humans, again from childhood onwards,[8] are said to be naturally inclined to engage in constant activity of a kind that expresses the natural capacities of their nature, even in cases when the people concerned do not recognise the power of this inclination (5.55–57).

This forms a prelude to the climactic section of the account, in which the analysis of natural development is presented as supporting the distinctively Antiochean conception of the *summum bonum* (58–74, subdivided into a number of stages). The first point (5.58) is that we are naturally disposed to carry out the activities which express the most important or valuable parts of our nature, presented here as being the study of natural philosophy, politics and ethics.[9] This is coupled with a restatement of the claim made earlier (5.41–43) about the gradual development of human understanding of what constitutes our nature. By contrast with physical functions such as perception, mental capacities only develop gradually. We have 'small inklings of great things to come' (*notitias parvas rerum maximarum*) and 'so to speak, the building blocks of virtue' (*tamquam elementa virtutis*, 5.59). But their development depends on the exercise of 'skill' (*ars*) to complete this process. The second point, and one much stressed, is that a special (and inherent) value is attached to the kind of 'perfection of the intellect' (*mentis … perfectio*) involved in realising the virtues. 'That is why honour, admiration and enthusiasm are directed exclusively at virtue and at actions consistent with virtue' (*Itaque omnis honos, omnis admiratio, omne studium ad virtutem et ad eas actiones quae virtuti sunt consentaneae refertur*, 5.60). Although this motive has so far been explained, broadly speaking, in terms of self-love, we are now told that 'what I am calling right actions are desirable for their own sake and not just because we love ourselves' (*haec honesta quae dico, praeterquam quod nosmet ipsos diligamus, praeterea suapte natura per esse expetenda*, 5.61). The point is elaborated, in rather rhetorical fashion, with examples designed to show that even children and uneducated people, in different ways express the idea that virtuous and right actions are inherently attractive to us (5.61–64).[10]

---

[7] See, e.g., (end of 5.52): 'We must therefore conclude that the attractions of learning and study are contained within the very things that we learn and study' (*Quocirca intellegi necesse est in ipsis rebus quae discuntur et cognoscuntur invitamenta inesse quibus ad discendum cognoscendum moveamur*).

[8] This is presented in 5.55 as being the 'Old Academic' or Peripatetic (*nostri*) version of the 'cradle argument' (on this argument, see Brunschwig 1986).

[9] For a helpful exposition of this (rather confusing) chapter, see Bénatouïl 2009: 20–24.

[10] See also the last sentence of 5.64, including the claim that 'all the virtues [and the right] are desirable in their own right' (*virtutes omnes et honestum … per se esse expetendum*).

This point is elaborated in a number of exceptionally compressed passages, which seem designed to outline positions relevant to current ethical debates. The passages are linked, in that they relate to virtue and the good, but they do not form a fully worked-out analysis. In 5.65, ethical concern and affection for human beings as such are presented as motives which naturally arise by extension of family bonds, progressively expanded in scope to take in 'the whole human race' (*totius gentis humanae*). These motives are characterised as an expression of justice, though combined also with other virtues. The interfusing of justice with other virtues that arises in this way is taken as a mark of the communal feeling (*politikon*) which is said to be in-built in human nature. This point in turn supports the idea that the combination of virtues which underlies right action (*honestum*) is a quality which is 'in harmony with nature' (*naturae congruens*, 6.66). It also provides a basis for presenting the four cardinal virtues as distinct in function but also interdependent, and as having both self-regarding and other-regarding dimensions (6.67).

These points form a bridge to the climactic section, which sets out the relationship between different kinds of good, including the distinctive Antiochean formulation on happiness. First, other people (such as family and country), and relationships with them, are said to form part of the class of external goods; these are intrinsically valuable but secondary in value to goods of the mind and body which together constitute the highest good (5.68). Thus, performing a right action towards other people forms an intrinsic part of the highest good, whereas the relationships maintained in this way form part of secondary (external) goods (5.69). Piso then waxes eloquent about the inherent value of virtue and the right, claiming that the possession of the virtues confers happiness in a way that is invulnerable to the vicissitudes of circumstances. However, this does not mean that bodily goods are entirely without significance for happiness, as some thinkers (primarily, the Stoics) maintain. The bodily goods provide, together with the virtues, the basis for the most or completely happy life (*beatissimam vitam*), though not the simply happy (virtue-based) life (*beata vita*, 5.70–72).[11] The ethical system thus outlined is presented as the most complete and perfect one (*completa et perfecta*), of which most other schools accentuate only one aspect, except for the Stoics who, allegedly, adopt the theory wholesale but disguise the fact by changing some of the names (5.73–74).[12]

---

[11] On this distinction, see the debate in 5.77–86, discussed in section 5 below. See also Cic. *Acad. Post.* 1 (=*Varro*), ch. 22, *Tusc.* 5.22; see further Dillon 1977: 69–87, Annas 1993: 419–425, Irwin 2012.

[12] Cf. the criticism of the Stoics for borrowing the theory but redescribing external goods as 'preferable indifferents' in *Fin.* 4.20–23, 29–31, 56–60.

2 Underlying rationale and source

What is the overall point of this account? Taken in its context (*De Finibus* generally, especially Books 4–5), the general objective seems rather clear. This discussion, like the Stoic accounts of *oikeiōsis* in Book 3, offers an account of human development which is designed to support a distinctive conception of the overall goal of life (*telos* or *finis*) or highest good (*summum bonum*). Although, in both theories, the account appears highly idealistic, it is presented as describing a process which is fully in line with natural human capacities and tendencies. As in the Stoic version, human ethical development is located in the context of animal motivation more broadly, and the account of development includes both individual and social dimensions. The main recurrent emphases in Antiochus' version are meant to lend support to his distinctive view on the relationship between virtue and happiness, a point which becomes increasingly explicit as the discussion proceeds. In particular, the account combines a stress on the idea that *some* of our natural functions are more inherently valuable than others, especially reason as exercised in the virtues, with the idea that we are constitutively disposed to care for our nature *as a whole*, including bodily functions. This combination matches, and supports, the Antiochean thesis that virtue is necessary and sufficient for virtue but that 'complete happiness' requires, primarily, bodily goods such as health and, secondarily, external goods including social ones.

This overview of the objectives of the account, obviously, needs closer scrutiny, particularly in connection with the question, which of the two accounts of development (Antiochean or Stoic) is presented by Cicero as being more self-consistent and cogent (see sections 4–5 below). But, first, I consider the question of the provenance and philosophical character of the Antiochean account. In her review of ancient ethical theories from Aristotle onwards, Julia Annas underlined two features of the Antiochean account. She argued, in contrast to much previous scholarship, that the account of *oikeiōsis* was a deliberate and (at least broadly) coherent one, and not a mere 'scissors-and-paste' collection of ideas taken from different schools. She presented Antiochus' theory as an attempt to adopt, from an Academic standpoint, the Stoic project of defining the goal of life by a theory of human development, while also challenging the Stoic version and improving on it.[13] Although there has been a good deal of subsequent work done on Antiochus' ethical theory, as

---

[13] Annas 1993: 180–187, also 277–279, 316–317, 419–425.

well as other aspects of his thought,[14] I think, these two points still hold good. As regards the Peripatetic tradition in the period 200 BC to AD 200, Robert Sharples' 2010 source-book has brought out the way in which Stoic thinking on ethics, including their ideas about *oikeiōsis*, stimulated thinkers from other schools to challenge their claims while adopting many of their assumptions.[15] Antiochus' work on ethics seems to illustrate this general tendency, although his formal allegiance was Academic, rather than Peripatetic.

From what intellectual standpoint, exactly, is Antiochus' project approached? In *Fin.* 5, his theory is presented as derived from the 'Old Academic' philosophical framework, which embraces not only followers of Plato such as Polemo but also Aristotle, taken as a pupil of Plato, and his adherents.[16] The Stoics are depicted as borrowing wholesale from this tradition, while also changing key elements, notably regarding terminology relating to value.[17] Recent treatments have taken differing views about which intellectual influence is most significant. Mauro Bonazzi, for instance, presents Antiochus' aim as being to 'subordinate' Stoicism to leading features of the Academic or Platonic tradition. Among other features, he underlines the influence of Carneades, whose famous division or classification of ethical theories plays a prominent role in *Fin.* 5. Carneades' division is generally interpreted as having been designed to isolate and undermine the distinctively Stoic approach to the goal of life, though in *Fin.* 5 it is also deployed for a positive objective, supporting the competing 'Old Academic' or Antiochean theory.[18] Thomas Bénatouïl also suggests that the thinking of *Fin.* 5 on the relationship between practical and theoretical knowledge makes best sense when this is seen as expressing a Platonic riposte to the Stoic approach to this topic.[19]

On the other hand, Georgia Tsouni, in a recent Cambridge PhD thesis (2010), stresses the Aristotelian side of Antiochus' intellectual framework. In some earlier scholarship, notably a study by Dirlmeier (1937), it was seen as derived *en bloc* from Theophrastus. Tsouni, while not reviving

[14] See esp. Sedley 2012.
[15] Sharples 2010: chs. 15–18, on ethics, esp. ch. 17 on 'the primary natural things, *oikeiōsis*'; see also Gill 2012.
[16] See *Fin.* 5.6–8, also 4.3–4.
[17] See *Fin.* 5.74, a view of the relationship between the two theories already presented in *Fin.* 4 (e.g. 4.2, 19–20); on the critical strategy of Book 4, see Bénatouïl in this volume.
[18] See Bonazzi 2009: 33–44, 2012: 307–316; also Lévy 1992: 353–376. On the 'Carneadean division' in *Fin.* 5.16–23, see Annas 2007a, with full references to previous treatments, and, on Antiochus' use of this division, Schofield 2012b.
[19] Bénatouïl 2009: 11–24, esp. 20–24.

Dirlmeier's view in its original form, argues that the account of development is consistently Aristotelian, or at least Peripatetic, in its provenance
and conception. She considers a salient set of themes that form an integral
part of the version of *oikeiōsis* presented in *Fin.* 5. These include the idea of
goods 'according to nature', the relationship between plants, non-human
animals and human children, the themes of self-love, contemplation and
the happy life, *philia* and justice. She argues that, on all these topics, we
can see how the Antiochean account reflects aspects of the Peripatetic
tradition. Her main focus is on Aristotle, as expressed both in the treatises
and in fragments of published works such as the *Protrepticus*, and also on
Theophrastus, taking account of evidence for biological and ethical works.
But Tsouni also highlights parallels with the broadly similar account of
development in Stobaeus, usually attributed to Arius Didymus (*c.* 70–*c.*
9 BC),[20] and also the much later work *Mantissa*, which is preserved as a
supplement to the *De Anima* of Alexander of Aphrodisias.[21] Tsouni takes
similarities between the *Fin.* 5 account and these later texts as substanti-
ating the claim that Antiochus draws on a distinctively Peripatetic line of
thought on this topic.

   Tsouni's treatment is valuable in underlining the Aristotelian dimension in the Antiochean version of *oikeiōsis*. But there are certain factors
which make it difficult to accept her claims in full. A problem in seeing
the account of *oikeiōsis* as consistently Peripatetic is that, as noted already,
the ethical theory is presented as reflecting a broad 'Old Academic' tradition, in which both Aristotle and (more tendentiously) the Stoics are
included.[22] A further complication, which Tsouni acknowledges, is
that we cannot tell exactly how well Antiochus knew the Aristotelian
school-texts. She suggests that his knowledge of them was probably medi-
ated by Theophrastus or subsequent Peripatetic writings.[23] Also, I think it
is not clear from the evidence we have that Theophrastus actually had a
full-scale theory of *oikeiōsis* of the type we find in *Fin.* 5 and other, later,
writings, as distinct from offering ideas which could be used to inform

---

[20] This forms part of a summary of Peripatetic ethics; the section on *oikeiōsis* is Wachsmuth and
    Hense 1958: II: 118.5–128.10; for translation, see Sharples 2010: 112–118 (ch. 15, sections 3–12). See
    further Fortenbaugh 1983: part 3, chs. 7–9.
[21] See Bruns 1887: 150.19–153.27 and Sharples 2004: 149–159, with extracts in Sharples 2010: ch. 17;
    also Tsouni 2010: 64–73, and Tsouni 2012 (on contemplation).
[22] See references in nn. 16–17 above.
[23] See Tsouni 2010: 26–31, 64–73: also Barnes 1997: 48–50, Irwin 2012: 153–155. See *Fin.* 5.12, where
    we find a rather vague reference to Arist. *EN* and a more specific reference to Theophrastus, *On
    Happiness*.

the construction of a theory of this type.[24] Also, like the other scholars noted, Tsouni acknowledges respects in which the *Fin.* 5 account is shaped by other (post-Theophrastean) influences, notably Carneadean sceptical method, and is also shaped in order to present a rival account to the Stoic version.[25]

The question whether Antiochus' thought was informed more by Academic (or Platonic) or Peripatetic influences will, no doubt, be a matter of continuing debate. However, it seems to me that, on either view, the Book 5 account of *oikeiōsis* is best understood as an intended replacement of the Stoic version, designed to support a competing ethical theory by reference to an account of ethical development which is presented as being in line with human nature.

3 Strengths of the Antiochean account of *oikeiōsis*

This view of the origin and purpose of the *Fin.* 5 account of development makes it especially appropriate to attempt a comparative assessment of the two versions as regards their coherence and credibility. First, I consider what Antiochus himself is likely to have regarded as the principal strengths of his version, and also highlight features which may strike us as cogent even if they are not obviously part of Antiochus' programme, as Cicero presents this. Subsequently (sections 4–5), I appraise the two theories, considered alongside each other, and consider what view Cicero himself may have taken on this question.

One prominent theme in the account reflects the critique of Stoic thought in Book 4. Although this is placed in the mouth of Cicero, he functions there (by contrast with Book 5) as a critic of Stoicism and one who largely shares the standpoint of Antiochus.[26] There, among other points, Stoic ethical theory is criticised for offering an incomplete or defective conception of human nature, since it presents only the mind, and not the body, as valuable, and thus implies that we are, in effect, just minds.[27] This is, on the face of it, an odd claim. From a wide range of

---

[24] Tsouni 2010: 152–70 does claim that Theophrastus had a theory of social *oikeiōsis*. But Fortenbaugh and Gutas 2011: 558–561, discussing her view, offers a more qualified estimate of what is shown by the relevant evidence.

[25] See Tsouni 2010: 8–16.

[26] See further section 5 below on the formal framing of *Fin.* 4–5 and its philosophical significance. Bénatouïl, in his analysis of Book 4 in this volume, brings out the Antiochean standpoint of 'Cicero' in Book 4 (though with some qualifications, see pp. 211–213); he identifies the views of this character with those of Cicero as author.

[27] Cic. *Fin.* 4.26–39, esp. 26–28; see also Aug. *Civ. Dei* 19.3 (translation in Dillon 1977: 71).

other evidence, it is clear that a distinctive feature of Stoicism, in partial contrast with Platonic and Aristotelian thought, is the presentation
of human beings and other animals as psychophysical and psychological
wholes.[28] But this is an Antiochean way of stigmatising the view of human
nature implied in their ethical theory, at least when the Stoic theory is
translated into Platonic-Aristotelian language. Stoic ethical theory is presented as holding that goodness is attached only to what are, in Antiochus'
terms, 'goods of the psyche', and not bodily or external goods; and this
is presented as amounting to the claim that we are nothing but minds.
This criticism seems to be directed, in part, at the Stoic account of development, especially the radical shift of motivation from securing natural
advantages to recognising that only virtue is intrinsically desirable and
that the other advantages are matters of relative indifference.[29] Although
the criticism, on the face of it, misdescribes the Stoic theory, the misde-
scription is intelligible, given Antiochus' assumptions.[30]

In spite of this criticism, what is recommended in Book 4 and provided
in Book 5 is an account of development which implies a conception of
human nature and value that has some features in common with Stoicism,
Notably, this account places supreme value on mental, and specifically
rational, functions, especially when directed towards virtue taken as an
object of inherent desire. But the Antiochean account does so while also
asserting that some goodness also attaches to bodily advantages and that
rational functions are properly devoted to taking care of 'the goods of the
body' and, to a lesser extent, 'external goods'.[31] This is the message con-
veyed especially in the image, deployed in both Books 4 and 5, of the vine
which has become 'humanised' by the addition of internalised viticulture
and rationality. While placing highest value on its highest (rational) functions – in this respect like Stoicism, as presented by Antiochus – the vine
still recognises that it is *a plant* and should take care of itself as such. By
the same token, the Antiochean account of development, while going
some distance towards the Stoic view, still recognises that each person is
an embodied human being and should take care of herself as that, a recognition which is denied in the Antiochean picture of Stoic anthropology.[32] Antiochus' account thus expresses what he would regard as a more

[28] See Gill 2006: 168–169, also on psychophysical and psychological holism in Stoicism, 29–46,
75–100.
[29] See *Fin.* 4.32–34, also 26, 28–29; for the Stoic account, see 3.16–22, discussed in section 4 below.
[30] On this point, see also Ioppolo in this volume, section 2 (pp 176–180); Bonazzi 2012: 325–326.
[31] See Cic. *Fin.* 4.32–39; see also the summary of the Book 5 account given in section 1 above.
[32] See Cic. *Fin.* 4.38–39, 5.39–40, and text to nn. 3–4 above. See also Annas 1993: 183–184, Gill
2006: 168–171.

credible and realistic picture of human nature (what Julia Annas calls 'the intuitive view')[33] than Stoicism, and this is clearly one of the main aims and intended strengths of the account.

A second salient feature of Antiochus' account is that self-love is taken to be a primal underlying motive throughout the whole process of ethical development, and one that, by implication at least, informs the (rather brief) statement on social *oikeiōsis* (5.65–66).[34] This feature might reasonably be taken as an implied criticism, or a deliberate improvement, of the Stoic theory. In the Stoic account, individual development is presented as consisting in two, apparently, rather discontinuous phases, the first focused on self-love (or at least the desire to maintain one's constitution), while the second brings a radical refocusing of desire on virtue.[35] Also, at least as presented by Cicero in *Fin.* 3, the motives underlying individual and social ethical development are distinct, with rather different focuses and explanatory frameworks.[36] Thus, there are two possible criticisms: (1) that the Stoic theory of individual appropriation points in two, quite different, directions, and (2) that the two strands (individual and social) are not combined in a coherent way.

The Antiochean pattern might be seen as preferable in positing a single underlying motive for all human, and indeed plant and animal, development, though one that allows for valid variations for different life-forms. When coupled with other assumptions (that self-love is properly expressed in the desire to realise one's nature, that acquiring knowledge of one's nature is a gradual process, and that there is an inherent desire for self-perfection), this idea may seem to provide a unified explanatory framework. Hence, although the emphasis falls at different stages either on self-realisation or on responding to *certain* features (especially, virtue) as being inherently desirable, these variations can be seen as compatible parts of a single explanatory pattern. Although it is unclear exactly how far Antiochus was familiar with the Aristotelian school-texts, it seems reasonable to see Aristotle's claim that self-love is, in principle, compatible with ethical virtue and with other-benefiting motivation as an important underlying influence.[37] This is so, although the framework chosen by

---

[33] Annas 1993: 180–187.
[34] See the summary of 5.24–76 (section 1 above) for the underlying theme of self-love, despite a partial shift of focus at 5.46.
[35] For the two phases of individual *oikeiōsis*, see Cic. *Fin.* 3.16–20, and 21–22.
[36] On social *oikeiōsis*, see *Fin.* 3.62–68. The social side of the process has sometimes been seen as a later addition to the Stoic theory, e.g., by Inwood 1983: 193–199; but this is denied by Annas 1993: 264–265.
[37] Arist. *EN* 9.4, 8: also Annas 1993: 285–287. Tsouni 2010: 111–113 refers also to Arist. *Pol.* 2.5 in this connection. On Antiochus' knowledge of Aristotle's school-texts, see text to n. 23 above.

Antiochus to express this idea, namely as an account of *oikeiōsis*, is based on Stoicism, rather than Aristotle. So here too, arguably, the Antiochean theory, when juxtaposed to the Stoic one, might seem to come off better, at least at first sight.

We might supplement these features with two, related, points made by Tsouni. Both Antiochean and Stoic accounts of the social sides of development have certain elements in common, including the key role allocated to parental love and the idea that we should come to have ethical concern for human beings in general and not just members of our family or community. Similar features appear in the treatment of the social side of development in the summary of Peripatetic ethics attributed to Arius Didymus.[38] The extension of ethical concern to human beings as such (which is not found in Aristotle's school-texts) is sometimes taken as reflecting an attempt by Peripatetic thinkers to match and improve Stoic theory, in which this is a well-marked feature,[39] though Tsouni thinks it goes back to Theophrastus.[40] However, more relevant here is the question of the coherence of the explanation offered in each case. In Stoic theory, including, but not limited to, Cicero's treatment in *Fin.* 3.62–68, Tsouni sees a rather uneasy mixture of strands, which combines parental love and community involvement with the more abstract ideals of cosmopolitanism and human brotherhood.[41] In the Antiochean version, Tsouni identifies a more straightforward line of explanation, with two salient strands. One, shared with Arius, is the idea that concern with humanity as a whole forms a linear extension of the progressive expansion of concern with one's own children in ever-widening circles. The other is the idea that this process develops out of a growing sense of the implications of what justice involves. Both strands are presented as derived from motives in-built in human nature, namely familial love and an instinctive sense of community (*to politikon*).[42]

---

[38] See Cic. *Fin.* 5.65–66, Wachsmuth and Hense 1958: II:120.8–121.21 (translated as Sharples 2010, ch. 15. section 4); see also the Stoic version in *Fin.* 3.62–68.

[39] See e.g. Annas 1993: 276–290, and 1995.

[40] Tsouni 2010: 156–160; for a more cautious view about the Theophrastean origins of this idea, see Fortenbaugh and Gutas 2011: 559–560.

[41] Tsouni 2010: 164–170; I offer a more positive assessment of the Stoic treatment in section 4 below.

[42] Tsouni 2010: 160–164. For a similar view see Schofield 2012a. The first strand is also found, framed as ethical advice, in a passage of Stobaeus ascribed to the Stoic Hierocles (Wachsmuth and Hense 1958: IV: 671.7–673.11), which Tsouni suggests was influenced by the Peripatetic approach (169–170). The idea of humans as naturally 'sociable' (*politikon*) is Aristotelian (*EN* I.7, 1097b8–11), though Aristotle sees this sociability as expressed only in family and communal relationships (on the contrast with later Peripatetic ideas, see Annas 1995: 75–83).

We can couple Tsouni's positive evaluation of this aspect of Antiochus' account with a related point about the relationship between human and animal capacities and motivation. Whereas Stoicism (as Tsouni claims) draws a rather rigid distinction between non-rational animals and rational (adult) humans, the Aristotelian or Peripatetic framework allows a more finely graded set of distinctions. This makes better sense of the presentation, in both versions of *oikeiōsis*, of a parallelism between human and animal motivation and development. In addition, while the Stoic view on this question is (as Tsouni supposes) anthropocentric,[43] Antiochus' framework, like Aristotle's, gives a central place to the idea that each species fulfils its own nature. Arguably, Antiochus offers in this way a broader and more realistic framework for analysing human motives and development against the background of other natural kinds.[44] Combining both her points, we might say that the Antiochean version of social development focuses more centrally on distinctively human motives (linear expansion of social bonds and the notion of justice) in explaining the extension of ethical concern to human beings as a whole.[45] In this way, his theory shows convincingly how self-love (the instinctive desire to realise one's – human – nature) issues in this extended form of other-concern.

4 Comparative appraisal of the Stoic and Antiochean accounts of *oikeiōsis*

So far, I have offered an analysis of the rationale of the Antiochean account, which brings out the ways in which it can be seen as an improvement on the Stoic version of *oikeiōsis*. I now offer a more critical assessment of the Antiochean theory. The question on which I focus is whether the account of *oikeiōsis* does, in fact, support the distinctive Antiochean position on the good. This is that virtue is both necessary and sufficient for the happy life, but that the happiest life (or completely happy life) also requires the addition of external goods. In considering this question, I take the Stoic account as a basis for comparison (as Antiochus seems to have done); but I suggest that the Stoic account is much more closely correlated with its theory of value than is Antiochus' account. For this purpose, I focus especially on the first phase of the Stoic account (*Fin.* 3.16–22); but I also return to the

[43] I think the idea that the Stoic world-view is anthropocentric is at least partly misleading; but I do not pursue this question here.

[44] Tsouni 2010: ch. 3, referring e.g. to *Fin.* 3.24, 38, 42; also to Theophrastus, cited by Porphyry *De Abstinentia* 3.25.1–4. On the Porphyry text, as evidence for Theophrastus, see also Fortenbaugh and Gutas 2011: 553–70.

[45] Cic. *Fin.* 5.65–66, and references in n. 42 above.

question of the comparative merits of the Stoic and Antiochean treatments of social development (in 3.62–68 and 5.65–66, respectively).

In broad terms, it is clear how Antiochus supposes that the account supports his distinctive account of the good life. The analysis of the natural development of self-love is intended to combine progression with inclusiveness. Thus, development leads one to see the expression of the virtues as an overwhelming or sovereign good without thereby surrendering wholly the belief that things such as health are also goods.[46] But there is room for argument whether what the account of *oikeiōsis* supports is the distinctively Antiochean position, as distinct from a competing position, which is more commonly found in the Peripatetic tradition before and after Antiochus, that happiness – as distinct from complete happiness – depends on a combination of virtue and external goods.[47]

For instance, a striking feature of Antiochus' account, as already underlined, is the picture of a vine which also embodies the art of viticulture and the vine-keeper's rational functions. This picture is used to support the claim that the development of higher (in this case, rational) functions need not involve a loss of concern for the more basic (vine-like) bodily condition (5.39–40). The moral as regards the nature of highest good is drawn out explicitly: it should be conceived inclusively as 'the combination of full bodily integrity with the perfection of reason' (*summum ... cumulatur ex integritate corporis et ex mentis ratione perfecta*, 5.40), and not solely defined by reference to the highest functions.[48] On the face of it, the position that seems to be supported by this point is the idea, maintained by the second-century BC Peripatetic Critolaus, for instance, that happiness is 'completed' (*sumplēromenon*) by the three kinds of good.[49] However, Antiochus maintains the distinct position that happiness is conferred by virtue (that is, the exercise of rational functions) *on its own*, whereas the other kinds of good confer an *extra* kind of happiness.[50] This

---

[46] See the summary of the account in section 1 and the discussion in section 3 of (what Antiochus probably regarded as) strong points in the account.

[47] For this position see e.g. (Arius Didymus), Wachsmuth and Hense 1958 II:133.7–134.1 (trans. Sharples 2010: ch. 15 (18)); Aspasius, *On Aristotle's Ethics* 16.32–17.17, 3.13–18 (trans. Sharples 2010: ch. 18 (Ab, Ac)). See also Annas 1993: 416–418, Sharples 2007: 631–633. On Critolaus, see below. In fact, according to Augustine, *De Civ. D.* 19.3, reporting Varro, Antiochus too presented the happy life as a combination of virtue and bodily goods, while the happier and most happy life contained yet more goods (in addition to virtue). See Dillon 1997: 71 and Bénatouïl 2009: 21, n. 82.

[48] See text to nn. 3–4, 32 above.

[49] Sharples 2010: ch. 18, H–I; see also Annas 1993: 413–414, Sharples 2007: 628–629. Inwood 2014 offers an illuminating discussion of the Aristotelian ethical tradition, which brings out the importance of Critolaus.

[50] See *Fin.* 5.68–72, also references in n. 11 above.

image, taken by itself, does nothing to support that distinction. On the contrary, one might read the image as expressing the view that concern for bodily condition is a primary motive and one that is not displaced by the development of the higher, rational (virtue-expressing) functions. Indeed, in so far as the image supports the idea of grades of happiness, it might be taken as suggesting that bodily well-being constitutes the core level (happiness), whereas rational development represents the higher level (complete happiness) – which is not at all what Antiochus claims.

Does Antiochus' account of development, taken as a whole, bring out the required combination of ideas? A prior question is how far Antiochus, at any point, supports the claim that virtue is necessary and sufficient for happiness (if not complete or 'extra' happiness). The answer to this question depends especially on the treatment of the relationship between self-love and the growing recognition of the inherent desirability of virtue, which are the dominant themes in the whole treatment of *oikeiōsis*. As highlighted in the earlier summary (section 1), there are two phases in Antiochus' account, before and after 5.46, which is signalled as a turning-point. In the first part, a latent tension between valuing features which are distinctive of *our nature* and those which are *intrinsically* valuable is resolved in favour of the latter in part by means of the image of the vine (5.39–40). The vine, imagined to have internalized (human-style) viticulture, places a higher value on these new, advanced and rational functions, while still using these to take care of the original vine nature (or bodily functions).[51] Although this image brings out the claim that higher (rational and virtuous) functions are to be preferred, this goes only part of the way towards showing that virtue is intrinsically valuable, and that it is necessary and sufficient for happiness. It is not clear why the expression of virtue, as distinct from other rational functions, should be seen as intrinsically valuable. Also, as just noted, the image is also intended to convey the point that the emergence of these higher functions does not exclude continuing concern for the lower ones. This second message is at odds with giving absolute priority to virtue, since doing so might, of course, conflict with the preservation of one's life or other bodily needs.

Does the second section (5.46–64) go further in this respect? This section has, more obviously, the form of a connected argument. In essence, it consists in the linked claims (1) that we are naturally disposed to realise our highest functions (rational ones, especially those expressed in the virtues), and (2) that we are naturally disposed to see the expression of the

---

[51] See also text to nn. 4, 32 above.

virtues as intrinsically desirable (5.46–60, 61–64).[52] These claims are supported by a series of generalisations about human behaviour, illustrated with some celebrated examples of Greek and Roman heroism.

Although both the linked claims are vigorously supported, at the rhetorical level, it is not easy to pin down their theoretical basis.[53] The questions raised in connection with the vine image still persist. These can be restated in this form: (1) Why does virtue have a special priority (among rational functions)? (2) What is it about the relationship between virtue and our distinctive (human or rational) nature that ensures that virtue will be necessary and sufficient for happiness? (3) How can the claim that virtue is sufficient for happiness be squared with the continuing attachment of (inherent) value to external goods, notably our bodily state?

These questions are the more pressing, because Antiochus' account seems to have been conceived as a replacement of the Stoic account. Antiochus' objectives seem to have been to offer an improved version both of the Stoic conception of the good or happiness and the correlated account of ethical development. But, in the case of the Stoic theory, it is much clearer how the account of *oikeiōsis* is consistent with, and designed to support, the theory of happiness. If we raise comparable questions to the first two just raised in connection with Antiochus (though not, obviously, the third), the answers are much more straightforward, at least in the first phase of the account (3.16–22). In the account of personal development, the spotlight falls on two features which are crucial for the theory of value. One is the idea that, in a complete (and allegedly natural) process of development, the person concerned comes to recognise the fact that virtue, alone, is intrinsically valuable and desirable. The other is that, although the progress towards this recognition proceeds by way of rational selection between other things conceived as good (such as health or wealth), when the process is complete, it is understood that such things, while naturally preferable, are matters of indifference compared with the absolute or inherent value of virtue. In these respects, the account of development is correlated exactly with the Stoic theory of value in which the account is embedded. The account thus lends support to the two distinctive features of the theory, underlined both in Book 3 and in the critical appraisal of Book 4. These are the idea that virtue is both necessary and sufficient for happiness, and that naturally beneficial things other

---

[52] These claims are prominent in Aristotelian ethics (e.g., *EN* 1.7, 2.4, esp. 1105a32); and perhaps for this reason Antiochus takes them for granted and does not see them as needing defence. But, given his aim of challenging the Stoic version of these claims, he does need to defend them effectively.

[53] See also text to nn. 6–10 above, including selective quotations.

than virtue, such as health, are to be seen as 'preferable indifferents', rather than goods.[54]

It is, of course, possible to challenge and contest the Stoic account of development and theory of value, on a variety of grounds, as *Fin.* 4 illustrates. But a criticism notably absent from Book 4 is that the Stoic account of development fails to correspond to the Stoic theory of value. It is precisely this criticism that, I have suggested, one might reasonably make in connection with Antiochus' account. Comparison with the Stoic account enables one to pose the questions in a more pointed form. How does Antiochus defend the idea that virtue has a unique and inherent desirability – given that he rejects the Stoic defence of this idea by means of the contrast between virtue and preferable indifferents? How does Antiochus, without the support of this distinction, confirm the claim that virtue is both necessary and sufficient for the happy life?[55] Comparison with the Stoic account and theory highlight the difficulty Antiochus would have in answering those questions. Also, as highlighted earlier, his account of development does not seem to provide support for the two grades of happiness identified in his theory (happy and happiest or completely happy), in a way that would show how virtue-based happiness provides a basic level to which we can add, as an extra, the other goods.[56]

The points just made in connection with the first phase of the Stoic account of development are the crucial ones, I think, for the appraisal of the two theories – and also for the question of Cicero's judgement on their validity to which I turn in the next section. But it is worth adding some comments on the second phase of Stoic ethical development. Earlier, I suggested that Antiochus' treatment of this topic (5.65–66) could be seen as more convincing than the Stoic one (3.62–68); but this view can be challenged. Tsouni argues that the Stoic version contains an uneasy fusion of ideals, particularly of local and universal allegiance, and that the Antiochean version offers a more coherent account of this combination. She also maintains that the Antiochean version provides a more credible account of human social development, though one placed in a broad

---

[54] See 3.16–22, esp. 21–22; also 3.23–29, 50–57; 4.20–23, 32–33, 37, 44–48, 58–60, 71–73. On the Stoic account of development, see Gill 2006: 129–166, with references to previous treatments. On the Stoic theory of value in *Fin.* 3, see Graver in this volume; and on the critical strategy of *Fin.* 4, see Bénatouïl in this volume.

[55] On the relevant features of his thought, see text to n. 50 above; and for the rejection of 'preferable indifferents', see 5.88–89, and Book 4 references in n. 54 above.

[56] See text to nn. 48–50 above. On the debate about happiness in *Fin.* 5.77–86, which is closely linked with the points made here, see section 5 below.

framework of social behaviour in different natural kinds.[57] However, I think the Stoic account is substantially more coherent and credible in its picture of human and animal motivation than she suggests, and that, in particular, it provides a more effective rationale than Antiochus does for the extension of moral concern to human beings as such.[58]

As presented by Cicero, the Stoic treatment of social development, like that of personal or individual development, starts from a primary motive which is presented as transformed by rationality. In the first phase, this is the motive to realise one's own constitution; in the second, it is the motive to benefit others of one's kind, a motive which is presented as primary and shared by animals and humans, and exemplified in parental love. The claim is that, in a complete or 'natural' process of development, this motivation becomes transformed, like other aspects of (adult) human experience, by rationality.[59] As a result, this motivation is expressed, with equal validity, in two main types of relationship that are characteristic of adult humans as rational animals. One is full-hearted engagement with one's own family and community. The other is the recognition that ethical concern should be extended, in principle, to any given human being whom one encounters, regardless of whether or not she is a member of our family or local community.[60] The broader history of Stoic thinking on this topic is not my concern here. But I think this set of ideas about social *oikeiōsis* also underlies a related discussion of social ethics in Cicero's *De Officiis* (1.50–58), and that this set of ideas may well have been part of Stoic thinking from a much earlier period.[61]

Why should we say that, as so interpreted, the Stoic account offers a better basis than the Antiochean one for the extension of ethical concern to humanity in general? Both accounts claim that human agents become disposed to expand the scope of ethical concern in ever wider circles. But

---

[57] See text to nn. 38–45. The Antiochean rationale, broadly speaking, is that one comes to see that social engagement and acting justly constitute a crucial part of actualising one's nature as a rational and ethical agent.

[58] For other evidence on the Stoic theory, see Long and Sedley 1987: 57 and 67.

[59] The role of developing rationality is implicit in 3.62–68, but is signalled by the contrast with other animals at *Fin.* 3.63: 'Yet the ties between human beings are far closer. Hence we are fitted by nature to form associations, assemblies and states.' The significance of developing rationality is explicit in the earlier account of (individual) *oikeiōsis* in 3.21–22, and the linkage between rationality, language and sociability is a common theme in Stoic (or Stoic-influenced) texts, e.g. Cic. *Off.* 1.11–14, 50.

[60] Ethical engagement with human beings as such is stressed in 3.63, and start of 67, but there is more stress on conventional (family or communal) bonds in 3.62, 64–66, end of 67 and 68.

[61] In line with some recent treatments, I think a single line of thought runs through Stoic social and political theory (albeit with varying emphases or nuances), at least from Chrysippus onwards; see Annas 1993: 302–311, Vander Waerdt 1994, Vogt 2008: chs. 1–2. Tsouni's rather critical view of this

the Stoic version supports this universalistic standpoint in two main ways. First, human other-benefiting motivation is explicitly placed in a broad, providential world-view which is not found in the Antiochean version. We are invited to see a wide range of types of animal and human motivation and behaviour (parental love, animal cooperativeness within and across species, and human sociability) as expressing a kind of *oikeiōsis* that is in-built in nature.[62] Second, the ideal of the universe as a providential order ('virtually a single city and state shared by humans and gods', 3.64) is presented as one that underpins the process of development presented. The thought may be that the natural capacity and tendency of human beings to conceive other human beings as our brothers (in addition to those who are more closely related to us) reflects, at some level, the fact that the universe has this providential character (especially in 3.63–64). Although Antiochus' account of *oikeiōsis* also expresses a kind of providential framework (for instance, in positing a universal animal desire to realise one's nature), this framework is not explicitly used to underpin the analysis of social development in *Fin.* 3.65–66.[63] Thus, the underlying presence of these aspects of Stoic theory provides a basis for the extension of ethical concern beyond members of one's family and community in *Fin.* 3.62–68 that is not present in the same way in Antiochus' version in 5.65–66. In the Antiochean version, it is harder to see why we should want to extend affection and concern beyond the family and local community or why we should think that justice requires us to do this.

Elsewhere in this volume, Brad Inwood offers a much less positive appraisal of the Stoic theory of social *oikeiōsis* and, more briefly, their theory of personal development. So, on the face of it, his comments might seem to challenge my favourable assessment of the Stoic account, when contrasted to the Antiochean version. However, some relevant considerations need to be noted. Inwood is not concerned with comparative evaluation of the two theories, as I am. His scepticism about the cogency of the appeal to nature in Hellenistic ethics applies very generally, and, indeed, applies to the Antiochean version of *oikeiōsis*, as Inwood himself recognises (see his notes 15 and 36). Also, Inwood does not dispute the point just made here, that the Stoic picture of social *oikeiōsis* is presented as

---

aspect of Stoic theory is based largely on Schofield 1991, who sees more discontinuity in the history of Stoic social and political thought.

[62] This framework is very clear in *Fin.* 3.62–63 (cf. 3.16, also D.L. 7.85–89).

[63] Although I suggested that *Fin.* 6.65–66 could usefully be linked with the Antiochean version of natural teleology (text to nn. 44–45 above), the explanation offered in the passage itself (outlined in text to n. 42) does not make this connection.

consistent with, and supported by, their providential world-view (whereas
this is not the case with the Antiochean account of social development
in 5.65–66). What he disputes is that the Stoic account is supported convincingly by their appeal to 'the voice of nature', especially regarding the
idea that parental love constitutes an instinctive human (and more generally animal) motive (3.62). The question whether Inwood's critique of the
appeal to nature in Hellenistic ethics is effective is a complex one, which
cannot be broached here.[64] However, his comments do not invalidate or
run counter to the comparison just made between the two accounts of
social development, even though he flags larger conceptual problems that
might affect both theories.

5   Cicero's assessment of the two accounts of *oikeiōsis*

In the two preceding sections, I have offered discussions, from different standpoints, of the question how far the Antiochean account of
oikeiōsis is successful in challenging and replacing the Stoic account, especially in supporting the relevant conception of happiness and the goal of
life. I conclude by considering what view Cicero himself takes on this
topic. In fact, answering this question is far from straightforward. This
is partly because it is difficult to distinguish Cicero's estimate of the two
accounts of *oikeiōsis* from his appraisal of the two ethical theories, taken
as a whole. Nor is it wholly easy to gauge his estimate of the strength
of the two theories in general. Also, determining the position of Cicero,
as author, as distinct from that of the various personae of 'Cicero' presented in the debate, is itself quite challenging.[65] A further puzzle is what
it means for an Academic sceptic, which is how Cicero typically presents
himself, to have a 'position' on these and other questions.[66] In spite of
this – rather daunting – set of interpretative difficulties, I believe it is possible to offer an answer to the question posed (Cicero's judgement on the
two theories of *oikeiōsis*), which is compatible with much of the relevant
evidence, including the features of *Fin.* 5 already discussed here. In broad

---

[64] I am inclined to think that Inwood attributes to the appeal to nature a more foundational and,
in particular, a more 'Archimedean' role (to use Bernard Williams' term) than is appropriate, at
least, for Stoicism (for a different view see Gill 1990: 147–153). I hope to address the issue raised by
Inwood more fully elsewhere.
[65] The philosophical significance of Cicero's use of dialogue – a greatly under-studied topic, by comparison with Plato's, for instance – is explored by Schofield 2008.
[66] See Powell 2007. See also the analysis of the types of scepticism presupposed by Cicero in Brittain
2006: xix–xxxviii; and on Cicero's own position (viewed against this background), Brittain 2001,
index under 'Cicero'.

terms, I think Cicero has presented the two accounts of this topic in a way designed to underline the respective strengths and weaknesses of both treatments, as of the theories of which they form a part. He sees the Stoic account as more internally coherent than the Antiochean, as well as more consistent with the broader theory of which it is part. However, he also sees the Antiochean theory as more prima facie plausible and as answering to more widely held beliefs than the Stoic one. This is as far as Cicero goes, I think, in determining the merits or defects of the theories; and it is consistent with what he (or his persona) states in related works.

I begin by considering the challenge for this topic posed by Cicero's use of dialogue form, and outlining the possible accounts one might give of Cicero's overall philosophical stance and attitude to the theories treated here. Charles Brittain, in this volume, underlines the significance of the unusual format chosen by Cicero for his enquiry in De Finibus, which consists of three distinct dialogues, set at three different periods, in each of which Cicero acts as a character. All three dialogues, including that of Book 5, include arguments for and against a specific theory; and in no case does Cicero, speaking as author as distinct from character, offer a definitive judgement on the matter under debate. Brittain argues that this format, along with other features of the argument, raises problems for the most common way of interpreting Cicero's epistemological stance in the work, namely as a 'mitigated' sceptic, who does not adopt any one position in a dogmatic way, but who accepts as 'plausible', one of the positions offered, namely that of Antiochus.[67] Rather, Brittain sees Cicero here as an 'unmitigated' or 'radical' sceptic, who applies a Carneadean critical strategy to *all* three positions, including that of Antiochus. Cicero, through his dialogue in De Finibus, thus displays what can be said for or against each of the theories, but presents the question addressed (the nature of the good or overall aim in life) as, ultimately, indeterminable.[68]

I would not want to go quite as far as Brittain in his analysis of the outcome of the argument;[69] but I do accept that the factors he highlights make it difficult to conclude that Cicero (as author) accepts in full, even as

---

[67] Reasons that have been taken as suggesting that Cicero favours Antiochus include the fact that Cicero, as character, is the spokesman for the (Antiochean-style) critique of Stoic ethics in *Fin.* 4, and that the exposition of Antiochus' views in *Fin.* 5, is not followed by a book-length critique (by contrast with Epicurean and Stoic ethical theories).

[68] Brittain in this volume: esp. section 2 (pp. 18–28). Brittain sees the Carneadean critical strategy (linked with the Carneadean classification of *Fin.* 5.16–23) as showing that the position being criticised in each case collapses into one of two positions rejected by the theory concerned.

[69] As brought out here, points made by Brittain himself suggest some (at least provisional) conclusions.

'persuasive' (*plausibile*), any one of the positions presented. In specifying further what judgements Cicero does make, even with these limitations, about the positions presented, it is useful to take note of two widely held beliefs that Brittain suggests play a key role in the whole debate in *Fin*. These beliefs, as formulated by Brittain, are: (a) 'virtue is a primary and intrinsic good' and (b) 'there are other kinds of good which are subject to fortune', and they are ones to which Brittain thinks Cicero is committed, in spite of his generally sceptical stance.[70] Reference to these beliefs enables us to characterise Cicero's view of the Antiochean and Stoic ethical theories, taken as a whole. Both theories adopt a strong version of the first belief, in the form of the principle that virtue is both necessary and sufficient for the happy life. Stoicism also adopts a set of related ideas which are consistent with this principle, notably the idea that benefits other than virtue are not 'good' in the full sense but are 'preferable indifferents', and that our happiness does not depend on them.[71] This excludes their adoption of the second widely held belief. Antiochus, by contrast, while taking the same position on the virtue–happiness relationship, seeks also to incorporate the second belief, and to allow that goods other than virtue make *some* contribution to our happiness, though much less than virtue.[72]

In seeking to accommodate these two widely held beliefs, as well as in the way it is presented, Antiochus' theory has a strong prima facie or intuitive appeal. On the other hand, the combination of the strong form of the first belief is inconsistent with the second belief; and so his theory fails in terms of doctrinal self-consistency. The Stoic theory is fully self-consistent in this respect and is to this degree stronger. But its denial that happiness is affected in any way by loss of the goods subject to fortune runs counter to most people's intuitive beliefs and prevents it from being widely accepted. This stand-off between the two theories seems to be the point at which Cicero leaves the debate, in *De Finibus* and elsewhere.

This presentation of the debate between Piso, Antiochus' spokesman, and Cicero, here acting as a critic of the Antiochean theory, at the end of Book 5 provides a vivid illustration of the contrast between the two positions (5.77–95, especially 77–86). The most damaging criticism made of Antiochus is that of outright inconsistency. If, as he accepts, virtue is both necessary and sufficient for happiness (normally taken as the ultimate goal

---

[70] Brittain (p. 35) thinks these beliefs form part of the Roman tradition (*mos maiorum*) but that they are also ones to which Cicero as thinker is committed.

[71] For the Stoic view, see *Fin*. 3.22, 33–34, 41–54; cf. the criticisms of this view in 4.20–23, 56–60, 70–73.

[72] *Fin*. 5.68–72, cf. 4.26–42 (part of the critique of Stoic ethics). See also references in n. 11 above.

and ceiling of human aspiration), it seems inconsistent to add requirements for an extra goal of 'complete happiness'.[73] One, especially cogent,
version of this criticism is that Antiochus will satisfy neither the general
public nor the philosophical experts (*prudentes*). The former will reject his
(Stoic-like) adoption of the claim that virtue alone is sufficient for happiness, while the experts will repudiate his logical or theoretical inconsistency.[74] The Antiochean response is not to challenge the self-consistency
of the Stoic position but to claim that denying that all things other than
virtue are really goods and that they increase someone's level of happiness
flies in the face of what most people can accept (5.82). This is followed by
a restatement of the Antiochean position (5.90–95), presented as consistent with ordinary, real-life beliefs, though one that adds nothing further
on the matter of logical inconsistency. Although we may feel at this point
that the Stoics are having the better of the argument, Cicero explicitly
leaves the matter open, with no final narrative or authorial comment, and
with divergent responses by different characters.[75]

In other works written around the same time as *De Finibus*,[76] Cicero,
speaking as character or author, articulates a similar view regarding
the relative merits and demerits of the two theories. In the *Lucullus*
(or *Academica Priora*), 2.134, the Cicero-character outlines the position in exactly this form, finally confessing that 'I am torn: sometimes
Zeno's view seems more persuasive to me, sometimes Antiochus'.[77] In
Book 5 of the *Tusculan Disputations*, Cicero (speaking as 'M'), referring to the dispute about goods in terms very similar to *Fin.* 5, embraces
whole-heartedly the Stoic view that the happiness of the virtuous life is
not qualified by loss of external goods (5.75–76). We might have expected
him at this point to reject the Antiochean view, but his response is more
nuanced. He urges 'Peripatetics and the Old Academy' to adopt the Stoic
position, even if they retain in some form their belief in kinds of good

---

[73] *Fin.* 5. 79–86, esp. 81, 83, 84. For this criticism, see also Cic. *Tusc.* 5.21–23, Sen. *Ep. Mor.* 85.19–20.

[74] *Fin.* 5.85; see further Annas 1993: 420–423, esp. her comment (p. 423): 'Antiochus could indeed be
said to get the worst of both worlds.' See also the notes in Annas and Woolf 2001: 143–148. Irwin
2012: 161–172 suggests that Antiochus' position is less inconsistent (and is closer to Stoicism) than
is usually supposed. Irwin's view depends on a rather intricate reinterpretation of the relationship
between the two theories and of their relationship to Aristotle, and would require fuller consideration than I can offer here.

[75] Lucius Cicero (5.76) and Quintus Cicero (5.96) accept the Antiochean position, while the
Epicurean Atticus praises the style of Piso's exposition (5.96). However, Marcus Cicero (*our* Cicero)
says of the Antiochean theory, though not the Stoic one, that it requires further strengthening (*confirmandus*), though he may still be speaking in his persona as critic of the Antiochean theory.

[76] *Acad.*, *Fin.*, *Tusc.*, and *Off.* were all written (in that order) during 45–44 BC.

[77] Trans. Brittain 2006: 79.

other than virtue. Also, at the end of *Tusc.* 5, he minimises the difference
between these two groups and presents them both as schools with shared
Socratic-Platonic roots who agree 'on the perpetual capacity of the wise to
live well' (5.119–120). In *De Officiis*, speaking in his own person, Cicero
depicts himself as a sceptic who adopts, on this occasion, as 'persuasive'
(*plausibile*) the view that virtue is an intrinsic good and that nothing expedient should be pursued which is in conflict with virtue. He claims that
this view is shared by Peripatetics and Academics as well as Stoics (though
not Epicureans), but does not explore the other differences between the
two groups (1.6, 3.11, 19–20). In *De Officiis* 3.33, as in *Ac.* 2.134, he admits
he is torn between the philosophical claims of these two groups. This is
the more striking since, in *De Officiis* as a whole, Cicero adopts Stoic ideas
wholeheartedly as the basis of his exposition, and in Book 3 especially, he
adopts what is, in effect, a rigorous version of the Stoic position, as distinct from the Antiochean one.[78] Each of these passages merits, of course,
closer examination than I can offer here; and, especially in the case of the
works in dialogue form, the dialectical context would need to be considered, as in *De Finibus*.[79] However, the fact that Cicero repeatedly presents
these two ethical theories as the most 'persuasive' or the ones to be given
greatest weight, and that he refrains from a decisive rejection of either of
them, is surely significant. It suggests that the stand-off depicted in *De
Finibus* remains as close to a final position as we can attribute to Cicero,
and that the grounds for reaching this impasse remain valid for him.

What indications do we have of Cicero's views (as author) on the validity of the competing (Antiochean and Stoic) accounts of *oikeiōsis*? In fact,
it is not easy to isolate comments directed specifically at these accounts,
as distinct from the larger ethical theories with which they are associated.
Also, such comments as we have are by Cicero speaking as character, and
as critic of one or other of the two theories. In Book 4, for instance, Cicero
comments negatively on an idea crucial for the first (personal) phase of
oikeiōsis in Stoicism, the idea that ethical development can lead someone to jettison (perhaps better, transform) the initial, instinctive attraction to primary advantages such as bodily health. He argues, by means of

---

[78] In *Off.* 3, Cicero argues that we should on each occasion, choose the virtuous course of action, even
if it is not expedient (3.17–19), a strategy defined, for instance, by means of the Diogenes-Antipater
debate (51–57) and by the presentation of the rigorously virtuous Regulus as an exemplar (99–110).

[79] See further Schofield 2008: 82–83, and 2012b: 243–249, including two discussions of *Tusc.* 5.32–34,
where Cicero addresses the question of the inconsistency between his pro-Stoic stance there and his
critique of Stoic ethics in *Fin.* 4.

two images (both linked with plants) that there is no reason to think that rational development in human beings would lead someone to abandon all concern for such primary needs.[80] This objection is, of course, entirely in line with the broader Antiochean stance taken up by Cicero, as critic of Stoicism, in Book 4. It is linked with the wider objection to Stoicism that it denies key facts of human nature, notably our continuing valuation of primary needs (or external goods) even when we have reached a complete understanding of the intrinsic value of virtue as the basis of happiness.[81] So it seems that the first phase, at least, of the Stoic account of *oikeiōsis* is linked in Cicero's mind with the denial of the second widely held belief noted earlier ('that there are goods of fortune other than virtue'). In so far as Cicero (as author) recognises this denial as a problem in accepting Stoic ethical principles in a full-hearted way (at least sometimes),[82] it seems likely that he could see what is potentially problematic in the strong motivational shift posited in the first phase of *oikeiōsis*.

Analogous points can be made about the attitude towards the Antiochean account of *oikeiōsis* taken up by Cicero in his role in Book 5 as critic of that theory (5.76–86). His objections are directed primarily at Piso's brief statement of the ethical implications of the account of development (5.69–72). But Piso's treatment of development moves seamlessly into his ethical conclusions; and, in any case, the contrast between the 'happy' and 'completely happy' life correspond to salient points made in the course of the preceding account.[83] So it makes sense to take Cicero's criticisms of the logical inconsistency or weakness of the theory as applying also to – what he sees as – competing strands in the account of development. These are, in fact, the same strands that were presented positively by Cicero in Book 4: the idea that developing rationality brings both a recognition of the overriding value of virtue as the basis of human happiness and the continuing valuation of other (external) goods.[84] I pointed out earlier a significant problem in the Antiochean account of development taken as supporting his account of the *telos*. This is that it fails to show how motivation towards virtue becomes in some sense primary or

---

[80] See 4.37–39 (images of corn and vine), also 3.16–22. The significance of this comment is stressed by Bénatouïl, in this volume (p. 212), though he takes this view to reflect Cicero's thinking as author rather than as a persona (critic of Stoicism in Book 4).

[81] Cf. 4.2–3 and 5.7–8; also 4.25, 40–42, 78, 5.71–72.

[82] On the fluctuations in Cicero's stance on this point, see text to nn. 77–78 above.

[83] See the summary of the Antiochean account in section 1, esp. that of 5.39–40, 60–61, 68–69.

[84] See text to nn. 80–81 above.

fundamental, so that other motives become secondary or additional, thus supporting the claim that virtue (alone) constitutes the happy life (though not the completely happy one).[85] Although this gap in the developmental account is not explicitly singled out by Cicero as critic in Book 5, it goes along with the features he does criticise and can perhaps be taken as implied by these criticisms. So we can infer that Cicero sees Antiochus' theory as vulnerable to the criticism of inconsistency in its account of human development, with its implied view of human psychology, as well as in its theory of value.

Finally, in gauging Cicero's thoughts as author, we can consider the significance of the very different mode of presentation used for each of the two versions of *oikeiōsis*. In the Stoic version, two relatively compressed treatments (3.16–22, 62–68) are embedded into a much fuller and tightly stated analysis of ethical doctrines. In the first phase especially, the conceptual linkage between the developmental account and the associated doctrines is very clear; in the second phase, there is strong internal coherence between key motifs.[86] In Book 5, the procedure is very different; Antiochus' theory is presented, almost entirely, by means of a long developmental narrative (5.24–68), with a short statement of doctrinal implications (5.69–72). Although there are evident links between the account of development and the conclusions, these links are neither as close nor as fully articulated as in the Stoic version (hence, the problem just noted as regards the matching of motivational strands with the distinction between the happy and most happy life). As indicated in the earlier summary of Book 5 (section 1), the account often has a rather rhetorical, rather than doctrinal or dialectical, character.[87] This contrast in modes of presentation – which reflects, at least in part, Cicero's decision as author – seems to match the contrast in evaluation of the philosophical content of the two theories discussed earlier. Antiochus' theory is presented largely in the form of a single and readily accessible narrative account which seems designed to reinforce the prima facie or intuitive appeal of its combination of the two widely held beliefs noted earlier. The Stoic account is presented primarily in terms of a set of interconnected claims or doctrines, into which Cicero inserts two illustrative developmental narratives. Both the narrative and doctrinal sections bring out the fact that the Stoic theory is internally coherent – but that it rejects outright one widely held

---

[85] See section 4 above, text to nn. 46–53.
[86] See section 4, text to nn. 53–64.
[87] See esp. comments in section 1 on 5.48–54, 61–64, as well as 69–72.

belief.[88] Thus, overall, it seems that Cicero's formal presentation of the two accounts of *oikeiōsis* has been carefully designed to prepare for the dialectical stand-off between the two theories that he stages at the conclusion of Book 5.

---

[88] See esp. the contrast in Annas and Woolf 2001: 150, n. 70, between 'philosophical argument' and 'elegantly presented theory'.

Bibliography

Algra, K. (1997) 'Chrysippus, Carneades, Cicero: The Ethical divisiones in Cicero's Lucullus', in Inwood and Mansfeld (eds.): 107–139.

(2003) 'The Mechanism of Social Appropriation and Its Role in Hellenistic Ethics', Oxford Studies in Ancient Philosophy 25: 265–296.

(2007) Conceptions and Images: Hellenistic Philosophical Theology and Traditional Religion. Amsterdam.

Allen, J. (1994) 'Academic Probabilism and Stoic Epistemology', Classical Quarterly 44: 85–113.

Annas, J. (1993) The Morality of Happiness. Oxford.

(1995) 'Aristotelian Political Theory in the Hellenistic Period', in Laks and Schofield (eds.): 74–94.

(2007a) 'Carneades' Classification of Ethical Theories', in Ioppolo and Sedley (eds.): 187–223.

(2007b) 'Ethics in Stoic Philosophy', Phronesis 52.1: 58–87.

(ed.) and Woolf, R. (tr.) (2001) Cicero: On Moral Ends. Cambridge Texts in the History of Philosophy. Cambridge.

Arnim, H. von. (1903–1924) Stoicorum Veterum Fragmenta, 4 vols. Leipzig.

Atkins, E. M. (2000), 'Cicero', in C. Rowe and M. Schofield (eds.), The Cambridge History of Greek and Roman Political Thought. Cambridge: 477–516.

Aubert, S. (2006) 'Recherches sur la rhétorique des Stoïciens à Rome, de ses origines grecques jusqu'à la fin de la République.' Dissertation, Sorbonne University, Paris.

(2008) 'Cicéron et la parole stoïcienne: polémiques autour de la dialectique', Revue de Métaphysique et de Morale 57.1: 61–91.

(forthcoming) 'De la phronêsis à la prudentia', Interférences.

Bailey, C. (1926) Epicurus: The Extant Remains. Oxford.

Baraz, Y. (2012) A Written Republic: Cicero's Philosophical Politics. Princeton.

Barnes, J. (ed.) (1984) The Complete Works of Aristotle: The Revised Oxford Translation. 2 vols. Princeton.

(1989) 'Antiochus of Ascalon', in M. Griffin and J. Barnes (eds.) Philosophia Togata I: Essays on Philosophy and Roman Society. Oxford: 51–96.

(1997) 'Roman Aristotle', in J. Barnes and M. Griffin (eds.), Philosophia Togata II: Plato and Aristotle at Rome. Oxford: 1–69.

Barney, R. (2003) 'A Puzzle in Stoic Ethics', Oxford Studies in Ancient Philosophy 24: 303–340.

Barton, C. (2001) Roman Honor: The Fire in the Bones. Berkeley.

Beard, M. (1986) 'Cicero and Divination: The Formation of a Latin Discourse', Journal of Roman Studies 76: 33–46.

Bénatouïl, T. (2004) 'Compte-rendu de Plutarque, Sur les notions communes contre les stoïciens, texte établi par M. Casevitz, traduit et commenté par D. Babut', Philosophie Antique 4: 220–224.

(2007) 'Le débat entre stoïcisme et platonisme à propos de la vie scolastique: Chrysippe, l'Ancienne Académie, Antiochus', in M. Bonazzi and Ch. Helmig (eds.), Stoic Platonism – Platonic Stoicism. Leuven: 1–20.

(2009) 'Theōria et vie contemplative du Stoïcisme au Platonisme: Chrysippe, Panétius, Antiochus et Alcinoos', in Bonazzi and Opsomer (eds.): 3–31.

Bett, R. (1989) 'Carneades' Pithanon: A Reappraisal of Its Role and Status', Oxford Studies in Ancient Philosophy 7: 59–94.

(1990) 'Carneades' Distinction between Assent and Approval', Monist 73.1: 3–20.

(1997) Sextus Empiricus: Against the Ethicists. Oxford.

Bobzien, S. (2006) 'Moral Responsibility and Moral Development in Epicurus' Philosophy', in B. Reis (ed.), Virtue in Greek Ethics. Cambridge: 206–229.

Boeri, M. (2009) 'Does Cosmic Nature Matter?' in R. Salles (ed.), God and Cosmos in Stoicism. Oxford: 173–200.

Bonazzi, M. (2009) 'Antiochus' Ethics and the Subordination of Stoicism', in Bonazzi and Opsomer (eds.): 33–54.

(2012) 'Antiochus and Imperial Platonism', in Sedley (ed.): 307–333.

Bonazzi, M. and Opsomer, J. (eds.) (2009) The Origins of the Platonic System: Platonisms of the Early Empire and Their Philosophical Contexts. Leuven.

Boyancé, P. (1936) 'Les méthodes de l'histoire littéraire: Cicéron et son œuvre philosophique', Revue des études latines 14: 288–309. Reprinted in P. Boyancé (1970), Etudes sur l'humanisme cicéronien. Brussels: 199–221.

Brennan, T. (2012) 'The Nature and Object of the Spirited Part of the Soul', in R. Barney, T. Brennan and C. Brittain (eds.), Plato and the Divided Self. Cambridge: 102–127.

Bringmann, K. (1971) Untersuchungen zum späten Cicero. Göttingen.

Brittain, C. (2001) Philo of Larissa. The Last of the Academic Sceptics. Oxford.

(2006) Cicero: On Academic Scepticism. Indianapolis.

Brown, E. (2002) 'Epicurus on the Value of Friendship (Sententia Vaticana XXIII)', Classical Philology 97: 68–80.

(2009) 'Politics and Society', in J. Warren (ed.), The Cambridge Companion to Epicureanism. Cambridge: 179–196.

Brunner, Á. (2011) 'Totas paginas commovere? Cicero's Presentation of Stoic Ethics in De Finibus Book III.' Dissertation, Central European University, Budapest.

Bruns, I. (ed.) (1887) Supplementum Aristotelicum 2.1. Berlin.

Brunschwig, J. (1986) 'The Cradle Argument in Epicureanism and Stoicism', in Schofield and Striker (eds.): 113–144.

Brunschwig, J. and Nussbaum, M. (eds.) (1993) Passions and Perceptions: Studies in Hellenistic Philosophy of Mind. Cambridge.

Canto-Sperber, M. and Pellegrin, P. (eds.) (2002) Le style de la pensée: Recueil de textes en hommage à Jacques Brunschwig. Paris.

Cooper, J. (1980) 'Aristotle on Friendship', in A. O. Rorty (ed.), Essays on Aristotle's Ethics. Berkeley, Los Angeles and London: 301–340.

(1984) 'Plato's Theory of Human Motivation', Journal of Philosophy 74: 713–730. Reprinted in Cooper (1999b): 118–134.

(1996) 'Eudaimonism, the Appeal to Nature, and "Moral Duty" in Stoicism', in S. Engstrom and J. Whiting (eds.), Aristotle, Kant, and the Stoics. New York: 261–284. Reprinted in Cooper (1999b): 427–448.

(1999a) 'Pleasure and Desire in Epicurus', in Cooper (1999b): 484–524.

(1999b) Reason and Emotion. Princeton.

Dalfino, M. C. (1993) 'Ieronimo di Rodi: la dottrina della vacuitas doloris', Elenchos 14: 277–303.

De Lacy, P. (1969) 'Limit and Variation in Epicurean Philosophy', Phoenix 23: 104–113.

Diano, C. (1974) Scritti Epicurei. Florence.

Dillon, J. M. (1977) The Middle Platonists. Ithaca, NY.

(1997) The Great Tradition: Further Studies in the Development of Platonism and Christianity. Aldershot.

(2003) The Heirs of Plato: A Study of the Old Academy (347–274 BC). Oxford.

Dirlmeier, F. (1937) 'Die Oikeiosis-Lehre Theophrasts', Philologus Supp. 30. Leipzig.

Donini, P. L. (1982) Le scuole, l'anima, l'impero. Turin.

Douglas, A. E. (1962) 'Platonis Aemulus', Greece & Rome BS 9.1: 41–51.

(1995) 'Form and Content in the Tusculan Disputations', in Powell (ed.) (1995a): 197–218.

Dyck, A. (1996) A Commentary on Cicero, De Officiis. Ann Arbor, MI.

(1998) 'Cicero the Dramaturge: Verisimilitude and Consistency of Characterization in Some of His Dialogues', in G. Schmeling and J. D. Mikalson (eds.) Qui miscuit utile dulci: Festschrift essays for Paul Lachlan MacKendrick. Wauconda, IL: 151–164.

Dyroff, A. (1897) Die Ethik der alten Stoa. Berlin.

Engberg-Pedersen, T. (1986) 'Discovering the Good: oikeiōsis and kathēkonta in Stoic Ethics', in Schofield and Striker (eds.): 145–183.

(1990) The Stoic Theory of Oikeiosis. Aarhus.

Erler, M. (1999) 'Epicurean Ethics' in K. Algra, J. Barnes, J. Mansfeld and M. Schofield (eds.), The Cambridge History of Hellenistic Philosophy. Cambridge: 642–674.

Erler, M. and Schofield, M. (1999) 'Epicurean Ethics', in K. Algra, J. Barnes, J. Mansfeld, and M. Schofield (eds.), The Cambridge History of Hellenistic Philosophy. Cambridge: 642–669.

Evans, M. (2004) 'Can Epicureans Be Friends?' Ancient Philosophy 24.2: 407–424.

Fantham, E. (2004) The Roman World of Cicero's De oratore. Oxford.

Feldman, F. (2004) Pleasure and the Good Life: Concerning the Nature, Varieties, and Plausibility of Hedonism. Oxford.

Ferrary, J.-L. (2001) 'Réponse à Carlos Lévy', in C. Auvray-Assayas and D. Delattre (eds.), Cicéron et Philodème. La polémique en philosophie. Paris: 77–84.

Fortenbaugh, W. W. (ed.) (1983) On Stoic and Peripatetic Ethics: The Work of Arius Didymus. New Brunswick, NJ.

Fortenbaugh, W. W. and Gutas, D. (2011) Theophrastus of Eresus, Commentary, vol. vi.1. Leiden.

Fortenbaugh, W. W. and Steinmetz, P. (eds.) (1989) Cicero's Knowledge of the Peripatos. New Brunswick, NJ, and London.

Fortenbaugh, W. W. and White, S. A. (eds.) (2004) Lyco of Troas and Hieronymus of Rhodes: Text, Translation and Discussion. Rutgers University Studies in Classical Humanities xii. New Brunswick, NJ.

Fox, M. (2000) 'Dialogue and Irony in Cicero: Reading De Republica', in A. Sharrock and H. Morales (eds.) Intratextuality: Greek and Roman Textual Relation. Oxford: 263–286.

Frede, M. (1987a) Essays in Ancient Philosophy. Oxford.

(1987b) 'The Skeptic's Beliefs', in Frede (1987a): 179–200.

(1987c) 'The Skeptic's Two Kinds of Assent and the Question of the Possibility of Knowledge', in Frede (1987a): 200–222.

(1999) 'On the Stoic Conception of the Good', in K. Ierodiakonou (ed.), Topics in Stoic Philosophy. Oxford and New York: 71–94.

Gawlick, G. and Görler, W. (1994) 'Cicero', in H. Flashar (ed.), Die Philosophie der Antike, vol. iv.2: Die Hellenistische Philosophie. Basel: 991–1168.

Giannantoni, G. (1984) 'Il piacere cinetico nell' etica epicurea', Elenchos 5: 25–44.

Gildenhard, I. (2007) Paideia Romana: Cicero's Tusculan Disputations. Cambridge.

Gill, C. (1990) 'The Human Being as an Ethical Norm', in C. Gill (ed.), The Person and the Human Mind: Issues in Ancient and Modern Philosophy. Oxford: 137–161.

(2006) The Structured Self in Hellenistic and Roman Thought. Oxford.

(2012) 'The Transformation of Aristotle's Ethics in Roman Philosophy', in J. Miller (ed.), The Reception of Aristotle's Ethics. Cambridge: 31–52.

Giusta, M. (1964–1967) I dossografi di etica, 2 vols. Turin.

(1990) 'Antiocho di Ascalona e Carneade nel libro v del De Finibus Bonorum et Malorum di Cicerone', Elenchos 11: 29–49.

Glucker, J. (1988) 'Cicero's Philosophical Affiliations', in J. Dillon and A. A. Long (eds.), The Question of Eclecticism. Berkeley: 34–69.

(1995) 'Probabile, veri simile, and Related Terms', in Powell (ed.) (1995a): 115–143.

Goldschmidt, V. (1953) Le système stoïcien et l'idée de temps, Paris.

Görler, W. (1974) Untersuchungen zu Ciceros Philosophie. Heidelberg.

(1984) 'Zum "Virtus"-Fragment des Lucilius (1336–1338 Marx) und zur Geschichte der stoischen Güterlehre', Hermes 112: 445–468. Reprinted in Görler (2004a): 105–135.

(1989) 'Cicero und die "Schule des Aristoteles"', in Fortenbaugh and Steinmetz (eds.): 246–263.

(1990) 'Antiochos von Askalon über die "Alten" und über die Stoa. Beobachtungen zu Cicero, *Academici posteriores* 1 24–43', in P. Steinmetz (ed.), Beiträge zur hellenistischen Literatur und ihrer Rezeption in Rom. Stuttgart: 122–139. Reprinted in Görler (2004a): 87–104.

(1994) 'Älterer Pyrrhonismus, Jüngere Akademie, Antiochus aus Askalon', in H. Flashar (ed.), Die Philosophie der Antike, 4: Die hellenistische Philosophie. Basel: 717–989.

(1995) 'Silencing the Troublemaker: De Legibus 1. 39 and the Continuity of Cicero's Scepticism', in Powell (ed.) (1995a): 85–113.

(1997) 'Cicero's Philosophical Stance in the Lucullus', in Inwood and Mansfeld (eds.): 36–57.

(2004a) Kleine Schriften zur Hellenistisch-Römischen Philosophie. Leiden.

(2004b) 'Zum literarischen Charakter und zur Struktur der Tusculanae Disputationes', in Görler (2004a): 212–239.

(2011) 'Cicero, *De Finibus Bonorum et Malorum*, Buch 5. Beobachtungen zur Quelle und zum Aufbau', Elenchos 32.2: 329–354.

(2012) Review of Sedley (ed.) (2012), Elenchos 33: 376–382.

Gosling, J. and Taylor, C. C. W. (1982) The Greeks on Pleasure. Oxford.

Gourinat, J.-B. (2008) 'Les éclipses de la *phronèsis* dans le stoïcisme de Cléanthe à Marc Aurèle', in D. Lories and L. Rizzerio (eds.), Le jugement pratique: Autour de la notion de phronèsis. Paris: 167–197.

Graver, M. (2000) Review of Leonhardt (1999), Bryn Mawr Classical Review 2000.06.04.

(2002) Cicero on the Emotions: Tusculan Disputations 3 and 4. Chicago.

(2007) Stoicism and Emotion. Chicago.

(2012) 'Cicero and the Perverse: The Origins of Error in De legibus 1 and Tusculan disputations 3', in Nicgorski (ed.): 113–132.

Griffin, M. (1995) 'Philosophical Badinage in Cicero's Letters to His Friends', in Powell (ed.) (1995a): 325–346.

Hahm, D. E. (2007) 'Critolaus and the Hellenistic Peripatetic Philosophy', in Ioppolo and Sedley (eds.): 47–102.

Hirzel, R. (1877–1883) Untersuchungen zu Ciceros Philosophischen Schriften, 3 vols. Leipzig. Reprinted Hildesheim and New York, 1964.

(1895) Der Dialog, ein literarhistorischer Versuch. Leipzig.

Hossenfelder, M. (1986) 'Epicurus: hedonist malgré lui', in Schofield and Striker (eds.): 245–263.

Hutchinson, W. M. L. (ed.) (1909) M. Tulli Ciceronis De Finibus Bonorum et Malorum Libri Quinque. London.

Inwood, B. (1983) 'The Two Forms of oikeiōsis in Arius and the Stoa (Comments on Professor Görgemann's Paper)', in Fortenbaugh (ed.): 190–201.

(1985) Ethics and Human Action in Early Stoicism. Oxford.

(1990) '*Rhetorica Disputatio*: the strategy of De Finibus II', in M. Nussbaum (ed.), The Poetics of Therapy (= *Apeiron* 23.4): 143–164.

(ed.) (2003) The Cambridge Companion to the Stoics. Cambridge and New York.

(2005) Reading Seneca: Stoic Philosophy at Rome. Oxford.

(2012) 'Antiochus on Physics', in Sedley (ed.): 188–219.

(2014) Ethics after Aristotle (Jackson Lectures). Cambridge, MA.

Inwood, B. and Donini, P. (1999) 'Stoic Ethics', in K. Algra, J. Barnes, J. Mansfeld and M. Schofield (eds.), The Cambridge History of Hellenistic Philosophy. Cambridge: 675–738.

Inwood, B. and Gerson, L. (1988) Hellenistic Philosophy: Introductory Readings. Indianapolis.

Inwood, B. and Mansfeld, J. (eds.) (1997) Assent and Argument. Studies in Cicero's Academic Books. Leiden.

Ioppolo, A.-M. (1980) Aristone di Chio e lo stoicismo antico. Naples.

(2000) '*Decreta* e *praecepta* in Seneca', in A. Brancacci (ed.), La filosofia in età imperiale: le scuole e le tradizioni filosofiche. Naples: 15–36.

(2012a) 'Chrysippus and the Action Theory of Aristo of Chios', in R. Kamtekar (ed.), Virtue and Happiness: Essays in Honour of Julia Annas, Oxford Studies in Ancient Philosophy Supplementary Volume. Oxford: 197–222.

(2012b) 'Il concetto di piacere nella filosofia di Aristone di Chio', Elenchos 33, 43–68.

Ioppolo, A.-M. and Sedley, D. N. (eds.) (2007) Pyrrhonists, Patricians, Platonizers: Hellenistic Philosophy in the Period 155–86 BC. Proceedings of the Tenth Symposium Hellenisticum. Naples.

Irwin, T. (1974) 'Aristippus against Happiness', Monist 74.1: 55–82.

(1985) Aristotle: Nicomachean Ethics. Indianapolis.

(1998) 'Socratic Paradox and Stoic Theory', in S. Everson (ed.), Ethics. Companions to Ancient Thought 4. Cambridge: 151–192.

(2003) 'Stoic Naturalism and Its Critics', in Inwood (ed.): 345–364.

(2012) 'Antiochus, Aristotle and the Stoics on Degrees of Happiness', in Sedley (ed.): 151–172.

Karamanolis, G. (2006) Plato and Aristotle in Agreement? Oxford.

Kaster, R. (2005) Emotion, Restraint, and Community in Ancient Rome. New York.

Knoche, U. (1934) 'Der römische Ruhmesgedanke', Philologus 89: 102–124.

Konstan, D. (2006) 'Epicurean "Passions" and the Good Life', in B. Reis (ed.), The Virtuous Life in Greek Ethics. Cambridge: 194–205.

Laks, A. (1993) 'Annicéris et les plaisirs psychiques: quelques préalables doxographiques', in Brunschwig and Nussbaum (eds.): 18–49.

Laks, A. and Schofield, M. (eds.) (1995) Justice and Generosity: Studies in Hellenistic Social and Political Philosophy. Proceedings of the Sixth Symposium Hellenisticum. Cambridge.

Langlands, R. (2008) ' "Reading for the Moral" in Valerius Maximus: The Case of *severitas*', Cambridge Classical Journal 54: 160–187.

Leeman, A. (1963) 'The Styles of Philosophical Writing in the *Republic*', in A. Leeman, Orationis Ratio. Amsterdam: 198–216.

Leonhardt, J. (1999) 'Die Bestimmung des probabile im philosophischen Spätwerk', in J. Leonhardt, Ciceros Kritik der Philosophenschulen. Munich: 13–88.

Levine, P. (1958) 'Cicero and the Literary Dialogue', Classical Journal 53.4: 146–151.

Lévy, C. (1980) 'Un problème doxographique chez Cicéron: les indifférentistes', Revue des études latines 58: 244–245.

  (1984) 'La dialectique de Cicéron dans les livres ii et iv du *De Finibus*', Revue des études latines 62: 111–127.

  (1992) Cicero Academicus. Recherches sur les Académiques et sur la philosophie cicéronienne. Rome.

  (2001) 'Cicéron et l'épicurisme: la problématique de l'éloge paradoxal', in C. Assayas-Auvray and D. Delattre (eds.), Cicéron et Philodème. La polémique en philosophie. Paris: 61–75.

Long, A. A. (1967) 'Carneades and the Stoic Telos', Phronesis 12.1: 59–90.

  (1977) 'The Early Stoic Concept of Moral Choice', in F. Bossier *et al.* (eds.), Images of Man in Ancient and Mediaeval Thought. Symbolae Facultatis Litterarum et Philosophiae Lovaniensis, Series A. Leuven: vol. 1: 79–92.

  (1982) 'Soul and Body in Stoicism', Phronesis 27.1: 34–57.

  (1986) 'Pleasure and Social Utility – the Virtues of Being Epicurean', in H. Flashar and O. Gigon (eds.), Aspects de la philosophie hellénistique. Entretiens Hardt 32. Geneva: 286–324. Reprinted in Long (2006a): 178–201.

  (1991) 'The Harmonics of Stoic Virtue', in H. Blumenthal and H. Robinson (eds.), Aristotle and the Later Tradition. Oxford Studies in Ancient Philosophy, Supplementary Volume 1991. Oxford: 97–116.

  (1995a) 'Cicero's Politics in *De Officiis*', in Laks and Schofield (eds.): 214–240.

  (1995b) 'Cicero's Plato and Aristotle', in Powell (ed.) (1995a): 37–61.

  (1996) Stoic Studies. New York.

  (2006a) From Epicurus to Epictetus. Oxford.

  (2006b) 'Lucretius on Nature and the Epicurean Self', in Long (2006a): 202–220.

  (2006c) 'Hellenistic Ethics as the Art of Life', in Long (2006a): 23–39.

Long, A. A. and Bastianini, G. (1992) 'Hierocles: *Elementa Moralia*' in Corpus dei papiri filosofici greci e latini, part i vol. 1. Florence: 268–451.

Long, A. A. and Sedley, D. N. (1987) The Hellenistic Philosophers, 2 vols. Cambridge.

Lörcher, A. (1911) Das Fremde und das Eigene in Ciceros Büchern De Finibus bonorum et malorum und den Academica. Halle.

MacKendrick, P. (1989) The Philosophical Books of Cicero. London.

Madvig, I. N. (1876 [1839]) De Finibus bonorum et malorum libri quinque. Hanse. Copenhagen, 1876; Hildesheim, 1965.

Mansfeld, J. (1999) 'Sources', in K. Algra, J. Barnes, J. Mansfeld and M. Schofield (eds.) The Cambridge History of Hellenistic Philosophy. Cambridge: 3–30.

Martha, J. (ed. and tr.) (1928) Cicéron, Des termes extrêmes des biens et des maux. 2 vols. Paris.

Maso, S. (2008) Capire e dissentire. Cicerone e la filosofia di Epicuro. Naples.

Merguet, H. (1964) Handlexikon zu Cicero. Hildesheim.

Merlan, Ph. (1960) Studies in Epicurus and Aristotle. Wiesbaden.

Mette, H. J. (ed.) (1986) 'Philon von Larissa und Antiochos von Askalon', Lustrum 28: 9–63.

Mitchell, T. N. (1991) Cicero, The Senior Statesman. New Haven, CT.

Mitsis, P. (1988) Epicurus' Ethical Theory: The Pleasures of Invulnerability. Ithaca, NY.

Moreschini, C. (ed.) (2005) M. Tullius Cicero, De Finibus Bonorum et Malorum. Munich and Leipzig.

Nicgorski, W. (ed.) (2012) Cicero's Practical Philosophy. Notre Dame, IN.

Nikolsky, B. (2001) 'Epicurus on Pleasure', Phronesis 46.4: 440–465.

O'Connor, D. K. (1989) 'The Invulnerable Pleasures of Epicurean Friendship', Greek, Roman, and Byzantine Studies 30: 165–186.

O'Keefe, T. (2001) 'Is Epicurean Friendship Altruistic?' Apeiron 34.4: 269–305.

  (2002) 'The Cyrenaics on Pleasure, Happiness, and Future-Concern', Phronesis 47.4: 395–416.

Patzig, G. (1979) 'Cicero als Philosoph, am Beispiel der Schrift "De Finibus"', Gymnasium 86: 304–322.

Pease, A. (1914) 'The Conclusion of Cicero's *De Natura Deorum*', Transactions of the American Philological Association 44: 25–37.

Penner, T. and Rowe, C. (2005) Plato's Lysis. Cambridge Studies in the Dialogues of Plato. Cambridge.

Philippson, R. (1939) 'Die Philosophischen Schriften', in M. Gelzer (ed.), M. Tullius Cicero. *RE* 7.A.1: 1104–1192.

Powell, J. G. F. (ed.) (1995a) Cicero the Philosopher: Twelve Papers. Oxford.

  (1995b) 'Introduction: Cicero's Philosophical Works and Their Background', in Powell (ed.) (1995a): 1–35.

Powell, J. G. F. (1995c) 'Cicero's Translations from Greek', in Powell (ed.) (1995a): 273–300.

  (2007) 'Cicero', in Sharples and Sorabji (eds.): vol. II: 333–345.

Price, A. W. (1989) Love and Friendship in Plato and Aristotle. Oxford.

Prost, F. (2001) 'L'éthique d'Antiochus d'Ascalon', Philologus 145.2: 244–268.

  (2003) 'Aspects de la critique cicéronienne de l'épicurisme en De Finibus 2', Quaderni del dipertimento di filologia linguistica e tradizione classica. Università degli studi di Torino 2: 87–111.

Purinton, J. (1993) 'Epicurus on the Telos', Phronesis 38.3: 281–321.

Rackham, H. (trans.) (1914). Cicero's 'On Ends'. Loeb Library. Cambridge, MA.

Reid, J. (ed.) (1925) M. Tulli Ciceronis De Finibus Bonorum et Malorum Libri I, II. Cambridge.

Reinhardt, T. (ed.) (2003) Marcus Tullius Cicero. Oxford.

Reydams-Schils, G. (2002) 'Human Bonding and *Oikeiôsis* in Roman Stoicism', Oxford Studies in Ancient Philosophy 22: 221–251.

Reynolds, L. D. (ed.) (1998) M. Tulli Ciceronis De Finibus Bonorum et Malorum Libri Quinque. Oxford.

Rist, J. M. (1974) 'Pleasure, 360–300 BC', Phoenix 28: 167–179.

Ruch, M. (1969) 'La *disputatio in utramque partem* dans le Lucullus et ses fondements philosophiques', Revue des études latines 47: 310–335.

Schofield, M. (1983) 'The Syllogisms of Zeno of Citium', Phronesis 28.1: 31–58.

  (1986) 'Cicero for and against Divination', Journal of Roman Studies 76: 47–65.

  (1991) The Stoic Idea of the City. Cambridge.

  (1995) 'Two Stoic Approaches to Justice', in Laks and Schofield (eds.): 191–212.

  (1996) 'Epilogismos: An Appraisal', in M. Frede and G. Striker (eds.) Rationality in Greek Thought. Oxford: 221–223.

  (1999) 'Social and Political Thought', in K. Algra, J. Barnes, J. Mansfeld and M. Schofield (eds.), The Cambridge History of Hellenistic Philosophy. Cambridge: 739–770.

  (2002) 'Cicero, Zeno of Citium and the Vocabulary of Philosophy', in Canto-Sperber and Pellegrin (eds.): 412–428.

  (2003) 'Stoic Ethics', in Inwood (ed.): 233–256.

  (2009a) 'Ciceronian Dialogue', in S. Goldhill (ed.) The End of Dialogue in Antiquity. Cambridge: 63–84.

  (2009b) 'Republican Virtues', in R. Balot (ed.) A Companion to Greek and Roman Political Thought. Oxford: 199–213.

  (2012a) 'Antiochus on Social Virtue', in Sedley (ed): 173–187.

  (2012b) 'The Neutralizing Argument: Carneades, Antiochus, Cicero', in Sedley (ed.): 237–249.

  (2012c) 'The Fourth Virtue', in Nicgorski (ed.): 43–57.

Schofield, M. and Striker, G. (eds.) (1986) The Norms of Nature: Studies in Hellenistic Ethics. Cambridge and Paris.

Sedley, D. N. (1996) 'The Inferential Foundations of Epicurean Ethics', in G. Giannantoni and M. Gigante (eds.) Epicureismo greco e romano. Naples: 313–339.

  (1998) 'The Inferential Foundations of Epicurean Ethics', in S. Everson (ed.), Ethics. Companions to Ancient Thought 4. Cambridge: 129–150.

  (2002) 'Diogenes of Oinoanda on Cyrenaic Hedonism', Proceedings of the Cambridge Philological Society 48: 159–174.

  (ed.) (2012) The Philosophy of Antiochus. Cambridge.

Shackleton Bailey, D. R. (ed.) (1965–1970) Cicero's Letters to Atticus, 5 vols. Cambridge.

  (ed.) (1977) Cicero: Epistulae ad Familiares. 2 vols. Cambridge.

Sharples, R. W. (2004) Alexander of Aphrodisias: Supplement to 'On the Soul', trans., with introduction and notes. London.

  (2007) 'Peripatetics on Happiness', in Sharples and Sorabji (eds.): vol. II: 627–637.

(2010) Peripatetic Philosophy 200 BC to AD 200: An Introduction and Collection of Sources in Translation. Cambridge.

Sharples, R. W. and Sorabji, R. (eds.) (2007) Greek and Roman Philosophy 100 BC–200 AD, 2 vols. *Bulletin of the Institute of Classical Studies*, Supplement 94. London.

Shorey, P. (trans.) (1930) Plato's 'Republic'. Loeb Library. Cambridge, MA.

Smith, P. (1995) '"A self-indulgent misuse of leisure and writing?" How Not to Write Philosophy. Did Cicero Get it Right?' in Powell (ed.) (1995a): 301–323.

Spinelli, E. (2012) 'Sextus Empiricus et l'ombre longue d'Aristote', Philosophie Antique 12: 281–288.

Splawn, C. (2002) 'Updating Epicurus's Concept of Katastematic Pleasure', Journal of Value Inquiry 36: 473–482.

Steel, C. (2005) Reading Cicero: Genre and Performance in Late Republican Rome. London.

Stokes, M. (1995) 'Cicero on Epicurean Pleasures', in Powell (ed.) (1995a): 145–170.

Striker, G. (1980) 'Sceptical Strategies', in M. Schofield, M. Burnyeat and J. Barnes (eds.), Doubt and Dogmatism: Studies in Hellenistic Epistemology. Oxford: 54–83. Reprinted in Striker (1996): 92–115.

(1983) 'The Role of *Oikeiosis* in Stoic Ethics', Oxford Studies in Ancient Philosophy 1: 145–167. Reprinted in Striker (1996): 281–297.

(1991) 'Following Nature: A Study in Stoic Ethics', Oxford Studies in Ancient Philosophy 9: 1–73. Reprinted in Striker (1996): 221–280.

(1993) 'Epicurean Hedonism', in Brunschwig and Nussbaum (eds.) (1993): 3–17. Reprinted in Striker 1996: 196–208.

(1995) 'Cicero and Greek Philosophy', Harvard Studies in Classical Philology 97: 53–61.

(1996) Essays on Hellenistic Epistemology and Ethics. Cambridge.

Sullivan, F. A. (1941) 'Cicero and *gloria*', Transactions of the American Philological Association 72: 382–391.

Süss, W. (1966) Cicero: eine Einführung in seine philosophischen Schriften (mit Anschluss der staatsphilosophischen Werke). Wiesbaden.

Thiaucourt, C. (1885) Essai sur les traités philosophiques de Cicéron et leurs sources grecques. Paris.

Tsouna, V. (1998) The Epistemology of the Cyrenaic School. Cambridge.

(2002) 'Is There an Exception to Greek Eudaimonism?' in Canto-Sperber and Pellegrin (eds.): 464–489.

Tsouni, G. (2010) 'Antiochus and Peripatetic Ethics.' Dissertation, University of Cambridge.

Tsouni, G. (2012) 'Antiochus on Contemplation and the Happy Life', in Sedley (ed.): 131–150.

van der Blom, H. (2010) Cicero's Role Models: The Political Strategy of a Newcomer. Oxford.

vander Waerdt, P. A. (1987) 'The Justice of the Epicurean Wise Man', Classical Quarterly 37.2: 402–422.

(1994) 'Socrates and Stoic Natural Law', in P. A. vander Waerdt (ed.) The Socratic Movement. Ithaca, NY: 272–308.

Voelke, A.-J. (1973) L'idée de volonté dans le stoïcisme. Paris.

Vogt, K. (2008) Law, Reason and the Cosmic City: Political Philosophy in the Early Stoa. Oxford.

von den Hoff, R. (1994) Philosophenporträts des Früh- und Hochhellenismus. Munich.

Wachsmuth, C. and Hense, O. (eds.) (1958) Ioannis Stobaei: Anthologium, 5 vols. Berlin. Firsts published 1884–1912.

Warren, J. (2000) 'Epicurean Immortality', Oxford Studies in Ancient Philosophy 18: 231–261.

(2001) 'Epicurus and the Pleasures of the Future', Oxford Studies in Ancient Philosophy 21: 135–179.

(2002) Epicurus and Democritean Ethics: An Archaeology of Ataraxia. Cambridge.

(2004) Facing Death: Epicurus and His Critics. Oxford.

(2007) 'L'ethique', in A. Gigandet and P.-M. Morel (eds.) Lire Épicure et les épicuriens. Paris: 117–143.

(2009) 'Aristotle on Speusippus on Eudoxus on Pleasure', Oxford Studies in Ancient Philosophy 36: 249–281.

(2013) 'The Harm of Death in Cicero's First *Tusculan Disputation*', in J. S. Taylor (ed.), The Metaphysics and Ethics of Death. Oxford: 44–70.

White, N. (1979) 'The Basis of Stoic Ethics', Harvard Studies in Classical Philology 83: 143–178.

White, S. (2002) 'Happiness in the Hellenistic Lyceum', in L. Jost and R. A. Shiner (eds.), Eudaimonia and Well-Being: Ancient and Modern Conceptions (first published as *Apeiron* 35). Kelowna, British Columbia: 69–93.

(2004) 'Lyco and Hieronymus on the Good Life', in Fortenbaugh and White (eds.): 389–409.

Wolfsdorf, D. (2009) 'Epicurus on εὐφροσύνη and ἐνέργεια (DL 10.136)', Apeiron 42.3: 221–257.

(2013) Pleasure in Ancient Greek Philosophy. Cambridge.

Woolf, R. (2004) 'What Kind of Hedonist Was Epicurus?' Phronesis 49.4: 303–322.

Wright, M. R. (1991) Cicero: On Stoic Good and Evil. Warminster.

Wynne, J. P. F.(2014) 'Learned and Wise: Cotta the Sceptic in Cicero's *De Natura Deorum*', Oxford Studies in Ancient Philosophy 47: 245–273.

Zoll, G. (1962) Cicero Platonis aemulus. Untersuchungen über die Form von Ciceros Dialogen, besonders von De oratore. Zürich.

Subject index

Index locorum